GED

DeMYSTiFieD®

DeMYSTiFieD® Series

The DeMystified series publishes more than 125 titles in all areas of academic study. For a complete list of titles, please visit www.mhprofessional.com.

GED
DeMYSTiFieD®

Cynthia Johnson and Diane Milne

Mc
Graw
Hill

New York   Chicago   San Francisco   Lisbon   London   Madrid   Mexico City
Milan   New Delhi   San Juan   Seoul   Singapore   Sydney   Toronto

1 2 3 4 5 6 7 8 9 10 11 12 13 14 15 16 17   QFR/QFR   1 9 8 7 6 5 4 3 2

ISBN   978-0-07-177837-4
MHID   0-07-177837-3

e-ISBN   978-0-07-177838-1
e-MHID   0-07-177838-1

Library of Congress Control Number   2012938186

McGraw-Hill products are available at special quantity discounts to use as premiums and sales promotions or for use in corporate training programs. To contact a representative, please e-mail us at bulksales@mcgraw-hill.com.

This book is printed on acid-free paper.

Contents

GED

DeMYSTiFieD®

Part I

Introduction

chapter 1

About the Book

Congratulations on taking the first steps toward earning your GED credentials! Over the years, millions of people in the United States and Canada have taken the GED tests in order to reach their educational and occupational goals. You are definitely in good company.

Have you ever wondered exactly what is on the GED test, what tips and tools could be helpful in doing well on it, or how the test is scored? Well, you have come to the right place. This book will help explain and demystify the GED.

Why Do I Need This Book?

The key to many things in life is to be prepared. We purchase car insurance to prepare for the unexpected. We clean the house, blow up balloons, and bake a cake to prepare for a birthday party. We buy new notebooks and pens to prepare for the first day of school. We also study to prepare for a test. The most effective way to study is to learn about the test and find out what information will be on it. The better prepared you are, the more likely you will be to do well.

This book was designed to help you prepare for the GED in several ways:

- First, it will help you review the concepts that are assessed on the test.
- Second, it will familiarize you with the types of questions that appear on the test.
- Third, it will give you opportunities to take GED practice tests.
- Fourth, it will introduce strategies for selecting the best answers to the GED questions.

What Is in This Book?

The GED includes separate tests that assess your knowledge in five different content areas: language arts, social studies, science, reading, and math. In this book, each of these subject area exams is broken down into specific skills. Each of these skills is reviewed in a separate chapter dedicated solely to helping you master that concept. For example, the GED Science test measures your knowledge of life science, earth and space science, chemistry, and physics. So this book includes a separate chapter on each of these areas. Take a look at the chapter topics related to each of the GED tests.

Language Arts, Writing

- Basic English Usage
- Sentence Structure
- Mechanics
- Organization
- Preparing for the GED Essay

Social Studies

- World History
- US History
- Civics and Government
- Economics
- Geography

Science

- Life Science: Biology
- Earth and Space Science
- Physical Science: Chemistry
- Physical Science: Physics

Language Arts, Reading

- Interpreting Prose Fiction
- Interpreting Poetry
- Interpreting Drama
- Interpreting Prose Nonfiction

Mathematics

- Whole Numbers and Operations
- Number Sense
- Decimal Numbers and Operations
- Fractions and Operations
- Number Relationships
- Statistics and Data Analysis
- Percents
- Probability
- Data Analysis
- Algebra
- Measurements
- Geometry
- Formulas

What can be found in each chapter? We're so glad you asked!

In Each Chapter

Chapters 3 through 33 each discuss a specific topic found on one of the GED subject area tests. Let's take a look at what you will find in these chapters.

Review of Information

Each chapter reviews information you will need to know for the subject area tests and offers examples and tips for how to apply the information. For example, in the chapter that explains fractions and operations, you will find definitions and explanations of different types of fractions, examples of fractions, a review of how to perform various operations involving fractions, and step-by-step instructions for how to complete the operations. Since the majority of the information on the GED is stuff you already know, the chapters simply provide a quick refresher to jog your memory.

Some of the chapters also explain information about the number of questions on each test and the time limit for completing it. As you will see, the number of questions varies from one test to the next, and the time limits vary as well. This information will be important as you prepare for the test.

What to Do

Following the explanations and concept review in each chapter, you will find a section titled "What to Do." This section gives you six steps to use when answering questions relating to the subject of the chapter. Take a look at the following box, which shows the steps for answering fractions and operations questions.

Fractions and Operations Steps

Step 1: Read the Problem
Step 2: Determine What Is Being Asked
Step 3: Identify Pertinent Information
Step 4: Choose Which Operation(s) or Steps to Use
Step 5: Solve the Problem
Step 6: Check Your Work

Following the list is a brief explanation of how to apply each step and why it is necessary and important.

The steps suggested in each of the math chapters are the same, those suggested in each of the social studies chapters are the same, and so on. There are two reasons for this. First, the steps you will use to answer any math problem, for example, are basically the same regardless of whether you are dealing with fractions, decimals, or geometry. Likewise, the steps you will use to answer any social studies question are the same, regardless of whether the topic is geography, civics, or history. So there is no reason to follow a different set of steps for each topic. Second, since all topics within a subject area follow the same steps, you will only need to memorize a single set of steps for each test. That is much simpler and more practical than learning a different set of steps for each of the 33 chapters in the book.

Sample Items

Next are two or three sample questions that are similar to something you might see on the GED. We show you how to use the steps to answer the first question; then we provide writing space for you to use in answering the next example(s). This gives you the opportunity to think through the steps as you work and to practice using the process explained in the chapter.

Independent Practice Items

After the sample questions is a set of practice questions related to the specific topic of the chapter. On the GED, all of the questions related to the subject area of the test will be mixed together rather than separated by topic. For example, on the GED Science test, the life science questions will be mixed in with the earth and space science, chemistry, and physics questions. However, all the questions in each chapter address only the information from that chapter; the life science chapter includes only life science questions and so on.

The Final Section

After reviewing and practicing with the types of information found on the GED, the final section of this book offers two practice tests. They are similar in length and structure to the actual test and give you the chance to practice taking the tests and to become more familiar and comfortable with the GED.

Types of Questions in This Book

The GED assesses more than simply your ability to comprehend reading passages or compute sets of numbers. It also assesses your abilities at increasingly higher cognitive levels. The skills required to ace the GED test include the following:

- Apply information
- Assess data
- Compare
- Contrast
- Distinguish facts from opinions or hypotheses
- Draw conclusions
- Evaluate information
- Identify cause-and-effect relationships
- Identify implications
- Make inferences
- Recognize unstated assumptions
- Restate information
- Summarize
- Synthesize information

The sample items and practice questions in each chapter, as well as the questions on the diagnostic tests at the end of the book, allow you to practice using these skills. Hopefully, by the time you read the chapters and answer all of the practice questions, you will be confident in your knowledge of the subject matter and comfortable with the format of the test, and the secrets of the GED will be demystified for you.

chapter 2

How to Use This Book

As you are probably aware, the purpose of this book is to help you prepare for the GED test. That is probably the reason you got this book in the first place. Now you may be wondering, *How should I use this book?* That's a great question. Let's go over the ways it can help you get ready to do your best on the GED.

Review the Content

As mentioned in the previous chapter, this book breaks each of the GED subject areas into specific skills or content areas. For example, the GED Language Arts, Reading test assesses your ability to interpret and comprehend prose, poetry, drama, and nonfiction works, so each of these literary forms is discussed in a separate chapter. Each chapter reviews the skills and information that relate to the topic. Since the majority of the information on the GED is likely to be familiar to you already, the reviews in this book are not in-depth; they are meant to serve as a refresher.

That being said, use this book to go over the ideas, skills, and information that will be important when you take the GED. As you read through each chapter, take notes or highlight the skills you would like to go over again. If you find a concept that is unfamiliar or with which you are not completely comfortable, research it further. If you find a concept that you can breeze through in a snap, good for you! There is no reason to spend too much time going over skills you have already mastered.

You will notice that the social studies and science chapters are a bit different than the math and language arts chapters. Many social studies and science topics are ideas that you spend months or even years studying in school, such as World War I or the periodic table of elements. So rather than including all of the information related to World War I in the World History chapter, for example, we have simply included a list of topics with which you should be familiar. Read through the lists in these chapters, think about what you know pertaining to each topic, and spend a little time reading about or studying those you do not know well.

The required skills in the language arts and mathematics chapters are explained briefly and often illustrated by examples. Read each of the explanations, check out the examples, and determine how well you know the information. Keep in mind that although you may recognize some of the concepts, you must be able to apply them as well. Use these chapters to find out what you know and what you need to review in more depth.

Memorize the Steps

Each chapter includes a list of six steps that will help you solve the problems or answer the questions. The steps in each of the social studies chapters are the same, as are those in each of the science chapters, math chapters, and so on. Here is how to use these steps:

1. Read through all the steps.
2. Notice how the steps are used to answer the sample questions. Sometimes seeing how they are applied can be helpful in understanding how they are used.
3. Practice using the steps. Follow the steps as you answer the practice questions. See how each step works. You will find that they are sequential and often build off of one another to lead you toward selecting the best answer choice.
4. Memorize the steps. Since you will not be able to take this book or any other notes with you to the GED test, you need to know any pertinent information by heart. That includes the steps used to answer the questions. Remember, you will need to memorize only one set of steps for each of the five tests.

Practice Taking the Tests

The final section in this book includes practice tests that are similar to the actual GED. Use these diagnostics to:

- Become familiar with the test format
- Find your strengths and weaknesses
- Practice using test-taking strategies
- Plan your pace for test day

We will come back to these points shortly.

When you practice, pretend you are taking the GED. Turn off your phone, put a Do Not Disturb sign on the door, set a timer for the correct number of minutes, and start working. Consider writing your answers on a separate sheet of paper rather than in the book so you can take the tests again in a few weeks or months if you wish.

Now that we have discussed *how* to take the practice tests, let's go over the reasons *why* you should take them.

Become Familiar with the Format

Taking the diagnostic tests at the end of this book will help you become familiar with the format of the GED. You may already know that, with the exception of the language arts essay, all of the questions on the test are multiple choice; however, you will learn that the tests have a few other key features with which you should be familiar. For example, some of the questions on the Language Arts, Reading test will present a set of sentences and then ask you to select the most effective way to combine them. The sentences in each passage on this test will be numbered, and some questions will ask you to identify the best way to correct an error in a given sentence. Also, each passage on the reading test will be preceded by a purpose question to help you focus on the information. Knowing these things ahead of time and getting used to seeing passages and questions presented in this manner will help you be more comfortable with the format of the test.

Find Your Strengths and Weaknesses

After answering all of the questions on the diagnostics, go back and find out which questions you answered correctly and which you did not. Do not be discouraged if you made a few mistakes. See this as a learning opportunity. Now you know which skills to focus on as you study and prepare for the GED.

Look for patterns in your correct and incorrect answers. Did you answer all of the algebra questions correctly but struggle with those pertaining to data analysis? Are you a pro at interpreting plays but not so hot at understanding poetry? This information is all good to have! The more you know about your own strengths and weaknesses, the more effectively you can use your study time. Take this opportunity to brush up on the skills you will need to do well on the GED. Then, when test day arrives, you will be able to tackle all of the questions with confidence.

Keep in Mind

Keep in mind that these strategies can be used when answering the practice questions at the end of each chapter as well. If you missed any of the questions, go back through the chapter and review the corresponding information again before moving on to the next skill.

Practice Using Test-Taking Strategies

Over the years, you have probably picked up a trick or two for answering test questions. There are definitely strategies you can use to do your best. Practice using the following test-taking strategies as you work through the diagnostic tests. That way, when the big day comes, you will be ready to take on whatever the GED throws at you.

• **Try to answer the questions before looking at the answers.** Read the passage or information and read the question, but don't peek at the answer choices. Decide what the correct answer should be; then look at the choices. If your answer is there, great! If not, try again.

• **Read every choice.** The first answer choice may look tempting, but do not mark anything until you have read all the options. Several may appear to be at least partially correct, but only one is completely right. Make sure you read them all to find the one best answer.

• **Answer everything.** There is no penalty for guessing on the GED. This means that if you leave a question blank, it is the same as marking the wrong answer. So if you are stumped by a question, take your best guess and move on.

• **Make smart guesses.** Did we just tell you to guess on the GED? Actually, yes. You need to mark an answer for every single question. There may be times when a question leaves you completely baffled, and guessing is necessary. The trick to guessing well is first to eliminate as many of the incorrect answer choices as possible. Often, an answer choice that is extremely different from the rest can be eliminated. Also, answer choices that include absolutes such as *always*, *every*, and *never* may be incorrect. Math answer choices that are far off your estimate may be incorrect. Once you have eliminated as many incorrect options as possible, guess between those that remain. Keep in mind that randomly selecting between five answer choices gives you a one in five chance of getting the answer correct. That's only 20 percent. However, eliminating three of the incorrect choices improves your chances to one in two, giving you a 50 percent chance of selecting the right answer. That's much better!

• **Keep up.** You will mark your answers to the multiple-choice questions on the GED on a separate answer sheet. Make sure the answer to each question is correctly marked in the corresponding place on the answer sheet. In other words, be careful to mark the answer to question 10 in the correct space for answer 10.

• **Mark only one answer.** If you decide to change an answer, be sure to erase the original answer completely. Only one answer can be marked for each item.

Plan Your Pace for Test Day

As you work through the questions, notice how much time it takes you to complete the diagnostic test. Remember, each of the GED tests has a time limit. Figure out if you will need to work more quickly or if you can spend a little longer on each question and still finish before time is called. It is a good idea to try to leave a few minutes at the end of the test to check your work. That way, you also have a cushion of time at the end if a few of the questions take longer than anticipated.

Figure out how many questions are on each test and how long you will have to complete them. Then determine the pace at which you need to work. For example, the GED Mathematics test is divided into two 45-minute sections, each containing 25 questions. If you plan to spend approximately one and a half minutes on each question, you will finish the test with about seven minutes left to check your work. Here are a few ideas for how to stick to the pace you have set for yourself.

• **Keep an eye on the clock.** Focus on the test, but be aware of how much time has passed and how much time you have left. Check your pace every now and then. For example, to complete the 25 math questions before time is up, you will need to have eight or nine questions done by the time the first 15 minutes have passed. If you notice that you are running behind, try to work a little faster, without moving so quickly that you begin to make mistakes. If you are running ahead of time, keep moving along with the confidence that you will have a couple of minutes to spare at the end of the section.

• **Don't spend too long on any one question.** It is important not to get bogged down by a single question. If an item has you stumped, take your best guess and move on. You can always come back to it at the end of the test if time allows. It would be a shame to waste precious minutes on one question and not have enough time to answer a later question on something you know well.

• **Start marking answers as time runs out**. When you are down to only a minute or so, start randomly marking answers for any questions you have not yet completed. Yes, it sounds strange, but anything left blank will be marked wrong. At least by marking something, you have a chance of picking up a few extra points.

Now that you know how to use this book to review GED content, learn steps to answer questions, and practice taking the tests, let's get started!

Part II

Language Arts, Writing

chapter **3**

Basic English Usage

What's Being Tested?

Basic English usage questions on the GED assess your knowledge of subject-verb agreement, verb tense, and pronoun usage. These are skills you use every day, probably without even thinking about them. The questions that test your knowledge of usage will make up 30 percent of the Language Arts, Writing Test, Part I. To answer them, you will read a passage and then be expected to recognize errors related to verbs and pronouns in a particular sentence from the passage. You will then select the answer choice that shows the best way to correct the error.

Sounds pretty easy, right? Well, some of the grammar rules can get a little tricky at times. Sure, many of the answers will jump out as being correct, but you may have to put a little more thought into others. With a little effort, though, you'll be a grammar pro and breeze right through this section of the test.

What to Know

Let's go over some basic grammar rules related to verbs and pronouns. Keep in mind that this is just a quick review of a few of the basics and by no means an all-inclusive list of everything you should know about English usage.

Subject-Verb Agreement

Every sentence has a subject. This is who or what the sentence is about. Every sentence also has a verb, or action word. The subject and the verb must agree, or fit together.

> *Correct:* <u>Marcel</u> <u>was</u> the first to arrive.

> *Incorrect:* <u>Marcel</u> <u>were</u> the first to arrive.

Notice that the subject, Marcel, is singular, so the sentence requires a singular verb. When the subject is plural, a plural verb is needed.

> *Correct:* <u>Marcel and Harvey</u> <u>were</u> seated at the same table.

Groups

Some groups of people, such as teams, businesses, and institutions are considered singular and require a singular verb.

> <u>The debate club</u> <u>was</u> planning to meet on Thursday before school.

Keep in Mind

Keep in mind that determining whether a group of people or items is singular or plural may take a little thought on your part. Some collective nouns refer to a set of items or people as a group, such as a dozen eggs. In this case, *dozen* is singular.

> A dozen eggs is enough to bake several cakes.

However, if the collective nouns are seen as separate individuals, the nouns are plural, such as a dozen goldfish.

> A dozen goldfish share the tank in the dentist's office.

It is important to pay attention to the context in which words are used. It may be tempting to focus only on the subject of the sentence to decide whether it requires a singular or plural verb. But to make an accurate decision, you must consider the sentence and its message.

Gerunds

Gerunds are verbs that end with *-ing* and serve as nouns. When a gerund is the subject of a sentence, it is considered singular.

<u>Running</u> late on the first day of a new job <u>is</u> not wise.

Either *and* Neither

If the subject of a sentence is *either* or *neither*, the nouns are singular. However, when followed by *or* and *nor*, these tricky little words become plural.

Correct: <u>Either</u> of those months <u>was</u> fine for taking a trip.

Incorrect: <u>Either</u> October <u>or</u> November <u>was</u> a good time for a vacation.

Notice that adding the little word *or* in the second sentence changed the subject from singular to plural.

Correct: <u>Either</u> October <u>or</u> November <u>were</u> good times to travel.

Verb Tense

Verb tense indicates the time of an action and tells whether the sentence is happening in the past, present, or future.

Yesterday they went to the football game.

Today they are going to the soccer game.

Tomorrow they will go to the basketball game.

Past, present, and future—easy peasy. Now here's where things can get a little thorny.

Simple Present Tense

Simple present tense refers to an action that is currently taking place or an action that happens on a regular basis.

Mia lives on the third floor of her apartment building.

Julio attends acting classes three afternoons each week.

Present Perfect Tense

This is an action that started in the past but continues in the present. Alternatively, the action began in the past but continues to have an effect on the present. Perfect tense verbs use the words *have*, *had*, or *has* along with a past tense verb.

Isabel has walked to school every day since kindergarten.

Simple Past Tense

Use of the simple past tells you an action has already happened.

She learned to ride a bike 15 years ago.

Past Perfect Tense

A verb in the past perfect tense shows an action in the past that was completed before something else took place.

Andre had worked at a law office before becoming a police officer.

Notice that this includes *had*, since it is a perfect tense verb.

Simple Future Tense

This tense shows an action that will take place in the future.

Our family will go to the airport to pick up Grandmother next week.

Future Perfect Tense

An action in future perfect tense has not yet occurred but will take place by a specific time in the future.

Roger will have finished painting the entire house by Friday.

Pronoun Usage

As you already know, pronouns can take the place of nouns. The big rule with pronouns is that they must agree with the nouns they replace.

<u>Bradley</u> plans to study biology in college because <u>he</u> has always loved science.

In this sentence, *he* is the pronoun. *Bradley* is the antecedent, or the word that is replaced by the pronoun.

Gender

Pronouns must be the same gender as the antecedent in order to agree.

Correct: <u>Emma</u> was promoted to supervisor because <u>she</u> is a dedicated employee.

Incorrect: <u>Emma</u> was promoted to supervisor because <u>he</u> is a dedicated employee.

Notice that Emma is a female. For the pronoun to agree with the antecedent, the pronoun must be feminine.

Subject Pronouns

Pronouns that can be the subject of a sentence are known as subject pronouns. They include *he, I, it, she, they, we, who,* and *you.* Other pronouns, including *its, her, him, his, me, mine, my, ours, their, us, whose,* and *your,* cannot be used as the subject of a sentence.

Correct: <u>Beth and Carlos</u> were surprised! <u>They</u> had no idea about the party.

Incorrect: <u>Beth and Carlos</u> were surprised! <u>Their</u> had no idea about the party.

Infinite Pronouns

Pronouns and antecedents must agree in regard to number as well. Infinite pronouns represent more than one subject but are considered to be singular.

Correct: <u>Anyone</u> who wants to join the study group <u>is</u> welcome to do so.

Incorrect: <u>Anyone</u> who wants to join the study group <u>are</u> welcome to do so.

Anyone refers to more than one person but requires a singular verb. Other infinite pronouns include *each, everyone, neither, no one,* and *someone.*

Number

Singular pronouns must replace singular antecedents, and plural pronouns must replace plural antecedents.

<u>Students</u> attending the pep rally must return to <u>their</u> classes afterward.

Pronoun Shift

Pronouns in a passage must remain in the same person. For example, if a sentence begins by using a first person pronoun, all pronouns must be in the first person. Changing from one point of view to another is called a *pronoun shift*, which is a no-no.

Incorrect: The professor told us you could work together on the project.

Us is a first person pronoun; *you* is third person.

Correct: The professor told us we could work together on the project.

What to Do

Now that you know the basic grammar rules regarding subject-verb agreement, verb tense, and pronoun usage, what's the plan of attack for answering questions about them on the GED? We're glad you asked!

Let's go over the six steps for correcting errors in basic English usage.

Steps to Correcting Errors in Usage

Step 1: Read the Sentence
Step 2: Identify the Subject, Verb, and Pronouns
Step 3: Determine Whether the Subject and Verb Agree
Step 4: Determine Whether the Verb Tense Is Correct
Step 5: Determine Whether the Pronoun Is Correct
Step 6: Read Each Answer Choice

Step 1: Read the Sentence

This probably sounds like a no-brainer, but read the sentence carefully. As we talked about earlier, some of the errors stick out like a sore thumb. Others are better disguised and may appear to be correct if you're not on top of your game.

On Part I of the GED Language Arts, Writing Test, you will be selecting which answer choice corrects an error in the passage. On Part II, you will be writing your own essay and will need to be able to apply basic English usage rules to your own writing. In either case, always read the sentence alone as well as in the context of the paragraph so you can spot any corrections that need to be made.

Step 2: Identify the Subject, Verb, and Pronouns

Every complete sentence must have a subject and verb. To identify the subject, ask yourself who or what the sentence is about. To identify the verb, ask yourself what the subject or subjects did.

Remember that a sentence may have more than one subject or verb. Be sure to identify all of them. The subject or subjects are often found at the beginning of a sentence, but they can be anywhere. And while the verb often follows the subject, it can also come first.

The sentence may or may not contain a pronoun. If there is a pronoun, determine what noun or nouns it replaces in the sentence. You may need to look back to the previous sentence in the passage or possibly earlier in the paragraph to determine the antecedent.

Keep in Mind

Keep in mind that singular items can sometimes be plural subjects. For example, when *pants*, *scissors*, and *pliers* are the subject, they require a plural verb. But not always. When words such as these are preceded by the phrase *a pair of*, they are singular. The glasses on the table are Uncle Stu's. But the pair of glasses in the kitchen belongs to Auntie Em.

Step 3: Determine Whether the Subject and Verb Agree

As you know, a singular subject requires a singular verb, and a plural subject requires a plural verb. Groups and gerunds are considered singular when it comes to subject-verb agreement. *Either* and *neither* are also singular, unless followed by *or* and *nor*, in which case they are plural. One way to determine whether the subject and verb agree is to just read these words, and ignore the rest of the sentence. For example, read the following sentence:

> On Tuesday, Sofia and Reggie, who live in the same neighborhood, were caught in a terrible rainstorm.

With so many other words in the sentence, it can be easy to lose sight of the subject and verb and to overlook errors in agreement. Now focus only on the subject, or subjects, and the verb.

> Sofia and Reggie were

This has a plural subject and a plural verb, so they are in agreement.

What happens if the subject and verb do not agree? Determine what changes could be made to the sentence to correct the error. It may be tempting, but do not look at the answer choices just yet. Think about what revisions you would make to the sentence to best correct the disagreement. Then, when you do look at the answer choices, you can see if your answer is among them.

Step 4: Determine Whether the Verb Tense Is Correct

To know if the verb tense is correct, you'll have to determine if the events being discussed are taking place in the past, present, or future. You may have to look around a bit. No, don't look around the room at other people's tests! Look beyond this sentence, and check out the message in the rest of the passage to determine the timing. The verb or verbs in the sentence must match the tense of the entire paragraph.

As you read the paragraph, look for clues about when the events occurred. Words and phrases such as *yesterday, tomorrow, right now, last week, currently, someday, as of now,* or *at this time* suggest time frame and can let you know what verb tense should be used.

If you determine that the verb tense is wrong, figure out what changes are needed to correct it. When you look at the answer choices, see if your correction is on the list.

Step 5: Determine Whether the Pronoun Is Correct

To determine whether the pronoun is correct, you'll have to figure out what the antecedent is. These have to match in regard to gender and number. Also, if the pronoun is the subject of the sentence, it must be a subject pronoun.

What should you do if there is an error with the pronoun? Decide what pronoun would be correct. When you read the answer choices, look for your response.

Step 6: Read Each Answer Choice

Read every answer choice. Again, read carefully. See if the correction you had in mind is among the choices. If it is, super! But you still need to read all of the choices diligently. The difference of one little letter can cause a very tempting answer choice to be incorrect. As with any test, there is only one best answer. Make sure you find it.

After choosing the answer, substitute it in the original sentence, and read the corrected sentence. Does it sound right now? If so, awesome! If not, go back to Step 1 and take another stab at it, selecting the best correction for the sentence.

Examples

Let's take a look at a sample question that's similar to the ones you will find on the actual test. Keep in mind that you will be reading entire paragraphs. For practice purposes, we're going to check out isolated sentences in the next two examples.

After arriving at the test center, the student will sharpen their pencil and then find a seat.

Which correction should be made to the sentence?

1. replace *After* with *Before*
2. replace *arriving* with *arrives*
3. replace *will sharpen* with *has sharpened*
4. replace *their* with *his or her*
5. replace *find* with *found*

Here are our steps:

Step 1: Read the Sentence

Step 2: Identify the Subject, Verb, and Pronouns

Subject: student

Verb: will sharpen

Pronoun: their

Step 3: Determine Whether the Subject and Verb Agree

Yes. Both are singular.

Step 4: Determine Whether the Verb Tense Is Correct

Yes. The sentence is in future tense, and so is the verb.

Step 5: Determine Whether the Pronoun Is Correct

No. <u>Student</u> is singular and <u>their</u> is plural, so the pronoun does not agree with the antecedent. The pronoun should be <u>his or her</u>, since we don't know if the student is male or female.

Step 6: Read Each Answer Choice

Answer choice D matches the correction we came up with during Step 5, so we'll select this answer.

Now it's your turn. Take a look at the sentence. We'll prompt you on the steps you will need to practice the process.

Currently, we accepted applications for the receptionist and office clerk positions, which will be filled by the end of the month.

Which correction should be made to the sentence?

1. replace *Currently* with *Soon*

2. replace *we* with *they*

3. replace *accepted* with *are accepting*

4. replace *receptionist* with *secretary*

5. replace *will be* with *were*

Step 1: Read the Sentence

Step 2: Identify the Subject, Verb, and Pronoun

_____

_____

_____

Step 3: Determine Whether the Subject and Verb Agree

Step 4: Determine Whether the Verb Tense Is Correct

Step 5: Determine Whether the Pronoun Is Correct

Step 6: Read Each Answer Choice

The correct answer is C.

BASIC ENGLISH USAGE DRILLS

Fill in the blanks for question 1. For each of the subsequent questions, choose the best answer.

1. **What are the steps for correcting errors in usage?**

    Step 1: _____

    Step 2: _____

    Step 3: _____

    Step 4: _____

    Step 5: _____

    Step 6: _____

Questions 2–15 refer to the following passage.

Harbor View Accounting Services
3719 West Lakeside Lane
Chicago, IL 60610
April 2, 2012

Dear Ms. Lopart,

(1) We have reviewed your recent employment application and would like to further discuss opportunities within our company. (2) We believe you are well qualified for the customer service representative position, which was currently available. (3) Everyone in this position work full time. (4) Mr. Wong is the supervisor in this department. (5) The employees and him have built a strong working relationship. (6) Seldom does the representatives have problems in this department. (7) The employees and Mr. Wong demonstrates positive attitudes, which create an enjoyable work environment.

 (8) Harbor View Accounting Services are pleased to offer a comprehensive benefits package to their employees. (9) Health insurance, dental insurance, and optical benefits are provided for each employee and their family. (10) Both short- and long-term disability coverage are also available and will be popular options since they were added to our benefits menu. (11) Either of these begin immediately upon being hired. (12) Choosing which benefits your family needs are important. (13) A representative from the human resources department is available to further explain the insurance benefits available.

(14) Customer service representatives at Harbor View works five days each week, with weekends off. (15) We expect their employees to arrive promptly by 8:00 A.M. and to work until 5:00 P.M., with a one hour lunch break during the day (16) Anyone needing to adjust these hours due to appointments or emergencies are able to do so occasionally.

(17) We look forward to further discussing the customer service representative position with you. (18) Thank you for your interest in working with our company.

Sincerely,

Ms. Wilma Harrington

2. **Sentence 2:** We believe you are well qualified for the customer service representative position, which was currently available.

    Which correction should be made to sentence 2?

    A. replace *We* with *Our*
    B. replace *believe* with *believes*
    C. replace *you* with *we*
    D. replace *are* with *will be*
    E. replace *was* with *is*

3. **Sentence 3:** Everyone in this position work full time.

    Which correction should be made to sentence 3?

    A. replace *Everyone* with *Anyone*
    B. replace *Everyone* with *They*
    C. replace *this* with *their*
    D. replace *work* with *works*
    E. replace *work* with *worked*

4. **Sentence 5:** The employees and him have built a strong working relationship.

    Which correction should be made to sentence 5?

    A. replace *employees* with *they*
    B. replace *him* with *he*
    C. replace *have* with *has*
    D. replace *built* with *will build*
    E. replace *working* with *have worked*

5. **Sentence 6:** Seldom does the representatives have problems in this department.

    Which correction should be made to sentence 6?

    A. replace *Seldom* with *Often*
    B. replace *does* with *do*
    C. replace *representatives* with *them*
    D. replace *have* with *will has*
    E. replace *this* with *your*

6. **Sentence 7:** The employees and Mr. Wong demonstrates positive attitudes, which create an enjoyable work environment.

   Which correction should be made to sentence 7?

   A. replace *employees* with *them*
   B. replace *Mr. Wong* with *him*
   C. replace *demonstrates* with *demonstrate*
   D. replace *create* with *will create*
   E. replace *work* with *will work*

7. **Sentence 8:** Harbor View Accounting Services are pleased to offer a comprehensive benefits packages to their employees.

   Which is one correction that should be made to sentence 8?

   A. replace *Harbor View Accounting Services* with *They*
   B. replace *Harbor View Accounting Services* with *It*
   C. replace *are* with *were*
   D. replace *are* with *is*
   E. replace *are* with *will be*

8. **Sentence 8:** Harbor View Accounting Services are pleased to offer a comprehensive benefits package to their employees.

   Which is one correction that should be made to sentence 8?

   A. replace *pleased* with *pleasing*
   B. replace *offer* with *offering*
   C. replace *offer* with *offered*
   D. replace *their* with *your*
   E. replace *their* with *its*

9. **Sentence 9:** Health insurance, dental insurance, and optical benefits are provided for each employee and their family.

   Which correction should be made to sentence 9?

   A. replace *benefits* with *benefit*
   B. replace *are* with *is*
   C. replace *each* with *every*
   D. replace *employee* with *employees*
   E. replace *their* with *his or her*

10. **Sentence 10:** Both short- and long-term disability coverage are also available and will be popular options since they were added to our benefits menu.

    Which correction should be made to sentence 10?

    A. replace *are* with *were*
    B. replace *will be* with *have been*
    C. replace *they* with *it*
    D. replace *were* with *was*
    E. replace *our* with *your*

11. **Sentence 11:** Either of these begin immediately upon being hired.

    Which correction should be made to sentence 11?

    A. replace *Either* with *Neither*
    B. replace *Either* with *Each*
    C. replace *begin* with *begins*
    D. replace *begin* with *began*
    E. replace *begin* with *beginning*

12. **Sentence 12:** Choosing which benefits your family needs are important.

    Which correction should be made to sentence 12?

    A. replace *Choosing* with *Choose*
    B. replace *which* with *that*
    C. replace *your* with *you*
    D. replace *needs* with *will need*
    E. replace *are* with *is*

13. **Sentence 14:** Customer service representatives at Harbor View works five days each week, with weekends off.

    Which correction should be made to sentence 14?

    A. replace *Customer service representatives* with *They*
    B. replace *Customer service representatives* with *Them*
    C. replace *works* with *work*
    D. replace *works* with *worked*
    E. replace *each* with *every*

14. **Sentence 15:** We expect their employees to arrive promptly by 8:00 A.M. and to work until 5:00 P.M. with a one-hour lunch break during the day.

    Which correction should be made to sentence 15?

    A. replace *We* with *I*
    B. replace *their* with *our*
    C. replace *employees* with *them*
    D. replace *to arrive* with *will arrive*
    E. replace *to work* with *working*

15. **Sentence 16:** Anyone needing to adjust these hours due to appointments or emergencies are able to do so occasionally.

    Which correction should be made to sentence 16?

    A. replace *Anyone* with *Someone*
    B. replace *needing* with *needs*
    C. replace *to adjust* with *adjusting*
    D. replace *these* with *them*
    E. replace *are* with *is*

chapter 4

Sentence Structure

What's Being Tested?

Recognizing mistakes in how sentences are put together accounts for 30 percent of the questions on the GED Language Arts, Writing Test, Part I. You will not only need to recognize sentence fragments, run-ons, comma splices, and lack of parallel structure, but you will also need to know what changes to make to correct these sentence structure slipups.

When you get to Part II of the test, you will need to demonstrate proper sentence structure in writing your own essay, so think of this chapter as a two-for-one. By understanding what does and does not make a proper sentence, you will be preparing for both sections of the test.

The Basics of Sentence Structure

As you know, a sentence expresses a complete thought and has to have a subject and a verb. The subject is the *who* or the *what* that is completing an action. The verb is the action that tells what the subject is or what the subject does.

Addison walked her dog.

Addison is the subject, because she is the *who* that is completing the action. *Walked* is the verb because it tells what Addison, the subject, did.

Dependent and Independent Clauses

A *clause* is a group of words that contains a subject and a verb. A *dependent clause* cannot stand alone, because it does not express a complete thought, despite the fact that it has a subject and a verb. It *depends* on another clause to be able to create a complete sentence.

> After Selena heard the doorbell

An *independent clause* can stand alone. It has a subject and a verb and expresses a complete thought. It is a complete sentence.

> She rushed to the peephole to look outside.

Compound Subjects

A sentence may have more than one subject.

> <u>Addison</u> and <u>Chad</u> walked the dog.

Compound Verbs

A sentence may also have more than one verb.

> Addison <u>walked</u> the dog and <u>gave</u> him a bath.

Compound Sentences

Compound sentences are two independent clauses that are joined together to create a single sentence; in other words, two complete sentences put together. A coordinating conjunction, such as *and, but, for, nor, or, so,* or *yet,* is the glue that holds the independent clauses together and also shows how they relate to each other.

> Luis did not study for the final exam, <u>yet</u> he still managed to ace the class.

Notice that each of the clauses is independent and expresses a complete thought. Also notice that the end of the first clause is followed by a comma and then the conjunction.

Run-On Sentences

Like compound sentences, *run-on sentences* also include two independent clauses. The difference is, the clauses in a run-on sentence are not joined by a conjunction. The clauses literally run into one another.

Kailyn is a terrific dancer she has taken ballet classes since she was young.

You may be thinking, *So how does one correct a run-on sentence?* We're so glad you asked! There are three options: (1) Add a period to the end of the first clause, creating two complete sentences. (2) Place a semicolon at the end of the first clause to separate the two ideas. (3) Create a compound sentence by inserting a comma and coordinating conjunction at the end of the first clause. Here are ways our sample sentence can be corrected.

Kailyn is a terrific dancer. She has taken ballet classes since she was young.

Kailyn is a terrific dancer; she has taken ballet classes since she was young.

Kailyn is a terrific dancer, for she has taken ballet classes since she was young.

Comma Splice

Like a run-on sentence, a *comma splice* also includes two independent clauses. But in this case, a comma has been placed between the clauses.

Franklin is renting a house near campus, it is much larger than a dorm room.

That certainly looks a lot like a run-on, doesn't it? The comma is the only thing that causes this to be a comma splice rather than a run-on sentence. Again, there are several options for correcting this sentence snafu. As with a run-on, you could use a period or semicolon to separate the clauses. You could also add a coordinating conjunction after the comma to create a compound sentence. Or you could add a subordinating conjunction that would cause one of the clauses to become dependent. Check out how each of these options would look.

Franklin is renting a house near campus. It is much larger than a dorm room.

Franklin is renting a house near campus; it is much larger than a dorm room.

Franklin is renting a house near campus, and it is much larger than a dorm room.

Franklin is renting a house near campus because it is much larger than a dorm room.

Complex Sentences

Complex sentences include both an independent and a dependent clause, which are joined by a subordinating conjunction, such as *although, because, unless,* or *while*. The conjunction appears at the beginning of the dependent clause and highlights the relationship between the two clauses.

Tiffany got to work on time, even though her alarm did not go off this morning.

The order of the clauses does not matter; either can come first. When the sentence begins with the dependent clause, a comma separates the clauses.

Even though her alarm did not go off this morning, Tiffany got to work on time.

Keep in Mind

Keep in mind that a subordinating conjunction should point out how the clauses relate to one another. Check out a few examples of conjunctions to show certain situations.

- **Cause and effect:** because, now that, so, whether
- **Condition:** as long as, if, provided that, unless
- **Contrast:** although, even though, whereas
- **Time:** after, before, during, once, since

Sentence Fragments

A sentence fragment is a group of words that may look like a sentence but fails to express a complete thought. The fragment might be missing the subject or the verb, or it may be a dependent clause.

> Fixed eggs and bacon for breakfast
>
> The majority of the employees in that department
>
> Even though the stock market rose significantly yesterday

The good news is, once you identify what causes a group of words to be a sentence fragment, the error is easy to fix. Simply add whatever is missing—a subject, a verb, or an independent clause.

> <u>Malcolm</u> fixed eggs and bacon for breakfast.
>
> The majority of the employees in that department <u>work hard.</u>
>
> Even though the stock market rose significantly yesterday, <u>I have no plans to invest right now.</u>

Coordination

Combining two independent clauses with a coordinating conjunction is called *coordination*. This combining of ideas not only allows for varied sentence structure, but it also helps the ideas flow more smoothly. Sometimes, words may need to be removed to avoid repetition.

> *Incorrect:* Tara will stay for cheerleading practice. She will not stay for the game.
>
> *Correct:* Tara will stay for cheerleading practice but not for the game.

Subordination

Subordination combines independent clauses by adding a subordinating conjunction. This creates a complex sentence structure and causes one of the clauses to become dependent on the other.

> *Incorrect:* Shannon is planning to buy a new dress. She wants to look professional for a job interview on Friday.
>
> *Correct:* Since she wants to look professional for a job interview on Friday, Shannon is planning to buy a new dress.

Keep in Mind

Keep in mind that by making one of the clauses dependent on the other, you are establishing that clause as less important. Make sure you combine the clauses in such a way that the most important idea remains an independent clause and the less important idea becomes subordinate to that.

Modification

Modifiers, including adverbs and adjectives, are words or phrases that offer details to clarify and add information to a sentence. The important thing to remember about modifiers is that what they are intended to modify must be crystal clear. Dangling modifiers leave questions about this.

Incorrect: Having been tossed three feet in the air, the chef caught the pizza dough.

So, was the chef tossed three feet in the air? Not likely. To clarify the meaning here, you could do one of several things. You could change the modifying phrase to a dependent clause. You could also rearrange the words so that the modifier is beside the word it is supposed to describe.

After the pizza dough was tossed three feet in the air, the chef caught it.

After the chef tossed the pizza dough three feet in the air, he caught it.

Misplaced modifiers can also lead to confusion. While it might be clear which object is being modified, the intended message of the sentence is vague.

Incorrect: The shoes were too tight in the closet.

Does this mean that the shoes were supercomfortable when located elsewhere? Probably not. Moving the modifier can eliminate any confusion.

The shoes in the closet were too tight.

Parallelism

When a list of ideas is included in a sentence, they should be written using a parallel, or similar, grammatical form. *Parallelism* not only helps the writing flow more smoothly, it also helps to express the ideas clearly.

> *Incorrect:* Nick bought his train ticket, will find a seat, and is reading the paper before the train left the station.

> *Incorrect:* Katia spent her vacation on a cruise, at the beach, and went to New York.

The first sentence includes past, future, and present tense verbs. To create parallelism, the verbs should all be in the same tense. The second sentence includes a list of places Katia went. Two of the places begin with a preposition, but the third does not. The key to parallelism is consistency.

> Nick bought his train ticket, found a seat, and read the paper before the train left the station.

> Katia spent her vacation on a cruise, at the beach, and in New York.

What to Do

Now that you've gone over some of the main points you need to remember about sentence structure, let's go over the six steps you will use to answer sentence structure questions on the GED.

> *Steps for Correcting Errors in Sentence Structure*
> **Step 1:** Read the Sentence
> **Step 2:** Determine Whether or Not the Sentence Is Complete
> **Step 3:** Determine Whether or Not the Ideas Are Expressed Clearly
> **Step 4:** Look for Parallelism
> **Step 5:** Decide How to Improve the Sentence
> **Step 6:** Read Each Answer Choice

Step 1: Read the Sentence

Read the entire sentence carefully. This is pretty much a standing rule for any test. Always read any passages, questions, sentences, or directions thoroughly. There are times in life when skimming and scanning text come in handy, but generally, the GED test is not one of those times.

Step 2: Determine Whether or Not the Sentence Is Complete

As you read the sentence, look for the subject and verb and then decide whether or not a complete idea is expressed. If you find a subject, verb, and complete idea, you've found a complete sentence! If not, decide whether you're dealing with a run-on, sentence fragment, dependent clause, or comma splice.

Step 3: Determine Whether or Not the Ideas Are Expressed Clearly

If the message is not clearly expressed or leads to any confusion, there may be a better way to arrange the ideas in the sentence. Look for modifiers, and figure out what they are intended to modify.

Step 4: Look for Parallelism

Look at all the phrases in the sentence. Check to see whether or not they are all in the same form.

When reading the sentence as a whole, it can be easy to overlook errors in parallelism. Try reading just the verbs to see if they are in similar form. Then read just the prepositional phrases to see if they are similar in form. Continue this with each speech element.

Keep in Mind

Keep in mind that parallelism should hold true for any part of speech. Be sure to check for similar structure between verbs, adjectives, adverbs, nouns, and phrases.

Step 5: Decide How to Improve the Sentence

After completing Steps 1 through 4, you should have identified the error in the sentence. Now it's time to figure out how to fix any mistakes. For example, if you find that the sentence is a run-on, you'll know that the best way to revise it would be to add a period, insert a semicolon, or create a compound sentence using a comma and an appropriate conjunction. If you find a dangling modifier, determine the best way to rearrange the words in the sentence to make sure the intended meaning is clear. If you find two complete sentences that would be more effective if combined, determine which should be subordinate to the other and select an appropriate conjunction to join them.

Remember, it is best to determine how to correct the error in the sentence before reading the answer choices. As we saw with run-on sentences, there may be more than one correct way to revise the sentence. Think about all the options that would fix the mistake and create a sentence with sensational structure.

Step 6: Read Each Answer Choice

Now that you know what the corrected sentence should look like, read every answer choice. Again, read carefully, as the differences in the choices may be slight. Check to see if the correction you came up with in Step 5 is among the answer choices. If not, don't panic! There may be several options for correcting the mistake. Just because your answer is not there does not mean that you were wrong. It may mean that while you thought of a terrific way to revise the sentence, the test writers came up with something else. Carefully consider each choice and decide why it does or does not work. Be critical. There is only one best answer. Make sure you find it.

Examples

Now that you are a sentence structure superstar, let's look at some sample questions. Use the six steps we've discussed to help you identify the error and select the best revision.

Darnell spends every Saturday playing golf and swims laps in the pool.

Which is the best revision of the sentence?

1. spent every Saturday playing golf
2. has spent every Saturday playing golf

3. playing golf and swimming laps

4. playing golf and will swim laps

5. plays golf and swims laps

Here are our steps:

Step 1: Read the Sentence

Step 2: Determine Whether or Not the Sentence Is Complete

Subject: Darnell

Verbs: spends, playing, swims

Expresses a complete thought? yes

Step 3: Determine Whether or Not the Ideas Are Expressed Clearly

Yes

Step 4: Look for Parallelism

No; playing and swims are not parallel

Step 5: Decide How to Improve the Sentence

Possible corrections: Darnell spends every Saturday playing golf and swimming laps.

Darnell plays golf and swims laps every Saturday.

Step 6: Read Each Answer Choice

Answer 3 matches one of the possible corrections from Step 5.

Now it's your turn. Take a look at the following sentence. We'll give you the steps you will need to practice the process.

Colleen is planning to make chicken stew for Brian when he comes to dinner. Brian does not eat beef.

Which group of words would be included in the most effective combination of these sentences?

1. While Colleen is planning

2. Since Colleen is planning

3. dinner; yet Brian does not

4. dinner, because he does not

5. dinner, even though he does not

Step 1: Read the Sentence

Step 2: Determine Whether or Not the Sentence Is Complete

_____

_____

_____

Step 3: Determine Whether or Not the Ideas Are Expressed Clearly

_____

Step 4: Look for Parallelism

_____

Step 5: Decide How to Improve the Sentence

_____

Step 6: Read Each Answer Choice

The correct answer is 4.

Keep in Mind

Keep in mind that sometimes the sentence may not contain any errors. If this is the case, you are likely to see one of two things. First, answer A may show the original sentence, or the portion of the sentence, in question. If the original version is already correct, choose the answer that does not show any changes. Second, answer E may state that no corrections are necessary. If this statement is true, select this option as the best answer. Just because you are being asked to find errors in a sentence, it does not mean there will always be something wrong.

SENTENCE STRUCTURE DRILLS

For question 1, fill in the blanks. For each of the subsequent questions, choose the best answer.

1. **What are the steps for correcting errors in sentence structure?**

    Step 1: _____

    Step 2: _____

    Step 3: _____

    Step 4: _____

    Step 5: _____

    Step 6: _____

Questions 2–15 refer to the following passage.

(1) At some point, most people will need to fill out a job application. (2) This can cause feelings of excitement, fear, and being worried. (3) You may be nervous, since being well prepared can help this to be a positive experience.

(4) If you will be completing the application at the job site. (5) It is a good idea to bring your own pen never fill out an application in pencil. (6) Blue or black ink. (7) By having your own pen. (8) You will look better prepared than if you had to ask to borrow one. (9) Most applications will require certain personal information, have your social security number and previous addresses handy. (10) If you have had other jobs in the past you will need to provide information regarding your work history. (11) You may need to submit the names of your supervisors, the addresses of the companies, and when you worked with each.

(12) Many potential employers also require a list of at least three people to be personal references. (13) Write down people you can use. (14) Include teachers, previous employers, reputable friends, or not members of your family. (15) Make sure beforehand that the people are willing to give you a positive reference on the list.

(16) After completing it in neat handwriting, the supervisor should be given the application. (17) Leaving it on a service counter, table, or desk does not ensure that the application will get into the proper hands to be reviewed.

2. **Sentence 2: This can cause feelings of excitement, fear, and being worried.**
    Which correction should be made to sentence 2?
    A. change *excitement* to *being excited*
    B. insert a semicolon after *excitement*

C. change *fear* to *fearful*
D. insert a semicolon after *fear*
E. change *being worried* to *worry*

3. **Sentence 3: You may be nervous, since being well prepared can help this to be a positive experience.**

   Which correction should be made to sentence 3?

   A. replace the comma after *nervous* with a semicolon
   B. insert the word *and* after the comma
   C. remove the comma after *nervous*
   D. replace *since* with *but*
   E. replace *since* with *unless*

4. **Sentence 4: If you will be completing the application at the job site.**

   Which correction should be made to sentence 4?

   A. change the period to a comma
   B. change the period to a semicolon
   C. change the period to a comma and add *during regular business hours.*
   D. change the period to a comma and add *be sure to bring everything you might need.*
   E. change the period to a semicolon and add *it is important to be prepared for this process.*

5. **Sentence 5: It is a good idea to bring your own pen never fill out an application in pencil.**

   Which correction should be made to sentence 5?

   A. insert a period after *idea*
   B. insert a comma after *pen*
   C. insert a semicolon after *pen*
   D. insert a comma and *or* before *never*
   E. insert a semicolon and *because* before *never*

6. **Sentence 6: Blue or black ink.**

   Which correction should be made to sentence 6?

   A. add *Using* before blue
   B. change the period to a semicolon
   C. change the period to a comma
   D. insert *will look most professional* after *ink*
   E. insert a comma and *which are dark colors* after *ink*

7. **Sentences 7 and 8: By having your <u>own pen. You will look</u> better prepared than if you had to ask to borrow one.**

   Which is the best way to write the underlined portion of sentences 7 and 8?

   A. own pen. You will look
   B. own pen, you will look

C. own pen; you will look
D. own pen you will look
E. own pen, you will look,

8. **Sentence 9: Most applications will require certain personal information, have your social security number and previous addresses handy.**

   Which correction should be made to sentence 9?

   A. replace the comma with a semicolon
   B. insert *and* after the comma
   C. replace the comma with *and*
   D. insert a comma after *number*
   E. no changes are necessary

9. **Sentence 10: If you have had other jobs in the past you will need to provide information regarding your work history.**

   Which correction should be made to sentence 10?

   A. insert a comma after *jobs*
   B. insert a semicolon after *jobs*
   C. insert a comma after *past*
   D. insert a period after *past*
   E. no changes are necessary

10. **Sentence 11: You may need to submit the names of your supervisors, the addresses of the companies, and when you worked with each.**

    Which correction should be made to sentence 11?

    A. change *names* to *name*
    B. change *the companies* to *their companies*
    C. change *and* to *or*
    D. change *when* to *the dates*
    E. change *worked* to *have worked*

11. **Sentences 12 and 13: Many potential employers also require a list of at least three people to be <u>personal references. Write down people</u> you can use.**

    Which is the best way to write the underlined portion of sentences 12 and 13?

    A. personal references. Write down people
    B. personal references, so write down who
    C. personal references, write down people
    D. personal references, and write down who
    E. personal references; before write down people

12. **Sentence 14: Include teachers, previous employers, reputable friends, or not members of your family.**

    Which correction should be made to sentence 14?

    A. add *Also* before *include*
    B. insert *and* after *teachers*
    C. insert *or* before *reputable*
    D. change *or* to *and*
    E. change *or* to *but*

13. **Sentence 15: Make sure beforehand that the people are willing to give you a positive reference on the list.**

    Which correction should be made to sentence 15?

    A. move *beforehand* to follow *list*
    B. move *beforehand* to precede *make*
    C. insert a comma after *reference*
    D. insert a comma and *who are* after *reference*
    E. move *on the list* to follow *people*

14. **Sentence 16: After completing it in neat handwriting, the supervisor should be given the application.**

    Which is the best revision of sentence 16?

    A. After you complete it in neat handwriting, the application should be given to the supervisor.
    B. After he completes it in neat handwriting, the supervisor should be given the application.
    C. After you complete it in neat handwriting, the supervisor should be given the application.
    D. After completing the application in neat handwriting, the supervisor should be given it.
    E. no revisions are necessary

15. **Sentence 17: Leaving it on a service counter, table, or desk does not ensure that the application will get into the proper hands to be reviewed.**

    Which correction should be made to the underlined portion of sentence 17?

    A. the application will get into the proper hands to be reviewed
    B. the application, however, will get into the proper hands for review
    C. the application will get into the proper hands, to be reviewed
    D. the proper hands will review the application
    E. it will get into their hands to be reviewed

chapter **5**

Mechanics

One of the first things you probably learned about language arts is that a sentence begins with a capital letter and ends with a period. In a nutshell, that's what this chapter is all about. The mechanics of English include capitalization, punctuation, and spelling. On Part I of the GED Language Arts, Writing Test, you will use what you know about mechanics to revise and edit sentences. Such items will make up about a fourth of this part of the test.

In Part II, you will have to use mechanics correctly when writing your essay. In this chapter, we'll review language arts rules about when to use a capital letter, how to determine whether a sentence calls for a colon or a semicolon, and why you need to know the difference between *two*, *too*, and *to*. Best of all, by the time we're done, you'll be able to edit passages without the assistance of a spell-check tool!

The Big Three

As already mentioned, mechanics is all about three main areas of writing: capitalization, punctuation, and spelling. Let's go over some of the most important points regarding these keys to wonderful writing.

Capitalization

Your kindergarten teacher probably drilled into your head the importance of starting your name with a capital letter. Many more capital letter rules followed.

While some of them are pretty simple and are rules that you apply every day without even thinking, a few might trip up even the best English language users at times.

Proper Nouns

Proper nouns name specific people, places, or things. While you would not need to capitalize a common noun, such as *dog*, you would capitalize the proper noun that names a specific dog, such as *Fido*.

> The newest woman in our department, Racquel, will be in the corner office.

> We have lived in several states, including Illinois, Pennsylvania, and Georgia.

> While attending Riverview High School in Washington, D.C., we visited the Lincoln Memorial, as well as several other monuments, while on a school field trip.

Notice that common nouns such as *woman, states, monuments,* and *school* are not capitalized, but proper nouns naming specific people, places, and things are.

Titles of People

Titles are capitalized when they refer to a specific person.

> The students' talking stopped when Professor Rodriguez entered the room.

> I always call Mom and send flowers on her birthday.

On the other hand, when titles simply refer to an occupation or relationship, they are not capitalized.

> Have you heard who the professor will be for Biology 101 this semester?

> My mom goes to yoga class every day after work.

Keep in Mind

Keep in mind that when *Mom* is used as a name, it is capitalized. However, when you are referring to a relationship, *mom* is lowercase. Confusing? Think of it this way: you would capitalize your sister's name (Amanda) but would not capitalize her relationship to you (sister).

In my opinion, Amanda is the most amazing sister in the world!

The same is true of other relationship names, such as dad, grandmother, and uncle. Here's another hint: sometimes, the word *my* can be a clue. If *my* is before the title, such as *my grandpa*, the name is not capitalized.

Titles of Written Works

Since titles are actually the names of books, plays, songs, shows, or magazines, they should also be capitalized. The exceptions are short prepositions and articles; these should not be capitalized unless they are the first word of the title.

My nephew sings "The Farmer in the Dell" and reads *The Tale of the Big, Bad Wolf* over and over.

Groups

As you know, specific names are capitalized. This is true for the names of groups, teams, organizations, and clubs.

Kasper had season tickets to the Red Sox games last year, because this is his favorite team.

The purpose of the fund-raising event was to raise money for charities, including the American Cancer Society.

Locations

Cardinal directions are not capitalized when they are used as directions but do begin with a capital letter when naming a specific location.

> The Choo family saved for years to take a trip to the West.

> Drive west on Maple Avenue; then turn north on Market Street.

Special Days and Events

As you can see on any calendar, the names of days, months, and holidays are capitalized. Seasons, however, are not, unless they are part of a title.

> The school's Spring Fling carnival will be held on Friday, April 8, which is only a few days after Easter.

The names of historic events are also capitalized. Notice that both words begin with a capital letter, since both are part of the name of the event.

> Morgan's grandfather is a veteran of World War II.

Punctuation

Punctuation can do much more than simply end a sentence. When used correctly, it can help to clarify meaning. Take a look at a few of the types of punctuation you will need to understand to do well on the GED.

Commas in Dates

A comma should be placed between the day and the year when writing a date. A comma should also follow the year when a complete date, including month, day, and year, is given within a sentence. A comma is not necessary when only the month and year are given.

> The first semester will begin August 18, 2012, and run through the middle of December. January 2013 will bring the new semester.

Commas in a Series

Commas are used to separate a list of more than two items.

> At the market, please buy a dozen eggs, a loaf of whole-wheat bread, and a quart of orange juice.

Sometimes, a list of adjectives is used to describe a noun. If each of these adjectives can stand alone to describe the item, they are separated by commas.

James flashed a bright, cheerful smile upon hearing the election results.

Commas and Quotations

Commas are also used to introduce quotations, including dialogue and information being copied from a source, such as an encyclopedia or a website. The comma appears outside of the quotation marks when the source is named before the quote and inside the quotation marks when the source is named after the quote.

According to a recent article in the *New York Times*, "students have shown academic gains that exceed any reported over the past decade."

"My greatest accomplishment during this term," the mayor explained, "was improving the educational programs in our community."

The exception to these rules comes into play when the quotation ends with a question mark or exclamation point. When the source or speaker is named after the quotation, a comma only replaces a period. It does not replace a question mark or exclamation point, since these are essential to the message.

"What are you planning to do about that?" asked Caitlyn.

"Look out!" Abe shouted.

Commas and Phrases

A phrase that appears at the beginning of a sentence is an introductory phrase. Such phrases should be followed by a comma.

As you know, it is important to prepare for the GED test.

Other phrases may appear in the middle of a sentence and interrupt the idea being expressed by sticking in a piece of information that may be interesting but is not vital. In other words, the phrase could be removed without changing the meaning of the sentence. In such cases, a comma is placed both before and after the interrupting phrase.

Raphael, who has a degree in marketing, was just promoted to head of the human relations department.

Words or modifying phrases that explain, define, or identify the noun or pronoun preceding them are called *appositives*. When the appositive is crucial to understanding the meaning of the noun, commas are not used. If the noun can be understood without the appositive, use commas before and after it.

The woman who answered the phone is the owner of the company.

The owner of the company, who answered the phone, is a friend of our family.

Commas and Compound Sentences

A compound sentence is created when two independent clauses are joined by a conjunction. A comma must precede the conjunction in a compound sentence.

The Cape Hatteras Lighthouse is the tallest in the United States, and its light can be seen for more than 20 miles across the Atlantic Ocean.

Commas and Conjunctive Adverbs

Conjunctive adverbs, such as *accordingly, on the other hand*, and *for example*, can be used to join two independent clauses. In this instance, the clauses are separated by a semicolon or a period. The conjunctive adverb introducing the independent clause is followed by a comma.

Noah did not return a signed permission slip; consequently, he will not be going on the class trip to the fine arts museum.

When the conjunctive adverb is in the middle of a sentence, it is preceded and followed by commas.

He is, however, planning to visit the museum this weekend.

Commas and Dependent Clauses

When a sentence begins with a dependent clause, it is followed by a comma. When the dependent clause follows the independent clause, a comma is not used.

Even though they are both cities in Florida, Pensacola and Tallahassee are located in different time zones.

Pensacola and Tallahassee are located in different time zones even though they are both cities in Florida.

Semicolons in a Series

Generally, commas are used to separate a list of items or phrases. However, when the phrases in the list already include commas, the components of the list are separated by semicolons.

The Sullivans' three children were born on February 9, 2002; April 2, 2004; and March 24, 2007.

Semicolons and Clauses

Two related independent clauses can be combined with a comma and coordinating conjunction. They can also be joined using a semicolon and no conjunction.

Hunter entered his physics project in the school science fair; he won first place.

As mentioned earlier, a semicolon can also be used to join two independent clauses with a conjunctive adverb.

This weekend's weather is expected to include thunderstorms; therefore, the class picnic will be postponed until further notice.

Apostrophes and Singular Possessive Nouns

A possessive noun shows ownership. In a singular possessive noun, the apostrophe is placed before the *s*. This holds true even if the singular noun ends with an *s*.

Delaware's state flower is the peach blossom.

Arkansas's state flower is the apple blossom.

Keep in Mind

Keep in mind that some proper names, such as *Alexis* or *Chris*, end in the letter *s*. To show ownership, an apostrophe and another *s* are added to the end, as they would be with any other name.

We went to Alexis's graduation party on Saturday.

Apostrophes and Plural Possessive Nouns

If a plural noun already ends with *s*, the apostrophe follows the *s*.

The teachers' lounge is located beside the office.

If a plural noun does not end with *s*, an apostrophe and *s* are added to the end of the word.

Women's shoes can be expensive and uncomfortable.

Apostrophes and Possessive Pronouns

Possessive pronouns, such as *hers*, *his*, *its*, *ours*, and *theirs*, show ownership without including an apostrophe and *s*. So a better heading for this section would have been "No Apostrophes with Possessive Pronouns."

Logan said his shirt needs to be ironed.

The sign on the front of the building has lost one of its letters.

Apostrophes and Plurals of Letters

Apostrophes are used to indicate plurals of letters.

Mark earned four A's and two B's on his report card.

Apostrophes and Contractions

A contraction is created when two words are combined to make a single, shorter word, such as when *can* and *not* are used to create *can't*. An apostrophe takes the place of the missing letter or letters in the new word.

The student body president doesn't plan to run for reelection next year because she'll be involved in other activities.

Quotation Marks and Quotes

Quotation marks indicate the beginning and end of a direct quote and are placed around the exact words that were spoken or copied from a source.

"We are going to the football game," Meredith explained, "but we may not get there until halftime."

According to the *Atlanta Business Journal*, "Sales have risen by 23% over the past quarter."

Quotation Marks and Titles

Titles of short works, such as poems, chapters, songs, short stories, television shows, and articles, are enclosed in quotation marks.

Our homework tonight is to read "The Roosevelt Era," which is chapter four in the history book.

Spelling

When you think of spelling questions on the GED, don't think of the number-your-paper-from-1-to-20 spelling tests you took in third grade. On the GED, you will have to recognize whether homonyms, contractions, and possessives are used and spelled correctly in a sentence.

Homonyms

When you read the words *sale* and *sail*, or *blue* and *blew*, they sound identical. But, as you know, their definitions are nothing alike. Words that sound the same but have different meanings and spellings are *homonyms*.

Walter learned to write with his right hand.

The pitcher accidentally threw the ball through the windshield of the car.

We were not sure whether the weather would be warm or cool this morning.

On the GED, you will find sentences that include the wrong homonym. You will need to identify the incorrect word and recognize the correct spelling. When writing your essay, you will need to use the correct spelling of any homonyms that you include.

Incorrect: While on our for-day vacation, we saw the White House and the Capital building, witch are located in Washington, D.C.

Correct: While on our <u>four</u>-day vacation, we saw the White House and the <u>Capitol</u> building, <u>which</u> are located in Washington, D.C.

Contractions

As mentioned earlier, contractions such as *I'm* and *don't* are formed by combining two words. The apostrophe in a contraction replaces the letter or letters that are left out when the words are combined. In many cases, omitting the apostrophe creates a different word. Without the apostrophe, contractions are not spelled correctly.

> Kyle hasn't left for school yet because he's not finished eating breakfast.
>
> It's 7:00 now; we'll be at the party within an hour.

Possessives

As already discussed, possessives show ownership. An apostrophe and *s* are added to the end of singular nouns. An apostrophe is added to the end of plural nouns that already end in *s*. And an apostrophe and *s* are added to the end of plural nouns that do not already end in *s*.

> Jessica's house is two blocks south of the children's museum.
>
> Girls' clothing is located upstairs in that department store.

Possessive Pronouns

Possessive pronouns, such as *yours*, *ours*, and *his*, also show ownership. However, they do so without the use of an apostrophe and *s*.

> Lexi said that the yellow coat is hers.
>
> The basket on the table is ours; their basket is on the floor.

Keep in Mind

Keep in mind that it can be easy to confuse the spelling of certain possessive pronouns and contractions. For example *its* and *it's* are homonyms. *Its* shows ownership, whereas *it's* is a contraction for *it is*. Make sure you know when to use each spelling of words such as these.

How to Master the Mechanics Questions

Let's go over the six steps you'll need to use in correctly answering the questions related to mechanics.

> ### Steps for Correcting Errors in Mechanics
> **Step 1:** Read the Sentence
> **Step 2:** Look at the Letters
> **Step 3:** Peruse the Punctuation
> **Step 4:** Scope Out the Spelling
> **Step 5:** Fix What You Found
> **Step 6:** Examine the Answers

Step 1: Read the Sentence

As always, read the sentence very carefully. In this case, you are looking for errors that may not stand out at first glance. You may need to go over every single letter and punctuation mark with a fine-tooth comb. Remember, you are looking not only for what is there but also for what may be missing.

Step 2: Look at the Letters

Look at the capital letters in the sentence. Are they all necessary, or are some words capitalized incorrectly?

Next, look at each word in the sentence. Does it name someone or something? If so, look to see whether or not it begins with a capital letter.

Step 3: Peruse the Punctuation

First, look at the punctuation in the sentence. Is it all necessary, or is extra punctuation included? Commas are often overused in writing. Make sure that all commas in the sentence are necessary. Also ask yourself if the punctuation is placed correctly. For example, look to see that apostrophes are properly placed in possessives, that quotation marks include the correct words, and that commas are where they belong in relation to any quotes.

Then look to see what punctuation is missing. For example, look for dependent clauses that might be missing a comma or independent clauses that need a semicolon between them. See if there are any places in the sentence where adding punctuation could clarify meaning.

Step 4: Scope Out the Spelling

Check each word carefully to be sure that it is spelled correctly; then reread the sentence as a whole. Think about the spelling of each word as it relates to the meaning of the sentence. For instance, if you look at the word *well* in isolation, it appears to be spelled correctly. However, if you look at it in the context of the sentence *Well be there on Sunday*, it is misspelled. In this case, *well* should be *we'll*.

Step 5: Fix What You Found

Once you've found the problem in the sentence, determine how to fix it. Figure out what the corrected sentence should look like, how it should be spelled, and where punctuation should be included.

Step 6: Examine the Answers

Finally, look at each answer choice and find the one that matches the corrections you made in Step 5. Then look back at each of the other choices and determine why each is incorrect. Being able to recognize why an answer is wrong will help to ensure that you have not overlooked anything. Remember, the difference of a single letter can make an entire answer wrong. Examine each answer choice carefully before making your final decision.

Examples

Let's look at some sample questions. We'll use the steps to find which answer models the correct use of English mechanics.

We read Emily Dickinson's poem, the Bee in class.

Which is the best way to write the sentence? If the original is correct, choose answer choice A.

1. We read Emily Dickinson's poem, the Bee in class.
2. We read Emily Dickinson's poem, "The Bee," in class.
3. We read Emily Dickinson's poem the Bee in class.
4. We read Emily Dickinson's poem, "the Bee" in class.
5. We read Emily Dickinson's poem "The Bee" in class.

Here are our steps:

Step 1: Read the Sentence

Step 2: Look at the Letters

The is part of the title of the poem, so it should be capitalized.

Step 3: Peruse the Punctuation

There should not be a comma after <u>poem</u> since the name of the poem is important in understanding the sentence.

Step 4: Scope Out the Spelling

Everything is spelled correctly.

Step 5: Fix What You Found

We read Emily Dickinson's poem "The Bee" in class.

Step 6: Examine the Answers

Answer choice E matches our corrected sentence from Step 5, so we'll select this answer.

Now it's your turn. Take a look at the following sentence and select the best correction. We'll give you the steps you will need to practice the process.

Many students would rather cram for a test then plan ahead, study early, and be prepared.

Which correction should be made to the sentence?

    A. replace *for* with *four*

    B. replace *then* with *than*

    C. remove the comma after *ahead*

    D. replace both commas with semicolons

    E. remove the comma after *early*

Step 1: Read the Sentence

Step 2: Look at the Letters

_____

Step 3: Peruse the Punctuation

_____

Step 4: Scope Out the Spelling

Step 5: Fix What You Found

Step 6: Examine the Answers

The correct answer is B.

MECHANICS DRILLS

Fill in the blanks for question 1. For each of the subsequent questions, choose the best answer.

1. **What are the steps for correcting errors in mechanics?**
    Step 1: _____
    Step 2: _____
    Step 3: _____
    Step 4: _____
    Step 5: _____
    Step 6: _____

(1) Over time, many new words have been added to our Language. (2) Not to many years ago, no one had even heard of a cell phone. (3) A laptop was where you sat with your Grandmother on her front porch swing to enjoy the sunset. (4) And, a cloud only referred to something seen in the sky indicating possible rain showers. (5) Today, *telecommute* is a word that is familiar to many, yet, was unheard of only a few decades in the past.

   (6) *Telecommute* means to work from home rather than in an office via computer. (7) Thanks to today's technology many people around the world enjoy this employment option. (8) While its not convenient or possible for everyone telecommuting does offer advantages. (9) These employees save money on clothes, gasoline, and lunch, may be able to set flexible hours, and save time commuting. (10) Companies' reap benefits from this arrangement as well. (11) Fewer sick days are taken, medical and Doctor expenses decrease, and less office space is needed. (12) As more and more people become comfortable with this less traditional work environment, we can expect its popularity to increase.

2. **Sentence 1: Over time, many new words have been added to our Language. Which correction should be made to sentence 1?**
    A. remove the comma
    B. replace the comma with a semicolon
    C. replace *new* with *knew*
    D replace *Language* with *language*
    E. no corrections are needed

3. **Sentence 2: Not to many years ago, no one had even heard of a cell phone.**

   Which shows the best way to write sentence 2? If no change is needed, select answer choice A.

   A. Not to many years ago, no one had even heard of a cell phone.
   B. Not to many years ago no one had even heard of a cell phone.
   C. Not too many years ago, no one had even heard of a sell phone.
   D. Not too many years ago no one had even heard of a sell phone.
   E. Not too many years ago, no one had even heard of a cell phone.

4. **Sentence 3: A laptop was where you sat with your Grandmother on her front porch swing to enjoy the sunset.**

   Which shows the best way to write sentence 3? If no change is needed, select answer choice A.

   A. A laptop was where you sat with your Grandmother on her front porch swing to enjoy the sunset.
   B. A laptop was where you sat with your Grandmother, on her front porch swing, to enjoy the sunset.
   C. A laptop was where you sat with your Grandmother on her front porch swing too enjoy the sunset.
   D. A laptop was where you sat with your grandmother on her front porch swing to enjoy the sunset.
   E. A laptop was where you sat with your grandmother on her front porch swing, to enjoy the sunset.

5. **Sentence 4: And, a cloud only referred to something seen in the sky indicating possible rain showers.**

   Which correction should be made to sentence 4?

   A. remove the comma after *And*
   B. replace *seen* with *scene*
   C. insert a comma after *sky*
   D. insert commas around *in the sky*
   E. no change is needed

6. **Sentence 5: Today, *telecommute* is a word that is familiar to many, yet, was unheard of only a few decades in the past.**

   Which correction should be made to sentence 5?

   A. remove the comma after *Today*
   B. add a comma after *telecommute*
   C. remove the comma after *many*
   D. remove the comma after *yet*
   E. no change is needed

7. **Sentence 6:** *Telecommute* means to work from home rather than in an office via computer.

   Which correction should be made to sentence 6?

   A. insert quotation marks around *Telecommute*
   B. insert an apostrophe before the *s* in *means*
   C. insert a comma after *home*
   D. insert commas around *rather than in an office*
   E. no change is needed

8. **Sentence 7:** <u>Thanks to today's technology</u> many people around the world enjoy this employment option.

   Which correction should be made to the underlined portion of sentence 7?

   A. Thanks to today's technology,
   B. Thank's to today's technology,
   C. Thanks to todays technology
   D. Thank's to todays technology,
   E. no change is needed

9. **Sentence 8:** While its not convenient or possible for everyone telecommuting does offer advantages.

   Which is the best way to write sentence 8? If no change is needed, select answer choice A.

   A. While its not convenient or possible for everyone telecommuting does offer advantages.
   B. While it's not convenient or possible for everyone, telecommuting does offer advantages.
   C. While it's not convenient or possible for everyone telecommuting does offer advantages.
   D. While its not convenient or possible for everyone, telecommuting does offer advantages.
   E. While its not convenient, or possible, for everyone, telecommuting does offer advantages.

10. **Sentence 9:** These employees save money on clothes, gasoline, and lunch, may be able to set flexible hours, and save time commuting.

    Which correction should be made to sentence 9?

    A. replace *employees* with *employee's*
    B. replace *employees* with *employees'*
    C. replace *clothes* with *close*
    D. replace the commas after *clothes* and *gasoline* with semicolons
    E. replace the commas after *lunch* and *hours* with semicolons

11. **Sentence 10: Companies' reap benefits from this arrangement as well.**

    Which correction should be made to sentence 10?

    A. remove the apostrophe from *Companies'*
    B. replace *Companies'* with *Company's*
    C. insert a comma after *benefits*
    D. insert a comma after *arrangement*
    E. no correction is needed

12. **Sentence 11: Fewer sick days are taken, medical and doctor expenses decrease, and less office space is needed.**

    Which correction should be made to sentence 11?

    A. remove the comma after *taken*
    B. replace *Doctor* with *doctor*
    C. replace *expenses* with *expense's*
    D. remove the comma after *decrease*
    E. insert a comma after *less*

13. **Sentence 12: As more and more people become comfortable with this less traditional work environment, we can expect its popularity to increase.**

    Which shows the best way to write sentence 12?

    A. No change is needed.
    B. As more and more people become comfortable with this less, traditional work environment, we can expect its popularity to increase.
    C. As more and more people become comfortable with this less traditional work environment we can expect its popularity to increase.
    D. As more and more people become comfortable with this less traditional work environment, we can expect it's popularity to increase.
    E. As more and more people become comfortable with this less traditional work environment, we can expect its popularity to increase

chapter 6

Organization

What's Being Tested?

The way writing is organized helps readers to understand the meaning of the text. Think back to when you were little. You knew that the words *once upon a time* meant that a story was beginning. You knew that every story had a beginning, a middle, and an end and that the words *the end* signaled that the story was over. At this point, the materials you read are a little more complicated than that. However, you can still expect to find certain things when you read that will enhance your comprehension.

In this chapter, we'll review the proper way to organize writing in order to maximize comprehension. On Part I of the GED Language Arts, Writing test, you'll be expected to recognize well-organized writing and to make corrections to organization that would make the writing more effective. On Part II of the test, you will need to apply this knowledge to your own writing.

How Is Effective Writing Organized?

Just as a good story contains a beginning, a middle, and an end, good nonfiction writing contains an introduction, a body, and a conclusion. The introduction is exactly what it sounds like; it introduces the topic or idea. The body explains the idea using facts and examples. The conclusion sums up the idea, often by restating the main point introduced at the beginning of the essay.

Generally, paragraphs are the building blocks of these sections of an essay. Before we talk about the organization of an entire passage, let's go over what makes a good paragraph.

Strong Paragraphs

Suppose we wanted to write an effective paragraph about e-book readers—you know, those little handheld electronic devices that let you read pretty much any book in the library on a screen that is the size of a deck of cards. Let's go over exactly what might be included in our paragraph.

Main Idea

The sentences in a paragraph should focus on the same idea. The **main idea** of a paragraph is the main message that the writer wants to convey. Each paragraph should have a single main idea; the rest should help readers clearly understand this key concept.

E-book readers are a popular means of accessing information.

Topic Sentence

The **topic sentence** states the main idea of the paragraph. Usually, this is the first or last sentence; however, it can be anywhere in the paragraph. The purpose of the topic sentence is to give readers an idea of what the paragraph will be about. It is not intended to give all of the important information about the main idea.

Over the past few years, many companies have introduced their versions of e-book readers, which have become a popular means of accessing information.

Supporting Details

While the purpose of the topic sentence is to introduce the main idea of a paragraph, the purpose of the remaining sentences is to provide **supporting details**. These are data, details, definitions, or examples that help to explain or prove the main idea. They paint a picture for readers so they are able to understand the main point that the writer is trying to make.

E-book readers are smaller and lighter than traditional bound books. and they are being used by some school districts to replace traditional textbooks.

A single e-book reader is able to access countless books, offering the opportunity to begin reading a fiction or nonfiction selection within a matter of minutes.

Organizational Patterns

There are a number of ways by which authors may choose to organize information. The organizational pattern depends on the type of information included and the purpose of the writing. Using the correct organizational pattern helps readers better understand the ideas included in the paragraphs.

Chronological Order

Chronological order tells events in the order in which they occurred. This is most effective when the actual sequence in which the actions took place—or the sequence of steps in a process—is important for the reader to understand. Depending on the message of the passage, the events may be told in reverse chronological order, beginning with what took place most recently and moving backward in time.

Order of Importance

When a passage uses this organizational structure, the information may be arranged in one of two ways. First, the most important idea may be discussed at the beginning, followed by the second most important idea, and so on. The passage ends with the idea that the author believes is least important. The advantage of this type of organization is that the most important information catches the reader's attention at the very beginning.

Second, the least important idea may be discussed first, and the following ideas build in importance until the passage concludes with the most important one. The advantage of this type of organization is that the reader is left to ponder the most important idea, which is fresh in his or her mind.

Compare and Contrast

This organizational structure highlights the similarities and differences between people, ideas, or objects. This may be done by describing the first item completely and then describing the second completely. For example, an essay comparing and contrasting Hawaii and Bermuda might fully discuss one island and then the other.

Another way to organize a compare-and-contrast structure is to discuss how a particular attribute relates to each of the objects. Then discuss each of the items in reference to a second attribute, and so on. In this case, one paragraph might discuss the locations of Hawaii and Bermuda, the next paragraph might talk about each location's climate, and the following paragraph might describe sightseeing on both islands.

Cause and Effect

A cause-and-effect organizational structure points out how one idea or event impacts another. Words such as *consequently*, *as a result*, and *if . . . then* often signal a cause-and-effect relationship between concepts.

Keep in Mind

Keep in mind that a single event may be the cause of several other events. Likewise, several causes may lead to the same result. For example, the single event of forgetting to set your alarm clock may cause you to skip breakfast, miss the carpool, and be late for school or work. This one cause could lead to all three effects. On the other hand, studying hard, completing the practice questions, and carefully reading each of the chapters in this book could lead to you earning a great score on the GED! In this case, three causes could bring about one terrific effect.

Problem and Solution

This organizational structure is exactly what it sounds like. A problem is stated; then one or several possible solutions are discussed.

Question and Answer

Again, you can probably guess what this organizational structure entails. A question is posed, followed by an answer. An essay may include several sets of questions and answers. Are these generally difficult to recognize? No. Will you do great on recognizing and answering questions about this type of organizational structure? Absolutely!

Transitions

Transitions are words or phrases that help to organize effective writing by pointing out the correct order of ideas or by highlighting how ideas are related. Different transitions serve different purposes. On the GED test, you will be asked to select the transition that could improve a given passage. Let's take a look at a few transitions that signal different types of relationships in writing.

Cause and effect: accordingly, as a result, because, consequently, hence, since

Comparison: as well as, both, in common, likewise, similarly

Contrast: although, however, on the other hand, nevertheless, rather, unlike, yet

Introducing examples: for example, in fact, specifically

Showing addition: also, furthermore, in addition

Time or sequence: first, finally, initially, meanwhile, next, preceding, then, until

What to Do

Now that you know what is involved in effectively organizing a passage, how will you use this information to answer questions on the GED? Great question! Here are six steps that will help you.

> ### Steps in Identifying Effective Organization
> **Step 1:** Read the Passage
> **Step 2:** Read the Question
> **Step 3:** Identify the Main Idea and Supporting Details
> **Step 4:** Identify the Organizational Pattern
> **Step 5:** Look for Transitions
> **Step 6:** Select the Best Revision

Step 1: Read the Passage

By now, you get the idea. Read the passage. All of it. Carefully.

Step 2: Read the Question

After reading the paragraph, you probably have a few ideas about revisions that should be made to improve the writing. Well, you're about to have the chance to make those corrections. Read the question without peeking at the answer choices, and find out exactly which part of the passage the question addresses. Then reread not only the sentence or section in the question but the surrounding sentences in the passage as well. This will help you to see the sentence or paragraph in the context of the passage as a whole. Organization generally deals with a paragraph or large section of text. Do not try to answer the questions by focusing solely on a single word or sentence. It will be easier to make the correct revision when you view the information in context.

Step 3: Identify the Main Idea and Supporting Details

As you read, look for the main idea and supporting details. Pay attention to the order in which the ideas are presented. Keep in mind that what you are reading is not a perfect passage. In fact, it was purposely written to include errors, since the whole point of the test is for you to find the errors and fix them. So, as you go, think about which sentences belong and which ones do not. Think about which ones seem to be in the correct order and which do not. Think about which paragraphs have a clear main idea and which do not.

Depending on the content of the question, you may need to identify the main idea of the entire passage or of a specific paragraph. Read carefully, find the main point the author intended to convey, and look for details and information that support this key concept.

Step 4: Identify the Organizational Pattern

As you read the imperfect passage, try to figure out what organizational pattern the author used—or attempted to use. Once you have figured this out, you will know what information you should be looking for. For example, if the passage uses a cause-and-effect organizational pattern, you will need to identify the cause and then look for what happened as a result of this action or event. If the effects are not clear, you may have just found one revision that needs to be made when you answer the questions about the passage.

Step 5: Look for Transitions

There are several reasons you will be looking for transitions at this point. First, identifying transitions can help you connect the information in the passage. This, in turn, can help to clarify the information. Second, transitions can offer a clue about the type of organizational pattern being used. Third, if you do not find enough transitions to clearly understand the information or the organizational pattern, you may have determined one way to improve the passage. In this case, decide what transition would be helpful, as you may need to answer a question related to this issue.

Step 6: Select the Best Revision

Now read all of the answer choices. Do not stop reading once you find an answer choice that sounds good; it might not be the best choice or most effective revision. The only way to know for sure that any answer choice is the best one is to know what all of them say.

Once you have read every answer choice, select the best revision. Then, just to be sure, go back and reread the other answer choices and determine why they are not the most effective. This is a great way to double-check that your revision is the best one possible.

Examples

Let's look at some sample questions that address what you have learned about organization. Remember to use the steps we discussed to answer the question.

(A)

(1) Over the past few years, the popularity of virtual schools has increased. (2) More and more students, from elementary school through college, are receiving their educations through online learning. (3) Virtual schools have as many supporters as opponents, and there are definitely advantages and disadvantages to these nontraditional teaching forums.

(B)

(4) What is often viewed as one of the greatest benefits of virtual schools is the flexibility they offer. (5) Many programs allow students to learn at their own pace and set their own schedules. (6) This allows schoolwork to be completed around work or sports schedules. (7) This flexibility also offers students the opportunity to study at the times of the day when they are most ready to learn. (8) Many students pursuing professional sports careers find this to be a great advantage.

(C)

(9) Virtual schools do not offer the same type of socialization that students are exposed to in traditional classrooms. (10) While students do

interact with each other and with teachers via the computer, they do not have the face-to-face contact that traditional students experience. (11) Many educators agree that cooperative learning is essential in preparing children to enter the world, specifically the workforce. (12) The types of interactions offered through virtual learning are different than the types of interactions students will experience when dealing with other people in the world around them.

(D)

(13) While it is unlikely that virtual schools will ever completely replace traditional classrooms, some school districts are beginning to require students to take at least a few online classes prior to graduation. (14) There are undoubtedly some disadvantages to taking such classes. (15) However, there are some benefits to consider as well.

Now let's take a look at a few questions related to the organization of the passage.

1. Which of the following would be the best improvement for paragraph B?

   A. delete sentence 8

   B. move sentence 8 to follow sentence 4

   C. move sentence 8 to follow sentence 5

   D. move sentence 6 to follow sentence 8

   E. move sentence 4 to the end of the paragraph

Here are our steps:

Step 1: Read the Passage

Step 2: Read the Question

Since the question focuses on paragraph B, reread this section. Look for the main idea and supporting details of this paragraph.

Step 3: Identify the Main Idea and Supporting Details

Main idea: Virtual schools offer flexibility.

Supporting details: Students learn at their own pace; students set their own schedules; students learn at the time of day when they are most ready to learn

Step 4: Identify the Organizational Pattern

The entire passage compares and contrasts the advantages and disadvantages of virtual schools. This paragraph lists details in order of importance.

Step 5: Look for Transitions

Also

Step 6: Select the Best Revision

Sentence 8 discusses the flexibility of virtual schools in relation to sports. It would make more sense for this to follow sentence 6, which introduces the idea of a sports schedule.

Answer choice D rearranges the paragraph in this way.

Now it's your turn. The following question is also based on the preceding passage. Take a look at the question. We'll give you the steps you will need to practice the process.

Sentence 9: Virtual schools do not offer the same type of socialization that students are exposed to in traditional classrooms.

Which of the following would be the best improvement for sentence 9?

1. add *On the other hand* to the beginning of sentence 9
2. add *In addition* to the beginning of sentence 9
3. move sentence 9 to the end of paragraph B
4. move sentence 9 to the end of paragraph C
5. move sentence 9 to follow sentence 10

Step 1: Read the Passage

Step 2: Read the Question

_____

Step 3: Identify the Main Idea and Supporting Details

_____

_____

_____

_____

Step 4: Identify the Organizational Pattern

_____

Step 4: Look for Transitions

_____

Step 6: Select the Best Revision

The correct answer is A.

ORGANIZATION DRILLS

Fill in the blanks for question 1. For each of the subsequent questions, choose the best answer choice.

1. **What are the steps for identifying effective organization?**

   Step 1: _____

   Step 2: _____

   Step 3: _____

   Step 4: _____

   Step 5: _____

   Step 6: _____

Questions 2–10 refer to the following passage.

(A)

(1) Although many children can state what they want to be when they grow up, selecting a career path is a major decision. (2) Often people waver between several options before settling on the job that is just right. (3) Before making such a major decision, there are a number of factors that should be seriously considered.

(B)

(4) Everyone has certain things they like to do better than other things. (5) Someone who enjoys working with animals might consider a career in veterinary medicine, while someone who is allergic to dogs should think of other options. (6) Most dogs have to go to the vet for regular checkups. (7) A career as a coach or P.E. teacher might be a good choice for a person who enjoys being outside and staying active, whereas this would not be a good choice for someone who tries to avoid being in the sun.

(C)

(8) Next, the education required for a career should be considered. (9) Some careers require a high school diploma, while others require a college education. (10) This is important to think about, since someone who is not a strong student would likely be frustrated by the amount of schooling required by some careers.

(D)

(11) On the other hand, attending four years of college and then going on to law school to become an attorney might be an exciting adventure for students who like to study. (12) In addition to the amount of schooling needed to pursue a career, the types of classes required should also be considered. (13) A career in accounting would require taking a number of math classes in college. (14) While this might sound like a lot of fun for some people, others might cringe at the thought of studying numbers for four years.

(E)

(15) Then, lifestyle goals should be thought about as well. (16) While some of these goals may be financial, others may relate to leisure and family time. (17) Obviously, some careers will offer more substantial paychecks than others. (18) However, these same careers may also require more work hours, less flexible schedules, and more demands on personal time. (19) It is important to determine an acceptable balance between salary and self. (20) Some people are happy to work nights, weekends, and holidays in order to earn a larger paycheck, while other people choose to work more traditional business hours for a more modest paycheck in order to have time with their families. (21) There is no single job choice that is right for everyone. (22) Choosing a career path to follow is a very personal decision. (23) If you choose a career that requires a college education, be sure to apply to schools early. (24) The most important thing is to carefully consider each and every factor to ensure that the best option is chosen.

2. **Which sentence below would be the most effective at the beginning of para-graph B?**
    A. Second, it is important to think about what types of things one would enjoy.
    B. First, interests, talents, and hobbies should be taken into consideration.
    C. People should think about what types of jobs would interest them.
    D. Furthermore, different careers would be best for different people.
    E. There are thousands of career options to choose from.

3. **Which revision would improve the effectiveness of paragraph B?**
    A. remove sentence 6
    B. remove sentence 7
    C. reverse sentences 5 and 6
    D. move sentence 4 to the end of the paragraph
    E. move sentence 7 to the beginning of the paragraph

4. **Sentence 13:** A career in accounting would require taking a number of math classes in college.

   Which transition would best be added to the beginning of sentence 13?

   A. So
   B. In addition
   C. As a result
   D. For example
   E. Nevertheless

5. **Which revision would improve the effectiveness of this passage?**

   Begin a new paragraph with

   A. sentence 3
   B. sentence 7
   C. sentence 10
   D. sentence 13
   E. sentence 21

6. **Sentence 15:** Then, lifestyle goals should be thought about as well.

   Which revision should be made to sentence 15?

   A. replace *Then* with *Similarly*
   B. replace *Then* with *Finally*
   C. replace *as well* with *in addition*
   D. replace *as well* with *however*
   E. no revisions are needed

7. **Which revision would improve the effectiveness of this passage?**

   A. remove sentence 16
   B. remove sentence 17
   C. move sentence 1 to the end of paragraph A
   D. move sentence 11 to the end of paragraph C
   E. move sentence 10 to the beginning of paragraph D

8. **Which sentence could be removed to improve the effectiveness of the final paragraph?**

   A. sentence 18
   B. sentence 20
   C. sentence 22
   D. sentence 23
   E. sentence 24

9. **Which of the following sentences could best be added to paragraph B?**
   A. While dogs are one of the most popular pets, many people choose to have cats.
   B. Someone who enjoys exercise might also enjoy working as a personal trainer.
   C. These people should be sure to wear sunscreen any time they are outside.
   D. Some veterinarians are on call for emergencies over the weekend.
   E. Most states require that P.E. teachers obtain a bachelor's degree.

10. **To which paragraph would the following sentence best be added?**

    Someone planning a career in medicine should expect to take quite a few science courses, such as biology, chemistry, and anatomy.

    A. paragraph A
    B. paragraph B
    C. paragraph C
    D. paragraph D
    E. paragraph E

chapter **7**

Preparing for
the GED Essay

Part II of the GED Language Arts, Writing test will involve writing an expository essay on a familiar topic. You will be given a prompt and have 45 minutes to plan, write, and revise your writing. You may be thinking, *What if I don't know enough about the topic to write a decent essay?* Don't worry about that. The essay is not intended to be a research paper. The topic will be something of general interest and will likely ask you to state your opinion on a subject and use examples from your own knowledge and experience to support your opinion. Your score will not be based on whether or not you have the "right" answer. It will be based on how well you develop your essay and support your opinion. Check out the following information about scoring.

What's Being Scored?

The essay will be scored using a four-point rubric, meaning you will be able to earn up to four points for each of the following writing characteristics. The better each of these traits is addressed, the higher your score will be.

- **Response to the prompt.** To earn the highest possible score, your essay needs to include a clearly focused main idea that addresses the prompt, or topic, given.

- **Organization.** Your essay should clearly demonstrate a logical organizational pattern.

- **Development and details.** An essay that scores four points in this area is well developed and includes relevant supporting details and examples to support the main idea of the text.
- **Conventions.** You need to consistently and accurately apply the rules of sentence structure, grammar, capital letters, punctuation, and spelling to your essay.
- **Word choice.** Your essay should include varied and precise words to express your ideas clearly.

The Parts of an Essay

As we discussed when reviewing organization, an expository essay includes an introduction, a body, and a conclusion. Let's go over what belongs in each of these sections.

Introduction

The introduction is the first paragraph of the essay. The purpose of this paragraph is to catch the reader's attention, introduce the topic, and state the main idea of the entire passage. In an essay, the main idea is given in a sentence called the **thesis statement**, which is usually found at the end of the introduction. It states the point that the essay is going to make.

Keep in Mind

Keep in mind that you will be scored on how well your essay addresses the prompt. Make sure your thesis statement clearly refers to the ideas you're asked to discuss. If possible, word your thesis statement in such a way that it repeats some of the wording of prompt. By doing this and supporting your thesis statement in the body of the text, you should be able to stay on topic and clearly respond to the prompt given.

Body

The body of the essay is where all of the supporting details are found. If an essay were a sandwich, the introduction and conclusion would be the bread, and the body of the essay would be the meat. All of the facts, examples, definitions, and explanations that support the thesis statement are found in the body of the essay.

So, just how long *is* the body of an essay? There is no magic number for how many words, sentences, or paragraphs an essay should include. However, 45 minutes is not an extremely long time, meaning that the essay you write on the GED may be somewhat limited in length. On the other hand, the prompt will be direct enough that you should be able to address it completely within this time.

With that in mind, your essay will most likely include about five paragraphs; one will be the introduction, three will be the body, and one will be the conclusion. Of course, you may find that you need more than three paragraphs to fully develop the information in the body of your essay, which is fine. But five paragraphs will generally be sufficient to cover the topic.

Each paragraph in the body will have a main idea that supports your thesis statement. The remaining sentences in each paragraph will support the main idea of the paragraph.

Keep in Mind

Keep in mind that part of your score on this part of the test will be based on how well you develop your ideas. The body of the essay is where these points will be earned. Make sure that the main idea of each paragraph is a reason, fact, or example that helps to explain your thesis statement. Then make sure that each paragraph includes enough information to prove the main idea. Answer any appropriate question words about the main idea: *who, what, where, when, why,* and *how.*

Conclusion

The last paragraph of the essay is the conclusion. This paragraph should restate the main idea given in your thesis statement, reminding the reader of your answer to the prompt. The conclusion should also provide a sense of closure; readers should feel that the essay is complete. This final paragraph should let readers know this is the end, without actually saying *the end.*

How to Write the Essay

Now that you know what belongs in the GED essay, let's go over six steps for writing an effective passage.

Steps for Writing an Essay

Step 1: Read the Prompt
Step 2: Determine the Main Idea
Step 3: Select Supporting Details
Step 4: Write the Draft
Step 5: Revise the Draft
Step 6: Edit the Essay

Step 1: Read the Prompt

The prompt for the essay is not stated in the form of a simple question, such as *What is your favorite color?* It will most likely include several sentences, along with a directive regarding what you should write. Read it carefully, and know exactly what information you are being asked to give. If you realize halfway through the essay that you misunderstood the prompt, you probably will not have time to go back and start over, so read it carefully. (Read it twice if you need to.) Do whatever is necessary to make sure you understand exactly what you are being asked to write about.

It may be helpful to underline key words in the prompt. This can help you to focus on what and how you should write. Look for verbs such as *explain* or *describe.* Also look for words that state specifics that should be included, such as *one special person* or *three reasons.* A prompt that asks you to tell about *three important events in your life* is asking for something completely different than one that asks you to give *three reasons why one event was important.*

For the sake of reviewing the steps for writing an essay, let's use the following sample prompt.

What does it take to be a good student?

In your essay, describe the characteristics of a good student. Use specific details to explain your opinion. Use your personal knowledge, experience, and observations.

It may also be helpful to restate the prompt in your own words. This can help you to focus on exactly what you need to write.

Sample restatement of prompt: What are the characteristics of a good student?

Step 2: Determine the Main Idea

Before you begin writing, you must think about what information you want to include and plan how to organize it most effectively. The first step in planning will be to determine the main idea of your essay.

The main idea should be directly related to the requirements of the prompt. To make sure you are addressing the topic directly, try restating a few words from the prompt in the main idea. This can help you stay on track. Remember, there is no single correct way to write the thesis statement for any essay. If 10 people were to write effective essays on the same prompt, there's a good chance that they would use 10 different thesis statements. The most important thing is to be sure that your thesis statement addresses the prompt and is something you can adequately support.

Sample thesis statement: Good students share a number of positive characteristics.

Step 3: Select Supporting Details

The details you choose must provide strong support for the idea or opinion given in your thesis statement. These facts, examples, and opinions must clearly explain the main idea of the essay and convince readers that your thesis statement is true.

Before you start writing, decide which supporting details will be most effective in your essay. Begin by brainstorming a list of possibilities; then select about three to include. These supporting details will each become the main idea of one body paragraph. Make sure you select ideas that you will be able to write several sentences about. Also, select the three that best explain your thesis statement.

Sample supporting details: Good students are well prepared for class; good students are often well organized; good students take responsibility for their own learning.

What if you have brainstormed a ton of ideas? Well, that's a terrific problem to have! Be glad that you have so many options to choose from. Find the three that will best explain your thesis statement to readers, and use them. Then look at the remaining ideas on the list. See if some of these are closely related to the top three. If so, you may be able to use them as support in one of the paragraphs. For example, suppose one of your strongest supporting details is *good students are well prepared for class*. Other ideas on your list, such as *good students always complete their homework*, or *good students always do the required reading*, could fit into the paragraph about being well prepared.

Once you have selected the supporting details, determine how to organize them most effectively. Would they work best if arranged in a compare-and-contrast format? Would they be conveyed most effectively using a cause-and-effect organizational pattern? In the case of the sample prompt we're using, we'll organize the supporting details in order of least to most important.

Keep in Mind

Keep in mind that any planning and prewriting should be completed on scrap paper. Only the actual essay will be turned in. The good news here is that you do not have to work neatly as you complete Steps 2 and 3; you can cross things off, draw graphic organizers, or mark arrows to move information around. The bad news is that you will need to work quickly to get all of these ideas onto the actual page of the essay. You may have written awesome ideas on your planning page, but they will only be scored if they make it into your final essay.

Step 4: Write the Draft

Here's where the actual writing begins. So where is the best place to start? At the top. Begin by writing an introduction that is interesting enough to make readers want to hear what you have to say. Include your thesis statement in this first paragraph.

Sample Introduction

In any class, whether in elementary school, high school, or college, some students are stronger and more academically successful than others. What makes some students more likely to do well in school than others? While all of these successful learners are individuals, a number of positive characteristics are often seen in good students.

Then begin writing the body. Each of the supporting statements selected in Step 3 is now the main idea of its own body paragraph. Include enough examples, facts, details, and explanations about each main idea to justify clearly why you felt this statement was important enough to include. Remember to arrange the paragraphs according to the organizational structure that is most effective for the type of essay you're writing. Include appropriate transitions.

Sample Body Paragraph

One characteristic commonly demonstrated by good students is that they are well prepared for class. These students have completed their homework assignments and done any required reading before the beginning of class. They also have their textbooks, calculators, pencils, and class notes with them each day. So when the teacher or professor arrives, these students are ready to learn.

Finally, write the conclusion. Remember to revisit your thesis statement and to wrap up the essay in a way that leaves readers feeling that you have completely covered the topic.

Sample Conclusion

Being a good student often goes hand in hand with being well prepared, organized, and responsible. These characteristics of good students often make a significant difference in the level of academic success achieved in school.

Step 5: Revise the Draft

Once the draft is completed, take a few minutes to read your essay carefully. Ask yourself questions such as, *Does that make sense? Would more details help to explain this idea better? Does every sentence support the main idea?*

As you read, look for places where more information or additional details would make the piece more effective. Add words, clarify ideas, and rearrange information to improve the essay. Neatly draw a single line through any information that does not fit or is not relevant.

Step 6: Edit the Essay

Remember all that we discussed in Chapter 5 about mechanics? Here is where we apply all of that information about grammar, capitalization, punctuation, and spelling. Carefully check your writing to make sure that you have applied these conventions correctly. Make any necessary changes. Remember, errors in mechanics and conventions can impact the overall quality of writing, as well as the reader's ability to clearly comprehend your ideas, both of which can affect your score.

Keep in Mind

Keep in mind that you will have 45 minutes to complete this portion of the test. That means you have a total of 45 minutes to plan, draft, revise, and edit your essay. While that may sound like a lot of time, you will need to budget these minutes wisely to ensure that you have time to complete all six of the steps. The following is a basic guideline for how you may want to allot the time given to complete the essay.

- **Step 1:** Read the Prompt—2 minutes
- **Step 2:** Determine the Main Idea—3 minutes
- **Step 3:** Select Supporting Details—5 minutes
- **Step 4:** Write the Draft—25 minutes
- **Step 5:** Revise the Draft—5 minutes
- **Step 6:** Edit the Essay—5 minutes

Time yourself as you work through the sample prompts in this book. At first, try to follow this guideline for budgeting the time. Then customize the plan to fit your specific needs. If you find that you need a little bit longer to plan your writing, for example, take a couple of extra minutes to plan and shave a few minutes from the amount of time used for writing the draft. However you decide to allot the 45 minutes, make sure that you have plenty of time to complete the writing and leave time at the end to double-check your work.

It's Your Turn

Now it's your turn to put all of this information into practice. Read the following prompt, and follow the six steps for writing an effective GED essay. Grab a timer and set it for 45 minutes. When you are ready to begin, start the timer and begin with Step 1 by reading the prompt. If you finish before the timer stops, go back and check your work. If the timer rings before you are finished with your essay, stop and take a look at how far you have gotten. Then go ahead and finish the essay. Make sure to work through all six steps for practice, regardless of the time.

Here are our steps:

> ### Steps for Writing an Essay
> **Step 1:** Read the Prompt
> **Step 2:** Determine the Main Idea
> **Step 3:** Select Supporting Details
> **Step 4:** Write the Draft
> **Step 5:** Revise the Draft
> **Step 6:** Edit the Essay

Are you ready? Take a deep breath, start the timer, and begin working on your essay. Good luck!

What one place that you have never been would you like to visit someday?

In your essay, name one place you would like to visit someday, and explain why you would like to go there. Use your personal observations, experience, and knowledge to support your essay.

Step 1: Read the Prompt—restate it in your own words

_____

_____

_____

Step 2: Determine the Main Idea

_____

_____

_____

Step 3: Select Supporting Details

_____

_____

_____

_____

_____

Step 4: Write the Draft

_____

_____

_____

_____

_____

_____

_____

_____

_____

_____

_____

_____

_____

_____

_____

_____

_____

_____

_____

_____

_____

_____

_____

_____

_____

_____

_____

_____

_____

_____

_____

_____

_____

_____

_____

_____

_____

_____

_____

_____

_____

_____

_____

Step 5: Revise the Draft

Step 6: Edit the Essay

How did you do? Writing a sample essay such as this can be very informative. You may have learned that the 45-minute time limit should be adjusted a bit to fit your needs. You may have found that you are completely comfortable selecting a main idea and supporting details. If you found any areas in which you need a little extra practice or review, go back over these sections of the book. For example, if you were unsure of exactly where to place commas in your essay, glance back at the section that discusses punctuation.

Now take another look at the prompt and reread your essay. Be critical. Did you stay on topic? Does every part of the essay explain why you would like to visit a single place? Are there enough reasons included to show why visiting this location is important to you? If so, awesome! If not, go back and make any revisions that will improve your essay.

Are you ready to tackle another practice essay? Use the six steps for writing an essay, as well as what you have learned about yourself as a writer, and complete an essay for the following prompt.

Choosing a college is an important decision. Write an essay to explain what factors should be taken into consideration when selecting which college to attend. Use your personal observations, experience, and knowledge to support your essay.

Step 1: Read the Prompt—restate it in your own words

_____

_____

_____

Step 2: Determine the Main Idea

_____

_____

_____

Step 3: Select Supporting Details

_____

_____

_____

_____

_____

_____

Step 4: Write the Draft

_____

_____

_____

_____

_____

_____

_____

_____

_____

_____

_____

_____

_____

_____

_____

_____

_____

_____

_____

_____

_____

_____

_____

_____

_____

_____

_____

_____

_____

_____

_____

_____

_____

_____

_____

_____

_____

_____

_____

_____

_____

_____

Step 5: Revise the Draft

Step 6: Edit the Essay

Part III

Social Studies

chapter **8**

World History

During the GED Social Studies test, you will be given 70 minutes to answer a total of 50 questions in the areas of world and US history, civics and government, economics, and geography. About 40 percent of the questions will be based on reading passages containing 250 words or less. Another 40 percent will be based on graphics such as maps, tables, illustrations, diagrams, or graphs. The remaining 20 percent will combine a reading passage with a visual.

To answer these questions, you will need to demonstrate the ability to comprehend, restate, summarize, and draw inferences based on the information in the passage, document, quotation, or illustration. The good news is that you will not have to recall everything you have ever learned about social studies. However, you will need to rely on what you already know about important social studies concepts and events, and combine this information with the facts and data given in each question.

In this chapter, we will review the types of questions you may find that relate to world history. Keep in mind that many questions will cover more than one area of social studies. For example, a question asking about the Declaration of Independence deals not only with an important event in the history of our country but with our government as well.

You may be thinking, *How do I prepare for a test that could ask questions about any event since the beginning of time?* Great question! The best way to prepare is to read the newspaper each day; keep up with current events either on television or on the Internet; take a look at reputable news magazines; and be familiar with current issues in politics, economics, and world events. Your high school social studies textbooks are also a great source of information. Do you need to reread every one of them from cover to cover? Probably not. But it would be a good idea to take another look through them, familiarize yourself with the main topics, and refresh your memory a bit.

What's Being Tested?

Fifteen percent of the questions on the GED Social Studies test will deal with world history going as far back as beginning and early civilizations. That is definitely a long time to be familiar with, but don't panic. Remember that you will not have to recall facts about these events; you will simply need to read or review the information given on the test and consider it as it relates to what you know about history.

As you go through textbooks, library materials, and news magazines, pay close attention to the topics on the following list. Keep in mind that this is not a comprehensive list of everything that could be on the test. It simply suggests a few topics that some of the questions may tackle. Also, the topics are listed alphabetically, not by historical importance or by chronology. As you study, add any other topics you want to learn more about to the lists.

Civilizations and Countries

Ancient Egyptian Civilizations   Greek and Roman Empires

The Discovery of America   New Democracies of Africa, Asia, and
                                          South America
Chinese Dynasties

The French Revolution

_____

_____

_____

_____

Religions

Catholicism   Judaism

Christianity   The Reformation

The Crusades

_____

_____

_____

_____

Eras, Ages, and Historical Periods

The Dark Ages   The Middle Ages

The Enlightenment   The Renaissance

The First Global Age   The Stone Age

The Industrial Revolution   Urbanization

_____

_____

_____

_____

Leaders, Explorers, and Significant Historical Figures

John Cabot   Martin Luther

Julius Caesar   Karl Marx

Christopher Columbus   Napoleon

Ponce de Leon   Peter the Great

Leif Eriksson   Amerigo Vespucci

Gandhi

_____

_____

_____

_____

Wars and Revolutions

The Cold War   The United Nations

The Hundred Years' War   World War I

The Korean Conflict   World War II

The League of Nations

The Russian Revolution and
the Rise of Communism

_____

_____

_____

_____

Documents and Treaties

The Magna Carta

The Treaty of Versailles

_____

_____

_____

_____

What to Do

Now that you know what types of information to study in order to do well on the world history questions of the GED Social Studies test, let's go over the six steps you will use to find the correct answer.

World History Steps

Step 1: Read All the Information
Step 2: Identify the Question
Step 3: Underline Key Words and Phrases
Step 4: Determine Meanings
Step 5: Think About What You Already Know
Step 6: Select the Best Answer

Step 1: Read All the Information

The first step to correctly answer any question is to read all of the information carefully. Since so many of the questions on this test involve graphics, reading may include titles, captions, keys, graphs, charts, and labels, in addition to the reading passages and the questions themselves. Be sure to pay attention to what is included in illustrations, drawings, photos, and cartoons as well.

Keep in Mind

Keep in mind that certain types of social studies questions are more likely to depend on visual aids than others. For example, you can expect to find more graphs that relate to economics and civics questions than to other areas of social studies and more maps that relate to geography questions than to other types of questions.

Step 2: Identify the Question

After reading everything you can find, make sure you understand exactly what the question is asking. For example, you may need to identify what occurred during a given historical event, what lead up to the event, or what took place afterward. Carefully read the question and determine what information you are being asked to explain.

Step 3: Underline Key Words and Phrases

Now that you know what the question is asking, go back through the passage or graphics and underline any pertinent key words, dates, phrases, or facts. For example, if the question refers to artifacts from an ancient Egyptian civilization, underline the word *artifacts* as well as any examples mentioned. If the question asks about who discovered the artifacts or when they were found, underline relevant names and dates as well. Do not try to rely on your memory to recall this information. During the test, you will be reading a lot of facts in a relatively short time. It would be easy to confuse information from one passage to the next. Take a few seconds to underline important information to ensure that you are focusing on the correct facts.

Step 4: Determine Meanings

As you know, there are times when words or phrases in a reading passage are unfamiliar. Don't let that make you nervous. First, take a look at the word or words you are unsure of and then use contextual clues to try to figure out their meanings. Think about what would make sense in the context of the sentence or passage. Look for hints in the sentence and the surrounding sentences that can offer clues about what the word or phrase means. You might find a definition or example that can help you out.

If that doesn't work, break the word apart and see if the root word, prefix, or suffix looks familiar. Do you know another word with a similar root? If so, see if that gives you an idea of what the new word might mean. Think back to all of the reading tricks you learned in elementary and middle school and put them to use now. Also, take a look at Part V of this book that deals with reading comprehension. It reviews several helpful reading skills that could come in handy when you are faced with unfamiliar words.

Step 5: Think About What You Already Know

After reading everything you can find, figuring out what the question is asking, and determining the meanings of key words, consider what you already know about the topic. Remember that many of the questions will require some thinking on your part. In other words, the answers may not be directly stated in the passage. Try to make connections between your own prior knowledge and the facts presented on the test.

Step 6: Select the Best Answer

The key word in this final step is *best*. More than one answer may appear to be at least partially correct. Your job is to select the single *best* answer choice.

Examples

Let's look at some sample questions dealing with world history.

Julius Caesar is known as one of history's greatest military leaders, at one time even declaring that he would be dictator for life. In the early sixties B.C., he became a leading ruler in Rome, alongside Pompey the Great and Crassus, with the three men becoming the first triumvirate. Together, they controlled the region for several years, until Crassus died, and the remaining two men began a civil war against one another. After several battles, Caesar defeated his former partner the following year. By 45 B.C., he had enjoyed widespread victories across the Mediterranean, although his joy was short-lived. Caesar was assassinated in 44 B.C. by political rivals.

According to the passage, which of the following is true?

1. Caesar ruled Rome as a lone dictator during the sixties B.C.
2. Caesar and Pompey the Great ruled Rome as equal partners.
3. Caesar ruled the entire Mediterranean as a dictator for several decades.
4. Caesar, Pompey the Great, and Crassus formed a committee of three equal rulers.
5. Caesar became ruler of Rome in the midsixties B.C. following the death of his mentor Crassus.

Here are our steps:

Step 1: Read All the Information

Step 2: Identify the Question

Determine which statement is supported by the information in the passage.

Step 3: Underline Key Words and Phrases

We need to determine which answer choice contains accurate information. Since the men's names, several dates, and the names of countries are mentioned, we'll underline this information in the passage.

Step 4: Determine Meanings

The word triumvirate *is unfamiliar, so we can use information in the surrounding text to figure out what it means. Take a look at this section of the passage:*

. . . he became a leading ruler in Rome, alongside Pompey the Great and Crassus, with the three men becoming the first triumvirate. *Together, they controlled the region for several years.*

This shows that Caesar ruled alongside two other men. Together they controlled the region. Also, we know that the prefix tri- *means "three." So a triumvirate must be three rulers who work together to lead a region.*

Step 5: Think About What You Already Know

Consider what you have learned, heard, or read about Julius Caesar in the past. Use this information, along with the information in the text, to complete Step 6.

Step 6: Select the Best Answer

According to the passage, answer choice 4 is the best answer. Although Caesar did rule Rome during the sixties B.C., he did this with two other men, which eliminates answer choice 1. Also, since the three rulers were equal partners, answer choice 2 is not the best answer since it only mentions two of the rulers. Although Caesar did conquer much of the Mediterranean, he was assassinated within a short time afterward, making answer choice 3 incorrect. And since Caesar ruled Rome with Crassus while he was alive, answer choice 5 is not correct either.

Now it's your turn. Take a look at the following question, which is based on the same passage about Julius Caesar. We'll give you the steps you will need to practice the process.

Which conclusion can be drawn based on the information in the passage?

1. Caesar and Pompey the Great did not agree on the best way to rule Rome.
2. Caesar battled Pompey the Great because he wanted to rule Rome himself.
3. Crassus was the most experienced and most popular of the Roman leaders.
4. The death of Crassus caused conflict among the leaders of Rome at the time.
5. Much conflict surrounded Caesar, Pompey the Great, and Crassus at that time.

Step 1: Read All the Information

Step 2: Identify the Question

_____

_____

Step 3: Underline Key Words and Phrases

Step 4: Determine Meanings

_____

_____

Step 5: Think About What You Already Know

_____

_____

_____

_____

Step 6: Select the Best Answer

The correct answer is 2.

WORLD HISTORY DRILLS

Fill in the blanks for question 1. For each of the subsequent questions, choose the best answer.

1. **What are the steps for answering world history questions?**
   Step 1: _____
   Step 2: _____
   Step 3: _____
   Step 4: _____
   Step 5: _____
   Step 6: _____

Use the following information to answer questions 2–4.

The Reformation, a primarily religious revolt during the sixteenth century, is one of the greatest revolutions of all time and caused changes that extended far beyond the reaches of the church. In fact, it is considered to be a turning point in history. This major and oftentimes brutal conflict divided the Christians in Western Europe into two separate groups: Protestants and Catholics. Prior to this, Roman Catholicism was the only religion in Western Europe. The Catholic Church had been quite powerful, even insisting that no one else had the authority to interpret the Bible.

Martin Luther, a Saxon monk, had been influenced by the work of a fourteenth-century priest, John Wycliffe, who believed that people should have the opportunity to interpret the Bible for themselves. Like Wycliffe, Luther also developed ideas that contradicted those of the church and became a leader of the Reformation in Germany. Other scholars assisted him in spreading his ideas, some by encouraging the study of Hebrew and Greek languages, others by adding new ideas to those preached by Luther. The Reformation was supported in other countries by those with similar views, and soon new churches appeared. For example, John Calvin's work supported the Presbyterian and Reformed churches' foundation in Geneva, which became the world center for these religions.

Religion, however, was not the sole cause of the Reformation, although many believed political and social problems were spurred by the support of religious leaders. As a result of the loss of religious unity experienced up to this point, people began to consider their own religious interests for the first time, and the Modern Age began.

2. **Following the Reformation, new political, social, and economic problems began to arise. In what way did the religious conflict spur issues outside the church?**
   A. New religions developed that encouraged people to turn against all of their previous beliefs.
   B. The church encouraged people to revolt in social and political arenas in addition to taking a stand against their religion.
   C. People's diverse religious interests began to impact other areas of their thinking, causing new social and political beliefs as well.
   D. Since the church had been so powerful prior to the Reformation, the lack of support caused economic and financial problems.
   E. All of the political leaders prior to the Reformation had been members of the church, so it was difficult to determine which religion new leaders should support.

3. **In what way would learning a new language encourage religious change?**
   A. All of the religious leaders preached only in languages other than German.
   B. Only German religious leaders were able to study the Bible up to this time.
   C. Knowledge of Greek and Hebrew allowed people to study the Bible in its original language.
   D. By learning other languages, people could assist with translating the Bible into Greek and Hebrew.
   E. Learning Greek and Hebrew allowed people to talk with religious leaders who spoke only those languages.

4. **Which of the following inferences can be made based on the passage?**
   A. Religious leaders were the only people who were satisfied with the strong role of the church prior to the Reformation.
   B. People throughout Western Europe were becoming unhappy with the church prior to the Reformation.
   C. Without the influence of Martin Luther, the Reformation never would have taken place.
   D. The Reformation came on suddenly, as the result of the actions of a few people.
   E. Martin Luther could have prevented the Reformation from occurring.

Use the following information to answer questions 5–7.

In the early part of the twentieth century, Germany's leader believed it was best to side with the majority in any conflict among the five European powers and to remain on peaceful terms with Russia. However, when a new leader took the reins of Germany, he refused to maintain the country's relationship with Russia, leaving his country with only one European ally, Austria-Hungary, the weakest of the five.

In 1914, Austria declared war against Serbia following the assassination of the heir to the Austro-Hungarian throne by a Serbian supporter. As an ally of Serbia, Russia was pulled into the conflict. Likewise, as an ally of Austria, Germany was now involved in a war against Russia. France and Britain were bound by an alliance with

Russia, which brought them into the conflict as well. The result was that nearly the entire continent was at war. Russia, France, and Great Britain, through the Treaty of London, agreed not to make peace individually with the Central Powers, and from this point, the three countries and those supporting them were known as the Allies.

   Although this war was fought primarily in Europe, it is called World War I. In time, 27 countries became involved. Although the United States remained neutral at the beginning of the war, it did produce a significant amount of food and weapons for Great Britain and France. In fact, US exports to these countries quadrupled during the first two years of the war. Germany used submarines to prevent these supplies from being exported by the United States and later encouraged Mexico to become involved in a war with the United States. Consequently, the US Congress declared war on Germany in 1917, and the United States officially entered the Great War.

5. **In what ways can you infer that the United States benefitted from World War I?**
    A. Exports to all European countries increased.
    B. Relations with Germany were strengthened.
    C. An agricultural economy was replaced by an industrial economy.
    D. Industry prospered as a result of producing supplies for the Allies.
    E. An agreement was reached between Mexico and the United States.

6. **Based on the passage and the map, which conclusion can be drawn?**

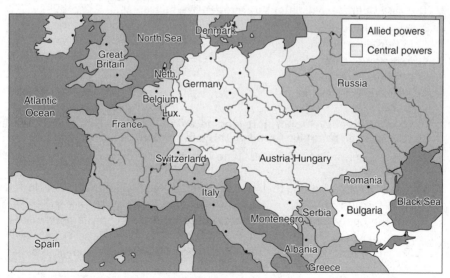

    A. Switzerland remained neutral throughout the war.
    B. Denmark and Russia supported the same war efforts.
    C. The same number of troops came from Serbia and Greece.
    D. Only Germany used submarines and watercraft during the war.
    E. Spain was not involved in the war because it is located so far from Russia.

7. **Why was World War I known as "The Great War"?**
   A. because the war lasted for so many years
   B. because so many countries were involved
   C. because every country in the world played a part
   D. because the war was fought by sea as well as by land
   E. because of how many countries benefitted from the war

Use the following information to answer questions 8–10.

From the beginning of civilization, agriculture has played a key role in the rise of permanent settlements. The development of farming practices allowed people to remain in an area without having to move their families, belongings, and herds in search of food. Communities began to develop in areas where the water supply could be used for irrigation.

8. **Which best explains the role of agriculture in the development of settlements?**
   A. Being able to grow their own food allowed people to settle in an area.
   B. Settlers built homes in communities in which they could purchase seeds.
   C. Having a common interest provided people with a sense of community.
   D. People were able to use the available timber to build permanent homes.
   E. The development of farming provided jobs and a source of income for settlers.

9. **The earliest great civilizations developed in which areas?**
   A. in dry valleys
   B. in cold climates
   C. in the mountains
   D. near oceans or seas
   E. near rivers or streams

10. **As communities developed, more food became available. Which of the following conclusions can be drawn based on this information?**
    A. Farmers were able to spend less time working since there was plenty of food for everyone.
    B. People gave up farming their own land and joined their efforts to develop community crops.
    C. Agriculture remained an important part of society, and only farmers were welcome to join the community.
    D. The importance of agriculture on civilization diminished, and people began to focus on learning a different trade.
    E. Communities had enough food to support workers who were not farmers, which enabled the growth of larger cities and populations.

chapter **9**

US History

Approximately one-fourth of the questions on the GED Social Studies test will deal with US history. As you know, you will not be required to recall facts about the history of our country; however, you will need to relate what you already know to passages and graphics provided on the test.

 Keep in Mind

Keep in mind that US history questions may also relate to other areas of social studies found on the test: world history, civics and government, economics, or geography. As long as you are familiar with the information, the area in which any topic is categorized is irrelevant.

What's Being Tested?

Although it is impossible to know exactly what questions will appear on the test, there will definitely be at least one question related to the Declaration of Independence, the Federalist Papers, the US Constitution, or an important Supreme Court landmark case. As you study, make sure to review each of these areas.

As you study textbooks, library materials, news magazines, and the Internet to prepare for this test, pay close attention to the topics that follow. Remember, this list does not include everything that could possibly be on the test. It simply suggests a number of people, events, and documents with which you should be familiar. As you study, add any other topics you want to learn more about to the lists.

Historical Periods and Events

The Boston Tea Party	Pearl Harbor
The Civil War	Reconstruction
Colonization	The Revolution
The Confederate States of America	The Roaring Twenties
The Contemporary United States	The Secession
The Emergence of Modern America	Settlement
The Expansion	The Spanish American War
The French and Indian War	Urbanization
The Great Depression	The Vietnam War
The Industrial Revolution	The War of 1812
The Louisiana Purchase	Watergate
The New Nation	World Wars I and II

_____

_____

_____

_____

Leaders, Explorers, and Significant Historical Figures

Abolitionists	Native Americans
Christopher Columbus	Thomas Paine
The Continental Congress	Pilgrims
Hernando de Soto	Presidents, past and present
Robert E. Lee	Paul Revere
Lewis and Clark	Dred Scott
Loyalists	

_____

_____

_____

_____

Documents

The Articles of Confederation	The Monroe Doctrine
Common Sense	The SALT Agreement
The Declaration of Independence	The Stamp Act
The Emancipation Proclamation	Supreme Court landmark cases
The Federalist Papers	The Townshend Acts
The Gettysburg Address	The Treaty of Ghent
The Intolerable Acts	The US Constitution

_____

_____

_____

_____

Concepts and Beliefs

Federalism	Popular Sovereignty
Isolationism	Progressivism
Manifest Destiny	Suffrage
The Peace Corps	Tariffs

_____

_____

_____

_____

What to Do

Now that you have an idea of the types of information with which you need to familiarize yourself in order to do well on the US history questions of the GED Social Studies test, let's go over the six steps you will use to determine which answer is the best.

> ### US History Steps
> **Step 1:** Read All the Information
> **Step 2:** Identify the Question
> **Step 3:** Underline Key Words and Phrases
> **Step 4:** Determine Meanings
> **Step 5:** Think About What You Already Know
> **Step 6:** Select the Best Answer

Step 1: Read All the Information

Before trying to answer any of the questions, read all of the information first. Remember that this includes not only the passage, but also any visual aids, labels, titles, or captions that are given. Understanding what type of information is included in a graph, for example, is key to understanding the data itself. One of the best ways to make sure you answer the questions correctly is to know as much as possible about the topic. Reading as much information as you have available is a great way to do this.

Now that we have told you to read all of the information first, let's throw you a curveball. There are exceptions to every rule. Some people actually find it helpful to read the questions before reading the passage. This allows them to focus on the information needed to answer the questions as they read. If you find this strategy helpful, then by all means, read the questions first and then the passage and associated information. Just remember to read only the questions associated with the passage you are about to read. And be sure to reread each question before selecting the correct answer to make sure you remember it correctly and that the answer you choose makes sense in the context of the question.

Keep in Mind

Keep in mind that everyone learns differently. Everyone also tests differently. Just because some people find it helpful to read the questions first does not mean that this is the best strategy. How do you know what works best for you? Try it! As you work through the questions in this book, try reading the questions first. If you feel that this strategy is helpful, awesome! Keep it up. If not, go back to reading the passage first and saving the questions for later. The key is to know what works best for you. Our suggestion? Figure this out before the day of the test so you know how to approach the questions before you pick up your pencil and the stopwatch begins.

Step 2: Identify the Question

Not only do you need to locate the question itself, you also need to make sure you understand exactly what it is asking. Try restating the question in your own words.

Step 3: Underline Key Words and Phrases

Once you have figured out what the question is asking, go back and find any important names, dates, vocabulary, and events that you will use to answer it. Underline or circle this information in the passage as well as in the visual, if one is included.

Step 4: Determine Meanings

Even the best readers come across unfamiliar words at times. If this happens, don't worry. Use the other information in the passage, as well as what you know about word parts, to get an idea of the meaning. If you are still unsure, even after applying every vocabulary recognition strategy you can think of, don't worry. It may be possible to determine the correct answer without knowing the meaning of every single word.

Step 5: Think About What You Already Know

You have probably studied US history in school, looked over information as you prepared for the GED test, and learned about our country on television. Now consider what the question is asking, think about the underlined information in the text, and try to remember anything you already know that relates to the topic. Many of the questions on the test require you to relate your prior knowledge to the information you read. You may not be an expert on history, but anything you already know about it could be helpful. Spend a few seconds trying to remember what you have learned in the past.

Step 6: Select the Best Answer

Remember that while several answers may appear to be partially correct, only one of the choices can be the best answer. Carefully read every word of each answer choice; then select the one that most completely and most accurately answers the question.

Examples

Let's take a look at a few sample questions dealing with US history.

In 1773 and 1774, the British Parliament enacted several measures over the United States colonies. The first of these was the Boston Port Bill, which closed the harbor until restitution was made for the tea destroyed during the Boston Tea Party. Following this, the Massachusetts Government

Act was imposed, which ended the agreements included in the colony's existing charter and required approval for any town meetings. The Administration of Justice Act protected British officials who were charged with serious criminal offenses while enforcing the law by allowing them to stand trial either in England or in a different colony. The fourth of these measures was the Coercive Act, which offered new arrangements allowing British troops to stay in occupied American houses.

Which conclusion can be drawn based on the passage?

1. The British desired to maintain control over the US colonies.
2. The British worked to help the colonies establish their own laws.
3. The US colonies wanted assistance from the British to pass new laws.
4. Parliament immediately recognized the colonies as an independent country.
5. The colonies were allowed to control their own government without interference.

Here are our steps:

Step 1: Read All the Information

Step 2: Identify the Question

Which statement does the passage support?

Step 3: Underline Key Words and Phrases

We must figure out which statement is most likely true, based on the information in the passage. Since the passage is about the measures enacted by Parliament, we should underline each. Clearly understanding these will help us determine which is the best conclusion.

Step 4: Determine Meanings

The word Parliament is unfamiliar. Let's use the information in the passage to determine what this word means.

In 1773 and 1774, the British Parliament enacted several measures over the United States colonies.

Since Parliament was able to make rules for the colonies, it must be a legislative group.

Step 5: Think About What You Already Know

You probably already know that the colonies were established by people who wanted to form their own country and come out from under British control.

Step 6: Select the Best Answer

According to the passage, choice 1 is the best answer. All of the acts were ways for Parliament to maintain some sort of control over what happened in the colonies.

Now it's your turn. Take a look at the next question, which is also based on the passage about the colonies. We'll give you the steps you will need to practice the process.

When were these acts put into place?

1. after the American Revolution
2. before the colonies were formed
3. before the Pilgrims arrived in America
4. after the development of the US Constitution
5. prior to the signing of the Declaration of Independence

Step 1: Read All the Information

Step 2: Identify the Question

_____

_____

Step 3: Underline Key Words and Phrases

Step 4: Determine Meanings

_____

_____

Step 5: Think About What You Already Know

_____

_____

_____

_____

Step 6: Select the Best Answer

The correct answer is 5.

US HISTORY DRILLS

Fill in the blanks for question 1. For each of the subsequent questions, choose the best answer.

1. **What are the steps for answering US history questions?**

    Step 1: _____

    Step 2: _____

    Step 3: _____

    Step 4: _____

    Step 5: _____

    Step 6: _____

Use the following information to answer questions 2–4.

For hundreds of years, European nations set their sights on beginning settlements in America as a means of increasing their wealth and expanding their influence around the world. Spain was the first European nation to successfully found a settlement in what we now know as the United States. Shortly thereafter, England's attempts to settle this new land met with success. Many of those who arrived had chosen to leave their homeland in order to gain religious freedom. English settlers in both Massachusetts and Virginia received help from Native Americans who taught them how to grow grains as a source of food and tobacco as a form of income.

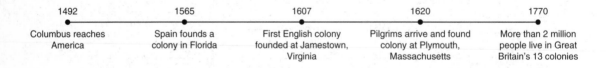

1492	1565	1607	1620	1770
Columbus reaches America	Spain founds a colony in Florida	First English colony founded at Jamestown, Virginia	Pilgrims arrive and found colony at Plymouth, Massachusetts	More than 2 million people live in Great Britain's 13 colonies

2. **Which is true?**
    A. Florida was one of Great Britain's successful 13 colonies.
    B. Columbus reached America before the Native Americans arrived.
    C. The Pilgrims founded the first successful British colony in America.
    D. Native Americans lived in the new land prior to the arrival of the Europeans.
    E. Virginia was home to the first successful European settlement in North America.

3. **Based on the details shown in the map, what can be said about the colonies?**

The 13 British Colonies

A. The first colonies settled were in the north, with later settlements moving toward the south.

B. Many of the first settlements were established near the coastline of the new land.

C. Current geographical state borders were established during the colonial period.

D. Most major settlements were located in the southern colonies.

E. Each colony occupied an equal amount of land area.

4. **Which of the following was *not* a reason that European countries wanted to establish settlements in the New Land?**

   A. to expand wealth
   B. to increase their power
   C. to spread organized religion
   D. to strengthen global influence
   E. to gain control of North America

Use the following excerpt from the Declaration of Independence to answer questions 5 and 6.

We hold these truths to be self-evident, that all men are created equal, that they are endowed by their Creator with certain unalienable Rights, that among these are Life, Liberty and the pursuit of Happiness.—That to secure these rights, Governments are instituted among Men, deriving their just powers from the consent of the governed,—That whenever any Form of Government becomes destructive of these ends, it is the Right of the People to alter or to abolish it, and to institute new Government, laying its foundation on such principles and organizing its powers in such form, as to them shall seem most likely to effect their Safety and Happiness. Prudence, indeed, will dictate that Governments long established should not be changed for light and transient causes; and accordingly all experience hath shewn, that mankind are more disposed to suffer, while evils are sufferable, than to right themselves by abolishing the forms to which they are accustomed. But when a long train of abuses and usurpations, pursuing invariably the same Object evinces a design to reduce them under absolute Despotism, it is their right, it is their duty, to throw off such Government, and to provide new Guards for their future security.—Such has been the patient sufferance of these Colonies; and such is now the necessity which constrains them to alter their former Systems of Government. The history of the present King of Great Britain is a history of repeated injuries and usurpations, all having in direct object the establishment of an absolute Tyranny over these States.

5. **The Declaration of Independence was signed in 1776. According to the document, which of the following practices of the time contradicted the beliefs of the United States?**

   A. women voting
   B. owning slaves
   C. religious freedom
   D. free public education
   E. presidential term limits

6. **Which supports the main idea of the Declaration of Independence?**
   A. Citizens have the right to have their voices heard in government.
   B. Only certain people have the right to pursue freedom and happiness.
   C. People have a responsibility to be loyal to the leaders of their country.
   D. Established systems of government should not be altered for any reason.
   E. Leaders should have the ability to establish and enforce laws as they see fit.

Use the following information to answer questions 7–9.

During the Civil War, President Lincoln issued the Emancipation Proclamation, a presidential order that declared that all slaves being held in the states that were in rebellion against the Union would be free within the following 100 days. Since these states were not under the control of the Union at the time, the proclamation essentially did not free anyone. However, as these states were recaptured, those enslaved in that region gained their freedom.

By proclaiming the anticipated end of slavery, the Emancipation Proclamation also turned the goal of the war into a battle against slavery. Although the president was strongly against slavery, he had been careful from the beginning of the war to frame its purpose as being to restore the Union rather than for abolition. This history-making order also announced that black men could serve in the Union army and navy. Following the issuing of the proclamation, about 180,000 African Americans joined the Union army, and an additional 18,000 joined the navy.

7. **Which is an opinion, rather than a fact, about the Civil War?**
   A. Freeing the slaves changed the goal of the war.
   B. The original goal of the war was to reunite the states.
   C. Many African Americans were anxious to support the efforts of the war.
   D. The Union expected to regain control of the states that had seceded.
   E. African Americans should have been able to fight from the beginning of the war.

8. **Which inference can be made based on the passage?**
   A. Only African Americans willingly fought in the Civil War.
   B. Everyone in the northern states shared Lincoln's beliefs about slavery.
   C. Lincoln wanted African Americans to remain in slavery for several more months.
   D. Lincoln originally had concerns that citizens would not support a war with the aim of freeing the slaves.
   E. The Emancipation Proclamation was a presidential order rather than a law since slavery was already unconstitutional.

9. **At the time of the Civil War, Britain was against slavery. Which of the following was *not* an effect of the Emancipation Proclamation?**

   A. Britain's opinion of the Confederate states was negatively impacted.

   B. Support for the Union greatly increased in foreign countries, including Britain.

   C. Political tensions deepened between the Union and many European countries.

   D. The Confederate states were viewed as a slave nation and were no longer able to receive foreign aid.

   E. The Confederacy's attempt to separate would no longer be viewed by Britain as an attempt to gain freedom but rather as a desire to support slavery.

10. **The Great Depression followed the stock market crash of 1929, causing a decrease in consumer spending, investing, and industry. Unemployment increased, leading to as many as 15 million Americans being jobless. Nearly half of the banks in the United States failed. Which of the following events helped to turn the American economy around?**

    A. the Battle of the Alamo

    B. Pearl Harbor

    C. the Vietnam War

    D. World War I

    E. World War II

chapter **10**

Civics and Government

Questions related to civics and government will comprise about 25 percent of the questions on the GED Social Studies test. They will address politics, government, the founding of our political system, our country's relationship with other nations, and the important role US citizens play in our democracy. As we mentioned in the previous chapter, at least one question on the test will come from the US Constitution, the Bill of Rights, a Supreme Court landmark case, the Declaration of Independence, or the Federalist Papers. These questions could be considered history questions, or they could be considered civics and government questions. Either way, it will be important to be familiar with these documents. You will also be asked questions based on practical documents, such as tax forms, voter's guides, a public notice, or political speeches. Keep in mind that you will need to demonstrate the ability not only to understand the information provided on the test, but also to apply, analyze, and evaluate this information.

What's Being Tested?

As you study for the GED Social Studies test, be sure to review information related to the topics listed in this chapter. As you know, the lists provided in this book are not comprehensive; they suggest topics with which you should be familiar before test day. Any subject regarding civics and government could pop up on the test, regardless of whether or not it is on these lists. Consider the lists a starting point. Remember, you will need to combine your prior knowledge of civics and government with the information provided to answer the test questions completely.

So dig out your old textbooks, take a trip to the library, surf the Web, watch the news, and browse a few good newspapers or news magazines. Become familiar with topics related to civics and government. As you study, keep your eyes peeled for information related to the following topics. And be sure to add any other topics that strike you as interesting or important.

Concepts and Terms

Branches of US Government

The Census

The Chief Justice

Citizenship

Congress

Council-Manager Form of Government

Democracy

Dictatorship

Divine Right

The Electoral Process and Voting

Federalism

The House of Representatives

Immigration and Naturalization

Interest Groups

Judicial Restraint

Judicial Review

Lobbying

Mayor-Council Form of Municipal Government

Monarchy

Oligarchy

Political Continuum

Political Parties

Popular Vote

The Senate

The Supreme Court

System of Checks and Balances

Veto

_____

_____

_____

_____

Legislation and Landmark Supreme Court Cases

Brown v. Board of Education

Civil Rights Act of 1957

Cooper v. Aaron

Dred Scott v. Sandford

Gibbons v. Ogden

Gideon v. Wainwright

Hazelwood v. Kuhlmeier

Korematsu v. United States

Mapp v. Ohio

Marbury v. Madison

McCulloch v. Maryland

Miranda v. Arizona

New Jersey v. T.L.O.

Plessy v. Ferguson

Regents of the University of California v. Bakke

Roe v. Wade

Terry v. Ohio

Texas v. Johnson

Tinker v. Des Moines

United States v. Nixon

Documents

The Bill of Rights

The Declaration of Independence

The Federalist Papers

Political Speeches

The US Constitution and Amendments

Practical Documents

Driver's License Manual

Tax Forms

Voter's Guide or Handbook

Voter's Registration Form

_____

_____

_____

_____

What to Do

Now that you know what types of information to look over as you prepare to answer civics and government questions on the GED Social Studies test, let's go over the six steps you will use to select the best answer for each question.

> ### Civics and Government Steps
> **Step 1:** Read All the Information
> **Step 2:** Identify the Question
> **Step 3:** Underline Key Words and Phrases
> **Step 4:** Determine Meanings
> **Step 5:** Think About What You Already Know
> **Step 6:** Select the Best Answer

Step 1: Read All the Information

As you already know, reading all of the information includes any passages or paragraphs, as well visual aids such as graphs, charts, cartoons, timelines, or maps. Be sure to pay close attention to titles, labels, and captions, since these often include pertinent information.

Step 2: Identify the Question

Once you have carefully read all of the information associated with a question, go ahead and read the question itself. Remember, some people find it helpful to read the question first and then read the information. Either way is fine, as long as you read everything. If you do read the question first, make sure you go back and read it one more time after completing the passage. That way, the question is fresh in your mind, and you are able to select the best answer choice in Step 6.

Step 3: Underline Key Words and Phrases

Now that you know what the question is asking, which words or phrases in the paragraph or graphics will be important in selecting the correct answer? Determine to what information the question is referring and underline it.

Step 4: Determine Meanings

If there are any unfamiliar words or phrases, use what you know about context clues and word parts to figure out what they mean. Remember, even the best readers encounter new words sometimes. Look for clues such as definitions or examples. Figure out what would make sense in the context of the sentence and passage. Then see if the root word, prefix, or suffix offer any hints to the word's meaning.

Step 5: Think About What You Already Know

Ask yourself questions about the topic, such as *Does this topic sound familiar?* and *What do I know about this subject?* and *Have I read or heard any of this information before?* There is a good chance that you will at least be familiar with many of the topics on the test, which is great! For example, you probably know that presidential elections in the United States occur every four years. You also probably already know that citizens over the age of 18 can register to vote and have a voice in who is chosen to lead our country. See? Civics and government are familiar subjects. Use what you already know to help you analyze the information given.

Step 6: Select the Best Answer

There is only one completely correct answer to any question on the test. Carefully analyze each of the five options; then select the one that best and most completely answers the question.

Examples

Let's take a look at a couple of civics and government sample questions.

In 1954, the Supreme Court ruled on *Brown v. Board of Education*, which challenged a ruling established by the 1896 case *Plessy v. Ferguson*. The 1954 case was brought against the school system of Topeka, Kansas, by the NAACP. Which best summarizes the outcome of this case?

1. Separate schools are inherently unequal.

2. All citizens are eligible to vote, regardless of race.

3. Schools segregated by race are separate but equal.

4. The First Amendment does support obscene speech in schools.

5. School-initiated prayer in public schools is protected by the First Amendment.

Here are our steps:

Step 1: Read All the Information

Step 2: Identify the Question

What was the outcome of Brown v. Board of Education?

Step 3: Underline Key Words and Phrases

To answer this question, it is important to note the date as well as who was involved in the ruling. Key information to underline includes 1954; school system of Topeka, Kansas; and NAACP.

Step 4: Determine Meanings

The words inherently and segregated in the answer choices may be unfamiliar. Inherently is an adjective that modifies unequal. The word means "basically"; however, omitting an adjective from a sentence does not necessarily change the meaning. So if you were unable to determine the meaning, you would still be able to understand answer choice A: Separate schools are unequal.

In answer choice C, the words race and separate are clues to the meaning of segregated. You probably know that in 1954, students were separated by race. So you can infer that segregated means "separated."

Step 5: Think About What You Already Know

You probably already know that an issue in 1954 was that students were assigned to schools based on the color of their skin. You probably also know that the NAACP is the National Association for the Advancement of Colored People, and its goal was equality for all citizens, regardless of race.

Step 6: Select the Best Answer

In 1954, the NAACP challenged the constitutionality of schools being segregated. Today, as a result of this Supreme Court ruling, students are no longer separated by race. Answer choice 1 best summarizes the outcome.

Now it's your turn. Take a look at the next question, which refers to the IRS income tax form shown. We'll give you the steps you will need to practice the process.

Form **1040** Department of the Treasury—Internal Revenue Service (99)
U.S. Individual Income Tax Return **2011** OMB No. 1545-0074 IRS Use Only—Do not write or staple in this space.

For the year Jan. 1–Dec. 31, 2011, or other tax year beginning , 2011, ending , 20 See separate instructions.

Your first name and initial	Last name	Your social security number
If a joint return, spouse's first name and initial	Last name	Spouse's social security number

Home address (number and street). If you have a P.O. box, see instructions. | Apt. no.

▲ Make sure the SSN(s) above and on line 6c are correct.

City, town or post office, state, and ZIP code. If you have a foreign address, also complete spaces below (see instructions).

Presidential Election Campaign

Foreign country name	Foreign province/county	Foreign postal code

Check here if you, or your spouse if filing jointly, want $3 to go to this fund. Checking a box below will not change your tax or refund. ☐ You ☐ Spouse

Filing Status

Check only one box.

1 ☐ Single
2 ☐ Married filing jointly (even if only one had income)
3 ☐ Married filing separately. Enter spouse's SSN above and full name here. ▶
4 ☐ Head of household (with qualifying person). (See instructions.) If the qualifying person is a child but not your dependent, enter this child's name here. ▶
5 ☐ Qualifying widow(er) with dependent child

Exemptions

6a ☐ **Yourself.** If someone can claim you as a dependent, **do not** check box 6a . . . . .
b ☐ **Spouse** . . . .
c **Dependents:**

(1) First name Last name	(2) Dependent's social security number	(3) Dependent's relationship to you	(4) ✓ if child under age 17 qualifying for child tax credit (see instructions)
			☐
			☐
			☐
			☐

If more than four dependents, see instructions and check here ▶ ☐

d Total number of exemptions claimed . . . .

Boxes checked on 6a and 6b
No. of children on 6c who:
• lived with you
• did not live with you due to divorce or separation (see instructions)
Dependents on 6c not entered above
Add numbers on lines above ▶

Income

Attach Form(s) W-2 here. Also attach Forms W-2G and 1099-R if tax was withheld.

If you did not get a W-2, see instructions.

Enclose, but do not attach, any payment. Also, please use Form 1040-V.

7 Wages, salaries, tips, etc. Attach Form(s) W-2 . . . . | 7
8a **Taxable** interest. Attach Schedule B if required . . . . | 8a
b **Tax-exempt** interest. **Do not** include on line 8a . . . | 8b | |
9a Ordinary dividends. Attach Schedule B if required . . . . | 9a
b Qualified dividends . . . . | 9b | |
10 Taxable refunds, credits, or offsets of state and local income taxes . . . . . | 10
11 Alimony received . . . . | 11
12 Business income or (loss). Attach Schedule C or C-EZ . . . . | 12
13 Capital gain or (loss). Attach Schedule D if required. If not required, check here ▶ ☐ | 13
14 Other gains or (losses). Attach Form 4797 . . . . | 14
15a IRA distributions . | 15a | | b Taxable amount . . . | 15b
16a Pensions and annuities | 16a | | b Taxable amount . . . | 16b
17 Rental real estate, royalties, partnerships, S corporations, trusts, etc. Attach Schedule E | 17
18 Farm income or (loss). Attach Schedule F . . . . | 18
19 Unemployment compensation . . . . | 19
20a Social security benefits | 20a | | b Taxable amount . . . | 20b
21 Other income. List type and amount ------------------------------ | 21
22 Combine the amounts in the far right column for lines 7 through 21. This is your **total income** ▶ | 22

Adjusted Gross Income

23 Educator expenses . . . . | 23 |
24 Certain business expenses of reservists, performing artists, and fee-basis government officials. Attach Form 2106 or 2106-EZ | 24 |
25 Health savings account deduction. Attach Form 8889 . | 25 |
26 Moving expenses. Attach Form 3903 . . | 26 |
27 Deductible part of self-employment tax. Attach Schedule SE . | 27 |
28 Self-employed SEP, SIMPLE, and qualified plans . . | 28 |
29 Self-employed health insurance deduction . . . | 29 |
30 Penalty on early withdrawal of savings . . . . . | 30 |
31a Alimony paid **b** Recipient's SSN ▶ | 31a |
32 IRA deduction . . . . | 32 |
33 Student loan interest deduction . . . . . . | 33 |
34 Tuition and fees. Attach Form 8917 . . . . . . | 34 |
35 Domestic production activities deduction. Attach Form 8903 | 35 |
36 Add lines 23 through 35 . . . . | 36
37 Subtract line 36 from line 22. This is your **adjusted gross income** . . . . . ▶ | 37

For Disclosure, Privacy Act, and Paperwork Reduction Act Notice, see separate instructions.   Cat. No. 11320B   Form **1040** (2011)

Which is *not* true?

1. Income tax must be paid on interest earned on investments.
2. Unemployed citizens are not required to pay any income taxes.
3. Small business owners may deduct a portion of the cost of health insurance.
4. School teachers are permitted to deduct some of the costs of classroom supplies.
5. A waitress is required to pay income tax on both her hourly wage and any tips she earns.

Step 1: Read All the Information

Step 2: Identify the Question

_____

_____

Step 3: Underline Key Words and Phrases

Step 4: Determine Meanings

_____

_____

Step 5: Think About What You Already Know

_____

_____

_____

_____

Step 6: Select the Best Answer

The correct answer is 2.

CIVICS AND GOVERNMENT DRILLS

Fill in the blanks for question 1. For each of the subsequent questions, choose the best answer.

1. **What are the steps for answering civics and government questions?**

    Step 1: _____

    Step 2: _____

    Step 3: _____

    Step 4: _____

    Step 5: _____

    Step 6: _____

Use the Voter Registration Application shown to answer questions 2–3.

New Jersey
Voter Registration Application

76

Please print clearly in ink. All information is required unless marked optional.

1 Check boxes that apply:
- ☐ New Registration
- ☐ Name Change
- ☐ Address Change
- ☐ Signature Update
- ☐ Political Party Affiliation or Non-affiliation Change

FOR OFFICIAL USE ONLY

Clerk

2 Are you a U.S. Citizen? ☐ Yes ☐ No
(If No, DO NOT complete this form)

Will you be 18 years of age by the next election?   Yes   No
(If No, DO NOT complete this form)

Registration #

3 Last Name   First Name   Middle Name or Initial   Suffix *(Jr., Sr., III)*

Office Time Stamp

4 Date of Birth

5 NJ Driver's License Number or MVC Non-driver ID Number

If you DO NOT have a NJ Driver's License or MVC Non-Driver ID, provide the last 4 digits of your Social Security Number. __ __ __ __

☐ "I swear or affirm that I DO NOT have a NJ Driver's License, MVC Non-driver ID or a Social Security Number."

6 Home Address *(DO NOT use PO Box)*   Apt.   Municipality   County   State   Zip Code

7 Mailing Address if different from above   Apt.   Municipality   County   State   Zip Code

8 Last Address Registered to Vote *(DO NOT use PO Box)*   Apt.   Municipality   County   State   Zip Code

☐ by mail
☐ in person

9 Former Name if Making Name Change

a. Day Phone Number *(Optional)*

b. E-Mail Address *(Optional)*

10 Do you wish to declare a political party affiliation?   ☐ Yes, the party name is ___
(Optional)   ☐ No, I do not wish to be affiliated with any political party.

11 Gender
☐ Female
☐ Male

Declaration - I swear or affirm that:
- I am a U.S. Citizen
- I live at the above address
- I will be at least 18 years old on or before the next election

- I will have resided in the State and county at least 30 days before the next election
- I am not on parole, probation or serving a sentence due to a conviction for an indictable offense under any federal or state laws

- I understand that any false or fraudulent registration may subject me to a fine of up to $15,000, imprisonment up to 5 years, or both pursuant to R.S. 19:34-1

Signature: Sign or mark and date on lines below

If applicant is unable to complete this form, print the name and address of individual who completed this form.

Name ___

Date ___

X _____   Date ___   Address ___

Important Instructions for sections 5, 6 and 10

5) Registrants who are submitting this form by mail and are registering to vote for the first time: If you do not have any of the information required by section 5, or the information you provide cannot be verified, you will be asked to provide a COPY of a current and valid photo ID, or a document with your name and current address on it to avoid having to provide identification at the polling place.

   Note: *ID Numbers are Confidential and will not be released by any governmental agency. Any person who uses such numbers illegally shall be subject to criminal penalties.*

6) If you are homeless, you may complete section 6 by providing a contact point or the location where you spend most of your time.

10) You may declare a political affiliation or you may declare to be unaffiliated, regardless of any prior party affiliation. Completing section 10 is OPTIONAL and will not affect the acceptance of your voter registration application.

Need More Information? Check boxes below if you would like to receive more information about:

- ☐ voting by mail
- ☐ becoming a poll worker
- ☐ polling place accessibility
- ☐ voting if you have a disability, including visual impairment
- ☐ available election materials in this alternative language: ___

For further information visit **Elections.NJ.gov** or call toll-free **1-877-NJVOTER** (1-877-658-6837)

NJ Division of Elections - 6/22/12

2. **According to the form, which is true?**
   A. Only US citizens are eligible to vote.
   B. Only residents born in the US may vote.
   C. Residents of New Jersey must have a driver's license in order to vote.
   D. New Jersey residents must be 18 years old before registering to vote.
   E. People new to the state may vote as long as they reside in New Jersey on election day.

3. **Which group of people may *not* register to vote?**
   A. those with disabilities
   B. those who are homeless
   C. those who are on parole
   D. those who do not speak English
   E. those not affiliated with a political party

Use the following information to answer questions 4–5.

The US Constitution was written in 1787. Since that time, portions of the document have been amended or superseded. Read the excerpt of the original document and answer the questions that follow.

The House of Representatives shall be composed of Members chosen every second Year by the People of the several States, and the Electors in each State shall have the Qualifications requisite for Electors of the most numerous Branch of the State Legislature.

No Person shall be a Representative who shall not have attained to the Age of twenty five Years, and been seven Years a Citizen of the United States, and who shall not, when elected, be an Inhabitant of that State in which he shall be chosen.

Representatives and direct Taxes shall be apportioned among the several States which may be included within this Union, according to their respective Numbers, which shall be determined by adding to the whole Number of free Persons, including those bound to Service for a Term of Years, and excluding Indians not taxed, three fifths of all other Persons. The actual Enumeration shall be made within three Years after the first Meeting of the Congress of the United States, and within every subsequent Term of ten Years, in such Manner as they shall by Law direct. The Number of Representatives shall not exceed one for every thirty Thousand, but each State shall have at Least one Representative; and until such enumeration shall be made, the State of New Hampshire shall be entitled to chuse three, Massachusetts eight, Rhode-Island and Providence Plantations one, Connecticut five, New-York six, New Jersey four, Pennsylvania eight, Delaware one, Maryland six, Virginia ten, North Carolina five, South Carolina five, and Georgia three.

4. **Which state had the greatest population at the time the US Constitution was written?**
   A. Massachusetts
   B. New Hampshire
   C. New York
   D. Pennsylvania
   E. Virginia

5. **According to the document, which is true?**
   A. Representatives could live in any state.
   B. Slaves counted as three-fifths of a person.
   C. Residents had to be 25 years old to be able to vote.
   D. Each state was responsible for an equal amount of taxes.
   E. Men could join the House of Representatives as soon as they arrived from England.

Use the following table to answer questions 6–7.

Bill of Rights	
Amendment	Summary
I	Grants freedoms of religion, speech, and the press and to assemble and petition the government to remedy grievances.
II	Gives the right to bear arms.
III	Establishes that private citizens cannot be forced to house soldiers during times of peace.
IV	Guarantees protection against search and seizure without a warrant.
V	States the rights of citizens who are accused of crimes.
VI	Outlines the rights of citizens in regard to trials and juries.
VII	Gives the right to a trial by jury in a federal civil court case.
VIII	Offers protection against "cruel and unusual" punishments and extremely large fines for criminals.
IX	States that rights not specifically listed in the Constitution may still be respected.
X	Explains that powers that have not been granted to the federal government are either granted to the states or the people.

6. After being charged with a felony, Clarence Earl Gideon asked the judge to provide him with an attorney at no cost, based on the fact that he was unable to afford representation. The judge denied the request, so Gideon turned to the Supreme Court. Which amendment did the Court uphold in *Gideon v. Wainwright* (1963) when they ruled that indigent defendants must be provided legal representation without being charged?

   A. the Fourth Amendment
   B. the Fifth Amendment
   C. the Sixth Amendment
   D. the Seventh Amendment
   E. the Eighth Amendment

7. The Supreme Court case of *Tinker v. Des Moines* (1969) ruled in favor of Mary Beth Tinker and her brother, who wore black armbands to school in protest of the Vietnam War. The administrators of their school worried that the armbands would cause a disruption and prohibited students from expressing their opposition in this manner. The Court ruled that the Tinkers' actions were protected by which amendment?

   A. the First Amendment
   B. the Second Amendment
   C. the Third Amendment
   D. the Ninth Amendment
   E. the Tenth Amendment

8. In our country, the president is selected by the electoral college. Which type of political system is this?

   A. anarchy
   B. democracy
   C. dictatorship
   D. monarchy
   E. oligarchy

9. Queen Elizabeth II began ruling England at age 25, following the death of her father, King George VI. Which type of political system is practiced in her country?

   A. anarchy
   B. democracy
   C. dictatorship
   D. monarchy
   E. oligarchy

Use this page from the *2012 California Driver Handbook* to answer question 10.

MINORS' PERMIT RESTRICTIONS

Your permit is not valid until you begin driver training; your instructor will sign the permit to validate it. You must practice with a licensed California driver: parent, guardian, driving instructor, spouse, or an adult 25 years of age or older. The person must sit close enough to you to take control of the vehicle at any time. A provisional permit does not allow you to drive alone—not even to a DMV office to take a driving test.

MINORS' DRIVER LICENSE REQUIREMENTS

You must:

- Be at least 16 years old.
- Prove that you have finished both driver education and driver training.
- Have had a California instruction permit or an instruction permit from another state for at least six months.
- Provide parent(s) or guardian(s) signature(s) on your instruction permit stating that you have completed 50 hours of supervised driving practice (10 hours must be night driving) as outlined in the *California Parent-Teen Training Guide* (DL 603). Visit the Teen website at **www.dmv.ca.gov/teenweb/** or call 1-800-777-0133 to request this booklet.
- Pass the behind-the-wheel driving test. You have three chances to pass the driving test while your permit is valid. If you fail the behind-the-wheel driving test, you must pay a retest fee for a second or subsequent test and wait two weeks before you are retested.

Once you have your provisional driver license, you may drive **alone**, as long as you do not have any collisions or traffic violations.

When you become 18 years old, the "provisional" part of your driver license ends. You may keep your provisional photo license or pay a fee for a duplicate driver license without the word "provisional."

During the first 12 months after you are licensed, you cannot drive between 11 p.m. and 5 a.m. **and** you cannot transport passengers under 20 years of age, unless you are accompanied by a licensed parent or guardian, a licensed driver 25 years of age or older, or a licensed or certified driving instructor.

EXCEPTIONS - MINORS' DRIVER LICENSE RESTRICTIONS

The law allows the following exceptions when reasonable transportation is not available and it is necessary for you to drive. A signed note explaining the necessity to drive and the date when this driving necessity will end must be kept in your possession for the following exceptions (emancipated minors are excluded from this requirement):

- Medical necessity to drive when reasonable transportation alternatives are inadequate. The note must be signed by a physician.

10. **Which assumption can be made based on this information?**

   A. Drivers must be at least 25 years old to legally operate a car alone.
   B. After obtaining a California driver license, minors have the same driving privileges as adults.
   C. A driver education class is required for anyone under the age of 18 wishing to obtain a California driver license.
   D. High school students may carpool to campus, as long as the driver is at least 16 years old and has his license.
   E. Minors with driving permits are encouraged to practice driving after dark extensively before obtaining their license to drive alone.

chapter 11

Economics

One definition of *economics* is "the study of goods and services." Another is "the financial aspect of something." Basically, economics involves money matters. Twenty percent of the questions on the GED Social Studies test will address this area of learning.

Believe it or not, you dabble in economics every day. For example, grabbing the last pair of jeans off the department store shelf during a sale, while a handful of other customers stomp away empty-handed is an example of supply and demand. This is part of the study of goods and services. And when you decide that the amount of money in your wallet is not quite enough to purchase the jeans and a new belt too, that is an example of the financial aspect of something. Welcome to the world of economics!

As you know, you will need to combine your own knowledge and experiences of economics with the information and graphics provided to answer the questions completely on the GED Social Studies test. Remember, you will be demonstrating your ability not only to comprehend the information, but also to analyze, restate, summarize, and draw inferences based on the data.

In this chapter, we will go over a few of the types of economics questions you might encounter on the test. To prepare effectively, make sure to check out any information related to economics in your textbooks. The newspaper is also a great source of material on the topic. And as mentioned in previous chapters, the Internet, news magazines, and television can be valuable sources of information.

What's Being Tested?

Economics questions on the test may cover quite a range of subject matter. Be comfortable with your understanding of economic reasoning, different types of economic systems, how businesses operate in a free enterprise system, financial institutions, the role of the government in economics, labor, production, consumers, global markets, and foreign trade. The following lists suggest a few topics to review; however, pretty much anything related to economics could be fair game. Start by reviewing the ideas on the lists. As you study, add any other important or interesting economic concepts you come across.

Keep in mind that practical documents such as tax forms, bank statements, workplace benefits forms, and contracts may be included on the test. Make sure you are comfortable working with these everyday papers.

Types of Economic Systems

Capitalism

Communism

Mixed Economy

Socialism

_____

_____

_____

_____

Economics and the Government

Child Labor Laws

The Economic Opportunity Act

Minimum Wage Laws

The Sherman Anti-Trust Act

_____

_____

_____

_____

Economic Terms Related to Goods and Services

Capital	Labor
Consumers	Natural Resources
Demand	Production
E-commerce	Shortage
Equilibrium	Surplus
Free Enterprise	

_____

_____

_____

_____

Economic Terms Related to Finance

Balanced Budget	Fixed Expense
Budget Surplus	Flexible Expense
Consumer Price Index	Gross Domestic Product (GDP)
Deficit Spending	Gross National Product (GNP)
Deflation	Inflation
Discount Rate	Inflationary Spiral
Econometrics	Luxury Expense
The Federal Reserve Board	Money
Fiscal Policy	Reserve Ratio

_____

_____

_____

_____

Keep in Mind

Keep in mind that economics questions are likely to involve graphs and charts. Make sure you are comfortable reading these data displays. Take a quick look at Chapter 29 in this book to refresh your memory on data analysis.

What to Do

Now that we've reviewed what types of economics information you may find on the GED Social Studies test, let's go over the six steps you will use to find the best answer for each of the questions.

> ### Economics Steps
> **Step 1:** Read All the Information
> **Step 2:** Identify the Question
> **Step 3:** Underline Key Words and Phrases
> **Step 4:** Determine Meanings
> **Step 5:** Think About What You Already Know
> **Step 6:** Select the Best Answer

Step 1: Read All the Information

Make sure you read any and all information associated with each question. That includes not only the passage but also the visual aids. If an illustration includes a caption, read it. If a cartoon includes dialogue, read it. You get the idea.

Since graphs are often used to display economic data, it is likely that you will find a graph or two associated with these questions. It may be tempting to assume that you know what type of information is included in the graph and skip over titles, labels, and keys to save time. Spend the few extra seconds it takes to read this information. It can make a tremendous difference in your understanding of the data.

For example, without reading the vertical axis of a graph, how would you know the increments by which the data are shown? Let's do a little experiment.

Take a look at the following bar graph, which is missing the information on the vertical axis.

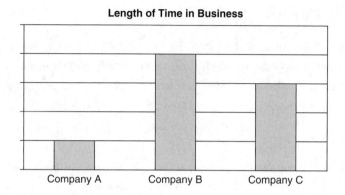

Without knowing the information shown along the left side of the graph, how can someone confidently interpret these data? Has Company A really only been in business for a single year? Are the data even reported in years or shown in days, weeks, or months?

Now take a look at the revised graph.

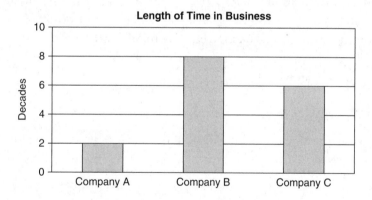

By reading the labels, we now know that Company A has been in business for two decades, or 20 years. Knowing all the material makes a big difference. Make sure you take time to read as much information as you can find before trying to answer any questions on the GED Social Studies test.

Step 2: Identify the Question

Once you have read every bit of information related to each question, including the question itself, determine exactly what is being asked. For example, are you supposed to identify a company's profit for a single year, its increase in profits over the previous year, or its total profits over a period of several years? Try restating the question to be sure you clearly understand the task.

Step 3: Underline Key Words and Phrases

What are the most important facts or details in the passage? What information will you need to answer the question? Underline these words and phrases in the passage or graphic so you can locate them quickly and easily when selecting the best answer.

Step 4: Determine Meanings

Were there unfamiliar words in the passage, question, or answer choices? If so, look for clues in the given information that can help you figure out the meaning. Ask yourself what meaning would make sense in the context of the paragraph. Also, look for familiar word parts, such as roots or prefixes, that may offer hints about the definition.

Step 5: Think About What You Already Know

Now think about the information you have been given, and figure out what you already know about the topic. You may have studied similar information in school, read about it in the newspaper, or heard a related story on the news. Combine your prior knowledge with the ideas included on the test to best understand the subject matter.

Step 6: Select the Best Answer

Before answering the question, reread it and all of the answer choices one more time. Then select the answer that gives the best and most complete response to the question.

Examples

Let's look at a few sample economics questions.

Supply and demand work together to determine the market price for goods. The graph shows the supply and demand for a product.

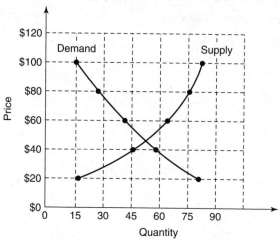

Supply and Demand for Product X

According to the chart, what is the market price for the item?

1. $20
2. $45
3. $50
4. $100
5. $120

Here are our steps:

Step 1: Read All the Information

Step 2: Identify the Question

At what price does supply equal demand?

Step 3: Underline Key Words and Phrases

The information needed to solve this problem is on the graph. Underline the axis labels <u>Price</u> and <u>Quantity</u> and the <u>Supply</u> and <u>Demand</u> labels on each line.

Step 4: Determine Meanings

Suppose the phrase <u>market price</u> is unfamiliar. The information states that supply and demand work together to determine market price. Take a look at the graph to see how supply and demand work together, and notice that the lines meet where the quantity and price are balanced. So market price is the point at which quantity and price balance.

Step 5: Think About What You Already Know

What have you learned, heard, or read about supply and demand and market price in the past? Use this information, along with the information in the statement and the graph, to complete Step 6.

Step 6: Select the Best Answer

Supply and demand are balanced at approximately $45, so the best answer choice is 2.

Now it's your turn. Take a look at the following question, which is based on the same supply and demand graph. We'll give you the steps you will need to practice the process.

Based on the graph, which is true?

1. Less of the product would sell if it were priced below $40.
2. When the price is lower, the demand is lower as well.
3. When the supply is greatest, the price is also greatest.
4. When the price is increased, the demand is decreased.
5. The company would sell the most products if it were priced at $100.

Step 1: Read All the Information

Step 2: Identify the Question

_____

_____

Step 3: Underline Key Words and Phrases

Step 4: Determine Meanings

_____

_____

Step 5: Think About What You Already Know

_____

_____

_____

_____

Step 6: Select the Best Answer

The correct answer is 4.

ECONOMICS DRILLS

Fill in the blanks for question 1. For each of the subsequent questions, choose the best answer.

1. **What are the steps for answering economics questions?**
    Step 1: _____
    Step 2: _____
    Step 3: _____
    Step 4: _____
    Step 5: _____
    Step 6: _____

2. **Following a successful advertising campaign, the demand for a certain product increases. Which of the following can most likely be expected?**
    A. product surplus
    B. increase in supply
    C. decrease in market price
    D. increase in market price
    E. decrease in product sales

Use the following information to answer questions 3–4.

In 1964, President Johnson passed the Economic Opportunity Act, which established the Office of Economic Opportunity to help combat poverty. The Economic Opportunity Act stated, "It is the policy of the United States to eliminate the paradox of poverty in the midst of plenty in this nation by opening, to everyone, the opportunity for education and training, the opportunity to work, and the opportunity to live in decency and dignity." And so, the act became known as "the war on poverty."

   This act was the first of several antipoverty steps taken by the US government during the 1960s. Through this first step, a range of programs were established that could be used by communities to access federal funds and professional help to deal with causes of poverty. Although health care and loans were offered, educational programs were at the center of the act. One such program, HEAD START, enrolled more than half a million preschool-aged students during the first summer it was in operation, providing children from economically and culturally deprived families with health care, welfare, and academic training. The act also supported the National Youth Corps, the Job Corps, and Upward Bound, which were each related to education and offered job training to help tackle high unemployment rates among teens from low-income families.

The following year, the act was amended to include the creation of offices at the state level to support economic opportunity and encourage state governments to help fight the war on poverty.

3. **Which can be inferred from the passage?**
   A. Adolescents were not looking for jobs.
   B. President Johnson saw education as key to ending poverty.
   C. Undereducated children were one cause of poverty in the nation.
   D. Most communities were not interested in assisting low-income families.
   E. President Johnson believed local government should take full responsibility for ending poverty.

4. **Upon signing the Economic Opportunity Act, President Johnson stated, "This is not in any sense a cynical proposal to exploit the poor with a promise of a handout or a dole. We know—we learned long ago—that answer is no answer. The measure before me this morning for signature offers the answer that its title implies—the answer of opportunity. For the purpose of the Economic Opportunity Act of 1964 is to offer opportunity, not an opiate."**

   Which inference can be made?
   A. At this time, everyone in the country was dealing with issues related to poverty.
   B. This was the first time the government had done anything to help those faced with poverty.
   C. People from low-income families were given plenty of opportunities but were not taking advantage of them.
   D. President Johnson believed programs that offered financial assistance to low-income families were sufficient.
   E. President Johnson believed that past programs had not done enough to solve the underlying problems that caused poverty.

5. **Which of the following did the Economic Opportunity Act do?**
   A. give money to the unemployed
   B. offer jobs to unemployed citizens
   C. eliminate poverty in the United States
   D. supply homes and food for those facing poverty
   E. provide education and job training to adolescents

Use the following information to answer questions 6–8.

The Rivera family bought a new home. They obtained a 30-year mortgage for $100,000 at 6 percent interest. The amortization schedule shows the amount of principal and interest they will pay each month for the life of the loan.

Payments	Yearly Total	Principal Paid	Interest Paid	Balance
Year 1 (1–12)	$57,194.61	$1,228.00	$5,967.00	$98,771.99
Year 2 (13–24)	$57,194.61	$1,304.00	$5,891.00	$97,468.24
Year 3 (25–36)	$57,194.61	$1,384.00	$5,810.00	$96,034.07
Year 4 (37–48)	$57,194.61	$1,470.00	$5,725.00	$94,614.53
Year 5 (49.00)	$57,194.61	$1,560.00	$5,634.00	$93,054.36
Year 6 (61–72)	$57,194.61	$1,656.00	$5,538.00	$91,397.95
Year 7 (73–84)	$57,194.61	$1,759.00	$5,436.00	$89,639.39
Year 8 (85–96)	$57,194.61	$1,867.00	$5,328.00	$87,772.35
Year 9 (97–108)	$57,194.61	$1,982.00	$5,212.00	$85,790.17
Year 10 (109–120)	$57,194.61	$2,104.00	$5,090.00	$83,685.72
Year 11 (121–132)	$57,194.61	$2,234.00	$4,960.00	$81,451.48
Year 12 (133–144)	$57,194.61	$2,372.00	$4,823.00	$79,079.44
Year 13 (145–156)	$57,194.61	$2,518.00	$4,676.00	$76,561.09
Year 14 (157–168)	$57,194.61	$2,674.00	$4,521.00	$73,887.42
Year 15 (169–180)	$57,194.61	$2,839.00	$4,356.00	$71,048.84
Year 16 (181–192)	$57,194.61	$3,014.00	$4,181.00	$68,035.19
Year 17 (193–204)	$57,194.61	$3,200.00	$3,995.00	$64,835.66
Year 18 (205–216)	$57,194.61	$3,397.00	$3,798.00	$61,438.79
Year 19 (217–228)	$57,194.61	$3,606.00	$3,588.00	$57,832.40
Year 20 (229–240)	$57,194.61	$3,829.00	$3,366.00	$54,003.59
Year 21 (241–252)	$57,194.61	$4,065.00	$3,130.00	$49,938.62
Year 22 (253–264)	$57,194.61	$4,316.00	$2,879.00	$45,622.93
Year 23 (265–276)	$57,194.61	$4,582.00	$2,613.00	$41,041.06
Year 24 (277–288)	$57,194.61	$4,864.00	$2,330.00	$36,176.59
Year 25 (289–300)	$57,194.61	$5,165.00	$2,030.00	$31,012.09
Year 26 (301–312)	$57,194.61	$5,483.00	$1,712.00	$25,529.05
Year 27 (313–324)	$57,194.61	$5,821.00	$1,373.00	$19,707.84
Year 28 (325–336)	$57,194.61	$6,180.00	$1,014.00	$13,527.58
Year 29 (337–348)	$57,194.61	$6,561.00	$633.00	$6,966.14
Year 30 (349–360)	$57,194.61	$6,966.00	$228.00	$50.00
Totals	$215,838.19	$100,000.00	$115,838.19	

6. **How much principal will the family have paid on the loan by the end of the fifth year?**
   A. $1,560.00
   B. $5,385.47
   C. $5,634.00
   D. $6,945.64
   E. $7,194.61

7. **How much interest will the family pay over the life of the loan?**
   A. $6,000.00
   B. $15,838.19
   C. $100,000.00
   D. $115,838.19
   E. $215,838.19

8. **Which is true based on the table?**
   A. The total amount of interest owed will be repaid during the first 20 years of the loan.
   B. Approximately one-fourth of the principal will be repaid during the final five years of the loan.
   C. The amount of interest paid over the life of the loan will be 6 percent of the total amount of principal paid.
   D. After the first 15 years of payments, approximately half of the total loan amount will have been repaid.
   E. During the first 10 years, the amount of interest paid each month is approximately twice the amount of principal.

9. *Capitalism* **refers to a type of economic system that includes private ownership and operation of all, or most, means of production that are motivated by profit. Which of the following is associated with capitalism?**
   A. Fascism
   B. dictatorship
   C. free enterprise
   D. social equality
   E. state ownership

10. **The Federal Reserve System was established, in 1913 by the Federal Reserve Act, as the central banking system of the United States, partially as a result of several serious financial panics in our country. The purpose for the act was to maximize employment, to provide stability in prices, to moderate long-term interest rates, and to give the United States a safer and more stable financial system. However, these goals have since been expanded to include a number of other objectives, including influencing financial and credit conditions, protecting consumers' credit rights, and providing financial services not only to banks but also to our government.**

Based on the information, as well as your own knowledge, which of the following is true?

A. The idea of a central banking system is unique to the United States.

B. Financial issues in our country were limited to certain rural areas in the 1900s.

C. The establishment of the Federal Reserve has eliminated financial crisis in our country.

D. Widespread financial problems afflicted our country during the late nineteenth and early twentieth centuries.

E. The banking system in the United States was stable and secure from the time the country gained independence.

12

Geography

For many people, the word *geography* brings to mind spinning globes and pull-down world maps in the front of a classroom. These items would definitely be studied in a geography class, but this branch of social studies is much more than simply learning about location, location, location. Geography also includes learning about the physical features of our planet, including bodies of water, mountains, climate, and the impact these have on our lives.

Fifteen percent of the questions on the GED Social Studies test will address your understanding of geography. You will be asked questions about places and regions, physical systems, the environment and society, and the uses of geography. So break out your atlas and let's get started!

What's Being Tested?

Geography questions may cover a wide range of topics. While you probably will not have to identify the capital of Tajikistan, you will need to be comfortable using a variety of types of maps and be able to understand the characteristics of each. It will also be important for you to understand how geographic features impact other factors, such as weather, population, and international relations. The following lists cover a few topics to review. Keep in mind that these lists include suggestions and are by no means exhaustive. Check out the information in your geography textbook. Pay attention to geographic concepts mentioned in the news. Think about how geography has affected historical events in the past and how it affects events today. As you study, add any important or interesting concepts to the lists.

And just in case you're wondering, the capital of Tajikistan is Dushanbe.

Maps and Publications

Almanac

Atlas

Climate Map

Conic Map

Economic or Resource Map

Gnomic Map

Mercator Map

Physical Map

Political Map

Thematic Map

Topographical Map

_____

_____

_____

_____

Geography Vocabulary

Contour Lines

Equator

Hemispheres

Key

Latitude

Legend

Longitude

Prime Meridian

Time Zones

_____

_____

_____

_____

Geographic Features

Climate

Hills

Mountains

Plains

Plateaus

Sea Level

_____

_____

_____

_____

Keep in Mind

Keep in mind that geography questions are likely to involve maps. Make sure you are comfortable using many kinds of maps. Look through books, magazines, and newspapers, and pay attention to the different maps. Notice the features of each. Pay close attention to the key and what type of information is being displayed.

What to Do

Now that you have a basic idea of some of the geography topics you may find on the GED Social Studies test, let's go over the six steps you will use to find the best answer for each of the questions.

> *Geography Steps*
> **Step 1:** Read All the Information
> **Step 2:** Identify the Question
> **Step 3:** Underline Key Words and Phrases
> **Step 4:** Determine Meanings
> **Step 5:** Think About What You Already Know
> **Step 6:** Select the Best Answer

Step 1: Read All the Information

Read, read, read. On this or any other test, always read as much information as you can find. The more you know, the more likely you are to select the correct answer. Since this is a geography test, it will be important to know how to read maps. Remember that the title, key, legend, and any labels that are included may contain valuable information. Take the time to read each of them.

Step 2: Identify the Question

After reading all of the information, figure out exactly what is being asked. For example, when reading a time zone map, are you supposed to tell how many hours later it is in New York than in Los Angeles, or are you supposed to tell what time it is in New York when it is 4:00 in LA? One way to make sure you completely understand the question is to restate it in your own words. Being unable to do this could be a clue that you do not quite understand what is being asked. And being able to recognize what is being asked is key to selecting the correct answer.

Step 3: Underline Key Words and Phrases

Once you have carefully read all of the information and are confident you know what is being asked, identify the important facts and details in the passage and graphics. This will help you focus on the key concepts and make it easier to locate pertinent ideas when answering the question.

Step 4: Determine Meanings

If any words or phrases in the passage, visual aids, or answer choices were unfamiliar, take a minute to determine their meaning. Use clues in the passage, such as definitions, examples, or synonyms, as well as your prior knowledge about root words, prefixes, and suffixes. Often, these will offer enough hints and information to make it possible to figure out the meaning of the unknown word.

Step 5: Think About What You Already Know

You probably already know quite a bit about geography. Think about how your existing knowledge on the topic relates to the information given on the test. Combining these ideas can help you gain a more complete understanding of the subject matter and can improve your ability to select the correct answer.

Step 6: Select the Best Answer

Read the question one more time. Then reread each of the answer choices. Finally, select the one answer that is the best response to the question.

Keep in Mind

Keep in mind that it is important to read each and every answer choice completely. If the first answer sounds good, it might be tempting to stop there and not look at the other options. However, more than one answer could be partially correct. Take the time to read all of the choices carefully. Another answer further down the list could be even better.

Examples

Now let's check out a few sample geography questions.

Julio was traveling on business. The current location of his airplane is approximately 9.5° N latitude and 43° E longitude. Over which location is the airplane currently located?

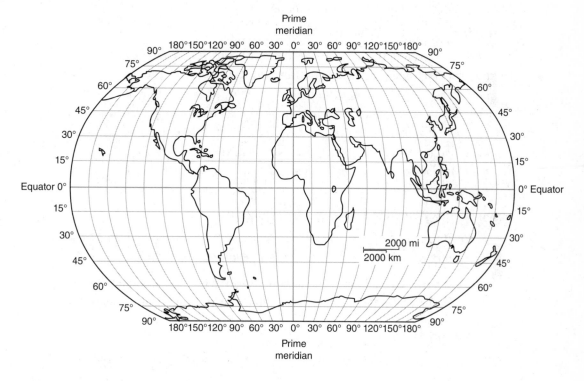

1. Africa
2. the Atlantic Ocean
3. Europe
4. the Pacific Ocean
5. South America

Here are our steps:

Step 1: Read All the Information

Step 2: Identify the Question

Which location is found at 9.5° N latitude and 43° E longitude?

Step 3: Underline Key Words and Phrases

The information you need to solve this problem are the latitude and longitude, 9.5° N <u>latitude</u> and <u>43° E longitude.</u>

Step 4: Determine Meanings

Suppose you cannot remember the directions in which latitude and longitude run. The letter N in 9.5° N latitude can be used as a clue that latitude is north of the equator. The letter E in 43° E longitude can be used as a clue that longitude is east of the prime meridian.

Step 5: Think About What You Already Know

In the past, you may have learned some type of trick to remind you the direction in which lines of latitude and/or longitude run. For example, you may have been taught that <u>longitude</u> lines are <u>long</u>, as a way to remember that these lines are vertical. O, you may have learned that the t's in latitude must be crossed, so these lines run across, or horizontal. You also probably already know the names of the oceans and continents, which will be important since the map does not label any landmasses or bodies of water. Anything you already know about the topic could be helpful in answering the question.

Step 6: Select the Best Answer

The point given is approximately 10 degrees north of the equator and about 45 degrees east of the prime meridian, so the location is in Africa.

Now it's your turn. Take a look at the next question, which is based on the same world map as the previous question. We'll give you the steps you will need to practice the process.

Which of the following points indicates a location in the United States?

1. 17° S latitude and 64° W longitude
2. 17° N latitude and 88° W longitude
3. 34° S latitude and 92° W longitude
4. 40° N latitude and 72° E longitude
5. 67° N latitude and 153° W longitude

Step 1: Read All the Information
Step 2: Identify the Question

_____

_____

Step 3: Underline Key Words and Phrases

Step 4: Determine Meanings

_____

_____

Step 5: Think About What You Already Know

_____

_____

_____

_____

Step 6: Select the Best Answer

The correct answer is 5.

GEOGRAPHY DRILLS

Fill in the blanks for question 1. For each of the subsequent questions, choose the best answer.

1. **What are the steps for answering geography questions?**

   Step 1: _____

   Step 2: _____

   Step 3: _____

   Step 4: _____

   Step 5: _____

   Step 6: _____

2. **Many countries around the world export oil. Saudi Arabia and Russia export the most, with Saudi Arabia exporting nearly 8 million barrels per day and Russia exporting more than 6 million barrels per day. Which inference can be made based on the map?**

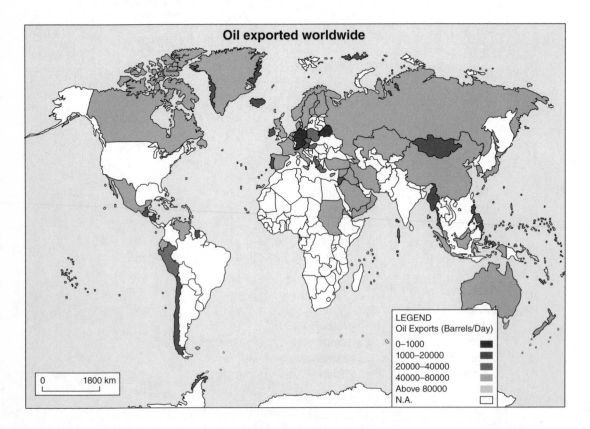

A. The United States does not use oil.
B. There is very little oil in South America.
C. Africa's economy is dependent on exporting oil.
D. The majority of the world's oil comes from Europe.
E. Less oil is exported from Mexico each day than from Australia.

Use the following map to answer questions 3 and 4.

World climates

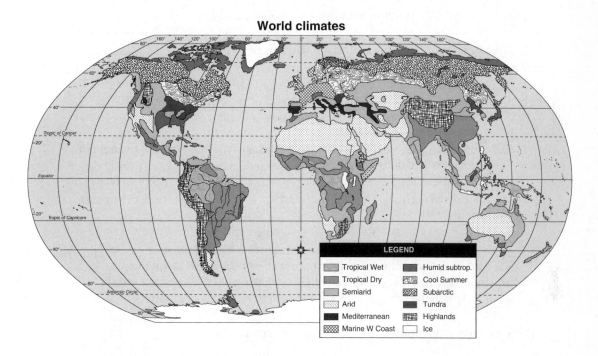

3. **Which conclusion can be drawn based on the map?**

   A. Longitude correlates to the climate of an area.
   B. Locations with similar latitudes have similar climates.
   C. Locations nearest to the equator have the driest climates.
   D. Areas with the warmest climates receive the least rainfall.
   E. Climate is uniform across most locations within the same continent.

4. **Which statement is true?**

   A. Arid climates are found only near the equator.
   B. All islands experience tropical, wet climates.
   C. Climate refers only to the temperature of a region.
   D. Areas bordering an ocean experience wet climates.
   E. A range of climates can be found in both hemispheres.

Use the following information to answer questions 5 and 6.

As altitude increases, temperature decreases. For this reason, mountains have colder climates than surrounding flatlands. They also receive more rainfall. This is due to the fact that as moist air rises to move above the mountain, it cools, allowing it to carry less moisture, resulting in precipitation. In fact, some mountaintops are covered with snow year-round due to weather conditions associated with the altitude rather than the climate of the surrounding areas.

5. **Based on this information, which conclusion can be drawn?**
    A. Plains located in mountainous regions have cold climates.
    B. Flatlands surrounding a mountain range generally have dry, arid climates.
    C. Deserts are not found in the same geographic regions as mountain ranges.
    D. The land on one side of a mountain range may be rainy, while the other side may experience drought conditions.
    E. Mountains that are located in warm climates, such as those nearest the equator, have a lot of rain but no snow.

6. **Which best describes the characteristics of plant life found on or near mountains?**
    A. Mountain peaks often have sparse grasses or bare rocks.
    B. Broad, lush forests are located near a mountain's highest points.
    C. Plant life found at the base of a mountain is similar to that at the top.
    D. Mountains are mostly covered with rock, making plant life uncommon.
    E. Thin, sparse trees are generally found near the foothills of a mountain.

Use the following information to answer questions 7–10.

The largest tropical rain forest in the world is located in the Amazon Basin. This area receives a measureable amount of rainfall nearly 200 days each year, with yearly totals of approximately 100 inches. The Amazon River, as well as more than 1,000 tributaries, runs through this area as well.

7. **Which conclusion can be drawn about this region?**

   A. The Amazon River drains into the Caribbean Sea.

   B. The amount of rainfall is comparable in all areas of the continent.

   C. The majority of the coastal regions of South America is at sea level.

   D. The Andes Mountains are the source of most rivers in South America.

   E. The lowest lying areas in South America are located near the Pacific coastline.

8. **Which is true about the Atacama Desert?**

   A. It is located in Peru.
   B. It is located in the Andes Mountains.
   C. It is found near the equator and has a warm climate.
   D. It is part of the Amazon Basin and has a damp climate.
   E. It is an island in the Pacific Ocean off the coast of South America.

9. **About how many miles in length are the Andes Mountains?**

   A. 200 miles
   B. 600 miles
   C. 2,000 miles
   D. 4,500 miles
   E. 7,200 miles

10. **Based on the physical features of South America, where are the most highly populated cities located?**

    A. near Cape Horn
    B. along the east coast
    C. in the Amazon Basin
    D. along the northwest coast
    E. along the southwest coast

11. **In 2007, approximately 10–20 percent of the residents of the United States were under the age of 15 years old. The map below shows these data worldwide. Which inference can be made based on this information?**

Percent of Population Under 15 Years of Age (2007)

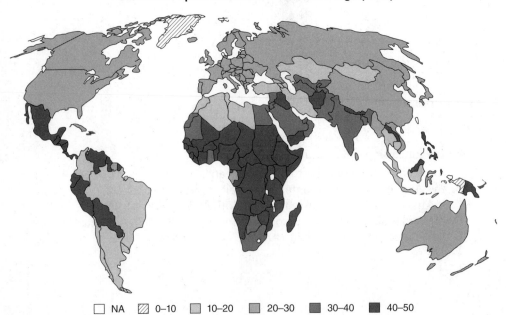

☐ NA   ▨ 0–10   ☐ 10–20   ▨ 20–30   ▨ 30–40   ■ 40–50

A. Nearly one-third of the North American population is under 15 years old.

B. The annual birth rate in much of Europe is greater than the mortality rate in the region.

C. There are more teen-aged residents than elderly residents in most of Central America.

D. The average number of children per family is greater in the United States than in South America.

E. The life expectancy in many African countries is less than that of most other places in the world.

12. **Craig's flight from Anchorage, Alaska, leaves at 3:00 P.M., local time and arrives in Dallas approximately six hours later. About what time will it be in Dallas when the flight lands?**

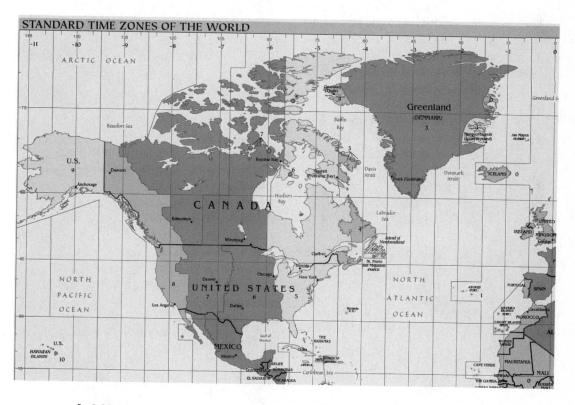

A. 9:00 A.M.

B. 11:00 A.M.

C. 5:00 P.M.

D. 7:00 P.M.

E. 9:00 P.M.

Part IV

Science

chapter **13**

Life Science

In the next few chapters, we will discuss information related to the GED Science test. This test will include 50 questions covering basic science concepts relating to life science and biology, earth and space science, chemistry, and physics. You will be given 1 hour and 20 minutes to complete the test. As many as 60 percent of the questions will include some type of visual aid, such as a graph, table, chart, or diagram. Some of the questions will simply require that you comprehend the information given in the passage or graphic. To answer other questions, you will need to restate or summarize data, evaluate the information, identify assumptions related to the material, and make judgments or hypotheses based on the facts. You may also need to relate the information to your prior knowledge of the topic.

About 45 percent of the questions on the GED Science test will relate to life science, or biology. Basically, you will be asked about living things, including humans, plants, and animals. It will be important to understand the cell, heredity, the interdependence of organisms, and the behavior of organisms. In this chapter, we will go over some of the concepts you can expect to find on the test.

What's Being Tested?

Life science questions may cover a large range of subject matter. The following are lists of suggested topics to understand before the test. Keep in mind that these lists are by no means exhaustive; however, understanding these ideas will put you on the right track.

In addition to topics related to life science, the lists also include subjects about scientific inquiry. You probably learned this process when completing science experiments in school or a science fair project at home, so the concepts will most likely be familiar. Questions about scientific inquiry may address any area of science, but we will review it now, since this is the first science chapter.

To prepare for the test, watch TV shows that discuss science- and health-related topics. Read newspaper and magazine articles related to life science. Take a look at the list of ingredients on the grocery items in your kitchen. Think about how everyday life is affected by disease and improvements in medical technology; be aware of current events. There are a few blank lines at the end of each list for you to jot down any applicable topics you find interesting or important as you research and study.

Scientific Inquiry (the Scientific Method)

Control Group	Independent Variable
Dependent Variable	Result
Experiment	Trial
Hypothesis	

_____

_____

_____

_____

Cells

Active Transport	Gametes
Anaphase	Golgi Apparatus
Animal Cells	Haploid Cell
Cell	Meiosis
Cell Membrane	Metaphase
Cell Wall	Mitochondrion
Chromosome	Mitosis
Cytoplasm	Nucleus
Diffusion	Nucleolus
Diploid Cell	Organelles
Endoplasmic Reticulum	Osmosis

Plant Cells   Telophase
Prophase

_____

_____

_____

_____

Human Body

Alveoli	Involuntary Muscles
Aorta	Ligaments
Artery	Liver
Axons	Marrow
Ball-and-Socket Joints	Muscular System
Blood	Nervous System
Brain	Occipital Lobe
Bronchial Tubes	Pancreas
Capillaries	Pivot Joints
Cardiac Muscles	Plasma
Cerebellum	Platelets
Cerebrum	Red Blood Cells
Circulatory System	Reproductive System
Dendrites	Respiratory System
Diaphragm	Senses
Digestive System	Sensory nerves
Endocrine System	Skeletal System
Enzymes	Smooth Muscles
Epiglottis	Spinal Cord
Esophagus	Synapses
Excretory System	Temporal Lobe
Fixed Joints	Tendons
Gallbladder	Trachea
Glands	Valve
Gliding Joints	Veins

Heart   Ventricle
Hinge Joints   Voluntary Muscles
Hormones   White Blood Cells
Intestines

_____

_____

_____

_____

Animals

Amphibian   Mammal
Arthropods   Mollusks
Bird   Reptile
Cold-blooded   Sponges
Exoskeleton   Vertebrate
Fish   Warm-blooded
Invertebrate   Worms
Jellyfish

_____

_____

_____

_____

Keep in Mind

Keep in mind that some of the vocabulary in these lists relates to more than one topic. For example, *mammal* is listed under the "Animals" heading. However, since humans are mammals, the word relates to humans as well. Likewise, *heart* and *brain* are listed under "Human Body," but animals have hearts and brains too. The important thing is not so much where the words are located on the lists but that you understand each of them.

Plants

Amino Acids	Nitrogenase
Carotene	Nitrogen Cycle
Cellular Respiration	Nodules
Chlorophyll	Nonvascular Plants
Chloroplasts	Phloem
Fern	Photosynthesis
Fertilization	Pistil
Flowers	Pollen
Fungi	Roots
Gametophyte	Spores
Germination	Stamen
Glucose	Stem
Leaf	Vascular Plants
Moss	Xanthophylls
Nitrates	Xylem
Nitrogen	

_____

_____

_____

_____

Organisms

Class	Order
Eukaryotes	Phylum
Family	Prokaryotes
Genus	Simple Organisms
Kingdom	Species
Multicellular Organisms	Unicellular Organisms

_____

_____

_____

_____

Heredity

Chromosomes

Cloning

DNA

Dominant Gene

Fraternal Twins

Genes

Genetic Disorder

Genetics

Heredity

Identical Twins

Mitosis

Mutation

Recessive Gene

RNA

Species

_____

_____

_____

_____

Ecosystems and Nutrients

Calories

Carbohydrates

Carbon Cycle

Carbon Dioxide

Consumers

Decay

Decomposers

Ecosystem

Fats

Food Chain

Food Web

Glucagon

Habitat

Insulin

Minerals

Nutrients

Oxygen

Population

Primary Consumers

Producers

Proteins

Respiration

Secondary Consumers

Tertiary Consumers

Vitamins

_____

_____

_____

_____

Behaviors

Instinct	Reflex
Learned Behavior	Self-Preservation

_____

_____

_____

_____

Health

Acquired Immunity	Immunodeficiency
Age-related Diseases	Infection
Assimilation	Inflammation
Digestion	Life Cycle
Environmental Diseases	Medical Defenses
Hereditary Issues	Noninfectious Diseases
Immune System	Public Health
Immunization	Regulation

_____

_____

_____

_____

General Vocabulary

Adaptation	Energy
Creationist Theory	Interdependence
Darwinism	Natural Selection
Diversity	Theory of Evolution

_____

_____

_____

_____

What to Do

Now that you have a basic idea of some of the life science topics that may appear on the GED Science test. So let's go over the six steps you will use to find the best answer for each question.

Life Science Steps

Step 1: Read All the Information
Step 2: Identify the Question
Step 3: Underline Key Words and Phrases
Step 4: Determine Meanings
Step 5: Think About What You Already Know
Step 6: Select the Best Answer

Step 1: Read All the Information

The first step in correctly answering any test question is to carefully and completely read all of the information. This includes anything included in passages, graphs, tables, and captions, as well as the question and all of the answer choices.

Some people find it helpful to read the question before reading the passage. This alerts you to what information you will need to use to answer the question and gives you the chance to look for it as you read. If this strategy works well for you, great! The important thing is to make sure that you read all the information carefully, regardless of what you choose to read first.

Step 2: Identify the Question

Once you have read everything, the next step is to determine exactly what the question is asking. Try restating the question in your own words. This can be helpful in determining how well you understand what it is asking.

Step 3: Underline Key Words and Phrases

Now identify what facts and information will be needed to answer the question. Go back through the passage and graphics and underline or circle key words, pertinent facts, and other ideas that will help you select the correct answer. This draws your attention to the most important ideas and allows you to identify them quickly when it comes time to choose your answer.

Step 4: Determine Meanings

There may be times when a word in the passage is unfamiliar. Don't sweat it. Take a look at the surrounding information, which may offer a definition, explanation, or example that can help you determine the word's meaning. Such context clues can be great hints.

If you are still unsure of the meaning of the new word, try breaking it into parts, such as the root, prefix, and suffix. Do you know another word with a similar root? If so, this can be helpful in figuring out the meaning of the word in the passage.

Step 5: Think About What You Already Know

You have been learning science since kindergarten—or maybe even before. When you read information on the GED Science test, think about how it relates to what you already know. Combining the new information with your prior knowledge can help you fully understand the topic.

Step 6: Select the Best Answer

Before choosing the one best answer, reread the question, and carefully read every answer choice. Several of the choices may look good. The key is to select the single answer that gives the best and most complete response to the question.

Examples

Now, let's take a look at a few examples of life science questions.

For the school science fair, Liz wanted to determine the optimal amount of water for marigold plants. She planted the same number of marigold seeds in each of 30 pots. She divided the pots into three groups, with 10 in each group, and labeled the groups A, B, and C. She watered the plants in group A daily, group B twice a week, and group C once a week. The plants received an equal amount of water each time. She predicted that the plants watered daily would be the tallest at the end of one month. Which would NOT be necessary for the experiment to be valid?

1. using the same size pots
2. including a control group
3. planting all of the seeds in the same type of soil

4. having more than one pot in each of the groups

5. making sure the plants received an equal amount of sunlight

Here are our steps:

Step 1: Read All the Information

Step 2: Identify the Question

Which was not needed for the experiment?

Step 3: Underline Key Words and Phrases

In this question, it would be important to underline the word <u>NOT</u> in the question. Overlooking this word would completely change what is being asked.

Step 4: Determine Meanings

Suppose the word <u>optimal</u> is unfamiliar. What words have a similar root? <u>Optimistic</u> means "hopeful;" <u>optimum</u> means "best." Using these and considering what makes sense in the context of the sentence, we can figure out that optimal probably means "best" or "most favorable."

Step 5: Think About What You Already Know

What do you know about scientific inquiry? To test one variable, everything else must be the same, so answer choices 1, 3, and 5 are necessary. You also know that an adequate number of trials must be used, so answer choice 4 is also necessary.

Step 6: Select the Best Answer

Since three different watering schedules are being tested, a control group is not necessary. So answer choice 2 is correct.

Now it's your turn. The following question is based on the previously mentioned experiment. Use the information, as well as your own prior knowledge, to answer the question. We'll give you the steps you will need to practice the process.

The watering schedule Liz used in the experiment is the _____.

1. dependent variable

2. hypothesis

3. independent variable

4. result

5. trial

Step 1: Read All the Information

Step 2: Identify the Question

_____

_____

Step 3: Underline Key Words and Phrases

Step 4: Determine Meanings

_____

_____

Step 5: Think About What You Already Know

_____

_____

_____

_____

Step 6: Select the Best Answer

The correct answer is 3.

LIFE SCIENCE DRILLS

Fill in the blanks for question 1. For each of the subsequent questions, choose the best answer.

1. **What are the steps for answering geography questions?**
   Step 1: _____
   Step 2: _____
   Step 3: _____
   Step 4: _____
   Step 5: _____
   Step 6: _____

Use the following information to answer questions 2–4.

The CDC recommends that children in the United States receive certain vaccinations at given ages. Several of these vaccinations are repeated at specific intervals between birth and age six Many of the diseases for which children are routinely vaccinated today used to pose serious health concerns in the past; however, since vaccinations began, some of these diseases have declined by 100 percent. For example, in the years just prior to the introduction of the measles vaccine, more than 503,000 cases were reported annually. In 2007, there were only 43 cases of the disease. (See chart on following page.)

2. **According to the information given, which is a true statement?**
   A. Children receive the rotavirus vaccine one time between ages 2 months and 6 months.
   B. All children should receive the meningococcal vaccine between the ages of 2 and 6 years old.
   C. The vaccination for measles, mumps, and rubella is given three times before a child is six years old.
   D. The hepatitis B vaccine must be repeated at ages 6 months, 12 months, 15 months, and 18 months.
   E. Children are vaccinated against diphtheria, tetanus, and pertussis four times before their second birthday.

3. **A patient receives the same vaccination each winter. According to the chart, which disease is this vaccination preventing?**
   A. hepatitis A
   B. influenza
   C. pneumococcus
   D. rotavirus
   E. varicella

Recommended Immunization Schedule for Persons Aged 0 Through 6 Years—United States • 2011

For those who fall behind or start late, see the catch-up schedule

Vaccine ▼ / Age ▶	Birth	1 month	2 months	4 months	6 months	12 months	15 months	18 months	19–23 months	2–3 years	4–6 years
Hepatitis B[1]	HepB	HepB	HepB		HepB						
Rotavirus[2]			RV	RV	RV[2]						
Diphtheria, Tetanus, Pertussis[3]			DTaP	DTaP	DTaP	see footnote[3]	DTaP	DTaP			DTaP
Haemophilus influenzae type b[4]			Hib	Hib	Hib[4]	Hib	Hib				
Pneumococcal[5]			PCV	PCV	PCV	PCV	PCV			PPSV	
Inactivated Poliovirus[6]			IPV	IPV	IPV	IPV	IPV	IPV			IPV
Influenza[7]					Influenza (Yearly)						
Measles, Mumps, Rubella[8]						MMR	MMR		see footnote[8]		MMR
Varicella[9]						Varicella	Varicella		see footnote[9]		Varicella
Hepatitis A[10]						HepA (2 doses)				HepA Series	
Meningococcal[11]										MCV4	MCV4

Range of recommended ages for all children

Range of recommended ages for certain high-risk groups

4. Diphtheria, a disease caused by bacteria found in the mouth and throat, causes patients to suffer from a sore throat, as well as fever and chills. Untreated, it can lead to complications including heart failure and paralysis. It can be fatal in approximately 10 percent of those who contract the disease and used to be a major cause of death in children. As recently as the 1920s, about 15,000 people died from diphtheria each year. Which assumption can be made regarding this disease?

   A. More people die from diphtheria today than 100 years ago.
   B. The diphtheria vaccine has eliminated sore throats among young children.
   C. Diphtheria was the most serious health concern facing people in the 1920s.
   D. Widespread use of the diphtheria vaccine has significantly reduced its threat.
   E. The diphtheria vaccine is unnecessary since people no longer contract the disease.

5. Pertussis, also known as whooping cough, looks like the common cold; however, after a few weeks, it causes patients to suffer violent coughing spells and may lead to pneumonia, seizures, and brain infections. In some cases, it can be fatal. It is spread through the air from one person to the next but can be prevented through vaccination. Which type of disease is pertussis?

   A. age-related
   B. environmental
   C. hereditary
   D. infectious
   E. noninfectious

Use the information that follows to answer questions 6–7.

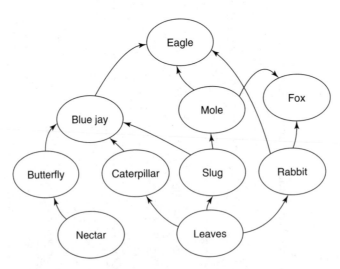

6. **What is the role of the mole in the food web shown?**
   A. producer
   B. decomposer

C. tertiary consumer
D. primary consumer
E. secondary consumer

7. **During which link in the food web is the most energy transferred?**
   A. caterpillar–blue jay
   B. nectar–butterfly
   C. rabbit–eagle
   D. mole–eagle
   E. rabbit–fox

8. **Behavior is the way in which organisms interact with other organisms and their environment. In both people and animals, behavior occurs in response to an external stimulus, an internal stimulus, or both. Some behaviors are innate, or built in. These innate behaviors include reflexes and instincts. Other behaviors are learned as a result of experiences.**

   Which is an example of a reflex?

   A. a person blinking when something is thrown toward them
   B. a baby crawling on the floor before it begins to walk
   C. a bird gathering material to build its nest
   D. a dog barking when it hears a doorbell
   E. a moth flying toward a bright light

9. **The anther and filament comprise which part of the flower?**

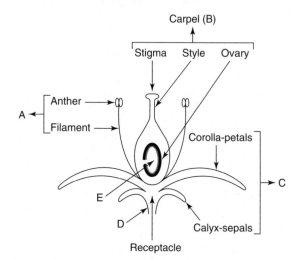

   A. ovule
   B. pedicel
   C. perianth
   D. pistil
   E. stamen

10. The brain controls nearly everything our bodies do, whether we are awake or asleep. There are five main parts of the brain. The cerebrum is the largest part and accounts for approximately 85 percent of the brain's weight. It is responsible for our thinking, short- and long-term memory, reasoning, and voluntary muscles. It is divided into two halves, with the right half controlling the left side of the body and the left half controlling the right side of the body.

The cerebellum is at the back of the brain and is located below the cerebrum. It is approximately one-eighth the size of the cerebrum. This part of the brain controls balance, movement, and coordination. Beneath the cerebrum and in front of the cerebellum is the brain stem, which connects the brain to the spinal cord. It is responsible for functions such as breathing; digestion; circulation; and involuntary muscle control, including the heart and stomach.

The pituitary gland is about the size of a pea and is responsible for releasing hormones into the body, which are responsible for many things, including growth and metabolism. The hypothalamus is the part of the brain that regulates the body's temperature. Reactions such as sweating and shivering are attempts to control temperature and help it to return to normal.

Which part of the brain would control the activities needed for riding a bicycle?

A. brain stem
B. cerebellum
C. cerebrum
D. hypothalamus
E. pituitary gland

Earth and Space Science

Does the phrase "My very excellent mother just served us nine pizzas" ring a bell? You may have learned this years ago as a mnemonic device for remembering the order of the planets. Each word in the phrase begins with the first letter of one of the planets, in order from the sun outward: Mercury, Venus, Earth, Mars, Jupiter, Saturn, Uranus, Neptune, Pluto. Well, now that Pluto's status as a planet has been questioned, the phrase should probably be "My very excellent mother just served us nachos." Regardless, the information you learned about our solar system will come in handy when answering earth and space science questions on the GED Science test.

Questions related to this area of science will account for 20 percent of the test. You may find information connected to geology, meteorology, oceanography, paleontology, geochemistry, ecology, and environmental science. That is a lot of *-ologies* to remember, but don't worry. By combining your own prior knowledge with the ideas presented in the passages and visual aids on the test, you will be ready to demonstrate your ability to comprehend, analyze, summarize, and apply earth and space science concepts.

What's Being Tested?

As we mentioned, earth and space science questions can cover a wide range of material. The following lists include suggested topics to study. Keep in mind that these lists are not all-inclusive; any ideas related to our planet and space may appear on the test. That's literally a whole world of possible topics. To prepare for the test, familiarize yourself with the ideas given here. As you watch science- and health-related TV shows, read newspaper and magazine articles, and look through science textbooks, add any other important or interesting ideas to the lists.

Earth

Atmosphere	Mesosphere
Axis	Metamorphic Rocks
Continental Drift	Minerals
Core	Ozone
Crust	Pangaea
Exosphere	Plate Tectonics
Fault Lines	Revolution
Geologic Time	Rotation
Glaciers	Sedimentary Rocks
Global Warming	Stratosphere
Greenhouse Effect	Subduction
Hydrosphere	Thermosphere
Igneous Rocks	Trench
Ionosphere	Troposphere
Magma	Volcanoes
Mantle	Water Cycle

Weather and Natural Disasters

Air Pressure	Landslides
Barometric Pressure	Precipitation
Cirrus Clouds	Relative Humidity
Cold Front	Richter Scale
Condensation	Runoff
Coriolis Effect	Seasons
Cumulonimbus Clouds	Seismic Waves
Cumulus Clouds	Stationary Front
Earthquake	Stratus Clouds
Evaporation	Temperature
Flooding	Tsunami
Front	Warm Front
Gulf Stream	Weather
Humidity	Wind
Hurricane	

_____

_____

_____

_____

The Environment

Air Pollution	Recycling
Conservation	Renewable Natural Resources
Hazardous Waste	Soil Pollution
Nonrenewable Natural Resources	Solid Waste Disposal
Prevention of Extinction	Water Pollution
Protection of Biodiversity	

_____

_____

_____

_____

Changes in the Earth

Abrasion	Gravity Erosion
Chemical Weathering	Leaching
Creep	Physical Weathering
Deposition	Water Erosion
Erosion	Weathering
Exfoliation	Wind Erosion
Fossils	

_____

_____

_____

_____

Space

Asteroids	Nebulae
Astronomy	Neutron Star
Black Dwarf Star	Nova
Black Hole	Open Clusters
Blue Star	Orbiters
Comets	Outer Planets
Copernican Theory	Planets
Elliptical Galaxy	Pulsar
Galaxies	Quasars
Gas Clouds	Red Giant Star
Giant Star	Satellite
Globular Clusters	Solar Nebula
Gravity	Solar System
Inner Planets	Spiral Galaxy
Irregular Galaxy	Star
Meteor	Sun
Milky Way Galaxy	Supernova
Light-years	White Dwarf Star
NASA	

_____

_____

_____

_____

The Moon

Lunar Eclipse   Solar Eclipse

Neap Tides   Spring Tides

Orbit   Tides

Phases

_____

_____

_____

_____

Theories

Big Bang Theory   Flat Universe Theory

Closed Universe Theory   Open Universe Theory

_____

_____

_____

_____

What to Do

Now that you have an idea of what types of earth and space science information to expect on the GED Science test, let's review the six steps you will use to select the best answer for each question.

> ### Earth and Space Science Steps
> **Step 1:** Read All the Information
> **Step 2:** Identify the Question
> **Step 3:** Underline Key Words and Phrases
> **Step 4:** Determine Meanings
> **Step 5:** Think About What You Already Know
> **Step 6:** Select the Best Answer

Step 1: Read All the Information

The first step in answering any type of question is to read all of the available information. This information may be found in a passage or statement, or it may be found in a graphic, such as an illustration, a table, a graph, or a diagram. It may be tempting to skip over some of the information to save time, but doing this could cause you to miss out on key facts. Take the time to read everything, including titles, captions, and labels. Reading all of the material will help you completely understand the concepts and select the best answer.

Step 2: Identify the Question

After you have read all of the information given, figure out exactly what the question is asking. For example, does it want to know which of the planets is closest to the sun or which of the *outer* planets is closest to the sun? Make sure you know what is being asked. Try restating the question in your own words as a way to monitor your understanding.

Step 3: Underline Key Words and Phrases

After identifying the question, you will probably recognize which facts or information will be pertinent to selecting the correct answer. Go back through the passage and underline the concepts you will use. If data in a graph or table will be important, underline or circle the information in the graphic as well.

Step 4: Determine Meanings

Sometimes an unfamiliar word will appear in the text. Even great readers face this situation. Look for contextual clues that offer hints about the meaning of the word. These clues could be examples, explanations, definitions, or synonyms. Check the sentence that contains the unfamiliar word first; then look at the surrounding sentences. Think about what meaning would make sense in the context of the passage.

Another strategy for determining meaning is to break the word apart into a root, prefix, and suffix. Sometimes finding a word with a similar root is helpful in determining meaning. Don't forget that prefixes and suffixes have meanings too.

Step 5: Think About What You Already Know

There's a good chance that you already know quite a bit about the world we live in. This could come in handy when answering earth and space science questions. Think about what you have read or learned about the topic at hand. Use your own prior knowledge, as well as any information given on the test, to form a complete understanding of the material.

Step 6: Select the Best Answer

Reread the question; then read every single answer choice. Determine which of the choices most completely answers the question. Remember, several answers may be tempting, but only one can be the *best* choice.

Examples

Now, let's take a look at a couple of sample earth and space science questions.

The physical structure of the Earth includes three basic layers. At the center of the planet is a solid, very dense inner core surrounded by a liquid outer core. The outer core, which contains iron, spins as the planet rotates, generating a magnetic field as it flows. Together, the inner and outer cores are approximately 2,200 miles thick and make up about one-third of the Earth's mass.

The core is covered by a layer called the mantle. It is semisolid, and although it is not the hottest layer of the planet, it is still so hot that some of the rock in this layer is molten. This rock flows slowly, similar to hot asphalt.

The mantle is covered by a rigid outside layer, or crust. This layer is about 25 miles thick beneath the continents and four miles thick beneath the oceans, which is relatively thin compared to the other two layers. The uppermost part of the mantle is cooler than the deeper parts and combines with the planet's thin crust to form the lithosphere. This layer has broken into pieces known as tectonic plates, which are constantly moving as they float on a layer of melted rock.

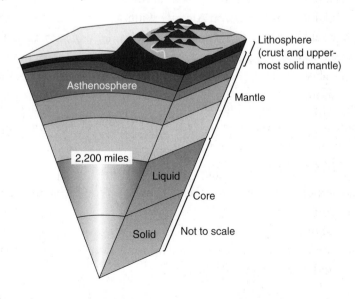

Which layer of the Earth is responsible for a compass pointing toward north?

1. crust
2. inner core
3. lithosphere
4. mantle
5. outer core

Here are our steps:

Step 1: Read All the Information

Step 2: Identify the Question

Which layer affects a compass?

Step 3: Underline Key Words and Phrases

To answer the question, it is important to understand each of the layers, so underlining these would be helpful. Since a compass points toward magnetic north, underlining any information about magnetism is also beneficial.

Step 4: Determine Meanings

The word lithosphere *may be unfamiliar. Clues in the sentence, as well as the following sentence, provide a definition of the word. Take another look:*

The <u>uppermost part of the mantle</u> is cooler than the deeper parts and <u>combines with the planet's thin crust to form the lithosphere</u>. <u>This layer has broken into pieces</u> known as tectonic plates, <u>which are constantly moving</u> as they float on a layer of melted rock.

Step 5: Think About What You Already Know

What do you already know about how a compass works? Most likely, you recognize the fact that a compass relies on magnetism to indicate direction.

Step 6: Select the Best Answer

Since you know that a compass relies on the Earth's magnetic field, and the passage states that the outer core generates a magnetic field, you can conclude that answer choice 5 is correct.

Now it's your turn. Select the best answer to following question, using the information about the layers of the Earth. We'll give you the steps you will need to practice the process.

Beneath which location is the Earth's crust the thickest?

1. Adriatic Sea
2. Atlantic Ocean
3. Grand Canyon
4. Mount Everest
5. Mojave Desert

Step 1: Read All the Information

Step 2: Identify the Question

_____

_____

Step 3: Underline Key Words and Phrases

Step 4: Determine Meanings

_____

_____

Step 5: Think About What You Already Know

_____

_____

_____

_____

Step 6: Select the Best Answer

The correct answer is 4.

EARTH AND SPACE SCIENCE DRILLS

Fill in the blanks for question 1. For each of the subsequent questions, choose the best answer.

1. **What are the steps for answering geography questions?**

   Step 1: _____

   Step 2: _____

   Step 3: _____

   Step 4: _____

   Step 5: _____

   Step 6: _____

Use the following information to answer questions 2 and 3.

Between the years of 1980 and 2010, the United States experienced 99 weather-related disasters with damages in excess of $1 billion each. The total cost for these events was more than $725 billion.

   In March 2010, flooding occurred in several states in the Northeast. Over the following two months, several states in the Mid-South faced severe weather, tornadoes, and flooding. That fall, Arizona dealt with unusually severe weather. In 2005, Hurricanes Dennis, Katrina, Rita, and Wilma pounded several states, while the Midwest faced a spring and summer drought. The year 2004 also brought a number of hurricanes, including Charley, Frances, Ivan, and Jeanne. Prior to this, only one $1 billion hurricane hit our country in 2003, one in 2001, and one in 1999.

   Northwestern Texas experienced severe weather disasters during six of the years between 1999 and 2010; however, it did not report any between the years 1980 and 1999. Likewise, Illinois reported eight flooding disasters between 1999 and 2009 and none during the nearly 20 years prior to this period.

2. **Which generalization can be made based on these data?**
   A. Flooding usually occurs in coastal regions.
   B. Damage from blizzards is most severe in northern states.
   C. Northern states are most likely to suffer high-cost damage from a freeze.
   D. Severe hurricanes are most likely along the Gulf and Atlantic coastlines.
   E. Areas with severe drought damage also suffer the most damage from fires.

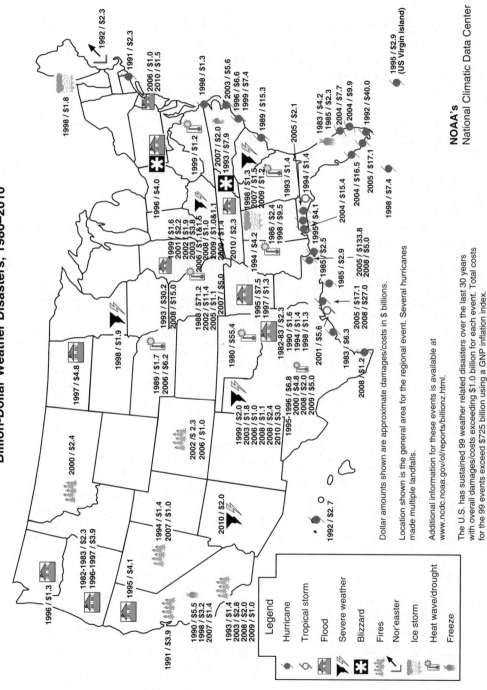

Billion-Dollar Weather Disasters, 1980–2010

1992 / $2.3

1991 / $2.3

1998 / $1.8

2006 / $1.0
2010 / $1.5

1998 / $1.3

2003 / $5.6
1996 / $6.6
1999 / $7.4

1995 / $2.9
(US Virgin Island)

1989 / $15.3

2005 / $2.1

1983 / $4.2
1985 / $2.3

2004 / $7.7
2004 / $9.9
1992 / $40.0

1999 / $1.2

2007 / $2.0
1993 / $7.9

1998 / $1.3
2007 / $1.5
2009 / $2.0

1993 / $1.4

1994 / $1.4

2004 / $15.4

1996 / $4.0

1999 / $1.6
2001 / $2.2
2002 / $1.9
2003 / $3.8
2006 / $1.1&1.5
2008 / $1.0
2009 / $1.0&1.1
2007 / $1.4
2010 / $2.3

1986 / $2.4
1998 / $9.5

2004 / $16.5
2005 / $17.1

1998 / $7.4

1994 / $4.2

1995 / $4.1

1985 / $2.5

2005 / $133.8
2008 / $5.0

1997 / $4.8

1998 / $1.9

1989 / $1.7
2006 / $6.2

1993 / $30.2
2008 / $15.0

1988 / $71.2
2002 / $11.4
2005 / $1.1

2007 / $5.0

1995 / $7.5
1997 / $1.3

1980 / $55.4

1985 / $2.9

1985 / $5.6

2005 / $17.1
2008 / $27.0

2000 / $2.4

2002 / $5 2.3
2006 / $1.0

1982-1983 / $2.3
1996-1997 / $3.9

1994 / $1.4
2007 / $1.0

2010 / $2.0

1999 / $2.0
2003 / $1.8
2006 / $1.0
2008 / $1.1
2008 / $2.4
2010 / $3.0

1982-83 / $2.3
1990 / $1.6
1994 / $1.4
1998 / $1.3

2001 / $5.6

1983 / $6.3

2008 / $1.2

1995-1996 / $6.8
2000 / $4.8
2008 / $2.0
2009 / $5.0

1996 / $1.3

1990 / $5.5
1998 / $3.2
2007 / $1.4

1993 / $1.4
2003 / $2.8
2008 / $2.0
2009 / $1.0

1991 / $3.9

1992 / $2.7

Legend

Hurricane	
Tropical storm	
Flood	
Severe weather	
Blizzard	
Fires	
Nor'easter	
Ice storm	
Heat wave/drought	
Freeze	

Dollar amounts shown are approximate damages/costs in $ billions.

Location shown is the general area for the regional event. Several hurricanes made multiple landfalls.

Additional information for these events is available at www.ncdc.noaa.gov/ol/reports/billionz.html.

The U.S. has sustained 99 weather related disasters over the last 30 years with overall damages/costs exceeding $1.0 billion for each event. Total costs for the 99 events exceed $725 billion using a GNP inflation index.

NOAA's
National Climatic Data Center

3. **Which statement can NOT be supported by the information?**
   A. Patterns of severe weather are consistent from one year to the next in any given region.
   B. Blizzards and snowstorms are less likely to cause high-cost damage than most other weather disasters.
   C. Tropical storms, while not as severe as hurricanes, have the potential to generate higher costs in damages.
   D. Most regions of the United States were affected by at least one major weather disaster during the reported period.
   E. Some areas of the country experience a range of severe weather, while other areas experience only specific types of weather events.

Use the following information to answer questions 4–6.

For centuries, people have been fascinated by our moon. The moon, Earth's only natural satellite, orbits our planet one time every 29½ days. It does not have any light of its own but rather reflects the light of the sun from its surface. As it circles around the Earth, the moon changes position with respect to the sun, causing it to go through a series of phases during which different amounts of the satellite are visible from Earth. A new moon cannot be seen from Earth, since the lighted side is pointed away from our planet. We can, however, view the other phases: new crescent, first quarter, waxing gibbous, full moon, waning gibbous, last quarter, and old crescent. Following the new moon, each phase allows a larger portion of the moon to be visible until reaching the full moon phase, during which the entire moon is visible during the entire night. From that point, each phase shows a decreasing amount of the moon until it reaches the new moon phase again.

Occasionally, the moon enters the shadow of our planet and is dimmed almost completely. Such a lunar eclipse can be partial or total and can last from less than half an hour to as long as several hours. An eclipse can occur only during the full moon phase and only if the moon passes through at least part of the shadow of the Earth. When the moon passes between the sun and our planet, this causes a different type of eclipse, known as a solar eclipse. Unlike a lunar eclipse, this is only possible during the new moon phase. When this takes place, the shadow of the moon is cast on the Earth, and we are unable to see a portion of the sun.

The gravitational interaction between the moon and the Earth is responsible for the tides in large bodies of water on our planet. The gravitational pull of the moon is stronger on the side of the Earth that is nearest to the moon. This causes the water in our oceans to bulge out toward the moon. The Earth, itself being pulled toward the moon, also causes a bulge on the opposite side of the planet.

Different circumstances cause different types of tides. Spring tides occur when the Earth, sun, and moon are in line. These are especially strong since the moon and the sun both have gravitational forces that act upon the tide. These occur during full moon and new moon phases. Proxigean spring tides are unusually high and occur when the moon is especially close to our planet during the new moon phase. This rare occurrence takes place only about every year and a half. Neap tides are the weakest type and take place when the moon, sun, and Earth form a right angle, with the Earth at the vertex. These take place during the quarter moon phase.

4. **Look at the following diagram. Which does the diagram show?**

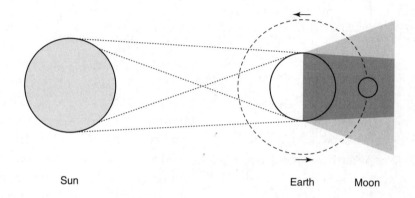

Sun   Earth   Moon

   A. first quarter
   B. lunar eclipse
   C. new moon
   D. solar eclipse
   E. waning gibbous

5. **Which conclusion can be drawn?**
   A. Tides occur at the same time each day.
   B. Spring tides only take place during the spring season.
   C. The moon's gravitational force only impacts water in the ocean.
   D. Differences occur in the extent of the tides experienced in different locations.
   E. The position of the sun has a greater impact on tides than the position of the moon.

6. **Which represents an opinion rather than a fact?**
   A. The length of time an eclipse is visible can vary.
   B. The phases of the moon occur in a repeated cycle.
   C. Certain types of tides are associated with the moon's phases.
   D. A lunar eclipse is more interesting to view than a solar eclipse.
   E. Gravity can have an impact on objects that are a great distance away.

7. Which best summarizes the information in the diagram?

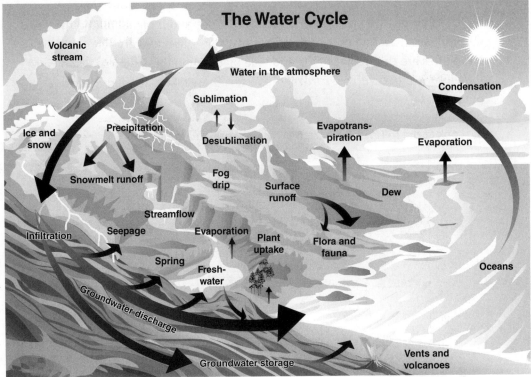

The Water Cycle

A. The sun heats water on Earth, causing some of it to turn to vapor in the air. Rising air currents carry the vapor into the atmosphere, where cooler temperatures cause the vapor to condense and form clouds. Air currents carry the clouds, which return the water to Earth as rain, ice, or snow.

B. Water in the Earth's oceans and streams is heated by the sun. The warm water then evaporates, becoming water vapor in the air. As the water meets the warmer temperatures in the atmosphere, the vapor forms clouds. The clouds then precipitate and return the water to the Earth as condensation.

C. The sun's energy causes the water to condense. It then evaporates and forms water vapor in the atmosphere. Cooler temperatures cause the vapor to become condensation, which then collects as clouds. The clouds are carried around the Earth, and they return the water to Earth as precipitation.

D. Energy from the sun warms water on the surface of the oceans. This causes some of the water to become vapor, which is carried into the atmosphere by rising air currents. The vapor meets cooler air in the atmosphere and precipitates to form clouds and fog. Wind carries the clouds. As the precipitation warms, it forms condensation.

E. Water in the ground, oceans, and springs is heated by the sun. The warm water evaporates and rises into the air as vapor. Once it rises, the warm water meets warm temperatures, causing the vapor to form condensation. The condensation becomes clouds and fog. As the condensation cools, it turns to precipitation and returns to Earth.

Use the following information to answer questions 8–10.

Relative humidity indicates how much moisture is in the air compared to how much moisture the air can hold at that temperature. Generally, the amount of moisture in the air is less than the amount needed to saturate the air. When the air is saturated, the relative humidity will be near 100 percent.

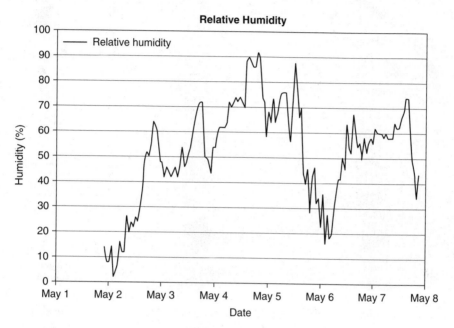

8. **On which day is precipitation most likely to occur?**
   A. May 2
   B. May 3
   C. May 4
   D. May 5
   E. May 6

9. **Suppose the temperature was 15 degrees higher on May 8 than originally reported. Which would occur?**
   A. The relative humidity would decrease.
   B. The relative humidity would increase.
   C. The relative humidity would not change.
   D. The relative humidity would be 100 percent.
   E. The relative humidity would be 0 percent.

10. **Which statement is true?**

   A. Snow is indicated by 100 percent relative humidity.
   B. A dry climate generally has 100 percent relative humidity.
   C. Fog and rain are indicated by 100 percent relative humidity.
   D. Relative humidity is generally highest in the afternoon.
   E. Relative humidity remains constant throughout the day.

chapter **15**

Physical Science: Chemistry

As you know, there are a total of 50 questions on the GED Science test. Thirty-five percent of the questions will be related to physical science. Of that 35 percent, some of the physical science questions will focus on chemistry, and some will focus on physics. In this chapter, we will review the types of information you should know to answer questions dealing with chemistry.

To answer the chemistry questions on the GED Science test, you will need to rely on your knowledge of atoms, the structure and properties of matter, and chemical reactions. So grab your lab coat, put on your safety goggles, and let's get started!

What's Being Tested?

As already mentioned, questions related to chemistry will focus on atoms, matter, and chemical reactions. Quite a few concepts fall under these topics. The following lists suggest some ideas for you to brush up on before the test. Being able to combine your own knowledge of the subject matter with the information given on the test will help you fully comprehend the material and select the best answer to each question.

Does this mean you need to memorize the periodic table of elements? No. But you should familiarize yourself with it well enough to know how to use it. The same holds true for other information related to chemistry. You will not be asked to recall facts, but you will need to be able to apply the concepts in order to analyze information, solve problems, and make judgments.

As you study your textbooks, science-related periodicals, and the Internet, add any other information that sounds interesting or important to the lists.

The Structure of Atoms

Allotrope	Isotope
Atom	Metalloids
Atomic Mass	Metals
Atomic Number	Nonmetals
Atomic Theory	Molecule
Chemical Bonding	Nuclear Fission
Chemical Formula	Nuclear Force
Compound	Nucleus
Covalent Bond	Neutron
Electric Force	Periodic Law
Electron	Periodic Table of Elements
Element	Proton
Ion	Radioactive
Ionic Bond	Symbol
Isobar	

_____

_____

_____

_____

Chemistry and Living Things

Carbon	Organic Chemistry
Hydrocarbons	Polymer
Organic	

_____

_____

_____

_____

Matter

Acids	Freeze
Aerate	Gas
Alkaline	Liquid
Alloy	Matter
Amalgam	Melt
Bases	Mixture
Boil	Oxidize
Chemical Change	Physical Change
Chlorinate	Plasma
Compounds	Solid
Condense	Solute
Distilled	Solution
Filtered	Sublimation

_____

_____

_____

_____

Changes

Activation Energy	Covalent Bond
Bond	Decomposition Reaction
Carnot Process	Law of Conservation of Matter
Catalyst	Nuclear Change
Chemical Change	Physical Change
Chemical Equation	Plastics
Chemical Reaction	Polymers
Chemical Reaction Rate	Products
Combination Reaction	Reactants
Combustion	

_____

_____

_____

_____

Keep in Mind

Keep in mind that questions relating to scientific inquiry can pop up in reference to any science topic. Make sure you are comfortable with this process.

What to Do

Now that you have an idea of the types of chemistry topics that may be covered on the GED Science test, let's go over the six steps you will use to find the best answer for each question.

Chemistry Steps

Step 1: Read All the Information
Step 2: Identify the Question
Step 3: Underline Key Words and Phrases
Step 4: Determine Meanings
Step 5: Think About What You Already Know
Step 6: Select the Best Answer

Step 1: Read All the Information

The best way to ensure that you have as much information as possible is to read everything you can find that is associated with each question. This includes not only the passage but also graphs, tables, and diagrams. Be sure you read the titles and labels on the graphic displays as well.

Step 2: Identify the Question

After reading all of the information, the next step is to figure out exactly what the question is asking. Read it carefully, paying close attention to words such as *not* or *except*. One little word can make a big difference. For example, "Which of the following is an element?" and "Which of the following is not an element?" are two very different questions. Likewise, "What is the atomic number of plu-tonium?" and "What is the atomic weight of plutonium?" may appear similar but are also very different. Make sure you read every word of the question closely and figure out what is being asked. Restating the question in your own words can be helpful in this effort.

Step 3: Underline Key Words and Phrases

Next, figure out which words, numbers, phrases, or facts will be most important in answering the question. Underlining these bits of information will help you to focus your attention and review key ideas, as well as allow you to locate the facts quickly when selecting the best answer to the question.

Step 4: Determine Meanings

Sometimes a passage may contain an unfamiliar word. No big deal. Use what you know about contextual clues and word parts to help you determine the meaning. Remember, passages often include hints, such as definitions, synonyms, or examples, that you can use to infer meaning.

Step 5: Think About What You Already Know

Next, take a few seconds to think about the topic. What have you read, heard, or learned that is related to the information given on the test? Adding your existing knowledge to what you have just read can help you gain a more complete understanding of the information.

Step 6: Select the Best Answer

Finally, reread the question, reread every answer choice, and then determine which option best answers the question. Remember, two or more choices may be at least partially correct. Make sure you find the one that answers the question most completely.

Examples

Now let's check out a few chemistry questions.

Both sucrose, or sugar, and salt will dissolve in water. The temperature of the water determines the amount of each solute that can be dissolved. Once a certain amount of the solute is dissolved in the water, the water becomes saturated, meaning no more of the salt or sugar will dissolve in the solution. Approximately how many grams of sugar will saturate 100 mL of water at 40°C?

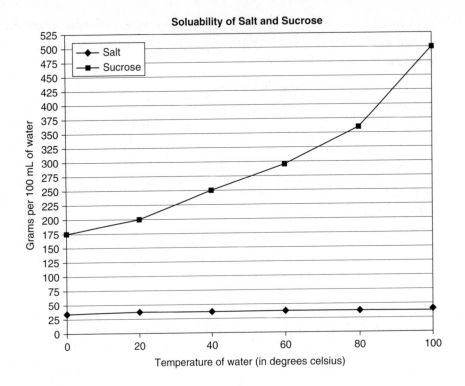

1. 45 g

2. 100 g

3. 175 g

4. 250 g

5. 500 g

Here are our steps:

Step 1: Read All the Information

Step 2: Identify the Question

How many grams of sucrose will dissolve in the water at 40°C?

Step 3: Underline Key Words and Phrases

The information you need to answer this question is in the graph. Identify the line that represents sucrose, and underline the value that corresponds to 40°C.

Step 4: Determine Meanings

Suppose the word <u>solute</u> is unfamiliar. The sentence that introduces this word explains that the solute can be dissolved. The previous sentence says *that sucrose and salt will dissolve in water. These are examples of solutes. Using these hints, you can determine that a solute is something that is being dissolved.*

Step 5: Think About What You Already Know

What do you know about dissolving sugar in water? What do you already know about reading a line graph? Use this information to help you determine the best answer to the question.

Step 6: Select the Best Answer

Since 250 g is marked directly above 40°C on the horizontal axis, answer choice 4 is correct.

Now it's your turn. The following question is based on the same information and graph. Use them, as well as your prior knowledge, to answer the question. We'll give you the steps you will need to practice the process.

Which conclusion can be drawn regarding the data?

1. When the temperature of the water increases, the amount of sucrose that can be dissolved decreases.

2. Increasing the temperature of the water significantly increases the amount of salt that can be dissolved.

3. When the temperature of the water increases, the amount of sucrose that can be dissolved increases as well.

4. Increasing the temperature of the water has no effect on the amount of sucrose or salt that can be dissolved.

5. Increasing the temperature of the water by 100 percent also increases the amount of salt that can be dissolved by 100 percent.

Step 1: Read All the Information

Step 2: Identify the Question

_____

_____

Step 3: Underline Key Words and Phrases

Step 4: Determine Meanings

_____

_____

Step 5: Think About What You Already Know

_____

_____

_____

_____

Step 6: Select the Best Answer

The correct answer is 3.

CHEMISTRY DRILLS

Fill in the blanks for question 1. For each of the subsequent questions, choose the best answer.

1. **What are the steps for answering geography questions?**

   Step 1: _____

   Step 2: _____

   Step 3: _____

   Step 4: _____

   Step 5: _____

   Step 6: _____

Use the following information to answer question 2.

Both sucrose, or sugar, and salt will dissolve in water. The temperature of the water determines the amount of each solute that can be dissolved. Once a certain amount of the solute is dissolved in the water, the water becomes saturated, meaning no more of the salt or sugar will dissolve in the solution.

2. **Based on the data, which statement is true?**
   A. All solutes are equally affected by changes in water temperature.
   B. All solutes have an equal saturation rate when the temperature of the water reaches a certain point.
   C. The amount of sucrose that will dissolve in boiling water is approximately 10 times greater than the amount of salt that will dissolve.
   D. The amount of sucrose that will dissolve in cold water is approximately the same as the amount of salt that will dissolve in the same water.
   E. At any temperature, the amount of sucrose that will dissolve in 100 mL of water is nearly 10 times greater than the amount of salt that will dissolve.

Use the following diagram to answer questions 3–4.

Sugar (Sucrose) Molecule

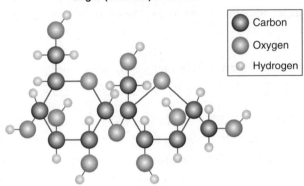

3. The diagram shows one molecule of sucrose, or sugar. Which shows the chemical formula of the molecule?

   A. $C_6H_{11}O_5$
   B. $C_{12}H_{22}O_{11}$
   C. $C_{22}H_{12}O_{11}$
   D. $Ca_6H_{11}O_5$
   E. $Ca_{12}H_{22}O_{11}$

4. Which best describes sucrose?

   A. atom
   B. compound
   C. element
   D. ion
   E. mixture

5. The smallest unit of magnesium that maintains all of its properties is a(n)

   A. atom
   B. electron
   C. ion
   D. molecule
   E. proton

6. Lester uses an axe to split an oak log. Which type of change occurs?

   A. atomic
   B. chemical
   C. electrical
   D. nuclear
   E. physical

7. Lester then burns the split oak log to start a campfire. Which type of change occurs?
    A. atomic
    B. chemical
    C. electrical
    D. nuclear
    E. physical

Use the following information to answer questions 8–10.

The periodic table of the elements arranges the elements in order of their atomic number, which generally also arranges them by their atomic mass. The rows of elements displayed in the table are known as *periods*. The number of electrons in each period increases as we move down the table. The columns of the table are known as *groups*.

   Each element is defined by the number of protons in the atom. This is known as the *atomic number*. Hydrogen (H) has an atomic number of 1, indicating that a single atom of this element contains one proton. The standard *atomic weight* for each element is the average mass of the element. The atomic number and the atomic weight appear in the table along with the element's symbol. As the table shows, the atomic weight of hydrogen is 1.008. The average number of neutrons can be determined by calculating the difference between the atomic number and the atomic weight.

8. Which element has an atomic weight of approximately 7?
    A. beryllium
    B. boron
    C. fluorine
    D. lithium
    E. nitrogen

9. Approximately how many neutrons does the average atom of iron contain?
    A. 26
    B. 29.85
    C. 55.85
    D. 77
    E. 115.2

10. The chemical formula for table salt is NaCl. Which elements does table salt contain?
    A. sodium and carbon
    B. sodium and chlorine
    C. nitrogen and chloride
    D. nitrogen, actinium, and lithium
    E. nitrogen, carbon, and aluminum

Periodic Table of the Elements

1A																	8A
1 hydrogen **H** 1.008	2A											3A	4A	5A	6A	7A	2 helium **He** 4.003
3 lithium **Li** 6.941	4 beryllium **Be** 9.012											5 boron **B** 10.81	6 carbon **C** 12.01	7 nitrogen **N** 14.01	8 oxygen **O** 16.00	9 fluorine **F** 19.00	10 neon **Ne** 20.18
11 sodium **Na** 22.99	12 magnesium **Mg** 24.31	3B	4B	5B	6B	7B	8B			11B	12B	13 aluminum **Al** 26.98	14 silicon **Si** 28.09	15 phosphorus **P** 30.97	16 sulfur **S** 32.07	17 chlorine **Cl** 35.45	18 argon **Ar** 39.95
19 potassium **K** 39.10	20 calcium **Ca** 40.08	21 scandium **Sc** 44.96	22 titanium **Ti** 47.88	23 vanadium **V** 50.94	24 chromium **Cr** 52.00	25 manganese **Mn** 54.94	26 iron **Fe** 55.85	27 cobalt **Co** 58.93	28 nickel **Ni** 58.69	29 copper **Cu** 63.55	30 zinc **Zn** 65.39	31 gallium **Ga** 69.72	32 germanium **Ge** 72.64	33 arsenic **As** 74.92	34 selenium **Se** 78.96	35 bromine **Br** 79.90	36 krypton **Kr** 83.79
37 rubidium **Rb** 85.47	38 strontium **Sr** 87.62	39 yttrium **Y** 88.91	40 zirconium **Zr** 91.22	41 niobium **Nb** 92.91	42 molybdenum **Mo** 95.94	43 technetium **Tc** 98	44 ruthenium **Ru** 101.1	45 rhodium **Rh** 102.9	46 palladium **Pd** 106.4	47 silver **Ag** 107.9	48 cadmium **Cd** 112.4	49 indium **In** 114.8	50 tin **Sn** 118.7	51 antimony **Sb** 121.8	52 tellurium **Te** 127.6	53 iodine **I** 126.9	54 xenon **Xe** 131.3
55 cesium **Cs** 132.9	56 barium **Ba** 137.3	*	72 hafnium **Hf** 178.5	73 tantalum **Ta** 180.9	74 tungsten **W** 183.9	75 rhenium **Re** 186.2	76 osmium **Os** 190.2	77 iridium **Ir** 192.2	78 platinum **Pt** 195.1	79 gold **Au** 197.0	80 mercury **Hg** 200.5	81 thallium **Tl** 204.4	82 lead **Pb** 207.2	83 bismuth **Bi** 209.0	84 polonium **Po** 209	85 astatine **At** 210	86 radon **Rn** 222
87 francium **Fr** 223	88 radium **Ra** 226	**	104 rutherfordium **Rf** 261	105 dubnium **Db** 262	106 seaborgium **Sg** 266	107 bohrium **Bh** 264	108 hassium **Hs** 277	109 meitnerium **Mt** 268	110 darmstadtium **Ds** 271	111 roentgenium **Rg** 272	112 copernicium **Cn** 285	113 **Uut** 286	114 **Uuq** 289	115 **Uup** 289	116 **Uuh** 291	117 **Uus** 294	118 **Uuo** 294

Lanthanide series*

57 lanthanum **La** 138.9	58 cerium **Ce** 140.1	59 praseodymium **Pr** 140.9	60 neodymium **Nd** 144.2	61 promethium **Pm** 145	62 samarium **Sm** 150.4	63 europium **Eu** 152.0	64 gadolinium **Gd** 157.25	65 terbium **Tb** 158.9	66 dysprosium **Dy** 162.5	67 holmium **Ho** 164.93	68 erbium **Er** 167.3	69 thulium **Tm** 168.9	70 ytterbium **Yb** 173.0	71 lutetium **Lu** 175.0

Actinide series**

89 actinium **Ac** 227	90 thorium **Th** 232.0	91 protactinium **Pa** 231	92 uranium **U** 238	93 neptunium **Np** 237	94 plutonium **Pu** 244	95 americium **Am** 243	96 curium **Cm** 247	97 berkelium **Bk** 247	98 californium **Cf** 251	99 einsteinium **Es** 252	100 fermium **Fm** 257	101 mendelevium **Md** 258	102 nobelium **No** 259	103 lawrencium **Lr** 262

11. **Cinnamon and sugar are combined for a recipe. What is produced by combining these ingredients?**

    A. atom
    B. compound
    C. chemical
    D. element
    E. mixture

12. **The law of conservation of matter explains that during an ordinary chemical change, the quantity of matter does not increase or decrease. Which best explains this law?**

    A. Different atoms combine to create new molecules.
    B. A portion of matter is destroyed when it changes form.
    C. Atoms are not created or destroyed in a chemical reaction.
    D. The atomic mass is greater in atoms with greater atomic numbers.
    E. Some types of changes do not alter the chemical makeup of the molecules.

16

Physical Science: Physics

As we mentioned in the previous chapter, 35 percent of the GED Science questions will relate to physical science. Some of them will address chemistry, and the rest will deal with physics. In this chapter, we will review the types of physics information you should know in order to do well on the test.

Physics is the study of matter, energy, force, and motion. On the GED Science test, you can expect to find questions about the different forms of energy, motion and forces, the conservation of energy, and how energy and matter interact with one another. Remember, you will need to add your own knowledge of physics to the information given on the test to best answer the questions.

What's Being Tested?

A number of concepts relate to matter, energy, force, and motion. The following lists suggest some ideas with which to familiarize yourself before the test. The good news is that you will probably recognize many of these ideas, regardless of whether or not you've ever found yourself sitting in an actual physics class. For example, the name Sir Isaac Newton is likely to ring a bell for you, even if physics isn't your forte. And do you remember learning about solids, liquids, and gasses back in about the first grade? Super! That's another physics-related concept that you already know.

To refresh your memory on some of the other information in the lists, flip through some of your science textbooks, read about these ideas in the newspaper and good-quality news magazines, look up related articles online, and keep your ears open for physics-related information on TV. As you review, add any other pertinent ideas or information you come across to the list.

Energy

Alternating Current	Magnetic Energy
British Thermal Unit	Magnetic Fields
Calorie	Magnetism
Celsius (Centigrade) Scale	Mechanical Energy
Conservation of Energy	Nuclear Energy
Convection	Nuclear Power
Diffraction	Polarization
Direct Current	Poles
Doppler Effect	Potential Energy
Electricity	Radiation
Electromagnetic Energy	Radio Waves
Energy	Reflection
Entropy	Refraction
Fahrenheit Scale	Rotational Energy
Frequency	Solar Energy
Gamma Rays	Sound
Geothermal Energy	Static Electricity
Heat Energy	Steam Energy
Hydroelectric Power	Transfer of Energy
Infrared Rays	Trough
Interaction of Energy and Matter	Transverse Wave
Interference	Ultrasonic Wave
Kinetic Energy	Ultraviolet Rays
Light Energy	Wave
Longitudinal Wave	Wavelength
Magnetic Domains	Wind Energy

_____

_____

_____

_____

Matter

Conductor	Liquid
Ductility	Luster
Electrical Conductivity	Malleability
Electric Current	Mass
Electromagnet	Plasma
Gas	Solid
Half-life	Temperature
Heat Conductivity	Viscosity
Insulator	Weight

_____

_____

_____

_____

Physics Laws and Theories

Kinetic Theory of Matter	Law of Inertia
Law of Acceleration	Law of Interaction
Law of Action and Reaction	Law of Universal Gravitation
Law of Applied Force	Particle Theory of Light
Law of Conservation of Energy	Wave Theory of Light

_____

_____

_____

_____

Keep in Mind

Keep in mind that you will not have to recite physics laws or give definitions, but you will need to be able to apply the concepts. With that in mind, don't spend a lot of time memorizing things such as the law of conservation of energy. Just make sure you understand it and are able to use the principles behind it.

Force, Work, and Machines

Centripetal Force	Magnetic Force
Electrical Force	Nuclear Force
Force	Power
Fulcrum	Pulley
Gravitational Force	Synergy
Lever	Wheel and Axle
Machines	Work

_____

_____

_____

_____

Motion

Acceleration	Position and Motion of Objects
Action	Pressure
Displacement	Properties of Objects and Materials
Distance	Reaction
Momentum	Resistance
Motion	Speed

_____

_____

_____

_____

Friction

Fluid Friction   Sliding Friction

Rolling Friction   Static Friction

_____

_____

_____

_____

What to Do

Now that you know what types of physics topics to expect on the GED Science test, let's go over the six steps you will use to select the best answer for each question.

> **Physics Steps**
>
> **Step 1:** Read All the Information
> **Step 2:** Identify the Question
> **Step 3:** Underline Key Words and Phrases
> **Step 4:** Determine Meanings
> **Step 5:** Think About What You Already Know
> **Step 6:** Select the Best Answer

Step 1: Read All the Information

By now you recognize the importance of reading all the information associated with each question. Even if you feel the pressure of the ticking clock, make sure to read everything. Carefully reading the information may actually save time in the long run. Having to go back to locate information you missed on the first pass could take longer than reading thoroughly enough to comprehend everything from the start.

Step 2: Identify the Question

The purpose of the test is to ask 50 questions that assess your knowledge of science. The only way to select the correct answer is to understand what is being asked.

Step 3: Underline Key Words and Phrases

At this point, you have read the information and identified the question. Next, locate and underline the pertinent words, phrases, and facts that you will use to determine the correct answer. Not only does this give you a chance to take a second glance at the key ideas, but it also allows you to find them quickly when it is time to answer the question.

Step 4: Determine Meanings

What should you do if a passage contains an unfamiliar word? First, don't panic. Second, look for contextual clues in the surrounding sentences and passages that can help you determine the meaning. Third, think of a word that contains a similar root and use this as a clue to the definition.

What if the meaning is still unclear? Think about what would make sense in the context of the passage and take your best guess.

Step 5: Think About What You Already Know

What have you read, heard, learned, or experienced related to this topic? Combine your existing knowledge with the information given on the test to form a complete understanding of the material. Integrating your own ideas with what you read can enhance your comprehension.

Step 6: Select the Best Answer

Read the question one more time. Then carefully reread each answer choice. Even if one of the first choices looks good, even if you are beginning to feel the time crunch, read every single answer. The only way to know that your selection is best is to know what all of the other options say. Finally, choose the one option that best answers the question most completely.

Examples

Let's take a look at a few sample physics questions.

Levers, inclined planes, and pulleys are all examples of simple machines. A lever pivots around a point and is used to move or lift an object by applying force to the opposite end. Which of the following is NOT an example of a lever?

1. crowbar
2. fork

3. scissors

4. screw

5. stapler

Here are our steps:

Step 1: Read All the Information

Step 2: Identify the Question

Four of the items are levers. Which is not?

Step 3: Underline Key Words and Phrases

The definition of <u>lever</u> is important to understanding the information. The word <u>not</u> is also important.

Step 4: Determine Meanings

Suppose that on the day of the test, the word <u>lever</u> is a bit baffling. The second sentence in the passage offers a definition of the word. What if that definition were not included? No worries! Take a look at the answer choices. Four are levers, and one is not. You can figure out which is not a lever by determining which of these things is not like the others.

Step 5: Think About What You Already Know

What is the first thing that comes to mind when you think of a lever? There's a good chance that you are picturing a playground teeter-totter. A weight on one end of the board lifts a weight on the opposite end. Use this example to help you determine which of the answer choices works in a similar way and which do not.

Step 6: Select the Best Answer

A crowbar, fork, scissors, and stapler all move by applying force to one end. A screw does not, so the correct answer is 4. A screw is actually a type of included plane.

Now it's your turn. Answer the following question about a simple machine. We'll give you the steps you will need to practice the process.

Which statement is true regarding levers?

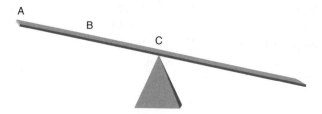

1. The force in the diagram is applied to point B.

2. The fulcrum in the diagram is located at point A.

3. The fulcrum in the diagram is located at point C.

4. The force in any lever must be applied to the end opposite the load.

5. The fulcrum of a lever must be located between the force and the load.

Step 1: Read All the Information

Step 2: Identify the Question

_____

_____

Step 3: Underline Key Words and Phrases

Step 4: Determine Meanings

_____

_____

Step 5: Think About What You Already Know

_____

_____

_____

_____

Step 6: Select the Best Answer

The correct answer is 3.

Keep in Mind

Keep in mind that the purpose of the practice questions in this book is to familiarize you with the type of questions that will be on the GED test, to help you figure out what topics you know well, and to alert you to concepts you should spend a little more time studying. If you select an incorrect answer while working on the sample questions, use the experience as a learning opportunity. Take the time to go back and study the topic further.

PHYSICS DRILLS

Fill in the blanks for question 1. For each of the subsequent questions, choose the best answer.

1. **What are the steps for answering physics questions?**
   Step 1: _____
   Step 2: _____
   Step 3: _____
   Step 4: _____
   Step 5: _____
   Step 6: _____

2. **A pulley is used to lift the 1,000-pound weight in the diagram. Which statement is true?**

   A. The weight can be lifted using 500 pounds of force.
   B. The weight can be lifted using 100 pounds of force.
   C. Adding a second pulley would allow the weight to be lifted using 500 pounds of force.
   D. Adding a second pulley would allow the weight to be lifted using 100 pounds of force.
   E. Adding a second pulley would not alter the amount of force required to lift the weight.

Use the following information to answer questions 3–5.

The United States uses a combination of fossil fuels, renewable sources, nuclear, and electricity net imports for energy. The chart shows the percentages of energy used from each source in 2008, as reported by the US Energy Information Agency.

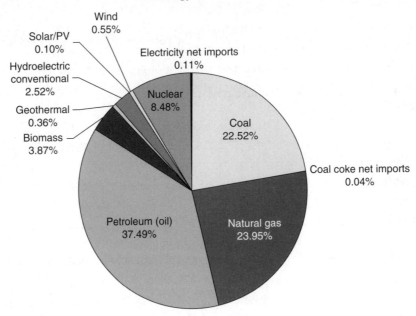

U.S. Energy Use—2008

Wind 0.55%
Solar/PV 0.10%
Hydroelectric conventional 2.52%
Geothermal 0.36%
Biomass 3.87%
Electricity net imports 0.11%
Nuclear 8.48%
Coal 22.52%
Coal coke net imports 0.04%
Natural gas 23.95%
Petroleum (oil) 37.49%

3. Fossil fuels include coal, coal coke net imports, natural gas, and petroleum. Approximately what percentage of the total US energy came from fossil fuels?

   A. 24%
   B. 37%
   C. 47%
   D. 62%
   E. 84%

4. According to the graph, approximately what percentage of the total US energy came from renewable sources?

   A. 4%
   B. 7%
   C. 10%
   D. 19%
   E. 23%

5. In 2008, 39.9 percent of Maine's energy came from renewable sources. Based on the data, which inference can be made?

   A. Most states used more renewable energy than Maine.
   B. Maine's use of renewable energy was the highest in the nation.
   C. Fossil fuels were less readily available in Maine than in other states.
   D. A greater amount of renewable sources than fossil fuels was used in Maine.
   E. Maine relied more heavily on renewable energy sources than most other states.

Use the following information to answer questions 6 and 7.

Sir Isaac Newton is widely known for his observations of apples falling from a tree and his resulting universal law of gravitation. It explains that any two objects exert a gravitational force of attraction on each other. The direction of this force is along the line that joins the centers of the objects, and the magnitude of the force is directly proportional to the product of the objects' masses and inversely proportional to the square of the distance between the objects. This explanation of gravity is but one of the scientist's contributions to our understanding of the world around us.

Newton also stated several other laws that are central to the study of physics. He presented his three laws of motion in 1686. His first law of motion, often called the law of inertia, states that every object in a state of rest or uniform motion remains in that state unless an external force is applied to it. His second law of motion explains that the rate of change of the momentum of an object is directly proportional to the resultant force acting on it. The relationship is shown by the equation $F = ma$, where F represents force, m represents mass, and a represents acceleration. Newton's third law of motion states that for every action, there is an equal and opposite reaction.

In addition to his work with gravitation and movement, Newton is also noted for his law of cooling, which states that the rate of change of an object's temperature is proportional to the difference between its own temperature and the temperature of its surroundings. In other words, the rate at which a hot object cools depends on its temperature and the temperature around it.

6. **Which of Newton's laws is demonstrated by the diagram of the rocket?**

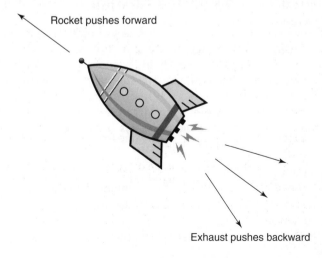

Rocket pushes forward

Exhaust pushes backward

    A. universal law of gravitation
    B. first law of motion
    C. second law of motion
    D. third law of motion
    E. law of cooling

7. The amount of force required to lift an airplane is different than the amount of force required to launch a rocket. Which of Newton's laws is this an example of?
    A. universal law of gravitation
    B. first law of motion
    C. second law of motion
    D. third law of motion
    E. law of cooling

8. Many daily tasks involve the changing of energy from one type to another. What type of energy change occurs when using an iron to press clothes before work or school?
    A. heat energy to light energy
    B. heat energy to electrical energy
    C. electrical energy to heat energy
    D. chemical energy to heat energy
    E. mechanical energy to heat energy

9. The universe, as well as everything it contains, is composed of matter and energy. Matter occurs as a solid, liquid, gas, or occasionally plasma. Which statement is true regarding the interaction between matter and energy?
    A. Matter is not impacted by the amount of energy applied.
    B. The amount of energy in matter remains in a constant state.
    C. As energy is added to matter, the movement of the molecules increases.
    D. As energy is added to matter, the movement of the molecules decreases.
    E. Matter is impacted by the type of energy added, not the amount of energy.

10. Friction is a force acting along the surfaces of objects that opposes motion. There are several types of friction. Static friction opposes the movement of a stationary object along a surface. Sliding friction is created when two surfaces slide over one another and is affected by the weight of the moving objects, the type and texture of the surfaces, and any temporary bonding between the two. Rolling friction is created when an object rolls over a surface and opposes less motion than sliding friction. Fluid friction is created when an object is moving through a fluid, such as a gas or liquid.

    A deer runs out into the road, causing a driver to slam on his brakes. Which type of friction is demonstrated when the car skids to a stop?
    A. fluid friction
    B. static friction
    C. rolling friction
    D. sliding friction
    E. friction not demonstrated

Part V

Language Arts, Reading

chapter **17**

Interpreting Prose Fiction

What's Being Tested?

On the GED Language Arts, Reading test, you will read passages and then answer questions based on the information in the text. Three-fourths of these passages will be fiction. Some of them will be prose, while others will be poetry or drama. *Prose* is just a fancy word that means the writing is not poetry. Basically, prose passages are written in regular, everyday paragraph style. In this chapter, we'll review some of the skills that will help you to answer questions about prose fiction.

The reading comprehension questions you will encounter on the GED go beyond simply recalling information that is directly stated in the text. You'll have to put on your thinking cap and be able to apply, analyze, and synthesize ideas to show that you truly understand what you have read.

Keep in Mind

Keep in mind that the comprehension strategies we review for the Language Arts, Reading questions do not apply to a single style of writing. What you read in this chapter may also be helpful in answering questions about prose nonfiction, even drama. Likewise, what you learn in the chapter about poetry may be helpful in answering prose fiction questions as well. The strategies are simply organized according to the type of passage in which they are most likely to be applied.

What to Expect

The prose fiction passages will be between 200 and 400 words. At least one of the passages will have been written before 1920; at least one will have been written between 1920 and 1960; and at least one will have been written since 1960.

There will be a purpose question before each of the reading selections. This question gives you a focus for reading. You will need to read the purpose question and think about what it is drawing your attention to as you read; however, you will not have to answer this question.

Following each passage, you will find between four and eight multiple-choice comprehension questions. You will select the one best answer for each question based solely on the information in the passage.

Determining Word Meanings

Every reading passage you will be given on the GED—or pretty much anywhere else—will include a bunch of words. What sense is there in reading something if you cannot understand the words, right? With that in mind, let's go over a few skills that can be helpful in figuring out the meanings of words.

Contextual Clues

Other words or phrases in a passage can offer hints about the meaning of an unfamiliar word. Look for synonyms, antonyms, examples, and definitions. These may be found within the same sentence as the word you would like to define, or they may appear in surrounding sentences.

> After only listening to the first few seconds of her <u>fabricated</u> account of what happened, we knew that the entire story was <u>made up</u>. On the other hand, Sam's story was completely <u>true</u>.

> Lucia was unsure which of her <u>culinary</u> masterpieces to enter in the contest. Her friends had given rave reviews to both her pineapple-coconut <u>cake</u> and her veal <u>stew</u>.

In the first example, the definition of *fabricated* can be found later in the same sentence. The opposite of *fabricated* is offered in the following sentence. In the second, examples of *culinary* items suggest that the word is related to cooking.

Multiple-Meaning Words

Many words in our language have more than one meaning. To determine which meaning an author has in mind for a particular sentence, pay close attention to how the word is used in the passage.

> Elliot's testimony was <u>instrumental</u> in the lawsuit.

> The <u>instrumental</u> piece on the CD is the most beautiful of all the songs.

Roots and Affixes

The **root** is the part of the word that contains the meaning. Often, the meaning of an unfamiliar word can be determined by thinking of another word that contains a similar root.

Words such as *recur* and *occurrence* have the same root as *occur*. Recognizing this fact can be helpful in determining the meanings of these words.

A **prefix** may be added to the beginning of a word to change its meaning; a **suffix** may be added to the end of a word to change its meaning.

> re + occur + ing = reoccurring

Recognizing roots and affixes—and knowing their meanings—can be helpful in determining the meaning of an unfamiliar word in a passage. A few affixes and their meanings are listed here. This list is by no means comprehensive; a number of prefixes and suffixes can be added to words. These are simply a few examples to show how their addition to a root word can change its meaning.

Prefixes	Suffixes
ex-: out of, previous	*-able, -ible*: able to, can be accomplished
inter-: among, between	*-ive*: likely to
mis-: badly, wrongly	*-ly*: in a particular way
post-: after	*-ous*: full of
trans-: not	*-tion*: an act or process

Comprehension Strategies

When you read a newspaper or magazine, you are doing so to learn about a topic or an event. When you read a novel, you are doing so to find out what happens next in the story. When you read a passage on the GED, you are doing so to answer questions correctly. The entire purpose of reading is to gain information. Let's go over a few strategies that can help you to make the most of what you read and fully understand the material.

Discovering the Author's Purpose

Knowing why a passage was written can be helpful in understanding the text. An author usually writes a selection to entertain, inform, or persuade. The purpose of most prose fiction passages is to entertain, although some are written to persuade. The purpose of nonfiction is generally to inform, although some of these are also written to persuade. The author's word choice, as well as the facts and opinions he or she includes, can offer clues about the purpose of the writing.

To entertain: The light of the silvery moon sparkled on the lake's surface.

To inform: The average distance of the moon from the Earth is 385,000 km.

To persuade: Spacecraft should not be sent to the moon again because the danger outweighs any potential benefits.

Making Predictions Based on Text

By considering information in the text, and thinking about what is likely to happen next, readers are able to increase their comprehension of a passage. Such predictions may be based on the events that have already taken place in the selection; titles and headings; and graphics such as illustrations, charts, or diagrams.

Understanding Theme

The theme of a story is the underlying message the author is trying to convey. Usually, rather than being stated directly, the theme is implied by the beliefs and attitudes in the passage that lead you to a particular idea or conclusion.

Many themes are ideas related to society or human nature. By considering the words and actions of the characters, ideas that are repeated throughout the story, and suggested opinions, you can figure out what "life lesson" the author wants you to take away from the passage. Here are some common themes.

True beauty is on the inside.

Do not give up when facing difficult situations.

It is important to accept people and their differences.

Synthesizing Information

To synthesize means to gather and combine information from more than one source or from more than one location within a single source. Putting ideas together in this way leads to a deeper comprehension of the topic.

The final question on the reading section of the GED test will be an extended synthesis question. Following the passage, an additional piece of information will be given in the question. You will need to consider this new information, along with what you read in the passage, to select the best answer to the question.

Determining Point of View

The type of information given in a passage depends on the point of view from which the story is told. A story written in the **first person** point of view is being told by one of the characters. Therefore, readers experience the events through the eyes of this character. In other words, readers only know the thoughts and feelings of this character. They are only aware of events involving the character telling the story. First person pronouns such as *I*, *we*, and *us* indicate this point of view.

> When we arrived at the museum, I headed directly to the large sculpture in the garden.

A story written in the **third person** is told by a narrator. Since the narrator is outside of the story, rather than being a character involved in the action, he or she is aware of the thoughts, feelings, and actions of everyone involved. Third person pronouns such as *they*, *he*, and *she* indicate this point of view.

> When Karen arrived at the museum with her family, she headed directly to the large sculpture in the garden.

What to Do

We've gone over how to understand words and passages. Now let's go over the steps you will use to answer questions on the GED Language Arts, Reading test.

Steps for Answering Questions About Prose Fiction

Step 1: Read the Purpose Question
Step 2: Read All of the Multiple-Choice Questions
Step 3: Read the Passage
Step 4: Reread the Question You Are Preparing to Answer
Step 5: State Your Answer
Step 6: Read the Answer Choices

Step 1: Read the Purpose Question

Remember, a purpose question will be given before each passage. You will not have to answer this question, but reading it will help you focus on the reason you are reading the selection.

Step 2: Read All of the Multiple-Choice Questions

Read the questions before reading the passages in this chapter and in the sample tests in the back of the book. Doing so will help you to locate important information in the text as you read.

Step 3: Read the Passage

Read the passage carefully. Your understanding of the material is crucial to answering the questions correctly and earning the best possible score on the test. Take your time. Read every word. Remember to use what you know about roots and affixes, contextual clues, and multiple meanings to figure out every word in the passage. If you come to the end of a sentence or paragraph and realize that you did not quite understand it, go back and read it again.

Step 4: Reread the Question You Are Preparing to Answer

Even though you may have already read every question before reading the passage, read the questions again, one at a time, as you are ready to answer them. Read each question carefully to be sure you understand exactly what it is asking. Do not look at the answer choices for that question yet. We'll get to those in a minute.

Step 5: State Your Answer

Figure out what the correct answer to the question is without peeking at the answer choices given. Think about what you read; then go back and find the answer in the passage. You may have to synthesize information from several parts of the passage to answer the question completely. Just make sure that your answer is based on the material.

Once you have found the necessary information in the passage, state your answer to the question. Make sure your response answers the entire question.

Step 6: Read the Answer Choices

Now that you know the correct answer to the question, go ahead and read the answer choices. Select the one that most closely matches the answer you stated in Step 5. You may find that more than one of the choices could be correct. That is entirely possible. Several answers may include correct information or be partially correct. Select the one that best and most completely answers the question.

Examples

Let's look at some sample questions, and use the six steps to select the best answer for each. Remember, the first step is to read the entire passage.

Will They Find the Perfect Piece?

Ding-ding.

The tiny, tarnished bell rang as we opened the door and entered the store. It somehow seemed fitting that the old-fashioned bell that was tied to the door frame had not been replaced by a more modern electronic chime to signal the entry of guests into the antique shop. Our hunt for pieces to furnish the historic farmhouse had led us to this destination. Upon entering, it appeared that we might have found the right place.

The walls of the crowded shop were lined with heavy chests, dressers, and armoires, standing side by side like heavy, wooden soldiers. The sizes of the large pieces of furniture seemed disproportionate in the tiny room. Slowly, we walked past each of the furnishings, rubbing our hands across the aged woods, sliding drawers open, examining discolored knobs and hinges. Then we came to a dark cherrywood china hutch and froze. A few seconds passed before I realized I was holding my breath. The hutch was the exact color of Grandmother's dining table. The decorative carving around the edges was identical to the carving on the backs of the dining chairs. Slowly, we walked toward the amazing piece, which would be the ideal complement to the furnishings already in the home. It was perfect. Despite its age, there was not a single scratch anywhere on the amazing cabinet.

Read the sentence from the third paragraph.

The sizes of the large pieces of furniture seemed <u>disproportionate</u> in the tiny room.

What is the meaning of *disproportionate*?

1. comparable
2. hefty
3. petite
4. size
5. unequal

Here are our steps:

Step 1: Read the Purpose Question

Will They Find the Perfect Piece?

Step 2: Read All of the Multiple-Choice Questions

What is the meaning of <u>disproportionate</u>? Now we know to look for this word and to use the strategies discussed in the chapter to determine its meaning in the passage.

Step 3: Read the Passage

Step 4: Reread the Question You Are Preparing to Answer

What is the meaning of <u>disproportionate</u>?

Step 5: State Your Answer

The root of <u>disproportionate</u> is <u>proportion</u>, which means "balanced in size." The prefix <u>dis-</u> means "not." So <u>disproportionate</u> means "not balanced in size." Does that make sense in the context of the passage? Yes, because the large furniture was not balanced in size with the tiny room.

Step 6: Read the Answer Choices

Answer choice 5 means about the same as "not balanced," so this is the best answer.

Now it's your turn. Take a look at the following question, which is based on the same passage. We'll give you the steps you will need to practice the process.

What will MOST LIKELY happen next?

1. They will purchase the china hutch.
2. They will return to the store on another day.
3. They will replace the dining table and chairs.
4. They will continue shopping in another store.
5. They will find a scratch on the piece of furniture.

Step 1: Read the Purpose Question

_____

_____

Step 2: Read All of the Multiple-Choice Questions

Step 3: Read the Passage

Step 4: Reread the Question You Are Preparing to Answer

Step 5: State Your Answer

_____

_____

Step 6: Read the Answer Choices

PROSE FICTION READING COMPREHENSION DRILLS

Fill in the blanks for question 1. For each of the subsequent questions, choose the best answer.

1. **What are the steps for answering questions about prose fiction?**

   Step 1: _____

   Step 2: _____

   Step 3: _____

   Step 4: _____

   Step 5: _____

   Step 6: _____

Questions 2–9 are based on the following passage.

What Will Happen When the Music Fades?

As was the case most days at this time, students wandered into the quad to cram for the afternoon's test, eat lunch, meet up with friends, or simply relax in the shade of the lush oak trees. For as many students as were present, the noise level remained surprisingly low. Laughter and chatter could be heard, but the sound was nowhere near what would be considered disruptive.

A young man with a guitar began to play quietly on one side of the lawn. Two friends beside him continued reading their textbooks as his music quietly floated through the air around them. Within a couple of minutes, another young man with a guitar began playing as well and slowly walked toward the first man. The two smiled at each other, and without a word being spoken, the solo became a duet. Around them, students began to look up from their laptops and notebooks. A couple of students slowly walked closer to the source of the melody in order to hear it better.

A few notes later, a girl with a flute wandered over, smiled at the men, and lifted her instrument to her lips. The duet became a trio, and more students gathered. Without a word, the trio was soon joined by a clarinet, a bongo drum, and a harmonica. The impromptu concert began to draw a crowd, which was as spontaneous as the music itself. The harmonies of the instruments eclipsed the students' plans to study, as nearly everyone on the lawn was drawn to gather near the musicians.

The single song grew into a medley, combining a number of familiar tunes, one after the other. A professor, on his way to his office, noticed the crowd and went to investigate. Upon hearing the music, he stopped. A glazed look came over his eyes, as he allowed his head to nod to the rhythm of the music, and his foot precisely tapped the beat.

A few minutes later, the music quieted, and the students clapped loudly. The musicians smiled and shook hands with each other, as the members of the crowd slowly returned to their routines. The professor anxiously approached the players and introduced himself. The group of six students, who had never before met one another, stood in a circle, and listened to the man whose words would impact them for years to come.

2. **What is the meaning of the word** *cram* **in the first sentence?**
   A. to study intensely
   B. to eat food greedily
   C. to force into a small space
   D. a time of rigorous learning
   E. the state of being packed tightly

3. **Which was MOST LIKELY the author's purpose for writing the selection?**
   A. to tell a true story about real events
   B. to persuade readers to take music lessons
   C. to inform readers about musical instruments
   D. to teach readers about how to play an instrument
   E. to entertain by telling a story that did not actually happen

4. **Which word tells the meaning of** *impromptu* **in the third paragraph?**
   A. eclipsed
   B. harmonies
   C. instrument
   D. spontaneous
   E. trio

5. **Read the sentence from the third paragraph.**
   The harmonies of the instruments <u>*eclipsed*</u> *the students' plans to study, as nearly everyone on the lawn was drawn to gather near the musicians. Which meaning of the word* <u>*eclipsed*</u> *is used in this sentence?*
   A. a loss of light
   B. a decline in status or power
   C. the partial or total hiding of the sun or moon
   D. to become more important than something else
   E. to cast a shadow by blocking the light on an object

6. **Read the sentences from the fourth paragraph.**

   The single song grew into a medley, combining a number of familiar tunes, one after the other. A professor, on his way to his office, noticed the crowd and went to investigate.

   What is the meaning of *medley*?

   A. assembly
   B. mixture
   C. recognizable
   D. teacher
   E. tune

7. **What is the meaning of the word** *glazed* **in the fourth paragraph?**

   A. fixed and staring
   B. enclosed with glass
   C. protected by a finish
   D. covered in a sweet coating
   E. having a shiny outside layer

8. **The professor is the director of the school's band and is also head of the performing arts department. Which sentence most accurately tells why he is probably speaking to the students?**

   A. to ask them not to disrupt the other students' study time
   B. to discourage them from drawing a crowd on school property
   C. to suggest the names of vocalists who might want to sing with them
   D. to find out if they will let him join them the next time they play together
   E. to encourage them to become involved in the school's music program

9. **What will MOST LIKELY happen next?**

   A. The musicians will plan to play their instruments together again in the future.
   B. The students will ask them to play music during their lunch break the next day.
   C. The two young men with guitars will continue to play together without the others.
   D. The group will decide that the concert was a one-time event and not perform again.
   E. The crowd will not gather on the lawn again the next time the musicians play their instruments.

chapter **18**

Interpreting Poetry

As you know, about 75 percent of the questions in the reading section of the GED will be based on fiction writing. At least one of the selections you will read and answer questions about will be poetry. Each poem on the test is between 8 and 25 lines in length. In this chapter, we'll review several reading comprehension skills that will help you to understand any poetry you may encounter on the GED. Keep in mind that some of the comprehension strategies reviewed in this chapter may also be useful in understanding other forms of literature as well.

What's the Difference?

So what's the difference between poetry and prose? Great question! A poem is usually arranged in short lines or phrases that are grouped into stanzas. Each line of a poem may or may not express a complete thought; often a single thought is spread over several lines. Prose, on the other hand, includes sentences that are grouped together in paragraphs. Each sentence, by definition, expresses a complete thought. Figurative language, a pattern of syllables, rhyming words, and rhythm are common characteristics of poetry.

You may think that poems are shorter than prose passages, but that is not actually the case. Some poems can be as long as a novel. Remember a little story called *Romeo and Juliet?* Shakespeare's famous play, which you may have spent weeks studying in high school, is also a poem. The Mahabharata, an Indian scripture, is actually the longest poem in the world, with a length of more than 1.8 million words.

Not only does poetry look and sound different than prose, interpreting poetry is different than interpreting other forms of literature. Let's go over a few things to look for when you read a poem.

Stanzas

As you know, poems are written in short lines or phrases. These phrases are arranged into groups called **stanzas**. Each stanza is set apart from the rest by a space. Poems may contain any number of stanzas.

 Keep in Mind

Keep in mind that unlike sentences, which end in a period, the lines of a poem do not necessarily express a complete thought. In other words, you should not stop reading at the end of a line and assume you've gotten the whole idea. Each line may begin with a capital letter, but that does not mean it is the beginning of a new sentence or idea. Read a line and then continue until you come to ending punctuation or the end of a stanza to make sure you have read the entire thought.

Rhythm

The **rhythm** of a poem is the musical pattern, or beat, that is created by the syllables. A poem's rhythm influences the feeling associated with the piece. Faster rhythms tend to suggest a lively, upbeat feeling, while slower rhythms suggest a calmer, possibly even somber, feeling.

Rhyme

Poems may or may not contain rhyming words at the ends of the lines. When a poem does include **rhyme**, these similar sounding words are arranged in a pattern.

For example, the words ending alternating lines may rhyme, or the words on every third line may rhyme. The pattern of rhyming words is the **rhyme scheme**.

Take a look at the rhyme scheme in this stanza from Elizabeth Barrett Browning's "The Poet's Vow." The letter A is given to the first line of the poem; any line that rhymes with this would also be given the letter A. The next line, since it does not rhyme with line A, is assigned the letter B, as is any line that rhymes with it, and so on.

Eve is a twofold mystery; (A)

The stillness Earth doth keep, (B)

The motion wherewith human hears (C)

Do each to either leap (B)

As if all souls between the poles (D)

Felt "Parting comes in sleep." (B)

So the rhyme scheme for this stanza is ABCBDB. It shows that lines 2, 4, and 6, which are all labeled B, rhyme with each other.

What to Know

Now that we've reviewed some of the ways in which poems look and sound different than prose, let's go over a few things that will help you understand poetry.

Mood and Tone

The **mood** of a poem is the feeling or emotion it suggests and is created by the words and details the writer selects. Notice the two descriptions of the same situation that follow. The first suggests a happy, cheerful, or excited mood. The second suggests an ominous, uncomfortable, or nervous mood.

After being introduced, Malcolm bounced across the stage to the podium, soaking in the cheers and applause of his supporters.

After being introduced, Malcolm trudged across the stage to the podium, cringing at the commotion created by the audience.

The **tone** is also created by the words and details a writer uses; it refers to his or her attitude about the topic.

The contagious excitement of the crowd continued long after the speaker had made his victorious march across the stage to deliver yet another awe-inspiring message.

The raucous noise of the crowd would not end soon enough, despite the fact that the speaker had already approached the podium to deliver a message that would not be unlike the sound of fingernails on a chalkboard.

Keep in Mind

Keep in mind that *mood* refers to the *emotions* the reader gets from a passage. The mood might be mysterious, romantic, serious, lighthearted, gloomy, or a hundred other feelings you may experience.

Tone refers to the *attitude* of the writer. The tone might be sarcastic, humorous, outraged, somber, or any other attitude you can think of.

Figurative Language

Figurative language helps literature be more descriptive by using words in a way that gives them meanings that are different than their ordinary meanings. This strategy helps to paint a clear picture in your mind and increases comprehension of the text. Here are several common types of figurative language.

Hyperbole

An overexaggeration, which may be used with humor, is a **hyperbole**. Such language is used for emphasis or effect rather than for giving a literal explanation.

Adrienne made her famous mile-high chocolate fudge cake for dessert.

The car stereo was so loud that the people in the next town could hear it.

Idioms

An **idiom** is an expression that has a different meaning than the words indicate literally.

She was <u>up a creek</u> when her dad found out she had not gone to the library to study.

The literal meaning of the phrase *up a creek* would mean that she was sitting in a narrow body of water, but as we know from the sentence, this was not actually the case. The figurative meaning of *up a creek* indicates that she was in trouble.

Metaphors

Metaphors compare two unlike things by stating that one is actually the other.

Trevor's eyes were stars when he saw her enter the coffee shop.

Did his eyes actually become stars? No. Do you understand what was happening? Probably. Is this more interesting and descriptive than saying, "Trevor was happy to see her"? You bet!

Simile

A **simile** is a comparison using the words *like* or *as*.

When the election results were posted, Madison was as happy as a clam.

Marcella sings like a canary, so she was given the starring role in the musical.

Personification

Sometimes, human characteristics are attributed to nonhuman things to provide a clear description. This type of figurative language is **personification**.

The waves danced across the surface of the lake.

Alliteration

Alliteration is one way writers emphasize and connect words by repeating similar sounds. The repeated sounds are often found at the beginning of words or at the beginning of stressed syllables. The two types of alliteration are assonance and consonance.

Assonance is the repetition of vowel sounds.

The <u>kite</u> <u>flies</u> <u>beside</u> the billowy cloud.

Consonance is the repetition of consonant sounds. Notice in the example that it is the repetition of the sound, not the letter, that creates alliteration.

He <u>gently juggled</u> the delicate items to ensure their safe arrival.

Style

The type of language a writer uses determines the style of the poem or passage. The appropriate style is determined by the purpose of the writing, the intended audience, and the feeling that the writer wants to achieve.

A **formal writing style** is often used for workplace documents and school assignments, as well as for passages or poems that deal with serious or somber topics. Complicated words and technical jargon may be included.

> During the current semester, students enrolled in Ancient Greek Literature for Modern Times will be required to research the history of poetry and present poems that serve as examples of iambic pentameter and dactylic hexameter.

An **informal style** uses words and information that are intended for pretty much anyone to be able to understand.

> Emily Dickinson is a famous poet who was born in 1830 in Massachusetts. She wrote nearly 2,000 poems. Only about a dozen of these poems were published while she was living.

A **conversational style** uses words and phrases that someone might use when talking with a friend. In fact, the writing sounds like a conversation.

> I read the most amazing poem today! It was hanging in this new store in the mall—you know, the one by the food court. The poem was written on kind of old-looking paper and was in the coolest frame. The dude at the store said they're having a sweet sale next week. I'll definitely check that out!

Word Usage

One factor that helps to set the style of a poem or passage is the words the writer selects to set the tone and express his or her ideas. **Word usage** can alter the impression you take away from the text. Take a look at how word usage affects the following examples.

> Kirk requested an extra-credit assignment to improve his final grade.

> Kirk begged for an extra-credit assignment to recover his final grade.

What to Do

So far in this chapter, we've reviewed the characteristics of poetry and the strategies needed to interpret the meaning of a poem. Now let's go over the six steps you'll use to answer questions about poetry on the GED. These steps may look familiar. Basically, they are the same as the steps used to answer questions about prose fiction passages.

Steps for Answering Questions About Poetry

Step 1: Read the Purpose Question
Step 2: Read All of the Multiple-Choice Questions
Step 3: Read the Poem
Step 4: Reread the Question You Are Preparing to Answer
Step 5: State Your Answer
Step 6: Read the Answer Choices

Step 1: Read the Purpose Question

As you know, you will not have to answer the purpose question. However, reading it will give you an idea of what the poem will be about. Let's face it; interpreting poetry can be tricky at times. Take advantage of any help that is offered. Read the purpose question and use it to determine what you should focus on as you read.

Step 2: Read All of the Multiple-Choice Questions

Reading all of the questions ahead of time can alert you to what information you should keep an eye out for as you read the poem. Will you need to look for examples of alliteration? Will you be expected to identify the tone or mood? Again, take advantage of any resource you have. Use these questions to focus your attention on which information and techniques will be most important.

Step 3: Read the Poem

By now you've figured out that the way you will read poetry is slightly different than the way you read prose. Remember not to read a poem line by line; rather, read it from the beginning of a thought to the end. A single idea may be expressed over several lines. To best understand the message of the poem, focus on identifying complete thoughts as you read.

Pay attention to punctuation. As with prose writing, punctuation can be helpful in separating ideas and keeping thoughts from running together. Pause where there are commas or semicolons. Stop where there are periods. Be careful not to pause or stop where there is no punctuation, regardless of whether you have come to the end of a line.

Also pay attention to the rhythm. The rhythm works to set the mood of the poem. You may find it helpful to read poetry aloud to hear the beats; however, you will have to listen to yourself read aloud in your head during the actual test. Practice doing this in the weeks and months beforehand.

Notice any figurative language, and read it carefully enough to be able to create the image in your mind that the poet intended. This will help you to understand exactly what he or she is describing.

Step 4: Reread the Question You Are Preparing to Answer

Read each question as you are ready to answer it. As always, read carefully and make sure you understand exactly what is being asked. Wait to read the answer choices though. We'll read those shortly.

Step 5: State Your Answer

Before reading the answer choices, determine what you believe the correct answer should be. Always look back at the poem to double-check your answer. Explain to yourself why your answer is correct, and make sure that it answers the question completely.

Step 6: Read the Answer Choices

Now check out the answer choices and see which one best matches the answer you came up with in Step 5. Be careful! The wrong answers that are included were put there for a reason. These are not just random options that test writers pulled out of their hats; they are based on test takers' common mistakes and misconceptions. Look at each option and explain to yourself why it is not the best answer. Then make sure the answer you chose is definitely the best choice.

Examples

Let's look at some sample questions about poetry. Read the following poem by William Butler Yeats.

What Do the Clouds Mean?

These are the Clouds

These are the clouds about the fallen sun,

The majesty that shuts his burning eye;

The weak lay hand on what the strong has done,

Till that be tumbled that was lifted high

(5) And discord follow upon unison,

And all things at one common level lie.

And therefore, friend, if your great race were run

And these things came, so much the more thereby

(10) Have you made greatness your companion,

Although it be for children that you sigh:

These are the clouds about the fallen sun,

The majesty that shuts his burning eye.

Which example of personification is found in the poem?

    1. The clouds fall.

    2. The sun shuts his eye

    3. The weak lay hands.

    4. A friend runs a race.

    5. Children sigh.

Here are our steps:

    Step 1: Read the Purpose Question

        What Do the Clouds Mean?

Step 2: Read All of the Multiple-Choice Questions

Step 3: Read the Poem

Step 4: Reread the Question You Are Preparing to Answer

Which example of personification is found in the poem?

Step 5: State Your Answer

The sun is the majesty that shuts his eye. Shutting eyes is a human trait and is attributed to the sun, a nonhuman object.

Step 6: Read the Answer Choices

Our answer in Step 5 is the same as answer choice 2.

Now it's your turn. Use the poem by Yeats to answer the following question. We'll give you the steps you will need to practice the process.

What is the rhyme scheme in the poem?

1. AABB
2. ABCD
3. ABAB
4. ABCB
5. ABCC

Step 1: Read the Purpose Question

_____

Step 2: Read All of the Multiple-Choice Questions

Step 3: Read the Poem

Step 4: Reread the Question You Are Preparing to Answer

_____

Step 5: State Your Answer

_____

_____

Step 6: Read the Answer Choices

The correct answer is 3.

POETRY READING COMPREHENSION DRILLS

Fill in the blanks for question 1. For each of the subsequent questions, choose the best answer.

1. **What are the steps for answering questions about poetry?**

    Step 1: _____

    Step 2: _____

    Step 3: _____

    Step 4: _____

    Step 5: _____

    Step 6: _____

Questions 2–6 are based on the excerpt from the poem by Henry Wadsworth Longfellow.

What Memories Are Associated with the Trees?

Voices of the Night

Pleasant it was, when woods were green,

And winds were soft and low,

To lie amid some sylvan scene.

Where, the long drooping boughs between,

(5) Shadows dark and sunlight sheen

Alternate come and go;

Or where the denser grove receives

No sunlight from above,

But the dark foliage interweaves

(10) In one unbroken roof of leaves,

Underneath whose sloping eaves

The shadows hardly move.

Beneath some patriarchal tree

I lay upon the ground;

(15) His hoary arms uplifted he,

And all the broad leaves over me

Clapped their little hands in glee,

With one continuous sound;—

A slumberous sound, a sound that brings

(20) The feelings of a dream,

As of innumerable wings,

As, when a bell no longer swings,

Faint the hollow murmur rings

O'er meadow, lake, and stream.

2. **Which word expresses the mood of the poem?**
   A. anxious
   B. content
   C. frightening
   D. gloomy
   E. surprising

3. **Which line contains an example of figurative language?**
   A. 1
   B. 5
   C. 12
   D. 17
   E. 24

4. **Which line contains an example of consonance?**
   A. *Alternate come and go*
   B. *No sunlight from above*
   C. *Underneath whose sloping eaves*
   D. *And all the broad leaves over me*
   E. *A slumberous sound, a sound that brings*

5. **Which line contains an example of assonance?**
   A. *The feelings of a dream*
   B. *His hoary arms uplifted he*
   C. *The shadows hardly move*
   D. *Where, the long drooping boughs between*
   E. *Pleasant it was, when woods were green*

6. **How does the poet feel about the sound of the leaves?**
   A. He feels that the sound is eerie.
   B. He thinks it sounds like a stream.
   C. The sound makes him feel afraid.
   D. He believes the sound is too quiet.
   E. The sound makes him feel peaceful.

Questions 7–10 are based on the following excerpt from the same poem.

(25) And dreams of that which cannot die,

Bright visions, came to me,

As lapped in thought I used to lie,

And gaze into the summer sky,

Where the sailing clouds went by,

(30) Like ships upon the sea;

Dreams that the soul of youth engage

Ere Fancy has been quelled;

Old legends of the monkish page,

Traditions of the saint and sage,

(35) Tales that have the rime of age,

And chronicles of Eld.

And, loving still these quaint old themes,

Even in the city's throng

I feel the freshness of the streams,

(40) That, crossed by shades and sunny gleams,

Water the green land of dreams,

The holy land of song.

Therefore, at Pentecost, which brings

The Spring, clothed like a bride,

(45) When nestling buds unfold their wings,

And bishop's-caps have golden rings,

Musing upon many things,

I sought the woodlands wide.

7. **Which use of figurative language is found in the poem?**
    A. A simile compares clouds to ships.
    B. A simile compares dreams and visions.
    C. A metaphor compares legends and monks.
    D. A metaphor compares the city and streams.
    E. A metaphor compares water and the land of song.

8. **Which shows the rhyme scheme of the final stanza?**
    A. AABBCC
    B. ABCABC
    C. ABAAAB
    D. ABABAB
    E. ABBABB

9. **Which of the following is included in a simile?**
    A. buds
    B. Pentecost
    C. sea
    D. Spring
    E. youth

10. **Which best expresses the tone of the poem?**
    A. angry
    B. amused
    C. humorous
    D. reminiscent
    E. suspicious

chapter **19**

Interpreting Drama

What's Being Tested?

Of the fiction selections on the GED Language Arts, Reading test, at least one will be drama, which means you will be reading a play and answering questions about it. If you have ever read a play in the past, you are aware that dramatic writing is different than prose, since the writer intended for the story to be performed by actors. In this chapter, we will go over some of the characteristics of drama, as well as several comprehension strategies that will help you to understand the text better and be prepared to answer questions about it.

What's All the Drama?

Like prose fiction, a drama includes a story and characters. You have a plot, characters, and dialogue. The major difference is the way in which the drama is written. As you read a drama, you will notice that it is written as a script rather than in paragraph form. The script is divided into acts and scenes rather than chapters. The script will also include a list of the characters and stage directions, which are not included in prose.

Now that you are aware of some of the differences between drama and prose, let's take a closer look at some of the characteristics of a drama.

Cast List

A **cast list** tells the names of all the characters who will have a part in the drama. Generally, the list appears at the beginning of the script. It may also include a short description of each character.

Acts and Scenes

A long story written in prose is generally divided into chapters; likewise, a long play may be divided into large sections, or **acts**. Whereas chapters may be named, acts are usually numbered sequentially. They may be further divided into smaller sections known as **scenes**, which are specific episodes from the drama. A scene takes place during a specified time in a single location. Whenever the location (or setting) changes, the scene changes as well.

Dialogue

The majority of a play is composed of conversations between the characters. This **dialogue** is what tells the story. In a script, the name of the character who is speaking is listed prior to his or her words. This takes the place of quotation marks and words such as *he said* or *she replied* in prose.

Tyra:	How did the job interview go this afternoon?
Gavin:	You know, I think it went really well. I was able to answer all of their questions, and the interviewer seemed to be impressed with my list of references.

Stage Directions

A drama also includes **stage directions** to let the actors know what expressions, emotions, and actions the characters should perform. These help to ensure that the drama is presented as the writer intended.

Kwan:	(reading the mail, gasps excitedly, and shouts) I can't believe it! It's an acceptance letter! I got into the university!

What's the Story?

Any time you read a story, you expect to encounter certain things. The story will be about someone. The events will occur someplace, either real or imaginary. And there will be some sort of conflict or problem that needs to be solved.

These **story elements** can be found in any story, whether it is written in a prose format or as a drama.

Characters

The people or animals that appear in a story are the **characters**. A story may include only one character or many. The **main character**, also known as the **protagonist**, is the one on whom the story focuses. There may be more than one main character if the story revolves around several people.

As you read, you get to know the characters. The way in which their personalities and behavior are shown is called **characterization**. Some writers choose to tell readers what characters are like by describing their interests, attitudes, thoughts, and appearances. This **direct characterization** *directly* explains their personalities.

Pedro was friendly and met everyone at the party.

Indirect characterization reveals the characters' personalities indirectly by showing, rather than telling, what they are like. The writer uses the characters' actions, speech, and interactions with other characters to give readers insight about the character.

At the party, Pedro introduced himself to each of the guests, flashing his broad smile, shaking every hand, and striking up a conversation with everyone in the room.

In the first example, we know Pedro is friendly because the author says so. In the second example, Pedro's actions reveal his personality.

Setting

When and where a story occurs is the **setting**. This includes not only the actual location of the events but also the time and atmosphere. Each of these elements works together to create the mood of the story and give readers a better understanding of the events.

Plot

All of the events in the story construct the **plot**. Basically, the plot is what happens and includes the conflict, rising action, and climax of the story.

The **conflict** is the problem the characters must deal with in the story. Generally, this is introduced toward the beginning of the story or play. The remaining part of the story is basically what happens as the characters try to solve the problem.

The **rising action** includes all the events that lead up to the **climax**, or most dramatic moment of the story. This is where the story reveals how the conflict will be solved.

Resolution

As you read, you expect that the conflict of the story will eventually be resolved. This part of the story is the **resolution** and is usually toward the end. The events following the resolution are the **denouement**.

What to Know

Now that we have reviewed the characteristics of drama and the parts of a story, let's talk about ways to make sense of it all. Knowing how to draw conclusions and make connections can help you to better understand what you read.

Drawing Conclusions

Authors often expect readers to consider the facts, details, and ideas in a text and to use this information to make a reasonable guess about what is happening. Being able to **draw conclusions** based on the text is one way to improve your comprehension. Not only are you understanding what is said, but you are also understanding what is *not* said.

Making Connections with Text

One way to increase your comprehension of drama or any other reading material is to **make connections** between the text and your prior knowledge.

Text-to-Self Connections

Connecting the information you read with your own experiences is a **text-to-self** connection, which helps to make the material more personal and relevant. To make this type of connection, ask yourself questions that will help you relate the characters and events in the text to your own life.

What does this remind me of that I have done?

What would I do if I were ever in a similar situation?

Text-to-Text Connections

Connecting the information you read with something you have read in the past is a **text-to-text** connection. Being able to make these connections helps you to relate information you have already encountered with the new information, which deepens your understanding. To make this type of connection, ask yourself questions that will help you relate the characters and events in the text to another selection, either fiction or nonfiction.

What else have I read that has involved similar characters or situations?

What have I learned by reading another book or article that relates to a similar topic?

How is this similar to other works I have read by the same author?

Text-to-World Connections

Connecting the information you read with real-world events is a **text-to-world** connection. Being able to make these connections helps you to relate the information in the story to actual occurrences in the world. To make this type of connection, ask yourself questions that will help you relate the characters, events, and information in the text to real life.

What does this text remind me of that I have seen on the news or the Internet?

What current events or factual information relate to this selection?

What to Do

As you know, you will have to read at least one drama and answer questions about it on the GED. Let's go over the six steps you will use to do that. These steps should look familiar by now; they are quite similar to the steps you used to answer prose fiction and poetry questions in the previous chapters.

> ### *Steps for Answering Questions About Drama*
> **Step 1:** Read the Purpose Question
> **Step 2:** Read All of the Multiple-Choice Questions
> **Step 3:** Read the Drama
> **Step 4:** Reread the Question You Are Preparing to Answer
> **Step 5:** State Your Answer
> **Step 6:** Read the Answer Choices

Step 1: Read the Purpose Question

Use this question to establish your purpose for reading and focus your attention. As you already know, you will not have to answer this question.

Step 2: Read the Multiple-Choice Questions

Reading the questions before reading the passage can alert you to what information you need to find in the text. Then, as you read, you can underline or circle any ideas that you recognize as being related to the questions. This can be a big time-saver when you need to locate information in the passage and actually answer the questions.

Step 3: Read the Drama

Carefully read the drama and any information associated with it, including the cast list, stage directions, and names of the characters. All of this information is important to your understanding of the story. It may be tempting to overlook some of it, but doing so could prevent you from correctly interpreting the meaning of the text.

As you read, look for all the story elements. Identify the characters, setting, conflict, rising actions, climax, and resolution. Since the author intended the drama to be performed onstage, two tricks can be helpful in understanding this form of literature. First, visualize the actions in the drama as you read. In your mind, try to see the story as a play or a movie, the way it was meant to be experienced. Second, remember that dialogue is the main ingredient in a drama. As you read, picture what each of the characters looks like, and imagine the sounds of their voices. This can help you correctly associate each character with his or her words.

Step 4: Reread the Question You Are Preparing to Answer

We know, we know—you've already read all the questions. But you should reread each one immediately before answering it. After you have read the passage, read the first question again. Answer it, read the next question, and so on. As always, wait to read the answer choices.

Step 5: State Your Answer

Determine the best answer to the question before you actually read the answer choices. Remember that in a drama, some of the information needed to answer the questions may be found in the stage directions or in other unique places in the script. Make sure you refer to the text to find the best answer; do not try to rely on your memory alone. The GED is a long test, and you will likely have a lot on your mind on test day. You may be a little distracted during the test without even realizing it. Double-check the facts by taking a look back at the passage to find the best answer.

Step 6: Read the Answer Choices

Now go ahead and look at the answer choices. Is your answer from Step 5 among them? If so, great! If not, consider each of the choices carefully. Go beyond simply determining whether each answer is correct or incorrect; determine *why* each one is either correct or incorrect. Then select the best answer.

Examples

Let's use what you've learned in this chapter to answer some sample questions related to drama. Be sure to use the six steps.

The following is based on an excerpt from the play "The Gibson Upright" by Booth Tarkington.

What Happened While He Was Away?

ACT II

The yard beside GIBSON'S house.

Autumn has come, and the foliage is beginning to turn; but the scene is warm and sunlit.

After a moment a young housemaid brings out a tray with a chocolate pot, wafers, and one cup and saucer and a lace-edged napkin.

Ella: The cook thought you might like a cup of chocolate after a long trip like that—just getting off the train and all, Mr. Gibson.

Gibson: Thank you, Ella, I should.

Ella: I'll bring your mail right out.

[She goes into the house and returns with a packet of letters.]

Gibson: Thanks, Ella!

Ella: Everything is there that's come since you sent the telegram not to forward any more.

Gibson: It's pleasant to find the house and everything just as I left it.

Ella: My, Mr. Gibson, we pretty near thought you wasn't never coming back. Those June roses in that bed round yonder lasted pretty near up into August this year, Mr. Gibson. For that matter, it's such mild weather even yet some say we won't have any fall till Thanksgiving.

Gibson: Yes, it's extraordinary.

Ella: Shall I leave the tray?

Gibson: No, you can take it. [She moves to do so.] Wait a minute. Here's a letter from John Riley, up at the factory. Don't I remember his son Tom coming here to see you quite a good deal?

Read the following question, and use what you read in the drama to select the best answer.

Who are the characters in this part of the play?

1. Ella
2. Ella and Gibson
3. Ella, Gibson, and the cook
4. Ella, Gibson, the cook, and John Riley
5. Ella, Gibson, the cook, John Riley, and Tom

Here are our steps:

Step 1: Read the Purpose Question

What Happened While He Was Away?

Step 2: Read All of the Multiple-Choice Questions

Step 3: Read the Drama

Step 4: Reread the Question You Are Preparing to Answer

Who are the characters in this part of the play?

Step 5: State Your Answer

Ella and Gibson are involved in this part of the play; others are mentioned but do not appear.

Step 6: Read the Answer Choices

Answer choice 2 lists the only characters in this part. Answer choice 5 lists everyone who is mentioned, but these characters are not involved in this scene.

Now it's your turn. Take a look at the following question, which is based on the same drama. We'll give you the steps you will need to practice the process. Use the space provided to work through the steps.

Which best describes Ella's relationship with Gibson?

1. She is his wife.
2. She is his sister.
3. She is his neighbor.
4. She is his colleague.
5. She is his employee.

Step 1: Read the Purpose Question

_____

Step 2: Read All of the Multiple-Choice Questions

Step 3: Read the Drama

Step 4: Reread the Question You Are Preparing to Answer

_____

_____

Step 5: State Your Answer

_____

_____

Step 6: Read the Answer Choices

The correct answer is 5.

Now try another example. Look over the following question. Use the six steps to help you find the correct answer.

Which best describes the setting?

1. outside of Ella's home on a fall afternoon
2. inside Ella's home on a summer evening
3. inside Gibson's home on a fall afternoon
4. outside Gibson's home on a fall afternoon
5. outside Gibson's home on a summer evening

Step 1: Read the Purpose Question

Step 2: Read All of the Multiple Choice Questions

Step 3: Read the Drama

Step 4: Reread the Question You Are Preparing to Answer

Step 5: State Your Answer

Step 6: Read the Answer Choices

The correct answer is 4.

Try the next two examples, based on the same drama. Use the six steps to help you find the correct answer.

Which conclusion can be drawn?

1. Gibson was gone on a short business trip.
2. The play takes place during modern times.
3. Gibson has been away for quite some time.
4. All of the characters in the drama appear in this scene.
5. Ella and Gibson have known each other for many years.

Which is most likely true about the characters?

1. Gibson is fond of John Riley.
2. Gibson is a successful attorney.
3. Ella did not have much schooling.
4. Gibson has a gardener for his roses.
5. Gibson returned from his trip in September.

How do you think you did on those two questions? The correct answer to the first question is 3. Since Gibson missed the changes in the garden over summer, and he sent a telegram to stop forwarding his mail, we can conclude that he has been away for at least the summer.

The answer to the second question is also 3. Judging from Ella's grammar, we can assume that she probably is not well educated. Did you recognize why the other answer choices were incorrect? Nothing is said regarding Gibson's feelings about John Riley, so there is no way to know whether or not the men are fond of each other. We can conclude that Gibson is most likely successful, but nothing suggests his occupation. We also know that he has a cook and a house-maid, so he may have a gardener, but there is no actual evidence to suggest this. And we are told that he was away for the summer and that it is now fall, but we do not know exactly which month he returned home from his trip.

DRAMA READING COMPREHENSION DRILLS

Fill in the blanks for question 1. For each of the subsequent questions, select the best answer.

1. **What are the steps for answering questions about drama?**
   Step 1: _____
   Step 2: _____
   Step 3: _____
   Step 4: _____
   Step 5: _____
   Step 6: _____

Questions 2–7 are based on this excerpt from "Aristotle's Bellows" by Lady Gregory.

When Will He Return?

ACT I

PERSONS

> The Mother
> Celia (HER DAUGHTER)
> Conan (HER STEPSON)
> Timothy (HER SERVING MAN)
> Rock (A NEIGHBOUR)
> Flannery (HIS HERD)
> Two Cats

Scene: A room in an old half-ruined castle

Mother: Look out the door, Celia, and see is your uncle coming.

Celia: (Who is lying on the ground, a bunch of ribbons in her hand, and playing with a pigeon, looks towards door without getting up.) I see no sign of him.

Mother: What time were you telling me it was a while ago?

Celia: It is not five minutes hardly since I was telling you it was ten o'clock by the sun.

Mother: So you did, if I could but have kept it in mind. What at all ails him that he does not come in to the breakfast?

Celia: He went out last night and the full moon shining. It is likely he passed the whole night abroad, drowsing or rummaging, whatever he does be looking for in the rath.

Mother:	I'm in dread he'll go crazy with digging in it.
Celia:	He was crazy with crossness before that.
Mother:	If he is, it's on account of his learning. Them that have too much of it are seven times crosser than them that never saw a book.
Celia:	It is better to be tied to any thorny bush than to be with a cross man.

2. **What do the stage directions reveal?**
   A. The uncle is missing.
   B. Celia is a young child.
   C. The uncle lives nearby.
   D. Celia went out the previous night.
   E. The mother has not had much sleep.

3. **Which word best describes the mother?**
   A. anxious
   B. confident
   C. intelligent
   D. livid
   E. wealthy

4. **Based on the characterization used by the author, which word best describes Celia?**
   A. excited
   B. impatient
   C. jovial
   D. upset
   E. wise

5. **Which is true about this act of the drama?**
   A. It is the end of the play.
   B. It takes place in the evening.
   C. The setting is not described.
   D. There are both human and animal characters.
   E. It only involves the mother, Celia, and the uncle.

6. **What is the conflict in this section of the drama?**
   A. The uncle is crazy.
   B. The mother has not had breakfast.
   C. Celia's mother needs help telling time.
   D. The uncle went out the previous night.
   E. Celia's uncle did not come home this morning.

7. **Which describes the setting?**
   A. long ago in a shabby castle in the afternoon
   B. in a half-ruined home on a modern morning
   C. recently in a fancy throne room in the evening
   D. an exclusive home during a full moon, long ago
   E. a run-down castle in the morning, many years ago

8. **Read the following lines from the drama.**

   Mother: What time were you telling me it was a while ago?

   Celia: It is not five minutes hardly since I was telling you it was ten o'clock by the sun.

   Which is an example of a text-to-self connection that could be made with this part of the script?
   A. My mom gave me a watch as a gift for my birthday once.
   B. I know that long ago people used to tell the time by looking at the sun.
   C. I read a book once in which the characters were a mother and daughter.
   D. I remember being nervous about something and repeatedly checking the time.
   E. My coworkers and I usually take a breakfast break at ten o'clock in the morning.

chapter **20**

Interpreting Nonfiction

What's Being Tested?

As you know, 75 percent of the reading selections you will find on the GED Language Arts, Reading test will be fiction. That means the remaining 25 percent will be nonfiction, or factual, passages. There will be two nonfiction passages that are either prose, reviews of visual and performing arts, or workplace and community documents. That means you may have to read legal documents, manuals, or other types of employee communications.

After reading, you will answer questions that require you to show how well you understood the material. This may call for making inferences, summarizing the information, identifying relationships between ideas, and interpreting the text. In this chapter, we will review a few comprehension strategies to help you do your best on this section.

Comprehension Skills for Nonfiction

Nonfiction writing is different than fiction writing in several ways. For example, since the purpose of nonfiction is generally to share information, you will not usually see the story elements that are common to fiction passages. Sure, a true story about an actual person will include characters and a plot. However, a literature review, employee handbook, or company mission statement will not.

With that in mind, recognizing other characteristics of nonfiction can improve your comprehension of the material. Let's take a look at some of the skills that will prove helpful.

Identifying the Main Idea and Supporting Details

In Chapter 6, we discussed the main idea and supporting details, so you already know that these are important to writing. Recognizing them in a nonfiction reading passage can help you organize the information and gain a better understanding of the text.

The **main idea** is the most important point the author wants to make. It is the central message of the text, the single most important idea the author wants you to gain from the passage. In reality, sharing the main idea is the author's reason for writing a nonfiction piece.

The **supporting details** are the facts, examples, and definitions the author uses to explain the main idea so that you clearly understand the most important piece of information.

To identify the main idea, you must first recognize the topic of the passage. The **topic** is what the passage is about and can generally be identified in one word, or possibly a couple of words. For example, *dress code* might be a topic.

Once you recognize the topic, ask yourself what idea about the topic was so important to the author that he or she wrote a passage about it. The main idea is a complete sentence and tells what the author wants to share about the topic.

Employees will be required to follow new dress code guidelines.

After identifying the main idea, look for details that support it.

All employees must wear closed-toe shoes. Jeans will not be permitted. Male employees must wear collared shirts.

Each paragraph of a nonfiction passage contains its own main idea, which is generally one of the supporting details of the overall paragraph. For example, take a look at the following paragraph. One of the supporting details about the new employee dress code is the main idea of this paragraph, which supports the main idea of the overall passage.

Male employees must wear collared shirts. These shirts may either be polo-style or button ups, and they can have either long or short sleeves. Men may wear a necktie with these shirts; however, neckwear is not required.

Distinguishing Facts and Opinions

Facts are true statements that can be proven or verified. Nonfiction texts will contain mostly facts.

All employees in the company are at least 18 years of age.

Opinions are personal views that cannot be verified.

Everyone should have some work experience by the time they reach 16 years of age.

Being able to differentiate between facts and opinions can help readers evaluate the importance of statements. In a nonfiction text, facts provide the information about the topic; opinions tell how the writer feels about it.

Summarizing Information

Being able to restate the most important information from a passage in your own words shows how well you understood what you read. When summarizing information, be sure to include the main idea and key details, since these are the most pertinent facts. A summary of our dress code example might look like the following:

The dress code requires male employees to wear collared shirts; both males and females must have closed-toe shoes and must not wear jeans.

Making Inferences

Making inferences is similar to drawing conclusions. Authors will suggest information without stating it directly. Readers then consider the information in the text, as well as their own knowledge and experiences, and read between the lines to fully understand the selection. The key to making inferences is to focus on ideas that are implied and steer away from guessing.

Recognizing the Organizational Structure

As we discussed in Chapter 6, text can be organized in various ways, depending on the type of information being shared and the purpose of the passage. Recognizing the **organizational structure**, or the way the writer chose to arrange the information, can help you identify what type of information will likely be found in the text and lets you know what information to look for as you read. The way information is organized tells you how the ideas are related.

Cause and Effect

When a **cause-and-effect** structure is used, the author focuses on how ideas or events are related. An event that makes something else happen is a **cause**; the resulting event or events are **effects**. When a cause is discussed in a passage, you know to look for effects. If you recognize effects, read to find out why they happened.

Classification

Some writers elect to group related ideas together in a **classification** structure. The information is arranged so that it is categorized according to similarities. When you recognize this structure in a passage, watch for several ideas that have something in common and then look for another set of ideas that have something in common.

Compare and Contrast

A **compare-and-contrast** organizational structure focuses on similarities and differences between the topics being discussed. When you recognize that the author is using this structure, you know to look for ways in which the topics are alike and ways in which they are different.

Authors may use this structure in one of two ways. They may completely describe the first topic and then completely describe the second. This is known as **whole-to-whole comparison**. On the other hand, authors may use **part-to-part comparisons**, in which both topics are discussed in light of one aspect, and then both are discussed in light of another, and so on.

Description

A **description** is exactly what it sounds like; a topic is introduced and its characteristics are described. Recognizing this structure is a red flag that you should expect to find facts and details that explain and clarify the topic.

Problem and Solution

Can you guess how this organizational structure works? When a **problem-and-solution** structure is used, a problem is introduced; then one or more possible ways of solving it are discussed. So when you encounter this type of organization, you know to keep an eye out for the problem and then search for solutions.

Sequence

Sequence is the order in which events and ideas are presented in a passage. **Time order** means that the sequence of events is chronological. **Order of importance** means exactly what it says; the events and ideas are presented according to which ones are most important. Some passages are arranged to present ideas in order from most to least important; others go from least to most important.

What to Do

Now that you are familiar with the comprehension skills that will help you understand the nonfiction passages on the GED, what should you do with all this information? We're glad you asked! Here are the six steps you will use to answer the questions. They are much like the steps you will use to answer other types of reading comprehension questions, so they probably look familiar. But be sure to read the information explaining each step. There are some differences in the ways you will approach questions about nonfiction selections.

Let's go over the six steps one more time.

Steps for Answering Questions About Nonfiction

Step 1: Read the Purpose Question

Step 2: Read All of the Multiple-Choice Questions

Step 3: Read the Passage

Step 4: Reread the Question You Are Preparing to Answer

Step 5: State Your Answer

Step 6: Read the Answer Choices

Step 1: Read the Purpose Question

Although you do not have to answer the purpose question, it can be helpful in focusing your attention on the type of information that will be included in the passage. It can also be a great tool in helping you predict what information you may encounter in the selection.

Step 2: Read All of the Multiple-Choice Questions

You may be thinking, *Isn't it a waste of time to read the questions first, since I'll have to read them again later?* Not at all! Taking a sneak peak at the questions ahead of time can let you know what information to look for as you read. Then, when you come across this information in the selection, the answers will grab your attention. You can underline, circle, or put a star beside any information you want to be able to locate quickly when selecting answers to the questions. This time-saving strategy can come in extremely handy, since you will be working within a time limit on the GED.

Suppose one of the questions asks for the meaning of the word *converse* as it is used in the passage. By reading the questions prior to reading the passage, you will know to look for this word in the text. When you encounter it, you can circle the word, use context clues to define it, and make a mental note of its meaning. Then, when answering the questions, you can quickly locate the circled word to double-check the answer. If, on the other hand, you do *not* read the questions, the word *converse* will not be significant to you when you come across it in the passage, and you will not pay any special attention to it. Then, when you read the questions after completing the text, you may be left scratching your head and thinking, *I know I saw that word somewhere. Where was that?* And you will have to look through the entire passage again to locate and define the word. That will be an unnecessary waste of the precious minutes available to complete the test. Tick-tock, tick-tock; wisely use the time on the clock.

Step 3: Read the Passage

Be sure to read the entire passage, even if the questions appear to be super-simple and the topic is something you could easily write a book about on your own. You might have been president of the science club, built model rockets since you were old enough to say "Blast off!" and seen video footage of every launch NASA ever made, but that does not mean you should skip reading a passage about the space shuttle.

As you read, mentally evaluate the information. Sort facts from opinions, distinguish supporting details from irrelevant information, and determine how the passage is organized. Do not just read; think about what you are reading.

Keep in Mind

Keep in mind that reading for pleasure is different than reading for information. When reading for information, your purpose is to learn something or to locate facts. To do this, focus on the details as you read. Monitor your comprehension of the selection by stopping periodically to think about how well you understand the passage. If you are unsure about any of the information or do not completely understand the text, go back and reread the section that is unclear. Continuing to read when you are not 100 percent sure of the previous information can prevent you from fully comprehending the remainder of the passage as well.

Step 4: Reread the Question You Are Preparing to Answer

Read the questions as carefully and completely as you read the passage. Overlooking a single word such as *not* or *except* can completely change what the question is asking. If extra information is given within a question, be sure to use it. If the question refers to a certain sentence or paragraph, check it out. It may be helpful to restate the question in your own words or to underline key words and phrases in the question. Make sure you understand exactly what is being asked. As always, wait to read the answer choices.

Step 5: State Your Answer

Once you have read the question and are sure you understand exactly what it is asking, use the information in the story to compose your answer. Remember that many of the questions will require analyzing the text, piecing information together, summarizing facts, and inferring meaning, as opposed to simply restating a few words from the passage. Carefully think about what you read, and use the information to answer the question completely.

Keep in Mind

Keep in mind that all of the correct answers are based solely on information included in the passage, not on what you might already know about the topic. Sure, you may happen on a topic that you already know a ton about. That's great, because you can easily make connections, and you have the opportunity to read about something you are interested in. However, you should not consider any of your prior knowledge when selecting the best answer.

Step 6: Read the Answer Choices

You have carefully and completely read the passage and the question; now carefully and completely read each of the answer choices. Remember that several of the options may be partially correct. Only one is entirely correct. See if your answer from Step 5 is among the choices. Once you select the best answer, explain to yourself why it is correct and why the others are not.

Examples

Let's take a look at a couple of sample questions and use the six steps to answer each. Here we go!

How Does One Species Protect Another?

The Anatolian shepherd is a breed of guard dog originally from areas of Turkey and Asia Minor. These large canines are known for their terrific eyesight and keen sense of hearing, as well as for being very dedicated to their herd. These qualities have allowed them to become protectors of an endangered species that is generally their enemy, the cheetah.

The number of cheetahs has declined by nearly 90 percent since 1900, leaving only between 10,000 and 12,000 worldwide. One of the reasons for the decrease of the fastest land animal is the fact that these cats feed on livestock in areas where their natural prey is not plentiful. As a result, farmers have killed the cheetahs in order to protect their herds.

Anatolian shepherds have been used to guard livestock for hundreds of years. In 1994, the Cheetah Conservation Fund's Anatolian Shepherd Livestock Guarding Dog program in Namibia introduced the dogs as a way to protect farmers' herds in Africa without harming the cheetah predators. Young Anatolian shepherds were raised with the livestock. When cheetahs or other animals threaten their herd, the dogs bark to frighten the intruders, who then run away.

Now the cheetahs are not being killed for attacking the livestock. And the livestock is no longer being preyed upon by the cheetahs. By protecting its herd, the Anatolian shepherd is also protecting the cheetah.

Now answer the following questions based on the nonfiction passage.

Which most likely states the opinion of the author?

1. Farmers using the dogs are no longer losing their livestock to predators.
2. Cheetahs are the most dangerous predator attacking the farmers' herds.
3. Anatolian shepherds are protective of the herds with which they are raised.
4. Purchasing an Anatolian shepherd would be a wise investment for farmers.
5. Predators that attack livestock should be stopped by any means necessary.

Here are our steps:

Step 1: Read the Purpose Question

Step 2: Read All of the Multiple-Choice Questions

Step 3: Read the Passage

Step 4: Reread the Question You Are Preparing to Answer

Which most likely states the opinion of the author? This is asking us to infer which statement is an opinion with which the author would probably agree. The correct answer will not be a fact, even if the statement is true.

Step 5: State Your Answer

The author seems to think that the dogs are a good way to protect the herds. He or she also seems to believe that the dogs are beneficial to the cheetahs and to the farmers.

Step 6: Read the Answer Choices

Answer choice 4 reflects the same ideas stated in Step 5. Several of the other answer choices include facts rather than opinions. The other opinion listed does not seem to agree with the beliefs of the author.

Now you try one. Answer the following question, which is based on the same passage. We'll give you the steps you will need to practice the process.

Which does *not* correctly state a cause-and-effect relationship discussed in the passage?

1. There are more of the dogs in Africa as a result of the cheetahs increasing in number.
2. The cheetahs' food supply was insufficient; therefore, they began to approach the farmers' herds.
3. The number of cheetahs is increasing because the dogs do not kill them when they approach the herds.
4. Cheetah populations are no longer declining because the cats are retreating from potentially deadly situations.
5. Anatolian shepherds have historically provided protection for herd animals, since these dogs are devoted by nature.

Step 1: Read the Purpose Question

Step 2: Read All of the Multiple-Choice Questions

Step 3: Read the Passage

Step 4: Reread the Question You Are Preparing to Answer

_____

_____

Step 5: State Your Answer

_____

_____

Step 6: Read the Answer Choices

The correct answer is 1.

NONFICTION READING COMPREHENSION DRILLS

Fill in the blanks for question 1. For each of the subsequent questions, choose the best answer.

1. **What are the steps for answering questions about nonfiction?**
   Step 1: _____
   Step 2: _____
   Step 3: _____
   Step 4: _____
   Step 5: _____
   Step 6: _____

Questions 2–8 are based on the following passage.

How Will These Changes Affect the Employees?

To: All Employees

From: Dwayne Callahan, director of human resources

As you are aware, our company has recently come under new management. Many changes will be taking place as a result of this restructuring. Many of these changes will affect our product lines. There will also be several changes that will affect you, our valued employees.

First, a new evaluation system will be put in place as of the first of next month. Under this new system, employee performance will be reviewed each quarter. Each employee will complete a self-evaluation checklist prior to his or her individual conference with a group of three management representatives. During the conference, the team will discuss the checklist, as well as the employee's progress toward performance goals and the observations of the direct supervisor. Employee performance will then be rated on a five-point scale, with five being the highest score. Employees receiving an exemplary review will receive an increase in hourly wages.

Another change will be the implementation of a bonus system based on customer satisfaction surveys. Each quarter, the department earning the highest scores on these surveys will be rewarded. Each employee in the department will earn a bonus based on the number of hours worked during that time period. This is a fair means of determining the size of each employee's bonus.

The final change that we are pleased to share with you is the addition of three more paid vacation days each year. Current guidelines for requesting vacation time will remain in place. These days are available immediately.

We appreciate your dedication during the recent change of management. We look forward to implementing these changes for our employees and believe that they will have a positive impact on our staff.

2. **What organizational structure is used for the overall passage?**
    A. sequence
    B. classification
    C. cause and effect
    D. order of importance
    E. compare and contrast

3. **What organizational structure is demonstrated in the second paragraph?**
    A. description
    B. classification
    C. problem and solution
    D. question and answer
    E. compare and contrast

4. **Which is the main idea of the passage?**
    A. Additional paid vacation time will be offered.
    B. The company has recently come under new management.
    C. Employees will be subjected to a new system of evaluations.
    D. Upcoming changes in the company will affect the employees.
    E. Employees will earn bonuses based on customer satisfaction.

5. **Which statement can be inferred by reading the section?**
    A. Customer satisfaction surveys are only used in some of the departments.
    B. Employees with lower evaluation scores will not receive an increase in salary.
    C. Employees with less than adequate scores on their reviews will be terminated.
    D. Those working in larger departments have a greater likelihood of earning bonuses.
    E. Bonuses given to full-time employees will be double those of part-time employees.

6. **Which of the following statements from the passage is an opinion?**
    A. As you are aware, our company has recently come under new management.
    B. There will also be several changes that will affect you, our valued employees.
    C. Each employee will complete a self-evaluation checklist prior to his or her individual conference with a group of three management representatives.
    D. This is a fair means of determining the size of each employee's bonus.
    E. The final change that we are pleased to share with you is the addition of three more paid vacation days each year.

7. **Which best summarizes the passage?**

   A. Three additional paid vacation days are available to all employees, effective immediately.

   B. Employees have the opportunity to earn bonuses if their department receives the highest scores on customer satisfaction surveys.

   C. Many of these changes will affect our product lines; however, there will also be several changes that will affect our valued employees.

   D. Upcoming changes that will affect the employees include a new evaluation system, a bonus opportunity, and an increase in the amount of vacation time.

   E. The new employee evaluation system includes a self-checklist, an interview with a team of management representatives, and progress toward performance goals.

8. **Which of the following statements is a fact that can be inferred from information in the passage?**

   A. The new system of evaluations will be an improvement over the current plan.

   B. The changes being put in place have the potential to benefit the employees.

   C. All of the employees will earn a bonus for positive customer survey results.

   D. Employees will be able to take time off anytime they would like.

   E. Bonuses given in the past were not large enough.

Part VI

Mathematics

Whole Numbers and Operations

The GED Math test is divided into two 45-minute sections, each containing 25 questions. The good news is that you will be given a calculator to use for Part I of the test! The bad news is you may not use it for Part II. The other good news is that you will be given a formula sheet that includes any formulas you will need to use on the test.

The majority of the questions—80 percent to be exact—are multiple choice. For the remaining 20 percent, you will record your answer on a standard grid or on a coordinate plane grid. Questions relating to number operations and number sense will make up between 20 and 30 percent of the test items, respectively. In this chapter, we will review whole numbers and operations; number sense will be the topic of the next chapter.

Basically, **whole numbers** are not fractions or decimals. **Operations** include the big four: *addition, subtraction, multiplication,* and *division*. So, in the next few pages, you can expect to review adding, subtracting, multiplying, and dividing numbers that are not fractions or decimals. We will also throw in a little review of exponents and square roots. Let's get started.

Words Related to Whole Numbers

Before we talk about the four operations you will use on the GED Math test, let's go over some vocabulary related to whole numbers.

Even numbers are those that are divisible by 2: 0, 2, 4, 6, 8, 10, 12, 14 . . .

Odd numbers are not evenly divisible by 2: 1, 3, 5, 7, 9, 11, 13, 15 . . .

Consecutive numbers follow one another in counting order: 5, 6, 7, 8 . . .

Prime numbers are evenly divisible only by 1 and themselves: 3, 5, 7, 11, 13, 17 . . .

Composite numbers are evenly divisible by a number besides 1 and themselves. For example, 4 is a composite number, because it is evenly divisible by 1, 2, and 4; 12 is a composite number, because it is evenly divisible by 1, 2, 3, 4, 6, and 12.

Factors are numbers by which another number is evenly divisible. For example, the factors of 10 are 1, 2, 5, and 10, because 10 can be divided evenly by these numbers.

Operations

As you know, the four basic operations used in math are addition, subtraction, multiplication, and division.

Addition

The numbers being added together in addition are the **addends**; the total is the **sum**.

$$3 + 2 = 5$$

In this example, 3 and 2 are the addends, and 5 is the sum.

Clue words such as *in all, altogether, increase,* and *total* often suggest that a problem calls for addition.

Subtraction

The answer to a subtraction problem is the **difference**. Two other words you might encounter when dealing with subtractions are **subtrahend** and **minuend**. In a subtraction problem, the minuend is the amount you start off with and the subtrahend is the amount you take away from it. The difference is, well, the "difference"—the solution to that problem, as just explained.

$$7 - 4 = 3$$

In this example, 3 is the difference.

Clue words such as *decrease*, *have left*, and *less than* often indicate that subtraction is needed.

Multiplication

The numbers being multiplied are the **factors**; the answer is the **product**.

$$5 \times 6 = 30$$

In this example, 5 and 6 are the factors, and 30 is the product.

Clue words such as *by*, *times*, and *twice* often suggest that multiplication should be used to solve a problem.

Division

The number being divided is the **dividend**; the number that is divided into the dividend is the **divisor**; and the answer is the **quotient**.

$$24 \div 3 = 8$$

In this example, 24 is the dividend, 3 is the divisor, and 8 is the quotient.

Clue words such as *average*, *equal parts*, and *per* may indicate that division is required to find the correct answer.

Exponents and Roots

An **exponent** is a small number positioned slightly higher and to the right of another number; it indicates repeated multiplication. For example, 4^3 is read as "four to the third power." Here, 4 is the **base**, and 3 is the exponent. The exponent tells how many times the base should be multiplied by itself: $4^3 = 4 \times 4 \times 4 = 64$.

On the Casio fx-260 calculator, which is issued during the GED test, use the x^2 key to solve exponents.

When an exponent is 2, we say that the number is *squared*. For example, 7^2 is read as "seven squared." **Square numbers** are those that result from multiplying a number by itself. Square numbers are the product of two identical factors.

$$2^2 = 2 \times 2 = 4$$
$$3^2 = 3 \times 3 = 9$$
$$4^2 = 4 \times 4 = 16$$
$$5^2 = 5 \times 5 = 25$$

and so on. Numbers such as 4, 9, 16, and 25 are squares.

The opposite of exponents are **roots**. The **square root** is the number that can be multiplied by itself to equal a given number: $36 = 6^2$. Since $6 \times 6 = 36$, 6 is the square root of 36. The symbol $\sqrt{}$ indicates square root: $\sqrt{36} = 6$.

On the calculator you will be given during the test, use the $\sqrt{}$ key to find roots.

Order of Operations

Some math problems require using more than one operation. In this case, it is necessary to solve the operations according to a certain sequence. The **order of operations** is a set of rules stating the order in which operations must be performed.

- Parentheses
- Exponents
- Multiplication, from left to right
- Division, from left to right
- Addition, from left to right
- Subtraction, from left to right

Keep in Mind

Keep in mind that solving arithmetic problems from left to right, or in any other sequence that does not follow the order of operations, may result in the wrong answer. To remember the correct sequence, take a look at the first letter of *each* of the steps: P, E, M, D, A, and S. The saying *Please excuse my dear Aunt Sally* is often used as a reminder of the order of operations, since each word in the phrase begins with the same letters as the steps.

Gridding Answers

As you know, most of the questions on the GED Math test will be multiple choice; however, some will be gridded response items. That means you will have to mark your answers on a number grid. Once you find the correct answer, it will be important to record it correctly on the grid.

First, write your answer in the boxes at the top of each column of the grid, making sure that all answers are aligned to the right. Write one digit, decimal point, or fraction bar in each box. Then, completely shade one bubble in each column to correspond to the number or character written at the top of the column.

You may find that you have more columns than you need. That's fine. You may leave any extra columns blank.

Keep in Mind

Keep in mind that there will not be a minus symbol on the grids, so negative numbers cannot be gridded. That means, all gridded response answers will be positive numbers. So if you come up with a negative answer, double-check your work.

What to Do

What process should we use to solve problems involving whole number operations? Great question! Let's go over the six steps.

> ### *Whole Number Operations Steps*
>
> Step 1:   Read the Problem
> Step 2:   Determine What Is Being Asked
> Step 3:   Identify Pertinent Information and Key Words
> Step 4:   Choose Which Operation(s) to Use
> Step 5:   Solve the Problem
> Step 6:   Check Your Work

Step 1: Read the Problem

Most of the questions on the GED Math test are word problems. Just like any other question involving words, read everything very carefully. Look for words such as *not* or *except*, which can completely change the question.

Step 2: Determine What Is Being Asked

After reading the problem, make sure you understand what the question is asking you to find. For instance, a question may mention that an item is on sale. You could be asked to determine the sale price, the original price, the amount of sales tax charged, the total price including tax, the amount of the discount, or the total cost for purchasing several of the same item. Make sure you know exactly what the question is asking.

Step 3: Identify Pertinent Information

Here's a little test-taking secret: some math problems include more information than is needed to solve the problem. Yes, it is sneaky but true. To correctly solve the problem, you must determine which pieces of information are important and which are not. When a problem includes the word *sum*, it may be tempting to add all of the numbers you can find. However, extra numbers may have been written into the problem. Including these would result in an incorrect answer.

Once you have figured out what the question is asking, you should be able to determine what information will be necessary to solve the problem. Reread the question, underlining or circling the numbers or information that you will need to find the correct answer. Cross out any information that you will not need to use.

Step 4: Choose Which Operation(s) to Use

Look for key words in the question that offer hints about which operation, or operations, will be required to solve the problem. These clues can be a great help! However, not every problem will be straightforward. Think about what is being asked and then decide what operations you need to use.

Step 5: Solve the Problem

Use the order of operations to solve the problem. Be sure to show each step as you work. Not only will this help you focus on using the correct process, but it can also come in handy if you determine that you've made a mistake. Rather than having to start over from scratch, you can see where the error occurred and rework the problem from that point.

Step 6: Check Your Work

Once you have solved the math question, go back and check your work. Look over the steps you used, make sure you correctly applied the order of operations, and double-check that you carried out each operation accurately. It is easy to make careless mistakes when you are working quickly. Leaving out a negative sign, not regrouping an addition or subtraction problem correctly, or reversing the base and the exponent can make a huge difference in your answer.

Next, think about the problem and determine whether or not your answer is reasonable. For example, if the question asks for the cost of an item including tax, a reasonable answer would be slightly higher than the original cost. If your answer is *less* than the original cost, your answer is not reasonable. Likewise, if your answer is *double* the original cost, it is not reasonable.

Keep in Mind

Keep in mind that just because your answer is among the answer choices, it is not necessarily correct. The incorrect choices are based on common errors and misconceptions. They reflect incorrect answers that test takers are likely to come up with. Even if your answer is among the choices, it is still important to double-check your work

Examples

Let's look at some sample questions involving the skills we reviewed in this chapter.

A bookstore is having a three-day sale that offers customers a 20 percent discount on all items. Leroy finds several books by his favorite author on sale for $14.75 each. What is the final price of four books, including 6 percent sales tax?

1. $46.91
2. $50.03
3. $59.00
4. $60.77
5. $62.54

Here are our steps:

Step 1: Read the Problem

Step 2: Determine What Is Being Asked

Find the final cost of four books, plus tax.

Step 3: Identify Pertinent Information

We need to know that the books are $14.75 each, he wants four books, and tax is 6 percent. We do not need to know that it is a three-day sale or that the items are 20 percent off, since the sale price is already given. Here's what the problem might look like if we underlined important information and crossed off unnecessary ideas.

Leroy finds several books by his favorite author <u>on sale for $14.75 each</u>. What is the <u>final price of four books, including 6 percent sales tax</u>?

Step 4: Choose Which Operation(s) to Use

We will multiply $14.75 by 4 to find the price of the books and then multiply the result by 1.06 to find the price including tax.

Step 5: Solve the Problem

$14.75 \times 4 = $59.00

$59.00 \times 1.06 = $62.54

Step 6: Check Your Work

Now it's your turn. Take a look at the following sample problem. We'll give you the steps you will need to practice the process.

The art museum has a special exhibit on display for the weekend. Tickets are $15 each. On Saturday, 462 people attended the exhibit, and on Sunday, 513 people attended. Which shows the total dollar amount of the tickets sold for both days?

1. $15 + 462 + 513$
2. $15 \times 462 + 513$
3. $15(462 + 513)$
4. $462 + 513 \times 15$
5. $(462 \times 15) + 513$

Step 1: Read the Problem

Step 2: Determine What Is Being Asked

_____

_____

Step 3: Identify Pertinent Information

_____

_____

Step 4: Choose Which Operation(s) to Use

_____

_____

Step 5: Solve the Problem

_____

_____

_____

_____

Step 6: Check Your Work

The correct answer is 3.

Now try another example. Look over the following problem. Use the six steps to help you find the correct answer and the space provided to work through the steps.

The square root of 2,975 is between which pair of numbers?

1. 50 and 60
2. 60 and 70
3. 70 and 80
4. 80 and 90
5. 90 and 100

Step 1: Read the Problem

Step 2: Determine What Is Being Asked

_____

_____

Step 3: Identify Pertinent Information

_____

_____

Step 4: Choose Which Operation(s) to Use

_____

_____

Step 5: Solve the Problem

_____

_____

_____

_____

Step 6: Check Your Work

The correct answer is 1.

WHOLE NUMBER AND OPERATIONS DRILLS

Fill in the blanks for question 1. For each of the subsequent questions, choose the best answer.

1. What are the steps for solving whole number and operations problems?

    Step 1: _____

    Step 2: _____

    Step 3: _____

    Step 4: _____

    Step 5: _____

    Step 6: _____

2. Which of the following problems has an answer called a *product*?

    A. 12(8)

    B. 25 – 17

    C. $\sqrt{64}$

    D. 15 + 13

    E. 81/9

3. Which of the following is equal to $144 \div (9 - 3)$?

    A. $6 \times 2 + 1$

    B. $4 + 5 \times 4$

    C. $36 \div 2 - 2$

    D. $2 \times (12 + 4)$

    E. $36 \div (5 - 2)$

4. Keisha is buying a new washing machine, which is on sale for $1,479. She can either pay the entire amount at the time of purchase or make a down payment of $250 and make monthly payments of $125 for one year. How much more will it cost her to choose the payment plan than to pay the full sale price?

    A. $21

    B. $102

    C. $229

    D. $271

    E. $3,021

5. Evaluate the expression.

$7 + 8(15 - 9)^2$

A. 8,100
B. 2,311
C. 540
D. 295
E. 70

6. Hunter bought a new computer desk that was on clearance for $485 and a chair for $199. The desk was originally $350 more than the price he paid for it. What was the original price of the desk?

A. $835
B. $684
C. $450
D. $334
E. $135

Questions 7 and 8 are based on the following information.

The owners of an apartment complex took out a loan for $35,000 to remodel some of the units. They put new carpeting in 12 of the units for $975 each and bought new appliances for 8 of the units for $1,350 each. They also repainted the interior of 15 of the units.

7. How much of the loan money do they have left after purchasing the carpeting and appliances?

A. $22,500
B. $16,400
C. $12,500
D. $11,700
E. $10,800

8. The owners paid a total of $2,460 for paint. If the same amount of paint was used for each of the apartments, what was the cost of paint per unit?

A. $70.29
B. $123
C. $164
D. $205
E. $307.50

9. On Friday, Saturday, and Sunday, a theater sold 665 tickets each day for a newly released movie. The theater sold 220 fewer tickets per day from Monday through Thursday. Which shows how to find the total number of tickets sold during the seven-day period?

   A. $3 \times 665 + 4 \times 665 - 220$

   B. $3 \times 665 + 4(665 - 220)$

   C. $3 \times 665 + 4 \times 220$

   D. $7 \times (665 - 220)$

   E. $7 \times 665 - 220$

10. A chef purchased 26 pounds of beef, 38 pounds of chicken, and 16 pounds of pork. He prepared an equal amount of meat for each of four dinner parties. Which explains how to find the number of pounds of meat he served at each party?

   A. add 26, 38, and 16; then divide the total by 4

   B. add 26 and 38; then add 16 divided by 4

   C. add 26, 38, and 16; then subtract 4

   D. divide 26 and 38 by 4; then add 16

   E. multiply 26, 38, and 16 by 4

Number Sense

What's Being Tested?

In this chapter, we will review a few things about how numbers work. As you know, where a digit appears in a number affects its value. As you also know, there are times when an estimate is good enough, and an exact answer is not necessary. Understanding skills such as these and being comfortable applying them is important to doing your best on the GED Math Test.

Classifying Numbers

Before we begin reviewing the skills you will use to answer the GED Math questions, let's go over the terms that are used to identify different types of numbers.

Natural Numbers

Natural numbers are those we use when we count, beginning with 1: 1, 2, 3, 4, 5 . . .

Whole Numbers

Whole numbers include all of the natural numbers, as well as 0: 0, 1, 2, 3, 4, 5 . . .

Integers

The whole numbers, as well as the negatives of the natural numbers, are **integers**: . . . –5, –4, –3, –2, –1, 0, 1, 2, 3, 4, 5 . . .

Rational Numbers

Integers and the fractions formed by dividing one integer by another are **rational numbers**. Rational numbers can be written as a fraction or a ratio, and they include decimals, repeating decimals, and terminating decimals. Take a look at a few examples of rational numbers: 7/8, 3¼, 0.721, 0.592592592 . . ., 8.3.

Irrational Numbers

As we just discussed, rational numbers can be written as fractions. **Irrational numbers**, on the other hand, cannot be written as fractions. Square roots of numbers that are not perfect squares are irrational. Decimals that are nonterminating or nonrepeating are also irrational. Check out a few examples of irrational numbers: $\sqrt{5}$, 0.325487 . . . , π.

Real Numbers

Real numbers are any that can name a position on a number line, and they include all rational and irrational numbers: –17.5, 0 26, 0.59204 . . ., 5/6, $\sqrt{23}$.

Place Value

The position of each digit in a number determines its value. Take a look at the 4 in each of the following numbers.

2<u>4</u>

<u>4</u>7

<u>4</u>91

In 24, the 4 is in the ones place, giving it the value of 4 ones, which is 4. In 47, it is in the tens place, giving it the value of 4 tens, which is 40. In 491, it is in the hundreds place, giving it the value of 4 hundreds, or 400.

From right to left, here is the place value of the digits in a number:

Ones

Tens

Hundreds

Thousands

Ten thousands

Hundred thousands

Millions

Ten millions

Hundred millions

Billions

That means that the value of the 4 in 5,348,912 is 4 ten thousands, or 40,000.

Rounding Numbers

When a number is rounded, it ends with a zero. When we round numbers to the nearest ten, for example, we find the ten to which the number is closest (10, 20, 30, 40, 50, and so on). Each place value to the right of the tens will be a zero. For example, 58 rounded to the nearest ten is 60, because 60 is the ten that is closest to 58 on a number line.

When we round to the nearest hundred, we find the hundred to which the number is closest (0, 100, 200, 300, and so on). Each place value to the right of the hundreds place will be a zero. So there will be a zero in the tens and ones places. For example, 732 rounded to the nearest hundred is 700, because 732 is closer to 700 than 800 on a number line.

To round a number, underline the digit in the place to which it is being rounded. For example, when rounding to the nearest ten, underline the digit in the tens place. When rounding to the nearest hundred, underline the digit in the hundreds place.

Then look at the digit immediately to the right of the underlined digit. If the number is less than 5, do not change the underlined digit. If the number to the right is 5 or greater, round up by increasing the underlined digit by 1. Change all digits to the right of the underlined number to zero.

Round 82,764 to the nearest thousand.

Underline the place value to which we are rounding.

82,764

Look at the digit to the right, which in this example is 7. Since 7 is greater than 5, we will change the underlined digit by adding 1 to it. Then change the hundreds, tens, and ones places to zeros.

83,000

Estimating

Suppose you went to a concert in a venue that accommodates 3,000 people. The concert was nearly sold out. You might make an educated guess and say that about 2,800 people were there. This is not an exact amount; you did not actually count every single person in the audience. This amount is an **estimate**, or an approximate value. Sometimes, an estimate is good enough. You do not need to know an exact answer.

One way to estimate is **front-end estimation**, in which you round a number to the greatest place value. For example, the greatest place value in 26,983 is the ten thousands place. Front-end estimation would round this number to the nearest ten thousand, or 27,000.

Keep in Mind

Keep in mind that estimation can be great for determining the reasonableness of a computed answer. After performing the operations to find an exact answer, you can estimate approximately what the answer should be and then make sure the answer you came up with is about right.

Properties of Numbers

You probably learned about the properties of numbers way back in elementary school, but by now you have had plenty of time to forget all about them. The good news is that whether you realize it or not, you most likely use these mathematical rules without even thinking. Let's see if any of them ring a bell.

Commutative Property of Addition

Basically, this rule states that the order of the addends does not matter.

$$a + b = b + a$$

Let's try it out.

$$3 + 5 = 5 + 3$$

Yep. Both sides equal 8, so the order of the addends did not make any difference. The same holds true even when a whole list of numbers is added together.

Commutative Property of Multiplication

Like the commutative property of addition, this rule states that the order of the factors will not affect the product. In other words, when we multiply, the numbers can be in any order.

$$a \times b = b \times a$$

Take a look at the example.

$$2 \times 6 = 6 \times 2$$

Both sides equal 12, so it does not matter which factor is listed first. Again, this is true if you are multiplying three, four, five, or even more numbers.

Associative Property of Addition

This rule refers to the fact that addends can be grouped, or associated, in any way without changing the sum.

$$(a + b) + c = a + (b + c)$$

Let's see how this works using real numbers.

$$(5 + 2) + 8 = 5 + (2 + 8)$$

The way the addends are grouped on the left side, $(5 + 2) + 8$, results in $7 + 8$. Suppose you want to group addends together to form a set of 10. By grouping the 2 and 8 together, as on the right side, you can add $5 + 10$.

Associative Property of Multiplication

Just like the associative property of addition, this multiplication rule states that factors can be grouped in any way. This can come in handy when you find it easier to multiply certain factors together first.

$$(a \times b) \times c = a \times (b \times c)$$

Take a look at the problem below.

$$(17 \times 25) \times 4$$

Multiplying 17×25 would probably require you to write down the factors and work out the problem the long way. But check this out:

$$17 \times (25 \times 4)$$

You already know that $25 \times 4 = 100$. So by grouping these factors together, you can now multiply them first and then multiply 17×100.

$$17 \times (25 \times 4) = 17 \times 100 = 1,700$$

Easy peasy! Grouping the factors differently turned a long multiplication problem into one you could do in your head.

Distributive Property of Addition

This addition rule actually involves both addition and multiplication. Basically, it means that multiplication is distributed over addition.

$$a(b + c) = ab + ac$$

As you can see on the left side of the equation, a is being multiplied by the sum of $b + c$. On the right side, a is multiplied by b and then multiplied by c, and the products are added together. Let's see what this looks like using actual numbers.

$$5(7 + 4) = 5 \times 7 + 5 \times 4$$

$$5(11) = 35 + 20$$

$$55 = 55$$

Distributive Property of Subtraction

This property is essentially the same as the previous one, except that it includes multiplication and subtraction rather than multiplication and addition.

$$a(b - c) = ab - ac$$

Now take a look at an example.

$$8(6 - 4) = 8 \times 6 - 8 \times 4$$

$$8(2) = 48 - 32$$

$$16 = 16$$

Using this property, you can either subtract first and then multiply the difference by 8, or you can multiply both numbers by 8 and then find the difference between the products.

Number Sequences

A **number sequence** is a list of numbers that follows a particular pattern or order. In the following sequence, for example, each number is three more than the number to its left: 2, 5, 8, 11, 14.

To determine what number comes next in a number sequence, or number series, you must determine the pattern that is being followed. Make sure the pattern holds true for the entire sequence.

What to Do

Now that we have reviewed the skills and information you should be familiar with to answer questions related to number sense, let's go over the steps you will use to find the answers.

Number Sense Steps

Step 1: Read the Problem

Step 2: Determine What Is Being Asked

Step 3: Identify Pertinent Information and Key Words

Step 4: Make a Plan

Step 5: Solve the Problem

Step 6: Check Your Work

Step 1: Read the Problem

Carefully read all of the information included in the problem. Many of the items will be word problems. Make sure you read all of the words, numbers, and directions given. Since the GED is a timed test, it may be tempting to skim quickly over the wording in the questions to save a few seconds. That is probably not the best idea. Carefully reading the question can make the difference between knowing what to do and misunderstanding the directions. If you do not understand the directions, it will be difficult to select the correct answer.

Step 2: Determine What Is Being Asked

Once you have read the problem, make sure you understand what it is asking. Do you need to estimate or find an exact answer? Are you supposed to identify a pattern or determine the next number in a sequence? Figure out what the problem is asking you to do, and restate the question in your own words. If you are not completely confident that you understand the question, read it again.

Step 3: Identify Pertinent Information and Key Words

Now that you know what the question is asking, determine what information, key words, and numbers you will need to solve the problem; underline or circle them. For example, if a question asks you to round a number, underline the place value to which you will be rounding it. Also pay close attention to words such as *estimate*, *not*, and *except*.

Remember that extra information that you will not need may be included. Cross this out so it does not confuse you.

Step 4: Make a Plan

You know what the question is asking, and you have identified the information you will need; now determine how to solve the problem. Will you add or subtract? Will you round a number? Do you need to make an estimate? Figure out what you need to do.

Step 5: Solve the Problem

Now use the plan you selected in Step 4 to solve the problem. Work carefully! You know what to do to find the correct answer. Make sure a careless mistake does not cost you points for this problem.

Step 6: Check Your Work

Before you mark your answer, always go back and double-check your work. Take a second look at the question, review the steps you followed to solve the problem, and make sure your answer is reasonable and makes sense in the context of the problem. Remember, estimating is a great way to gauge quickly if your answer is in the right ballpark.

Examples

Now, let's take a look at a few examples of questions dealing with number sense.

Which is the next number in the sequence? 1, 4, 9, 16, 25, ___

1. 28
2. 30
3. 34
4. 36
5. 49

Here are our steps:

Step 1: Read the Problem

Step 2: Determine What Is Being Asked

Find the next number in the pattern.

Step 3: Identify Pertinent Information and Key Words

The word <u>sequence</u> is important, and the number pattern itself is important.

Step 4: Make a Plan

We need to determine what pattern is used to get from one number to the next. Each of the numbers is a perfect square; 1 is the square of 1, 4 is the square of 2, 9 is the square of 3, and so on. Since 25 is the square of 5, we need to find the square of 6.

Step 5: Solve the Problem

$6^2 = 36$

Step 6: Check Your Work

Now it's your turn. Take a look at the following example. We'll give you the steps you will need to practice the process.

In the number 5,972,341, which digit is in the hundred thousands place?

1. 2
2. 3
3. 5
4. 7
5. 9

Step 1: Read the Problem

Step 2: Determine What Is Being Asked

_____

_____

Step 3: Identify Pertinent Information and Key Words

_____

_____

Step 4: Make a Plan

_____

_____

_____

_____

Step 5: Solve the Problem

_____

_____

Step 6: Check Your Work

The correct answer is 5.

Now try another example. Look over the following question. Use the six steps to help you find the correct answer and the space provided to work through the steps.

Which is the best estimate of the sum of 2,402 + 101,873 + 75,601?

1. 170,000
2. 182,000
3. 193,000
4. 200,000
5. 202,000

Step 1: Read the Problem

Step 2: Determine What Is Being Asked

_____

_____

Step 3: Identify Pertinent Information and Key Words

_____

_____

Step 4: Make a Plan

_____

_____

Step 5: Solve the Problem

_____

_____

Step 6: Check Your Work

The correct answer is 2.

NUMBER SENSE DRILLS

Fill in the blanks for question 1. For each of the subsequent questions, choose the best answer.

1. **What are the steps for answering number sense questions?**

   Step 1: _____

   Step 2: _____

   Step 3: _____

   Step 4: _____

   Step 5: _____

   Step 6: _____

The following information will be used to answer questions 2 and 3.

The Earth's orbit around the sun is a distance of 92,956,050 miles.

2. **What is the value of the underlined digit?**

   9<u>2</u>,956,050

   A. two
   B. two hundred
   C. two thousand
   D. two million
   E. two hundred million

3. **What is the distance of the Earth's orbit around the sun, rounded to the nearest hundred thousand?**

   A. 90,000,000
   B. 92,000,000
   C. 92,900,000
   D. 92,956,000
   E. 93,000,000

The following information will be used to answer questions 4 and 5.

The following table shows the number of employees a company had each year between 2006 and 2010.

Year	Employees
2006	13
2007	39
2008	117
2009	351
2010	1,053

4. If the pattern continues, how many employees will the company have in 2011?
   A. 1,404
   B. 1,755
   C. 2,106
   D. 3,159
   E. 9,477

5. Which is the best estimate of how many employees the company will have in 2013 if the pattern continues?
   A. 10,000
   B. 30,000
   C. 50,000
   D. 70,000
   E. 90,000

6. Which of the following is an example of a rational number that is an integer and a whole number?
   A. 47
   B. 0
   C. 3/8
   D. 0.25
   E. −19

7. Which is equal to 15(24 − 18)?
   A. $15 \times 24 - 15 \times 18$
   B. $18 \times 15 - 24 \times 15$
   C. $15 \times 24 - 18$
   D. 18(24 − 15)
   E. 15(18 − 24)

8. The answer to $(43{,}987 + 12{,}302) - 27{,}546$ is between which of the following pairs of numbers?

   A. 80,000 and 85,000
   B. 55,000 and 60,000
   C. 25,000 and 30,000
   D. 15,000 and 20,000
   E. 0 and 5,000

9. Which accurately describe $\sqrt{95}$?

   A. real and rational
   B. real and irrational
   C. rational and whole
   D. integer and rational
   E. natural and irrational

10. Which is equal to $(23 + 17) + 31$?

    A. $(23 + 31) + (17 + 31)$
    B. $23 + 17 + 31 + 17$
    C. $(23 + 17) \times 31$
    D. $23 + (31 + 17)$
    E. $31 + 17 \times 23$

chapter 23

Decimal Numbers and Operations

As you know, whole numbers represent whole amounts. **Decimal numbers**, on the other hand, represent parts of a whole. Whether you realize it or not, you probably use decimals every day. Remember that soda you bought from the snack machine for 75 cents? Those coins represent part of a whole dollar and can be represented by the decimal $0.75. How about the 14.6 gallons of gasoline you pumped into your car yesterday? That amount is also a decimal.

In this chapter, we'll go over the skills you will need to understand in order to do well on the GED Math questions related to decimal numbers. Remember, you will be able to use a calculator to answer some of these questions on the test; you will have to use pencil and paper or mental math to answer the rest.

Understanding Decimals

A decimal number may include both a whole number and a decimal, as you probably noticed in the preceding example that referred to 14.6 gallons of gasoline. The whole number is separated from the decimal, or the partial number, by a decimal point. The digits to the left of the decimal point are the whole number part. The digits to the right of the decimal point are the decimal places.

14.6 gallons of gas

Here, there are 14 whole gallons of gas; since the 6 is to the right of the decimal point, it represents part of a gallon of gas. Let's find out what each of the places to the right of the decimal point means.

Decimal Place Value

Just like the digits in whole numbers each represent a specific place value, the values of the digits in decimal numbers also depend on their positions. Take a look at the 5 in each of the following decimal numbers.

1.<u>5</u>

3.8<u>5</u>

0.47<u>5</u>

In 1.5, the 5 is in the tenths place, giving it a value of five-tenths, or 0.5. In 3.05, the 5 is in the hundredths place, giving it a value of five-hundredths, or 0.05. In 0.475, the 5 is in the thousandths place, giving it a value of five-thousandths, or 0.005.

Here, from left to right, is the place value of the digits to the right of the decimal point in a number. Notice that the value of each decimal place ends with the letters *-ths*.

Tenths

Hundredths

Thousandths

Ten-thousandths

Hundred-thousandths

The value of each place follows the same pattern as the values of the digits in whole numbers.

Reading and Writing Decimal Numbers

When reading decimal numbers, pay attention to the place value position of the final digit.

0.54 is fifty-four hundredths

0.927 is nine hundred twenty-seven thousandths

If both a whole number and a decimal are included, read the whole number first, say *and* for the decimal point, and then read the decimal according to its place value.

> 273.9 is two hundred seventy three and nine-tenths

> 1,804.0236 is one thousand, eight hundred four, and two hundred thirty-six ten-thousandths

Noticing the place value is key to writing decimal numbers as well. Write the final digit in the number in the corresponding place value position, and use zeros as place holders when necessary.

> Write four hundred twenty and seventeen thousandths in standard form.

You already know how to write the whole number part, so let's look at the decimal. *And* indicates the position of the decimal point. The 7 in *seventeen* is the final digit and must be in the thousandths place value position, which is three places to the right of the decimal point.

> 420.017

Rounding Decimals

Rounding decimals is basically the same as rounding whole numbers. Underline the digit that is in the place value to which you are rounding. Then take a look at the digit to the right of the underlined digit. If the number to the right is less than 5, leave the underlined digit as it is. If the number to the right is 5 or greater, add 1 to the underlined digit.

Here's the difference between rounding whole numbers and decimals: when rounding whole numbers, all digits to the right of the underlined digit become zeros. When rounding decimals, all digits to the right of the underlined digits are dropped.

> Round 2,361 to the nearest hundred.

> 2,361 rounded to the nearest hundred is 2,400.

> Round 0.2361 to the nearest hundredth.

> 0.2361 rounded to the nearest hundredth is 0.24.

Operations with Decimals

Adding, subtracting, multiplying, and dividing decimals is quite similar to performing these operations with whole numbers. There are just a few important differences to remember.

Keep in Mind

Keep in mind that some of the questions on the GED Math Test require gridded responses. Make sure to use a separate box for the decimal point when filling in decimal answers and to fill in the corresponding circle containing a decimal point.

Adding and Subtracting Decimals

When adding and subtracting decimal numbers, make sure to align the decimal points in each addend and the sum, and in the subtrahend, minuend, and difference. In other words, make sure the decimal points line up. Then add and subtract as always.

$$
\begin{array}{r}
24.901 \\
5.76 \\
+\ 308.7236 \\
\hline
339.3846
\end{array}
\qquad
\begin{array}{r}
65.13 \\
-\ 7.926 \\
\hline
57.204
\end{array}
$$

Multiplying Decimals

Decimal numbers are multiplied in the same way as whole numbers. The difference comes in placing the decimal point in the product.

After multiplying the factors, count the number of digits to the right of the decimal point in each of the factors. Then place the decimal point so that there are the same number of digits to the right of the decimal point in the product. Take a look at the following example. There are three digits to the right of the decimal point in the first factor and two digits to the right of the decimal point in the second factor. Since $3 + 2 = 5$, there must be five digits to the right of the decimal point in the product.

$$4.697$$
$$\times\ 1.18$$
$$5.54246$$

Dividing Decimals

As with multiplying decimal numbers, dividing decimal numbers is similar to dividing whole numbers, with the exception of placing the decimal point. First, if the divisor has a decimal point, move it to the right to make the divisor a whole number. Then move the decimal point in the dividend the same number of places to the right. If the dividend does not have enough digits to move the decimal point the necessary number of places, add zeros to the end of the number.

Once the decimal points have been moved, divide as always. Make sure to place the decimal point in the quotient directly above its position in the dividend.

Take a look at the following example. Notice that the decimal point in the divisor, 4.36, must be moved two places to the right to make the divisor a whole number, 436. That means the decimal point in the dividend must also be moved two places. After the decimal point is moved, the dividend becomes 19,707.2.

$$4.36\overline{)197.072}$$

Move the decimal point two places in divisor and dividend; then solve.

$$436\overline{)19707.2}^{\,45.2}$$

Keep in Mind

Keep in mind that the divisor must be a whole number; however, the dividend does not. The dividend and the quotient can contain a decimal point. Only the divisor cannot have a decimal point.

Decimals and Scientific Notation

Scientific notation is a means of writing extremely large or extremely small numbers using a decimal number and a power of 10. Let's go over how to use this form for writing such numbers.

Using Scientific Notation for Large Numbers

In scientific notation, the decimal number must be between 1 and 10. So the first step in writing a large number in this form is to move the decimal point to the left until the number is greater than 1 but less than 10. Count the number of places the decimal point was moved, and use this number as the exponent beside the number 10.

Write 496,000,000,000 in scientific notation.

First, move the decimal point to create a whole number between 1 and 10. Count the number of places the decimal point is moved.

4.<u>96000000000</u>

The decimal was moved 11 places, so the exponent beside the power of ten will be 11.

4.96×10^{11}

Using Scientific Notation for Small Numbers

There are only two differences between writing large numbers and writing small numbers in scientific notation. First, when writing small numbers, move the decimal point to the right rather than to the left to create a number between 1 and 10. Second, after counting the number of places the decimal point is moved, write this number as a negative, rather than a positive, exponent.

Write 0.0000032 in scientific notation.

Move the decimal point to the right and count the number of places it is moved.

<u>000003</u>.2

The decimal point was moved six places, so the exponent beside the power of ten will be –6.

3.2×10^{-6}

What to Do

Now that you know about decimals, let's go over the six steps for solving GED Math questions involving decimal numbers and operations. You will probably recognize that these are basically the same steps you use when solving problems with whole number operations as well.

> ### Decimal Numbers and Operations Steps
> **Step 1:** Read the Problem
> **Step 2:** Determine What Is Being Asked
> **Step 3:** Identify Pertinent Information and Key Words
> **Step 4:** Choose Which Operation(s) or Steps to Use
> **Step 5:** Solve the Problem
> **Step 6:** Check Your Work

Step 1: Read the Problem

As you know, the majority of the questions you will find on the GED Math Test will be word problems, and the words that make up the problems are important. So it is imperative to read each and every word very carefully. Paying attention as you read will make the next few steps much easier.

Step 2: Determine What Is Being Asked

After reading the information, figure out what the question is asking you to do. Are you supposed to round a decimal to the nearest hundredth or round a whole number to the nearest hundred? Is the question asking for the total or the difference? Make sure you understand exactly what is wanted. It can be helpful to restate the question in your own words.

Step 3: Identify Pertinent Information

Now that you know what the question is asking, the next step is to determine which information you will need to find the answer. Remember that there may be extra information that is not necessary. Cross out anything extra so it does not confuse you. Underline or circle any words, numbers, or other data that you will need to find the correct answer.

Step 4: Choose Which Operation(s) or Steps to Use

Remember that key words often offer clues about which operation is needed to solve the problem. For instance, words such as *in all*, *total*, and *sum* suggest addition. Look for hints such as these that let you know whether to add, subtract, multiply, and/or divide. Keep in mind, however, that not every problem includes these key words.

Whether or not you find such clues, the information in the problem will suggest what operations or steps to use to find the answer. Think about what is being asked and what will be required. For example, if a question states that an item is discounted by $14.75 and asks for the new price, it would make sense that the new price would be lower, which means you would need to subtract.

As you know, more than one operation or step may be necessary to find the correct answer. Make sure you determine all the steps you will need. For example, if the question requires writing a number using scientific notation, you know to move the decimal, count the number of places it was moved, and then write a multiplication sentence using a power of ten.

Step 5: Solve the Problem

Now use the plan you devised in Step 4 to find the answer to the problem. Work carefully, keeping in mind what we discussed about decimals in this chapter. Remember to align the decimal points as you add or subtract, count the digits to the right of the decimal point when you multiply, and move the decimal to create a whole number divisor when you divide. Pay attention to the place value position when rounding. Count how many places the decimal is moved when writing a number in scientific notation; then use this as a positive exponent when writing large numbers and as a negative exponent when writing small numbers.

Step 6: Check Your Work

Always go back and check your work. Using estimation is a terrific way to determine the reasonableness of your answer. If estimation shows that your answer is not logical, try again. If it shows that your answer is reasonable, terrific! Even so, look back over the steps you used to find the answer, make sure that you aligned decimals accurately, performed operations correctly, and placed decimal points properly. Remember, the correct answer must be exactly right, not just close to right.

Examples

Now let's use what we have discussed in this chapter regarding decimal numbers to answer a few sample questions.

> When Marisol received her credit card statement this month, she owed a balance of $385.92. She made a payment of $127.13 and then charged a pair of shoes for $64.76 and a jacket for $84.79. What is the new balance on the card?
>
> 1. $258.79
> 2. $323.58
> 3. $385.92
> 4. $408.34
> 5. $450.68

Here are our steps:

Step 1: Read the Problem

Step 2: Determine What Is Being Asked

What is the balance on Marisol's card after making one payment and two purchases?

Step 3: Identify Pertinent Information

We need to know that the beginning balance was $385.92, her payment was $127.13, and the two purchases were $64.76 and $84.79.

Step 4: Choose Which Operation(s) or Steps to Use

There are no key words to suggest which operations to use; however, we know that making a payment lowers a credit card balance. Making purchases increases the balance. So we will subtract the payment from the beginning balance and then add the price of the purchases.

Step 5: Solve the Problem

$385.92 – $127.13 = $258.79

$258.79 + $64.76 + $84.79 = $408.34

Step 6: Check Your Work

Now it's your turn. Take a look at the following sample problem. We'll give you the steps you will need to practice the process.

The owner of a taxi cab company purchased a total of 189.48 gallons of gasoline. If he put an equal amount into each of his 12 cars, how many gallons of gas did he use for each car, rounded to the nearest tenth?

1. 15.7
2. 15.79
3. 15.8
4. 22.7
5. 22.73

Here are our steps:

Step 1: Read the Problem

Step 2: Determine What Is Being Asked

_____

_____

Step 3: Identify Pertinent Information

_____

_____

_____

Step 4: Choose Which Operation(s) or Steps to Use

_____

_____

Step 5: Solve the Problem

_____

_____

Step 6: Check Your Work

The correct answer is 3.

DECIMAL NUMBERS AND OPERATIONS DRILLS

Fill in the blanks for question 1. For each of the subsequent questions, choose the best answer.

1. **What are the steps for solving decimal numbers and operations problems?**

    Step 1: _____

    Step 2: _____

    Step 3: _____

    Step 4: _____

    Step 5: _____

    Step 6: _____

2. **What is the value of the 7 in the number 25.3479?**
    A. seven tenths
    B. seven hundredths
    C. seven thousandths
    D. seven ten-thousandths
    E. seven hundred-thousandths

3. **Carson's living room is 4.76 meters long. He bought a piece of carpeting that is 5.2 meters long. How many meters of carpeting will he have to cut off in order for the length to fit exactly into the room?**
    A. 0.24
    B. 0.26
    C. 0.44
    D. 1.74
    E. 4.24

4. **The speed of light is 300,000,000 meters per second. What is this number written in scientific notation?**
    A. 0.3×10^9
    B. 0.3×10^{-7}
    C. 3.0×10^7
    D. 3×10^8
    E. 3×10^{-8}

5. **What is four hundred sixteen thousand, seven hundred ten, and eighty-two thousandths in decimal form?**
    A. 416,710.0082
    B. 416,710.082
    C. 416,710.82
    D. 416,782
    E. 482,000

6. Last week, three packages arrived weighing 6.09 kg, 10.8 kg, and 0.72 kg. This week, two packages arrived, each weighing 3.147 kg. What is the total weight of the packages, rounded to the nearest hundredth?

   A. 24.7
   B. 23.91
   C. 23.9
   D. 20.76
   E. 20.75

7. On a four-day trip, Simone drove a total of 677.6 miles and used 30.25 gallons of gasoline. How many miles per gallon was she able to drive?

   A. 51.24
   B. 22.4
   C. 16.9
   D. 8.96
   E. 2.24

8. A pet supply store buys a 20-pound bag of dog food for $3.78 and sells it for $9.49. How much profit does the store make on 35 bags of food?

   A. $199.85
   B. $189.80
   C. $142.35
   D. $132.30
   E. $114.20

9. A restaurant uses 0.47 pound of ground beef in each burger and 0.53 pound in each serving of meatloaf. How many pounds of beef are needed to make 180 burgers?

   A. 8.46
   B. 9.54
   C. 77.4
   D. 84.6
   E. 95.4

10. Which shows nine hundred thirty-five ten-thousandths?

    A. 0.00935
    B. 0.0935
    C. 0.90035
    D. 0.9035
    E. 0.935

chapter 24

Fractions and Operations

What's Being Tested?

Fractions are a part of our daily lives. We put one-fourth of a cup of butter in a chocolate-chip cookie recipe. We watch a favorite TV show for half an hour. We walk five-eighths of a mile to the market. In fact, at this point, you have read approximately two-thirds of the chapters in this book.

Fractions are parts of a whole number. On the GED Math Test, some of the questions will involve working with fractions. In this chapter, we will review the processes for adding, subtracting, multiplying, and dividing fractions, and we will discuss how to change fractions to decimals.

Understanding Fractions

Like decimals, **fractions** also describe parts of a whole. The **denominator** is the bottom number in a fraction, and it tells how many equal parts make up the whole. The **numerator** is the top number, and it tells how many parts of the whole the fraction names. For example, the fraction ¼ names one out of a total of four parts. If your friend eats ⅜ of a pizza, we know that the pizza had a total of eight slices, and your friend ate three of them.

Now that you know what a fraction means, let's go over several types of fractions.

Proper Fractions

Proper fractions have a numerator that is less than the denominator. These fractions name a portion of a single whole: $\frac{1}{3}$, $\frac{7}{8}$, $\frac{5}{12}$.

Improper Fractions

Improper fractions have a numerator that is greater than or equal to the denominator. When the numerator is greater than the denominator, the fraction names more than the whole. In other words, improper fractions refer to at least one whole and part of another: $\frac{10}{3}$, $\frac{7}{5}$, $\frac{13}{9}$.

When the numerator is equal to the denominator, the improper fraction is equal to 1. For example, suppose you have $\frac{4}{4}$ of a dollar in your pocket. The denominator says that the dollar is divided into four equal parts, such as four quarters. The numerator says that you have four of those equal parts, or four quarters. If you have all four of the four equal parts, you have the whole thing. Any time the numerator and denominator are equal, the fraction is equal to 1: $\frac{8}{8} = 1$; $\frac{12}{12} = 1$.

Mixed Numbers

A **mixed number** contains a whole number and a fraction. It names one or more wholes, as well as a portion of another, such as $1\frac{1}{2}$, $3\frac{4}{5}$, $5\frac{1}{3}$.

Equivalent Forms of Fractions

Fractions that name equal amounts are called **equivalent fractions**. Here are several strategies for finding equivalent fractions.

Converting Mixed Numbers to Improper Fractions

There are times when mixed numbers need to be changed to improper fractions. Why? Good question! Often, it is easier to add or subtract improper fractions than it is mixed numbers. Also, mixed numbers must be changed to improper fractions before multiplying or dividing. To change a mixed number to an improper fraction, multiply the denominator by the whole number and then add the product to the numerator.

Convert $4\frac{3}{8}$ to an improper fraction.

Multiply the denominator by the whole number; then add the product to the numerator.

$4\tfrac{3}{8}$

$8 \times 3 + 4 = 28$

$\tfrac{28}{8}$

So $4\tfrac{3}{8}$ is equal to $\tfrac{28}{8}$.

Converting Improper Fractions to Mixed Numbers

To change an improper fraction to a mixed number, divide the numerator by the denominator. The result becomes the whole number part of the mixed number. The remainder becomes the numerator of the fraction part. The denominator stays the same.

Change $\tfrac{26}{7}$ to a mixed number.

Divide the numerator by the denominator.

$26 \div 7 = 3$, remainder 5

The quotient, 3, becomes the whole number part of the mixed number. The remainder, 5, becomes the numerator.

$\tfrac{26}{7} = 3\tfrac{5}{7}$

Reducing Fractions

Reducing fractions simply means using smaller numbers to express the same amount. Since the reduced fraction is the same amount as the original, the two fractions are equal. Take a look at the following squares. The first shows $\tfrac{2}{4}$ shaded. The second shows $\tfrac{1}{2}$ shaded. Notice that the shaded portions of the squares are equal. This shows is that $\tfrac{2}{4} = \tfrac{1}{2}$.

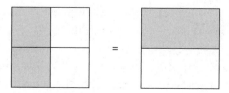

To reduce a fraction, divide both the numerator and the denominator by a common factor. In other words, divide the numerator and denominator by a number that goes into both evenly.

Reduce $^{16}\!/_{24}$.

Since 8 is a factor of both 16 and 24, divide both numbers by 8.

$$^{16}\!/_{24} = \frac{16 \div 8}{24 \div 8} = \,^2\!/_3$$

So $^{16}\!/_{24}$ is equivalent to $^2\!/_3$.

Finding Common Denominators

Before adding or subtracting, fractions must have common denominators, which means the bottom number of the fractions must be the same. To do this, you must find the smallest number that is divisible by both of the denominators. Start by checking the largest denominator. Will the other denominators go into it evenly? If not, mentally list the multiples of the largest denominator and see if the other denominators are also factors of the number. For example, look at the denominators of $^2\!/_3$ and $^4\!/_5$. The largest denominator is 5, but 3 is not a factor of 5. So let's list multiples of 5. Ten is a multiple of 5, but 3 is not a factor of 10. The next multiple of 5 is 15. Since 3 is a factor of 15, we'll use this as the common denominator for both fractions.

Once the common denominator is found, multiply the numerator and denominator of each fraction by the number that will create the common denominator. Take a look at the examples. Keep in mind that the common denominator will be 15.

Find the lowest common denominator for $^2\!/_3$ and $^4\!/_5$.

$^2\!/_3 \times \,^5\!/_5 = \,^{10}\!/_{15}$

$^4\!/_5 \times \,^3\!/_3 = \,^{12}\!/_{15}$

Operations with Fractions

On the GED Math Test, you will need to be able to add, subtract, multiply, and divide fractions. Let's review how to perform these operations.

Adding and Subtracting Fractions

To add or subtract fractions, they must have the same denominator. So the first step is to find a common denominator and then add or subtract the numerators. The common denominator will also be the denominator in the sum or difference.

$3/8 + 5/6 =$

$(3/8 \times 3/3) + (5/6 \times 4/4) =$

$9/24 + 20/24 = 29/24$

$29/24 = 1\,5/24$

Notice that the addends in this example have denominators of 8 and 6. The lowest number that is divisible by both 8 and 6 is 24, so 24 will be the common denominator.

To change $3/8$ to an equivalent fraction with a denominator of 24, multiply both the numerator and denominator by 3, since 3 multiplied by the denominator (8) equals 24. Because $3/3$ is equal to 1, multiplying the fraction by $3/3$ does not change its value. Multiply the second addend, $5/6$, by $4/4$ to create a fraction with a denominator of 24.

After finding common denominators, the addends $3/8$ and $5/6$ become $9/24$ and $20/24$.

Add the numerators, $9 + 20$. The numerator of the sum is 29, and the denominator remains 24. So the sum is $29/24$. This is an improper fraction and is equivalent to $1\,5/24$.

$2/3 - 5/18 =$

$(2/3 \times 6/6) - 5/18 =$

$12/18 - 5/18 = 7/18$

Keep in Mind

Keep in mind that if you do not find your answer among the choices, it may need to be put it in the simplest terms. Improper fractions may need to be written as mixed numbers, and proper fractions may need to be simplified, or reduced.

When adding or subtracting mixed numbers, convert them to improper fractions first and then find a common denominator. After that, add or subtract the numerators.

Multiplying Fractions

The steps to multiply fractions are actually much simpler than adding or subtracting. First, multiply the numerators and then multiply the denominators. No need to worry about finding common denominators. Remember that it may be necessary to convert the product to its simplest terms. In other words, reduce the fraction after finding the answer.

$$\frac{2}{5} \times \frac{3}{8} =$$

$$\frac{2}{5} \times \frac{3}{8} = \frac{6}{40}$$

$$\frac{6}{40} = \frac{3}{20}$$

As with other operations involving fractions, convert mixed numbers to improper fractions before multiplying. Simplify the product.

$$2\frac{7}{9} \times 4\frac{1}{2} =$$

$$2\frac{7}{9} \times 4\frac{1}{2} = \frac{25}{9} \times \frac{9}{2} = \frac{225}{18} = \frac{25}{2} = 12\frac{1}{2}$$

Dividing Fractions

Dividing fractions is also pretty straightforward. Simply invert one of the fractions; then multiply.

$$\frac{7}{12} \div \frac{3}{4} =$$

$$\frac{12}{7} \div \frac{3}{4} = \frac{36}{28} = \frac{9}{7} = 1\frac{2}{7}$$

Operations with Fractions and Whole Numbers

So far, we have discussed performing operations with two or more fractions. Sometimes, it will be necessary to add, subtract, multiply, or divide a fraction and a whole number. How do we do that? By turning the whole number into a fraction.

To convert a whole number to a fraction, simply create a fraction with the whole number as the numerator, and the number 1 as the denominator.

For example, 25 becomes $^{25}\!/_1$. Then perform the operation as usual with the fractions.

$36 \div 2\frac{1}{4} =$

$36 \div 2\frac{1}{4} = {}^{36}\!/_1 \div {}^9\!/_4 = {}^{36}\!/_1 \times {}^4\!/_9 = {}^{144}\!/_9 = 16$

Fractions and Decimals

As you know, both fractions and decimals name parts of a whole. Sometimes, it is necessary to change a fraction to a decimal or vice versa. Let's go over how to do this.

Changing Fractions to Decimals

The fraction bar, that little line between the numbers in a fraction, means to divide. So to change a fraction to a decimal, divide the numerator by the denominator.

Write $\frac{1}{4}$ as a decimal.

$1 \div 4 = 0.25$

Changing Decimals to Fractions

To change a decimal to a fraction, we have to remember the place value of the decimal. First, write the digits in the decimal places as the numerator. Leave out the decimal point and write them as a whole number. Then take a look at how many digits are to the right of the decimal point and determine which place value is represented. Write this number as the denominator. For example, two digits to the right of the decimal point indicate hundredths. So the denominator of the fraction will be 100.

Write 0.247 as a fraction.

$0.247 = {}^{247}\!/_{1,000}$

Look at the preceding example. The digits 247 are included in the decimal number, so these become the numerator of the fraction. There are three digits to the right of the decimal point, which is the thousandths place. The denominator of the fraction is therefore 1,000.

If digits are included to the left of the decimal point, the decimal becomes a mixed number. The digits to the left of the decimal point become the whole number, and those to the right become the fraction.

Write 9.7 as a fraction.

$9.7 = 9\frac{7}{10}$

Keep in Mind

Keep in mind that some of the questions on the GED Math Test require gridded responses. To grid a fraction, you have two choices. First, you can convert the fraction to a decimal and then grid the decimal answer. Second, you can grid the fraction by gridding the numerator first, then the fraction bar, and then the denominator. Mixed numbers cannot be gridded, so these must be reported as decimals or improper fractions.

What to Do

Now that we've reviewed fractions, operations with fractions, and relating fractions and decimals, let's go over the six steps to use in solving GED Math problems related to these parts of a whole.

Fractions and Operations Steps

Step 1: Read the Problem
Step 2: Determine What Is Being Asked
Step 3: Identify Pertinent Information and Key Words
Step 4: Choose Which Operation(s) or Steps to Use
Step 5: Solve the Problem
Step 6: Check Your Work

Step 1: Read the Problem

By now you recognize the importance of reading each problem carefully. It can be tempting to read quickly when facing a time limit, but skimming over key information could cost you time in the long run. Make sure you read carefully enough to catch each word, understand the scenario, and know what information you are being asked to find. Misunderstanding the information can lead to errors or the need to rework the problem.

Step 2: Determine What Is Being Asked

As you are reading, pay attention to what the question is asking you to find. Once you figure this out, try restating the question in your own words. This can be helpful in figuring out how to solve the problem.

Step 3: Identify Pertinent Information

Many of the word problems on the GED Math Test will include several sentences. You may or may not need all of this information to answer the question. Look back through the problem and underline or circle fractions, numbers, words, or directions you will need; cross out any information you will not need.

Step 4: Choose Which Operation(s) or Steps to Use

Wouldn't it be nice if every single question clearly told you what to do? *Divide 12 by ½. Multiply 3¾ by ⅝. Add ½ and ⅔.* That would be great, but it is not likely to happen. You will have to depend on key words and common sense to figure out what to do to solve the problems. Think about what answer would make sense; then decide which operations or steps can help you reach that solution.

One strategy that can be helpful is to draw a picture. Making a quick sketch of a fraction can help you visualize what you need to do to solve a problem. It can also be helpful in determining whether fractions are equivalent or checking whether you have correctly reduced a fraction.

Keep in Mind

Keep in mind that the word *of* is often a clue word indicating multiplication. When you are told to find ½ *of* 12, for example, you will multiply.

Step 5: Solve the Problem

Now that you have made a plan for finding the correct answer, it is time to solve the problem. Work carefully and remember everything we have reviewed about fractions. You know how to solve the problems; stay focused to avoid careless mistakes. Be sure to show your work as you solve each problem. This will not be scored, but it will make it easier to check your work in Step 6 and to identify and correct any mistakes if needed.

Step 6: Check Your Work

Look back over your work in Step 5, and double-check that you found the correct answer. Make sure you correctly counted place value positions when converting fractions to decimals, inverted one fraction when dividing, and correctly found the common denominator when adding and subtracting.

Examples

Let's put these six steps into practice by answering a few examples.

Each serving of hot spiced tea that Natalia gives her dinner guests calls for $\frac{1}{8}$ teaspoon of cinnamon and $1\frac{1}{2}$ teaspoons of sugar. How much more sugar than cinnamon will she use to make 6 servings of tea?

1. $1\frac{3}{8}$ tsp
2. $8\frac{1}{4}$ tsp
3. $8\frac{7}{8}$ tsp
4. 9 tsp
5. $9\frac{3}{4}$ tsp

Here are our steps:

Step 1: Read the Problem

Step 2: Determine What Is Being Asked

How much more sugar than cinnamon is needed for 6 servings of tea?

Step 3: Identify Pertinent Information

Each serving of tea uses $\frac{1}{8}$ teaspoon of cinnamon and $1\frac{1}{2}$ teaspoons of sugar.

Step 4: Choose Which Operation(s) or Steps to Use

First, to find out how much cinnamon and sugar are used, multiply each amount by the number of servings. The words <u>how much more</u> tell that we will need to subtract these amounts.

Step 5: Solve the Problem

$\frac{1}{8} \times 6 = \frac{1}{8} \times \frac{6}{1} = \frac{6}{8}$ *tsp of cinnamon*

$1\frac{1}{2} \times 6 = \frac{3}{2} \times \frac{6}{1} = \frac{18}{2} = 9$ *tsp of sugar*

$9 - \frac{6}{8} = (\frac{9}{1} \times \frac{8}{8}) - \frac{6}{8} = \frac{72}{8} - \frac{6}{8} = \frac{66}{8} = 8\frac{2}{8} = 8\frac{1}{4}$

Step 6: Check Your Work

Now it's your turn. Take a look at the next problem. We'll give you the steps you will need to practice the process.

At the market, Tyrone bought 4½ pounds of peaches, 2⅛ pounds of plums, and ½ gallon of milk. Which shows how many pounds of fruit he bought?

1. $6\frac{3}{8}$
2. $7\frac{1}{8}$
3. $7\frac{5}{8}$
4. $\frac{50}{8}$
5. $\frac{53}{8}$

Step 1: Read the Problem

Step 2: Determine What Is Being Asked

_____

_____

Step 3: Identify Pertinent Information

_____

_____

Step 4: Choose Which Operation(s) or Steps to Use

_____

_____

Step 5: Solve the Problem

_____

_____

_____

Step 6: Check Your Work

The correct answer is 5.

FRACTIONS AND OPERATIONS DRILLS

Fill in the blanks for question 1. For each of the subsequent questions, choose the best answer.

1. **What are the steps for solving fractions and operations problems?**

   Step 1: _____

   Step 2: _____

   Step 3: _____

   Step 4: _____

   Step 5: _____

   Step 6: _____

2. **Which of the following is greater than 2?**
   A. $\frac{3}{4} + 1\frac{1}{8}$
   B. $\frac{8}{6} + \frac{9}{12}$
   C. $\frac{13}{20} + \frac{11}{12}$
   D. $\frac{15}{16} \times \frac{3}{7}$
   E. $1\frac{2}{9} \times 1\frac{1}{6}$

3. **Becky made five deliveries for her employer.**
   Delivery A = 0.7 mile
   Delivery B = $\frac{5}{8}$ mile
   Delivery C = 0.45 mile
   Delivery D = $\frac{6}{10}$ mile
   Delivery E = $\frac{3}{4}$ mile

   Which shows the delivery distances in order from shortest to longest?
   A. A, D, B, C, E
   B. C, A, D, B, E
   C. C, D, B, A, E
   D. E, A, B, D, C
   E. E, C, B, D, A

4. **Raphael made 4½ pounds of fudge, which he wants to divide evenly among six friends. Assuming he gives away all of the fudge, how many pounds will each friend receive?**
   A. $\frac{1}{6}$
   B. $\frac{2}{3}$
   C. $\frac{3}{4}$
   D. $\frac{5}{6}$
   E. $\frac{7}{12}$

5. On Monday morning, $\frac{1}{12}$ of the total number of employees in an office called in sick. Throughout the day, $\frac{4}{15}$ of the employees went home early. What fraction of the total workforce remained in the office by the end of the day?

A. $\frac{2}{3}$

B. $\frac{7}{12}$

C. $\frac{7}{20}$

D. $\frac{13}{20}$

E. $\frac{33}{40}$

6. Two hundred people were surveyed about which of the four seasons is their favorite. Of those surveyed, $\frac{1}{8}$ selected spring, $\frac{2}{5}$ selected summer, and $\frac{3}{10}$ selected autumn. The remainder of the participants selected winter. How many people surveyed selected winter as their favorite season?

A. 25

B. 35

C. 60

D. 70

E. 80

7. Which of the following is equal to $\frac{-34}{-85}$?

A. −0.4

B. $\frac{-2}{5}$

C. 0.04

D. $\frac{2}{5}$

E. $\frac{5}{2}$

Keep in Mind

Keep in mind that the fraction bar is a division sign. The same rules for dividing negative and positive numbers apply to fractions as to whole numbers.

8. A baker uses $4\frac{2}{3}$ cups of flour in a cookie recipe. He has 36 cups of flour. What is the greatest number of times he can make the recipe?

A. 7

B. 8

C. 9

D. 10

E. 11

9. Jessica used 5⅛ pounds of coffee beans to make coffee for people attending a business seminar hosted by her company. She paid $7.84 per pound for the beans. What is the cost of the coffee she served?

   A. $39.20

   B. $39.98

   C. $40.18

   D. $40.61

   E. $45.47

10. Evaluate $(⅗)^3$.

    A. $\frac{9}{25}$

    B. $\frac{27}{125}$

    C. $\frac{81}{125}$

    D. $1⅘$

    E. $5⅖$

chapter **25**

Number Relationships

Number relationships span just about every area of math and are part of your everyday life as well. When you drive, you (hopefully) pay close attention to how many miles per hour you are driving. This number on your speedometer represents a number relationship. When you answer 8 out of 10 questions correctly on the "How Well Do You Know Your BFF" magazine quiz, you are dealing with another number relationship. In this chapter, we will review a few number relationship skills that will come in handy when answering questions on the GED Math Test.

Ratios and Proportions

Ratios and proportions involve comparing numbers. Let's take a look at each of these relationships.

Ratios

Ratios compare two numbers using words, numbers, or a fraction. Suppose you have 6 apples and 8 bananas in a fruit bowl. The ratio of apples to bananas is 6 to 8. Since the word *apples* was listed first in the statement, the number of apples is listed first in the ratio. Since the word *bananas* appeared second, the number of bananas is also second in the ratio.

Writing Ratios

Ratios can also be written using a colon. The ratio of apples to bananas is 6 to 8, or 6:8. Notice that the numbers stay in the same order as their labels appear in the statement.

Another way to write a ratio is as a fraction. So the ratio of apples to bananas can be written as $\frac{6}{8}$. Notice that this is different than a fraction in the sense that the total number of fruits in the bowl is not written as the denominator. The denominator in the ratio of apples to bananas is the number of bananas.

> There are 3 employees and 12 customers in a store. What is the ratio of employees to customers?
>
> The ratio of employees to customers is 3 to 12.

This answer can also be written in one of the other forms.

> 3:12
>
> $\frac{3}{12}$

Suppose this example had asked for the ratio of employees to the total number of people in the store. In this case, the denominator would be the total, since that is what the ratio reports. To solve this ratio, find the sum of the employees and customers to show the total number of people.

> The ratio of employees to the total number of people in the store is $\frac{3}{15}$.

Like fractions, ratios can be simplified.

> The ratio of employees to customers is $\frac{3}{12}$, or $\frac{1}{4}$.
>
> The ratio of employees to customers is 3:12, or 1:4.

Solving Problems with Ratios

Take a look at the following problem involving ratios.

> In a video store, the ratio of DVDs to Blu-rays sold is 3:7. If the store sells 90 movies, how many of the movies were DVDs?

The ratio explains that for every 3 DVDs sold, the store sells 7 Blu-rays. That means that if 10 movies are sold, 3 are DVDs and 7 are Blu-rays. The fraction $\frac{3}{10}$ shows that 3 out of 10 movies sold are DVDs. This fraction can be used to find how many DVDs were sold out of a total of 90 movies.

$$\frac{3}{10} \times 90 = \frac{270}{10} = 27$$

This tells us that of the 90 movies sold, 27 were DVDs. That means the remaining 63 movies sold were Blu-rays. Let's double-check the ratio again.

The ratio of DVDs to Blu-rays sold was 27:63.

27:63 = 3:7

Proportions

A **proportion** is an equation that states that two ratios are equivalent—for example, $\frac{3}{4} = \frac{6}{8}$. In the example, $\frac{3}{4}$ and $\frac{6}{8}$ are the **terms**, or **elements**, of the proportion. One way to verify that the terms of a proportion are equal is to cross multiply. To cross multiply the terms in the example, $\frac{3}{4}$ and $\frac{6}{8}$, first multiply 3×8, then multiply 4×6. Since these products are equal, the ratios are equal. So the proportion is true.

Solving Problems with Proportions

At times, one value in a ratio may be unknown. Solving a proportion reveals the missing value.

$$\frac{x}{15} = \frac{1}{5}$$

To find the missing value, cross multiply the terms.

$x \times 5 = 15 \times 1$

$5x = 15$

We know that $5 \times 3 = 15$, so the missing value is 3. Let's write the proportion using this value and make sure the ratios are equal.

$$\frac{3}{15} = \frac{1}{5}$$

These ratios are equal, so they form a proportion.

Comparing Numbers

One way to compare numbers is to determine if one is **greater than**, **less than**, or **equal to** another. As you know, 10 is greater than 4. We can compare these numbers using a symbol for *greater than*.

10 is greater than 4

10 > 4

As you also know, 15 is less than 25. This can also be represented using the symbol for *less than*.

15 is less than 25

15 < 25

When two numbers are equal, we use the equal sign to represent their relationship.

(3 + 2) = 5

Keep in Mind

Keep in mind that the greater than and less than symbols open toward the larger number. Think back to when you were in elementary school, and the teacher explained that the symbol looks like an open alligator mouth eating the biggest number. Corny, but it works.

Prime and Composite Numbers

Refer to Chapter 21 if you need a review about the definitions of prime and composite numbers. What follows is a bit of a repeat for those of you who like to skip around in these books!

Numbers can be classified based on how many factors they have. Numbers greater than 1 whose only factors are 1 and the number itself are **prime numbers**.

For example, since the only numbers that can be multiplied together to equal 5 are 1 and 5, 5 is a prime number. Take a look at the following list of prime numbers. The list could go on, but these are the prime numbers between 0 and 100. The number 1 is not included, since it is not greater than 1.

Prime Numbers between 0 and 100

2, 3, 5, 7, 11, 13, 17, 19, 23, 29, 31, 37, 41, 43, 47, 53, 59, 61, 67, 71, 73, 79, 83, 89, 97

Take a look at that list one more time. Do you notice any even numbers? Since all even numbers have 2 as a factor, they are not prime, with the exception of the number 2; it only has 1 and 2 as factors. So what do we call these other numbers that are not prime? Great question!

Composite numbers have more than two factors. For example, the factors of 10 are 1, 2, 5, and 10. So 10 is a composite number. To determine whether a number is prime or composite, determine whether it is divisible by another number. Remember, all even numbers are divisible by 2. All numbers with a 5 in the ones place are divisible by 5. And all numbers with a 0 in the ones place are divisible by 10. Another trick is that all numbers whose digits have a sum that is a multiple of 3 are divisible by 3. Likewise, all numbers whose digits have a sum that is a multiple of 9 are divisible by 9. These tricks will not help you determine whether every single number is prime or composite, but they will at least give you a starting point.

3,574 is even, so it is divisible by 2.

495 has a 5 in the ones place, so it is divisible by 5.

29,470 has a 0 in the ones place, so it is divisible by 10.

474 is divisible by 3 because the sum of its digits (4 + 7 + 4) is 15, which is a multiple of 3.

657 is divisible by 9 because the sum of its digits (6 + 5 + 7) is 18, which is a multiple of 9.

Greatest Common Factor

The largest number that is a factor of two or more given numbers is known as the **greatest common factor** (GCF). To find the GCF, list all the prime numbers that are factors of each number. Then identify which factors are common to both numbers and multiply these factors.

What is the greatest common factor of 30 and 75?

First, list the prime factors of each:

Prime factors of 30: $2 \times 3 \times 5$

Prime factors of 75: $3 \times 5 \times 5$

Second, identify the factors they have in common:

Prime factors of 30: $2 \times \underline{3} \times \underline{5}$

Prime factors of 75: $\underline{3} \times \underline{5} \times 5$

Third, multiply the factors they have in common:

$$3 \times 5 = 15$$

So the greatest common factor of 30 and 75 is 15. In other words, the largest number that is a factor of both 30 and 75 is 15.

Lowest Common Multiple

Multiples are numbers that can be evenly divided by a particular number. For example, 5, 10, 15, 20, and 25 are all multiples of 5 because they can be evenly divided by 5.

What numbers are multiples of 7?

7, 14, 21, 28, 35, 42 …

A **common multiple** is a multiple that two or more numbers have in common. For example, 36 is a common multiple of both 4 and 6, since it is evenly divisible by both of these numbers.

The **lowest common multiple**, also known as the least common multiple (LCM), is the lowest number that is a common multiple of two or more numbers. To find the lowest common multiple, list the multiples of each number. Then find the lowest number that appears on both lists.

What is the lowest common multiple of 8 and 12?

Multiples of 8: 8, 16, <u>24</u>, 32, 40, 48, 64, 92, 80, 88, 96 …

Multiples of 12: <u>12</u>, 24, 36, 48, 60, 72, 84, 96, 108, 120 …

Since 24 is the lowest number that is common to both sets of multiples, it is the LCM of 8 and 12.

Keep in Mind

Keep in mind that two numbers may have several common multiples. For example, 48 and 96 are also common multiples of 8 and 12. However, the LCM is the lowest number that is a common multiple of both.

What to Do

Let's go over the steps for answering questions related to number relationships. Do they look familiar? They're quite similar to the steps you will use to answer any of the questions on the GED Math Test.

> ### Number Relationships Steps
> **Step 1:** Read the Problem
> **Step 2:** Determine What Is Being Asked
> **Step 3:** Identify Pertinent Information and Key Words
> **Step 4:** Make a Plan
> **Step 5:** Solve the Problem
> **Step 6:** Check Your Work

Step 1: Read the Problem

Carefully read each word of the problem. As you read, think about the information given and what the question is asking you to do. You will use this in other steps of solving the problem.

Step 2: Determine What Is Being Asked

Once you have read the problem, figure out exactly what it is asking you to do. If you are unsure, go back and read it again. You must clearly understand what the question is asking in order to answer it correctly. Once you are confident that you understand the question, restate it in your own words.

Step 3: Identify Pertinent Information and Key Words

Once you know what the question is asking, you will be able to recognize which information you will need to solve the problem and what material is unnecessary. When reading number relationship problems, underline words such as *ratio, proportion, prime, composite, greatest common factor, lowest common multiple, greater than,* and *less than.* As always, cross out any numbers you will not need. That way, you will not focus on them unintentionally.

Remember, even though this is a math test, the vocabulary is crucial. For instance, there's a big difference between *greatest common factor* and *lowest common multiple.* Make sure you identify key words so you can determine the correct steps to solve the problem in Step 4.

Keep in Mind

Keep in mind that any symbols included in the answer choices are considered pertinent information as well. When selecting the correct answer to GED Math questions, consider underlining or circling any symbols in the answer choices as well. For example, make sure you do not mistake a greater than symbol (>) for a less than symbol (<).

Step 4: Make a Plan

In Step 2, you figured out what the question is asking. In Step 3, you found the information you will need to solve the problem. Now determine how you will use this information. Determine what steps you need and plan how you will find the correct answer.

Step 5: Solve the Problem

Work carefully to complete the steps you outlined in the previous step. Even if you are answering a question that allows the use of a calculator, you will want to focus on performing each step accurately.

Step 6: Check Your Work

Reread the question, look back over the steps you completed in solving the problem, and estimate whether your answer is reasonable. Working backward can be a great way to make sure you found the correct answer. For example, use subtraction to check addition, and use division to check multiplication. In number relationship problems, make sure multiples can be divided by each of the numbers given.

Examples

Let's look at a few sample questions dealing with number relationships.

On his third math quiz of the semester, Jamal answered 28 questions correctly and got 7 answers wrong. What is the ratio of the number of questions he got right on the quiz to the total number of questions?

1. 1:4
2. 1:5
3. 4:1
4. 4:5
5. 5:4

Here are our steps:

Step 1: Read the Problem

Step 2: Determine What Is Being Asked

What is the ratio of correct answers to the number of questions on the quiz?

Step 3: Identify Pertinent Information and Key Words

The phrases <u>answered 28 questions correctly</u>, <u>7 answers wrong</u>, and <u>ratio of the number of questions he got right ... to the total number of questions</u> are important.

Step 4: Make a Plan

First, find the total number of correct answers and then find the total number of questions. Write these numbers as a ratio and simplify the ratio.

Step 5: Solve the Problem

Number of correct answers: 28

Total number of questions: 28 + 7 = 35

28:35 = 4:5

Step 6: Check Your Work

Now you try it. We'll give you the steps you will need to practice the process.

What is the lowest common multiple of 16 and 40?

1. 640
2. 160
3. 80
4. 8
5. 4

Step 1: Read the Problem

Step 2: Determine What Is Being Asked

_____

_____

Step 3: Identify Pertinent Information and Key Words

_____

_____

Step 4: Make a Plan

_____

_____

Step 5: Solve the Problem

_____

_____

Step 6: Check Your Work

The correct answer is 3.

NUMBER RELATIONSHIP DRILLS

Fill in the blanks for question 1. For each of the subsequent questions, choose the best answer.

1. **What are the steps for answering number relationship questions?**

   Step 1: _____

   Step 2: _____

   Step 3: _____

   Step 4: _____

   Step 5: _____

   Step 6: _____

2. **The Alvarez family paid a handyman $930 for 60 hours worth of work on their rental property. At this rate, what would they pay him for 24 hours of work on their home?**
   A. $154
   B. $155
   C. $362.50
   D. $372
   E. $387.50

3. **What is the greatest common factor of 56 and 84?**
   A. 7
   B. 14
   C. 28
   D. 168
   E. 336

4. **A movie theater sold 112 student tickets and 144 adult tickets to a matinee showing of a newly released film. Which of the following is equal to the ratio of student to adult tickets sold?**
   A. 7:9
   B. 7:16
   C. 9:7
   D. 9:16
   E. 16:9

5. The ratio of men to women at a business conference was 3:7. How many women attended the seminar if there were a total of 420 men in attendance?

   A. 840

   B. 980

   C. 1,260

   D. 2,520

   E. 2,940

6. What is the lowest common multiple of 18 and 45?

   A. 3

   B. 9

   C. 90

   D. 180

   E. 810

7. Which correctly compares the greatest prime number less than 50 and the greatest composite number less than 50?

   A. $47 < 48$

   B. $47 < 49$

   C. $47 > 49$

   D. $48 < 49$

   E. $48 > 49$

8. The art museum will earn $6.75 for every $10 raised during a fund-raising auction. Which shows the ratio of the proceeds the museum will keep to the total amount raised?

   A. 13:27

   B. 13:40

   C. 27:40

   D. 27:67

   E. 40:67

Statistics and Data Analysis

You have probably read research involving facts and figures such as the average wingspan of a bald eagle is between 80 and 90 inches, or the median income in Dover, Massachusetts, is more than $143,000 per year. You may even have read that the average American family has 1.86 children (as if someone could have less than a whole child). Facts and figures like these fall under the mathematical category of **statistics**, which deals with analyzing and interpreting numerical data based on samples and populations.

In this chapter, we will review the definitions and skills you will need to know to correctly answer the statistics and data analysis questions on the GED Math Test. As with other types of questions, you will need to apply some of the other mathematical skills we have already reviewed in order to answer these questions. Get ready to put into practice what you know about whole numbers, operations, estimation, and decimals.

What's the Word?

First, let's start at the beginning. Here are a few words and definitions that will be helpful in understanding statistics.

Population

A **population** is an entire group of people or objects about which data is considered. To generalize about a specific population, a sample is often collected or surveyed—for example, all trees in a particular forest, all male students attending a certain university, all employees of a given company, or all residents of the United States.

Sample

A **sample** is a smaller group selected from the population. A sample is used when the population is too large to study every single element. For example, to determine the average age of the residents of a given city, *some* of the people's ages are recorded and analyzed. It would be difficult and time-consuming, if it were even possible, to record this information for every single resident. The portion of the population about which data are collected is the *sample*. The entire group, which would include every resident of the city, is the *population*. For a study to be accurate, the sample should be representative of the general population.

Random Sample

A **random sample** is often the best way to ensure that a study represents the general population, although there are many problems with random sampling, especially if the sample is small. A random sample is a sample in which every individual or object from the general population has an equal chance of being selected.

Biased

A sample is considered to be **biased** if some members of the populations are not represented or if certain members are more likely to be represented. Suppose you wanted to find out how the student population in a high school feels about increasing the budget for the music program. If only band members were surveyed, the sample would be biased, since it would not represent the entire school population.

Unbiased

A sample is considered to be **unbiased** if every member of the population has been chosen on characteristics not based on their inherent characteristics. In plain English, that means you didn't pick a woman because she is a woman or a child because he is a child. This may not seem much different from a random sample, described above. Technically, though, it is. Think of it this way:

surveyors trying for an unbiased sample make an *effort* not to consider given qualities. Let's go back to the example about the budget for the school music program. An unbiased sample would include some members of the band, some students who are involved in the sports program, and some students who are not involved in any after-school activities. To find an unbiased sample, the survey might be given to all students in the first lunch period, since this would be an equal representation of the school population as a whole.

Range

The **range** of a set of data is the difference between the highest and lowest values in the set. Suppose your math quiz scores this semester were 100 percent, 92 percent, 87 percent, and 98 percent. The highest score is 100 percent, and the lowest is 87 percent. The difference between these scores is 13, since $100 - 87 = 13$. So the range of your quiz scores is 13.

Outlier

An **outlier** is a data value that stands out from the rest of the set. Such values can affect measures of central tendency. For example, suppose you wanted to find the average test score of the students in your math class. Fifteen of the students scored between 85 percent and 95 percent on the test; one student scored a 37 percent. This score is an outlier. Including it in a report of the average test score would significantly lower the class average.

Measures of Central Tendency

Measures of central tendency are at the heart of statistics. Basically, these are different ways to report the values at the center of a set of data. These measures include *mean*, *median*, and *mode*. Let's take a closer look at each one.

Mean

When we think about the average of a set of data, we are generally referring to the **mean**. To find the mean, add the values in a set of data and divide the sum by the number of addends.

Example: The ages of the people living in Madeline's house are 17, 12, 47, 50, 14

What is the mean age of the members of her household?

To find the mean, first find the sum of the numbers.

$$17 + 12 + 47 + 50 + 14 = 140$$

Next, divide the sum, 140, by the number of values in the set. Since there are five ages, we will divide the total by 5.

$$140 \div 5 = 28$$

So the mean age in Madeline's household is 28. Did you notice that no one in her house is actually 28 years old? The mean may or may not be one of the values in the data set.

Median

The **median** is the number in the middle of a set of data. To determine the median, first arrange the data in order from least to greatest. Then find the value in the middle of the list.

> Terrell checked out five books from the public library for a research report. The numbers of pages in the books were 147, 653, 812, 92, and 281. What is the median number of pages in the books?

Begin by listing the values in order from least to greatest.

92, 147, 281, 653, 812

Find the number in the middle of the list.

92, 147, <u>281</u>, 653, 812

There are five values, so the third value is in the middle. That means the median of the set is 281.

Finding the median value in a set containing an odd number of items is really pretty simple. But what happens when the set contains an even number? In this case, arrange the items in order from least to greatest, identify the two values in the middle of the set, add them together, and divide by two. Let's try that.

> Find the median of the following set of data.
>
> 73, 10, 82, 141, 155, 26

First, list the values in order from least to greatest.

10, 26, 73, 82, 141, 155

Now, since there is an even number of values, identify which two are in the middle of the list.

10, 26, 73, 82, 141, 155

Add these numbers together and divide the sum by 2.

$$73 + 82 = 155$$

$$155 \div 2 = 77.5$$

So the median of the data set is 77.5. Notice that 77.5 is not one of the numbers in the set of data. When the set includes an odd number of items, the median will be one of the numbers in the set. However, when the set includes an even number of items, the median may not be included in the set.

Mode

The **mode** is the value that appears most often in the data set. To determine the mode, look for any value that appears more than once. It may be easier to do this if you first arrange the numbers in order from least to greatest.

Over the past two weeks, Lexi has traveled for work each day. The number of miles she drove daily is 72, 61, 25, 61, 43, 92, 84, 50, 71, 55.

What is the mode of the set of data?

First, arrange the data in order from least to greatest.

25, 43, 50, 55, 61, 61, 71, 72, 84, 92

Find any numbers that appear on the list more than once.

25, 43, 50, 55, 61, 61, 71, 72, 84, 92

Since 61 appears most frequently on the list, it is the mode of the data set.

What if more than one number appears on the list repeatedly? In this case, find which value appears most often.

What is the mode of the following set of data?

68, 42, 30, 21, 42, 64, 21, 35, 30, 21, 40

First, arrange the numbers from least to greatest.

21, 21, 21, 30, 30, 35, 40, 42, 42, 64, 68

Identify any numbers appearing more than once in the set.

<u>21, 21, 21</u>, <u>30, 30</u>, 35, 40, <u>42, 42</u>, 64, 68

Three numbers are repeated in the set: 21, 30, and 42. Since 21 appears three times, and 30 and 42 each appear only twice, the mode of the data set is 21.

Well, what if two or more numbers appear an equal number of times? Let's find out.

What is the mode of the following set of data?

43, 80, 43, 91, 52, 43, 91, 75, 67, 91, 75

Arrange the data in order.

43, 43, 43, 52, 67, 75, 75, 80, 91, 91, 91

Now identify any numbers that are repeated.

<u>43, 43, 43</u>, 52, 67, <u>75, 75</u>, 80, <u>91, 91, 91</u>

Notice that 75 appears twice, but 43 and 91 each appear three times. Thus, this data set is **bimodal**, meaning it has two modes—43 and 91.

Did you notice any differences between mode and the other measures of central tendency? Unlike mean and median, the mode is always a number that appears in the set.

What to Do

Do you feel like you understand statistics better than the average bear now? Super! Let's go over the six steps you will use to solve problems in this area of math.

```
┌─────────────────────────────────────────────────────────┐
│                    Statistics Steps                      │
│   Step 1:  Read the Problem                              │
│   Step 2:  Determine What Is Being Asked                │
│   Step 3:  Identify Pertinent Information                │
│   Step 4:  Choose Which Operation(s) or Steps to Use    │
│   Step 5:  Solve the Problem                            │
│   Step 6:  Check Your Work                              │
└─────────────────────────────────────────────────────────┘
```

Step 1: Read the Problem

Read each word of the problem carefully to make sure you understand the scenario and will be able to accurately complete Steps 2 and 3. You can even begin to search for key words and think about what the question is asking as you read it thoroughly the first time. As you know, rereading is a great idea if you are at all confused.

Step 2: Determine What Is Being Asked

Each word problem will state certain pieces of information and then ask a question that you will need to answer. As you read each problem, identify the question and figure out exactly what you are being asked to do, what information you are supposed to find, or what problem you will need to solve. Then restate the question in your own words.

Step 3: Identify Pertinent Information

When solving statistics questions, you will need to find the values that are included in the data set. Then find the key words that let you know what to do with this information. Look for words such as *mean*, *median*, *mode*, and *range*. Circle or underline information you will use to solve the problem, and cross off any unnecessary facts or numbers.

Step 4: Choose Which Operation(s) or Steps to Use

Once you identify key words and know what the question is asking, you will be able to plan which steps you need to solve the problem. For example, if you are finding the mean, you know that the first step will be to add, the next step will be to count the number of items in the set, and the third step will be to divide. If you are finding the median, you will first arrange the values in order from least to greatest, find how many numbers are in the set, and then identify the value or values in the middle. If there is an even number of items, you will also need to add—then divide—the middle two numbers.

Step 5: Solve the Problem

Now you are ready to find the answer to the question. Use the plan you devised in the previous step to solve the problem. Since finding measures of central tendency usually involves working with a list of numbers, make sure to include each one. It can be easy to overlook one of the values when adding them together to find the mean or to accidentally leave one out of the list when arranging the values from least to greatest. Work carefully. It might even be a good idea to count how many numbers are in a set and then count how many you have listed once they are arranged in ascending value. That way if one is missing or repeated, you can make any needed corrections before you completely work through the problem.

Step 6: Check Your Work

Before marking an answer, go back and double-check your work. If you have not already done so, make sure you correctly copied all of the values when arranging data in order from least to greatest. Make sure that you followed the correct steps for finding the specific measure of central tendency required to solve the problem. And estimate to make sure your answer is reasonable. If, for example, a question requires you to find the mean of a data set, and your answer is greater than any of the values in the set, you should be able to estimate that this would not be reasonable.

Examples

Let's use what you have learned about statistics to answer a couple of questions.

Gerald's power bills for the past six months have been approximately $174, $215, $183, $198, $225, and $192. What was his mean monthly payment during this time?

1. $195.00
2. $197.83
3. $199.00
4. $201.71
5. $202.60

Here are our steps:

Step 1: Read the Problem

Step 2: Determine What Is Being Asked

What is the mean of the payment amounts listed?

Step 3: Identify Pertinent Information

We need to know the amounts of each bill: $174, $215, $183, $198, $225, and $192. We also need to understand the word <u>mean</u>.

Step 4: Choose Which Operation(s) or Steps to Use

To find the mean, add the amounts of the power bills. Then divide the sum by 6, since this is how many addends you have.

Step 5: Solve the Problem

$174 + 215 + 183 + 198 + 225 + 192 = 1,187$

$1,187 \div 6 = \$197.83$

Step 6: Check Your Work

Now it's your turn. Take a look at the following example. We'll give you the steps you will need to practice the process.

Donna runs a mile each afternoon after work. Her times for the past four days were 6 minutes 12 seconds, 5 minutes 34 seconds, 6 minutes 50 seconds, and 7 minutes 3 seconds. What is the median length of time she ran?

1. 6 minutes 12 seconds

2. 6 minutes 19 seconds

3. 6 minutes 25 seconds

4. 6 minutes 31 seconds

5. 6 minutes 50 seconds

Step 1: Read the Problem

Step 2: Determine What Is Being Asked

_____

_____

Step 3: Identify Pertinent Information

_____

_____

_____

Step 4: Choose Which Operation(s) or Steps to Use

_____

_____

Step 5: Solve the Problem

_____

_____

_____

Step 6: Check Your Work

The correct answer is 4.

STATISTICS DRILLS

Fill in the blanks for question 1. For each of the subsequent questions, choose the best answer.

1. **What are the steps for solving statistics problems?**

    Step 1: _____

    Step 2: _____

    Step 3: _____

    Step 4: _____

    Step 5: _____

    Step 6: _____

Use the following information to answer questions 2 and 3.

The chart shows how many gallons of gasoline Rosa used each month.

Month	Gallons of Gasoline
February	53.5
March	48.7
April	61.9
May	54.8
June	82.3
July	45.6

2. **What is the mean number of gallons of gasoline Rosa used?**
    A. 57.8
    B. 54.8
    C. 54.2
    D. 53.5
    E. 52.9

3. **What is the range of the data set?**
    A. 4.8
    B. 7.9
    C. 16.3
    D. 36.7
    E. 54.1

Use the following information to answer questions 4–6.

The winning bids at an art auction were $250, $170, $225, $185, $160, $250, $995, and $215.

4. **What was the median winning bid?**
    A. $215
    B. $220
    C. $250
    D. $172.50
    E. $306.25

5. **What is the mode of the data set?**
    A. $172.50
    B. $215
    C. $250
    D. $306.25
    E. $835

6. **What would be the result of eliminating the outlier from the data set?**
    A. The mode of the data would increase.
    B. The mean of the data would increase.
    C. The mean of the data would decrease.
    D. The median of the data would increase.
    E. The median of the data would decrease.

7. **Jerome wants to conduct a survey to find out whether people feel that the restaurants in the mall's food court offer enough healthy options. Which would most likely be the best way for him to find an unbiased random sample to survey?**
    A. Ask every fifth person standing in line at the food court.
    B. Ask men shopping in the health food store in the mall.
    C. Talk with everyone currently eating in the food court.
    D. Talk with every tenth person who enters the mall.
    E. Ask women who are shopping in the mall.

8. **While shopping, Alyssa bought two blouses that were on sale for $18.95 each, a sweater for $25.70, and three T-shirts for $12.50 each. What is the mean price she paid for each item?**
    A. $12.50
    B. $13.20
    C. $15.73
    D. $16.85
    E. $19.05

chapter 27

Percents

In earlier chapters, we discussed the fact that fractions and decimals represent parts of a whole. Percents also describe parts of a whole. The difference is that percents always refer to parts of 100.

In this chapter, we will review how to solve problems involving percents, as well as how to relate percents to fractions and decimals. By the end of the chapter, you will be 100 percent ready to face these types of questions on the GED Math Test!

Understanding Percents

Percent means "per 100." In other words, 64% means 64 out of 100. The following model shows 100 squares. Sixty-four of the 100 squares are shaded. That means 64% of the squares are shaded.

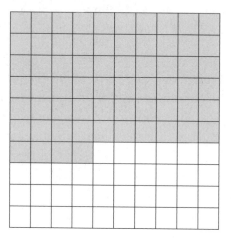

Suppose 100% of students are planning to go on the senior class trip. That means 100 out of every 100 students will be packing their bags. Everyone, the whole class, is going. That's because 100% is equal to one whole.

72 out of 100 = 72%

100 out of 100 = 100%

Percents can be greater than 100. If you were to be given a raise at work, for example, your salary might be 115% of what it was the year before. That means, you made 100% of what you made the previous year, plus an extra 15%.

Likewise, percents may be less than 1. For example, a survey might show that only 0.3% of employees feel that they earn too much money. That is less than 1% of the employees surveyed. The decimal indicates a number that is less than 1.

Decimals and Percents

Decimals and percents can easily be converted from one form to the other. To convert a decimal to a percent, simply move the decimal point two places to the right and add a percent sign.

Convert 0.23 to a percent.

0.23 = 23%

Make sure that you move the decimal two places to the right and do not simply drop it. While the decimal point is no longer needed if the original number includes only two digits to the right of the decimal, it is still needed when more digits are present.

Convert 0.547 to a percent.

0.547 = 54.7%

Also, be careful when there is only one digit to the right of the decimal point in the original number. Since percents are part of 100, the decimal must be moved to follow the digit in the hundredths place. When only one digit is to the right of the decimal point, add a zero in the hundredths place and move the decimal.

Convert 0.7 to a percent.

0.7 = 0.70 = 70%

Converting percents to decimals simply involves dropping the percent sign and moving the decimal point two places to the left.

Convert 91% to a decimal.

91% = 0.91

Convert 120% to a decimal.

120% = 1.20 = 1.2

Remember, the decimal point must be moved two places to the left, so you may need to add a zero.

Convert 3% to a decimal.

3% = 0.03

Convert 0.8% to a decimal.

0.8% = 0.008

Fractions and Percents

Since fractions and percents both name parts of a whole, fractions can be converted to percents and vice versa. To change a percent to a fraction, drop the percent sign. Then write the number as the numerator of a fraction that has a denominator of 100. Finally, reduce the fraction.

Convert 85% to a fraction.

85% = $^{85}/_{100}$

$^{85}/_{100}$ = $^{17}/_{20}$

To change a fraction to a percent, follow the same process you would to change a fraction to a decimal: divide the numerator by the denominator. Then write a percent sign rather than a decimal point.

Convert ¾ to a percent.

¾ = 3 ÷ 4

3 ÷ 4 = 0.75 = 75%

Again, be careful when the quotient only includes one digit. One digit to the right of the decimal point is tenths, not hundredths. Percents are always out of 100, so when you convert fractions to decimals and then to percents, there must be two digits to the right of the decimal point.

Convert $\frac{7}{10}$ to a percent.

$\frac{7}{10} = 0.7 = 0.70 = 70\%$

Solving Word Problems Involving Percent

As you know, most of the questions on the GED Math Test are word problems. Let's go over some of the skills you will need to solve word problems involving percents.

Finding the Percent of a Number

When a word problem on the GED Math Test asks you to find the percent of a number, you will need to change the percent to a decimal and multiply.

There were 400 people at the ballet performance. Of those, 72% were women. How many women attended the performance?

What we have to do: Find 72% of 400.

$72\% = 0.72$

$0.72 \times 400 = 288$

Finding What Percent One Number Is of Another Number

Other questions will require you to find what percent one number is of another.

In a box of 500 circuits, 25 of the circuits did not work. What percent of the circuits were faulty?

To do this, make a fraction with the part over the whole. In this example, 25 is the part, and 500 is the whole.

$\frac{25}{500}$

Then reduce the fraction and convert it to a percent.

$^{25}/_{500} = ^1/_{20}$

$^1/_{20} = 0.05$

$0.05 = 5\%$

Finding a Number When Given the Percent

Some questions will tell you a percent and ask you to find the original number.

Sixty-three percent of the books checked out from the public library yesterday were fiction. If the number of fiction books chosen was 315, what was the total number of books checked out?

To solve this problem, first change the percent to a decimal or a fraction.

$63\% = 0.63$

Then divide the number by the decimal or fraction.

$315 \div 0.63 = 500$

So the total number of books checked out was 500.

Finding the Rate of Change

The rate of change compares a new amount to an original amount.

According to a recent census, the population of Oakdale is 18,000. The previous census 10 years ago showed the population as 15,000. By what percentage did the population increase?

To solve rate of change problems, first determine how much change occurred.

$18,000 - 15,000 = 3,000$

Next, divide the amount of change by the original amount. Write the quotient as a percent.

$3,000 \div 15,000 = 0.2 = 20\%$

Finding Interest

You probably know that *interest* is the payment made by a bank for the use of money, such as the amount you earn on a savings account. It is also the charge paid for borrowing money, such as the monthly fee on a car loan or credit card. Interest is a percentage of the money in the savings account or a percentage of the amount of the loan.

The following formula is used to figure interest.

Interest = Principal × Rate × Time

Principal is the amount of money that is in an account or the amount of money that is borrowed for a loan. The *rate* is the percentage of interest. *Time* is the length of time the principal is saved or borrowed, and it is usually reported in years. For example, you might borrow the money for a car for a period of five years. In other words, you will pay the money back over this length of time.

Keep in Mind

Keep in mind that on the GED Math Test, you will be given a page of formulas to use to solve the problems. The formula for interest is on that list. So there is no need to memorize the formula; however, you will need to be familiar with how to use it.

Let's use this formula to solve a percent problem involving interest.

To buy a new car, Armando took out a loan of $16,500, which he will pay back over five years. His annual interest rate is 7.2%. What is the total amount of interest he will pay for the car?

To solve the problem, plug each of the amounts into the formula. Be sure to convert the interest rate to a decimal.

Interest = Principal × Rate × Time

Interest = 16,500 × 5 × 0.072 = 5,940

So Armando will pay $5,940 in interest on the loan over a period of five years.

What to Do

Now that we have reviewed 100 percent of what you will need to know about percents for the GED Math Test, let's go over the six steps you will use to solve these problems.

Percent Steps

Step 1: Read the Problem
Step 2: Determine What Is Being Asked
Step 3: Identify Pertinent Information and Key Words
Step 4: Make a Plan
Step 5: Solve the Problem
Step 6: Check Your Work

Step 1: Read the Problem

There is really not much chance of finding the correct answer without clearly understanding the question. Make sure you read the problem carefully enough to catch every piece of important information and to know exactly what the problem says.

Step 2: Determine What Is Being Asked

Determine exactly what information the question is asking you to find or what problem you will need to solve. Are you supposed to find the original amount when given a percentage or find the percentage of a given value? Does the question ask for the amount of interest earned on a savings account or the total amount in the account after a period of time? Figure out what the question is asking and restate it in your own words.

Step 3: Identify Pertinent Information and Key Words

Before you begin trying to solve any math problem, find the important information. This may include key words, bits of information, numbers, or symbols. As you solve problems involving percents, pay close attention to the numbers. There is a huge difference between 75% and 0.75%. There is also a big difference between 25 entrants winning a prize in a contest and 25% of the entrants winning a prize.

You already know what the question is asking, so think about what information you will need to find the answer. Then reread the question and determine which information is important and what you will need to know. Underline or circle this information, and cross off any extra numbers that are not needed to answer the question.

Step 4: Make a Plan

At this point, you have already figured out what the question is asking and selected the pertinent information. In this step, you must determine what to do with the information. Will you add, subtract, multiply, divide, convert fractions or decimals to percents, or some combination of these skills?

Percent problems may not be as straightforward as other questions. You may need to use a bit of logical reasoning to figure out what operations and steps you will need to answer the question. Other types of questions might direct you to *find the sum of apples and oranges*. It would be pretty simple to figure out that addition is needed to answer the question. A percent problem that asks you to *find the rate of change in the number of apples produced in an orchard over a 10-year period* will require a little more thought.

It is likely that solving percent problems will involve more than one step. For instance, finding the rate of change involves subtraction and division, followed by converting a decimal to a percent. Converting a decimal to a percent involves a few steps of its own. Figure out what steps will be required to solve the problem and what you will need to do to complete each of the steps. It might be helpful to quickly note the steps you will use in the correct order. Going back to the rate of change example, you might make a list similar to this one.

−

÷

move the decimal

add % sign

As you work through the problems in this chapter, as well as those in the sample tests at the end of the book, figure out what strategy works best for you. Making a few quick notes about which operations and steps may be helpful. If you find mental notes work well and save a few seconds, stick with that. The key is to find out what works for you and be comfortable with that strategy before test day.

Step 5: Solve the Problem

Really, the hard part was done in Step 4. Now all you have to do is follow the plan you've already made. Work carefully, making sure to follow each step of the plan.

Step 6: Check Your Work

Always double-check your work before marking an answer. Glance back over the solution, making sure that every step was followed accurately. Check the placement of any decimal points in percents that were converted to decimals. Quickly estimate what the correct answer should be and determine if the answer you found is logical. If you found that Joe has $500 in his savings account and is earning $150 per year in interest, you can pretty much figure that you made a mistake somewhere, because this is not likely to be true.

Examples

Now let's take a look at a few examples of percent questions.

Abby bought living room furniture costing $4,250. She made a down payment of 10% and financed the balance over three years at 9.5% interest. How much interest will Abby pay per month, rounded to the nearest penny?

1. $30.28
2. $31.88
3. $33.65
4. $90.84
5. $100.94

Step 1: Read the Problem

Step 2: Determine What Is Being Asked

What is the amount of interest for one month?

Step 3: Identify Pertinent Information and Key Words

The original cost of <u>$4,250</u>, the <u>down payment of 10%</u>, <u>9.5% interest</u>, and <u>per month</u> are important to know.

Step 4: Make a Plan

We will use the formula for interest, which is Principal × Rate × Time. To find the principal, we must find 10% of $4,250 and subtract this from the original price. We will convert the interest rate to a decimal. The time will be $\frac{1}{12}$, since we need to know the interest for one month rather than for the entire length of the loan.

Step 5: Solve the Problem

$4,250 × 10% = $4,250 × 0.1 = $425 down payment

$4,250 – $425 = $3,825 principal

Interest = $3,825 × 0.095 × $\frac{1}{12}$ = $30.28

Step 6: Check Your Work

Now you try it. Look at the next example. We will give you the steps you will need to practice the process.

There are approximately 12,500 students at a local university. According to school records, 2,200 students are business majors. What percentage of the student population is majoring in business?

1. 4.7%
2. 5.7%
3. 14.9%
4. 17.6%
5. 21.4%

Step 1: Read the Problem

Step 2: Determine What Is Being Asked

_____

_____

Step 3: Identify Pertinent Information and Key Words

_____

_____

Step 4: Make a Plan

_____

_____

Step 5: Solve the Problem

_____

_____

Step 6: Check Your Work

The correct answer is 4.

PERCENT DRILLS

Fill in the blanks for question 1. For each of the subsequent questions, choose the best answer.

1. **What are the steps for solving percent problems?**
   Step 1: _____
   Step 2: _____
   Step 3: _____
   Step 4: _____
   Step 5: _____
   Step 6: _____

2. **Which of the following fractions is equal to 16%?**
   A. ⅙
   B. ¹⁄₁₆
   C. ⁴⁄₂₅
   D. ¹⁶⁄₂₅
   E. ¹²⁄₅₀

Questions 3 and 4 are based on the information below.

Aiden opens a savings account with a deposit of $4,500. The account pays 3% simple interest.

3. **If he does not make any more deposits or withdrawals, how much will he have in the account at the end of two years?**
   A. $4,527
   B. $4,635
   C. $4,680
   D. $4,770
   E. $4,905

4. **At the end of the second year, Aiden makes a deposit of $300. How much will be in the account at the end of the third year?**
   A. $4,652.10
   B. $4,770
   C. $4,922.10
   D. $5,070
   E. $5,222.10

5. LaToya earned a score of 82% on her final math exam. She answered 123 questions correctly. How many questions were on the exam?

A. 101

B. 150

C. 189

D. 205

E. 223

6. A car dealership sold 4,120 automobiles during the past year. Approximately 58% of the vehicles sold were preowned, and the rest were new. About how many new cars did the dealership sell?

A. 174

B. 238

C. 1,730

D. 2,390

E. 3,882

7. Over the past four years, 5,620 students have graduated from Lake Jefferson High School. Following graduation, 70% of these students attended college. How many of the graduates attended college?

A. 393

B. 802

C. 3,934

D. 4,375

E. 5,227

8. A pair of boots that normally sells for $65.00 is on sale for 20% off. What is the final price of the boots, including 6% sales tax?

A. $47.70

B. $48.10

C. $52.00

D. $55.12

E. $55.90

9. Renee finished her first marathon in approximately 5.2 hours. She was able to complete her most recent marathon in about 3.9 hours. By what percent did her time decrease?

A. 25%

B. 30%

C. 33%

D. 40%

E. 75%

10. A survey showed that ⅜ of the customers in a bookstore prefer to read hardcover selections, and 21.6% of customers prefer reading paperbacks. The remaining customers have no preference. What percent of the customers have no preference between paperbacks and hardcovers?

    A. 37.5%
    B. 40.9%
    C. 48.2%
    D. 51.8%
    E. 59.1%

chapter 28

Probability

Suppose a friend asks you to choose a number between 1 and 2. You have a pretty good chance of selecting the correct number. Now suppose he asks you to choose a number between 1 and 100,000. You are much less likely to select the correct number this time. Determining the likelihood of a given event occurring is the basis of probability.

Whether you realize it or not, you likely use probability on a regular basis. When you flip a coin to see who picks up the check at dinner, enter your name in a drawing for an awesome prize, or cross your fingers and hope for a certain outcome when you roll dice, you are dealing with probability.

Some of the questions on the GED Math Test will address probability. In this chapter, we will go over definitions and strategies that will increase your likelihood of answering these questions correctly.

What's Being Tested?

As we discussed, **probability** is the chance of something happening. An event that is guaranteed to take place is **certain**. For example, it is certain that the Earth will continue to revolve around the sun all day today. On the other hand, an event that has no chance of happening is **impossible**. For example, there is no way the sun will rotate around the Earth tomorrow. This event is impossible.

A few other definitions will also be helpful in understanding probability. Let's take a look at them.

Experiment

You probably did science experiments starting in grade school. Math involves experiments too. When dealing with probability, an **experiment** is a controlled, repeatable situation that involves probability or chance.

Rolling a die, flipping a coin, or drawing a name from a hat are examples of experiments. Each is a situation of chance. When rolling a die, there is a chance of rolling a 1. There is also an equal chance of rolling a 2, 3, 4, 5, or 6.

Event

In probability, an **event** is the set of all possible outcomes for which a probability is assigned. Suppose you wanted to roll a 3 on a die. The event would be the cube actually landing with 3 facing up. If you wanted to roll a number greater than 4, the event would be the die landing with either 5 or 6 facing up.

Outcome

The **outcome** is one possible result of conducting a probability experiment a single time. As you know, the possible outcomes of rolling the die are 1, 2, 3, 4, 5, or 6. The possible outcomes of flipping a fair coin are heads or tails. The possible outcomes of drawing a name from a hat include each of the names entered.

When the result of rolling the die or flipping the coin is the outcome you were hoping for, we call it a **favorable outcome**. If you called "tails" while the quarter was in the air, and the coin landed with tails facing up, you experienced a favorable outcome.

Sample Space

The set of all possible outcomes for an event is the **sample space**. The sample space for rolling a regular six-sided die is {1, 2, 3, 4, 5, 6}. Notice that all of the possible results of rolling the die are listed, and that the list is written within braces.

Determining Probability

To determine the probability, or likelihood, of an event, we can use the following formula:

$$\text{Probability of an event} = \frac{\text{Number of favorable outcomes}}{\text{Total number of possible outcomes}}$$

The following is a shorthand version of this formula. Here, *P* represents probability, and *A* represents a particular event.

$$P(A) = \frac{\text{Number of favorable outcomes}}{\text{Total number of possible outcomes}}$$

Probability can be expressed as a ratio, a percent, or a fraction. A certain outcome, or one that is 100 percent likely to happen, has a probability of 1. An impossible outcome, or one that cannot occur, has a probability of 0. The probability of all other events range in value between 0 and 1.

Take a look at the following spinner.

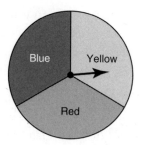

Notice that the sections of the spinner are equal. That means there is an equal chance of landing on any one of the colors. Let's find the probability of landing on yellow. Since landing on yellow is the only favorable outcome for this event, we will put 1 as the number of favorable outcomes. Since it is possible to land on yellow, red, or blue, we will put 3 as the number of possible outcomes.

$$P(\text{yellow}) = \frac{\text{Number of favorable outcomes}}{\text{Total number of possible outcomes}}$$

$$P(\text{yellow}) = \frac{1}{3}$$

So the probability of landing on yellow is ⅓.

What is the probability of landing on a primary color?

$$P(\text{primary color}) = \frac{\text{Number of favorable outcomes}}{\text{Total number of possible outcomes}}$$

$$P(\text{primary color}) = \frac{3}{3} = 1$$

The probability of landing on a primary color is 1. This event is certain, because there is a 100 percent chance of this outcome.

What is the probability of landing on green?

$$P(green) = \frac{Number\ of\ favorable\ outcomes}{Total\ number\ of\ possible\ outcomes}$$

$$P(green) = \frac{0}{3}$$

The probability of landing on green is 0 because this outcome is impossible.

When the probability of an event occurring is greater than 50 percent, we say that the event is **likely**. In other words, there is a good chance that it will take place. When the weather forecast says there is a 75 percent chance of rain, we know that there's a good chance of this event taking place; it is likely to rain.

On the other hand, when the probability of an event is less than 50 percent, there is a small chance of it happening, and the event is considered **unlikely**. When you roll a die one time, it is unlikely that you will roll a 2. It is possible; however, the probability of this happening is only $\frac{1}{6}$, so it is unlikely.

When two events have the same probability of taking place, the events are **equally likely**. Take another look at the spinner we just discussed. It is equally likely that the spinner will land on yellow or blue since the probability of each event is $\frac{1}{3}$.

Independent Probability

So far, the events we have discussed have involved **independent probability**—in other words, the probability of one event does not depend on the outcome of a previous event.

Suppose we flipped a coin twice. The outcome of the first flip has absolutely nothing to do with the outcome of the second. The probability of the second event is not affected by the outcome of the first.

Dependent Probability

Some events involve **dependent probability**, in which the outcome of one event depends on the outcome of a previous one. Suppose we have a standard deck of 52 playing cards. We will draw two cards, without returning the first to the deck. On the first draw, the probability of randomly drawing the ace of spades is $\frac{1}{52}$. However, on the second draw, there are no longer 52 cards in the deck; there are only 51. The probability of drawing the ace of spades on the second draw is now ⅟₅₁. The probability of the second event is affected by the outcome of the first.

Keep in Mind

Keep in mind that if a question states that an event occurred *with replacement*, the events are independent. The phrase *with replacement* means that whatever card was drawn, marble was pulled out of a bag, or name was removed from a hat, it was then replaced, or put back, following the experiment. If it was replaced, the outcome of the first event no longer affects the outcome of the second.

Take another look at the example involving the deck of playing cards. If, the first card was drawn and put back in the deck, the probability of drawing the ace of spades the second time is still ⅟₅₂ because there are still 52 cards in the deck. The probability did not change from one event to the next.

Mutually Exclusive Events

Events that cannot occur at the same time are considered to be **mutually exclusive**. Suppose you were to draw a single playing card from a standard deck. Drawing a heart and a queen would *not* be mutually exclusive because both events could occur at the same time. However, you could not draw a heart and a club at the same time; these events would be mutually exclusive.

Think about our spinner again. You could spin a primary color and red, so these events are not mutually exclusive; it is possible for them to happen at the same time. However, spinning blue and red would be mutually exclusive since these events cannot occur simultaneously.

What to Do

Now that we have reviewed probability, do you feel that you are likely to do well answering these questions on the GED Math Test? Hopefully, you said yes! Now, let's take a look at the six steps you will use to answer the questions.

Probability Steps
Step 1: Read the Problem
Step 2: Determine What Is Being Asked
Step 3: Identify Pertinent Information and Key Words
Step 4: Make a Plan
Step 5: Solve the Problem
Step 6: Check Your Work

Step 1: Read the Problem

Have we mentioned the importance of carefully reading each and every word of the problems on the test? Give yourself the best possible chance of doing well on the GED; read every set of directions, every problem, and every answer choice meticulously. This is certain to increase your likelihood of earning the best possible score.

Step 2: Determine What Is Being Asked

Make sure you know exactly what you are being asked to do or what information you will need to find. You might be given two events and need to determine the probability of the second. You might be asked to find the probability of spinning yellow *or* red. Read the problem carefully, figure out what the question is asking of you, and then restate the question in your own words. Being able to do this shows that you clearly understand the problem.

Step 3: Identify Pertinent Information and Key Words

Once you know what the question is asking, go back and underline any information that will be needed to solve the problem. Look for words such as *with* or *without replacement*. Also look for words explaining the event for which you are determining the probability. For example, are you finding the probability of drawing an ace, a spade, or the ace of spades from a deck of cards?

Step 4: Make a Plan

Now it is time to determine which steps to use to solve the problem. You may need to use the formula for determining probability. A formula page will be provided during the test; however, the formula for probability is not included. Keep this in mind as you prepare.

Since probability may be reported as a fraction, ratio, or decimal, be ready to convert answers from one form to another. Plan the steps needed to make these conversions.

Step 5: Solve the Problem

Now use the plan you created in Step 4 to find the answer to the problem. Work carefully. Remember what you have already learned about division, fractions, ratios, and decimals.

Step 6: Check Your Work

You are already aware that estimation is a terrific way to determine the reasonableness of an answer. Think about what the question is asking, and decide whether your answer is a good fit. For example, since you already know that probability is a value between 0 and 1, any negative answer or any answer greater than 1 is incorrect. Think about the situation given, and estimate whether the event is likely or unlikely. Use this estimate to gauge the reasonableness of your answer.

Examples

Let's use what we have discussed regarding probability and answer a few sample questions.

Lindsey has 2 red mittens, 6 black mittens, and 8 gray mittens in her drawer. She reached into the drawer without looking and pulled out a black mitten. What is the probability that the next mitten she pulls from the drawer will also be black?

1. $\frac{1}{3}$
2. $\frac{5}{6}$
3. $\frac{3}{8}$
4. $\frac{1}{15}$
5. $\frac{1}{16}$

Step 1: Read the Problem

Step 2: Determine What Is Being Asked

What is the probability of the second mitten being black, without replacing the first mitten chosen?

Step 3: Identify Pertinent Information and Key Words

There are 2 red mittens, 6 black mittens, and 8 gray mittens. She pulled out 1 black mitten.

Step 4: Make a Plan

Find the number of black mittens left in the drawer; then find the total number of mittens left. Divide the number of black mittens by the total number in the drawer.

Step 5: Solve the Problem

$$P(black\ mitten) = \frac{Number\ of\ favorable\ outcomes}{Total\ number\ of\ possible\ outcomes}$$

$P(black\ mitten) = \frac{5}{15}$

$\frac{5}{15} = \frac{1}{3}$

Step 6: Check Your Work

Now it's your turn. Take a look at the following example. We will give you the steps you will need to practice the process.

A case of light bulbs contains 60 bulbs. During shipping, 18 of the bulbs broke. What is the probability of randomly selecting a bulb that is not broken?

1. $\frac{3}{7}$
2. $\frac{3}{10}$
3. $\frac{7}{10}$
4. $\frac{1}{18}$
5. $\frac{1}{60}$

Here are our steps:

Step 1: Read the Problem

Step 2: Determine What Is Being Asked

_____

_____

Step 3: Identify Pertinent Information and Key Words

_____

_____

Step 4: Make a Plan

_____

_____

Step 5: Solve the Problem

_____

_____

Step 6: Check Your Work

The correct answer is 3.

PROBABILITY DRILLS

Fill in the blanks for question 1. For each of the subsequent questions, choose the best answer.

1. **What are the steps for solving probability problems?**
    Step 1: _____
    Step 2: _____
    Step 3: _____
    Step 4: _____
    Step 5: _____
    Step 6: _____

Use the following information to answer questions 2–5.

A bag contains 3 red marbles, 5 green marbles, 3 blue marbles, and 7 purple marbles.

2. **What is the probability of randomly selecting a purple marble from the bag?**
    A. $\frac{1}{7}$
    B. $\frac{1}{11}$
    C. $\frac{1}{18}$
    D. $\frac{7}{11}$
    E. $\frac{7}{18}$

3. **Mario pulled a purple marble from the bag and did not replace it. What is the probability that he will select a red marble next?**
    A. $\frac{1}{6}$
    B. $\frac{1}{18}$
    C. $\frac{3}{17}$
    D. $\frac{6}{11}$
    E. $\frac{6}{17}$

4. **What is the sample space of the experiment?**
    A. {red, green, blue, purple}
    B. {green, blue, purple}
    C. {red, green, blue}
    D. {red, red, red}
    E. {purple}

5. **Which two events are equally likely?**
    A. selecting purple and selecting a primary color
    B. selecting red and selecting a primary color
    C. selecting purple and selecting green
    D. selecting blue or selecting green
    E. selecting red or selecting blue

6. **Adrienne wrote her name on a piece of paper and cut the letters apart so that each was on a separate piece. She placed the pieces in a bag and selected one letter without looking. What is the probability that she chose the letter** *n*?
    A. ½
    B. ¼
    C. ⅓
    D. ⅙
    E. ⅛

Use the following spinner to answer questions 7 and 8.

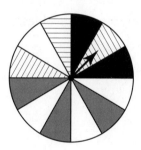

7. **Jordan spun the spinner one time. Which of the following is true?**
    A. It is impossible that he landed on striped.
    B. It is unlikely that he landed on a solid color.
    C. It is certain that he landed on black or gray.
    D. It is likely that he either landed on gray or white.
    E. It is equally likely that he landed on striped or black.

8. **What is the probability that he landed on either striped or gray?**
    A. 0.5
    B. ⅓
    C. 0.25
    D. ⅔
    E. ³⁄₂

9. Fourteen men and six women entered a raffle. What is the probability that the third name drawn will be a woman, if the first two names were both men?

A. ½

B. ⅓

C. ⅙

D. 3⁄7

E. 3⁄10

10. Ryan rolled two identical six-sided die, with sides numbered 1 through 6. What is the probability that the total value of the numbers he rolled is less than or equal to 9?

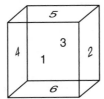 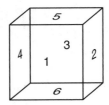

A. 90%

B. 75%

C. 66%

D. 30%

E. 25%

chapter 29

Data Analysis

Have you ever looked at the chart in the newspaper that gives the weather forecast? Have you ever looked at a graph in a textbook to find a piece of information? If so, you have used information from a data display. Some of the questions on the GED Math Test will require you to analyze and interpret data presented in various forms, such as graphs and tables. In this chapter, we will review bar graphs, circle graphs, line graphs, and tables, and go over a few strategies for figuring out the meanings of the information in each type of display.

Analyzing data often involves more than simply identifying information on a graph. To answer data analysis questions, you will use some of the skills already reviewed in this book, including whole numbers and operations, percents, and measures of central tendency. So dust off all that information in your mind, and let's get started.

Tables and Graphs

Tables and graphs are types of data displays. They are often used to organize and display large amounts of data in a way that is easy to interpret, compare, or analyze. Each display is different and is used to report different types of data.

Tables

A **table** displays information in rows and columns. One difference between a table and a graph is that tables present exact data, whereas data in a graph may be estimated or rounded for simplicity.

To interpret information in a table or chart effectively, pay close attention to headings and labels that indicate the type of information being displayed. Take a look at the following example.

According to the graph, how much more precipitation falls during March in Garden City than in Denver during the same month?

City	Average Precipitation for January	Average Precipitation for February	Average Precipitation for March
Denver, CO	0.64 in.	0.73 in.	1.88 in.
Miami, FL	2.09 in.	2.42 in.	3.0 in.
Garden City, NY	3.62 in.	3.17 in.	4.35 in.

First, look at each of the column headings and find the column that displays precipitation averages for March. Then find the rows that show these data for Garden City and Denver.

City	Average Precipitation for January	Average Precipitation for February	Average Precipitation for March
Denver, CO	0.64 in.	0.73 in.	**1.88 in.**
Miami, FL	2.09 in.	2.42 in.	3.0 in.
Garden City, NY	3.62 in.	3.17 in.	**4.35 in.**

Next, determine what strategy to use to solve the problem. Since the question asks *how much more*, subtract to find the difference.

$$4.25 - 1.88 = 2.37$$

So 2.37 more inches of precipitation falls in Garden City than in Denver during March.

Bar Graphs

Bar graphs organize information along a vertical axis and a horizontal axis. The bars on the graph may run either vertically or horizontally. Bar graphs are often used to compare amounts. One advantage of bar graphs, like other types of graphs, is that the information can quickly be interpreted visually.

As with tables, it is important to read the title of the bar graph and the labels on each axis and to notice the scale by which the data are listed. For example, are numerical data reported by ones, thousands, or millions?

Take a look at the following bar graph.

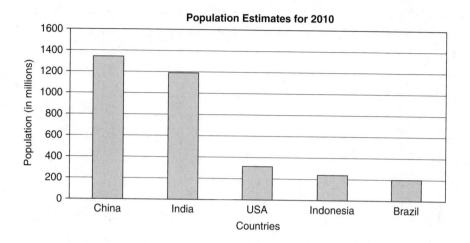

Notice that with a quick glance, you can easily compare the populations of the five countries. Take a look at the label on the y-axis, or vertical axis. It indicates that the data are reported in millions. As we mentioned, the data displayed in graphs may be rounded and may require estimation to interpret. For example, the estimated population of the United States for the year 2010 was 309,975,000. By looking at the graph, we can estimate that the population was probably slightly more than 300 million, but the display did not intend for us to determine an exact amount.

Now use the bar graph to answer the example question.

Which country has a population that is approximately five times that of Indonesia?

First, find the population of Indonesia. Since the bar indicating the population of this country is slightly above the line for 200, we can estimate that the population is about 230 million. Now determine what number would be about five times that amount.

$$230 \text{ million} \times 5 = 1{,}150 \text{ million}$$

Find 1,150 million on the vertical axis of the graph. It will be slightly below the line indicating 1,200 million. Since the bar for India reaches to about that point, we can determine that the population of India is about five times that of Indonesia.

Line Graphs

Line graphs are used to show trends, patterns, or changes over time. Each point on the line graph relates to a value on both the *x*-axis and the *y*-axis. As with other types of data displays, it is important to identify the title of the display, the labels on the axes, and the scale.

Take a look at this line graph.

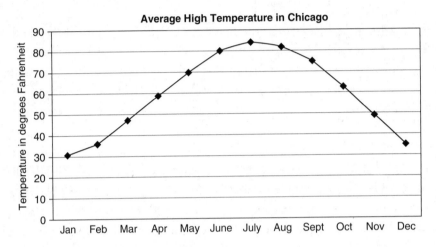

The graph clearly shows that the lowest temperatures in Chicago occur during January and the highest occur during July and August. It also shows more specific information, such as the fact that the average high temperatures in January are approximately 30°F and increase by about 5° the following month.

Some graphs will display more than one set of data at a time. Check out this sample line graph.

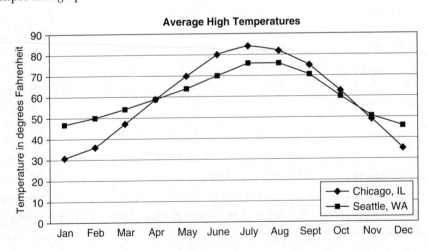

This includes the same data about the average high temperatures in Chicago; however, it also includes the average high temperatures for Seattle, Washington. A visual display such as this allows for a quick comparison of the temperatures in both cities. Use this graph to answer the following question.

> During which month do the high temperatures in Chicago and Seattle appear to be equal?

First, look for any points where the lines cross. Next, determine if the symbols for each city appear to be in the same location on the graph. Take a look at the symbols positioned above October and November for each city. These appear to indicate similar temperatures; however, the temperature in Chicago seems to be slightly higher for the month of September and slightly lower for the month of November.

Now take a look at the points for April. These seem to indicate the same number, which means the temperature is the same in both locations for this month. So the high temperatures in Chicago and Seattle appear to be equal in April.

Keep in Mind

Keep in mind that some types of data displays may include additional information in a key, such as the one seen on the right-hand side of the double line graph. Make sure you read all of the information included. Without reading the key on this graph, for example, it would be difficult to determine which line represents which city.

Circle Graph

A **circle graph**, sometimes called a *pie graph* or *pie chart*, represents a whole amount, and each section represents a percentage of that whole. The sum of the sections of the graph equal 100 percent. This type of visual display makes it easy to determine quickly what percent of the whole is represented by each group. Again, rather than giving exact numbers, the data are presented as percentages. Take a look at the following circle graph. Since the smallest section of the graph is labeled *seniors*, we know that this is the smallest class. Likewise, since the largest section is labeled *freshmen*, we know that this is the largest class.

The circle graph represents the student body of State High School. If the total number of students enrolled in the school is 960, how many students are in the freshman class?

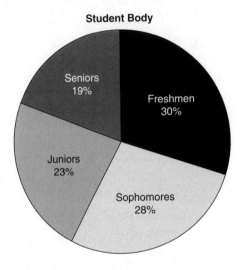

According to the graph, 30% of the students are freshmen. We can multiply the total number of students by 30% to find the number of freshmen in the school.

30% of 960 =

$0.3 \times 960 = 288$

So 288 students are in the freshman class.

What to Do

In this chapter, we have reviewed several types of data displays found on the GED Math Test. Now let's go over the six steps you will use to answer data analysis questions regarding these types of displays.

Data Analysis Steps

Step 1: Read the Problem

Step 2: Determine What Is Being Asked

Step 3: Identify Pertinent Information and Key Words

Step 4: Make a Plan

Step 5: Solve the Problem

Step 6: Check Your Work

Step 1: Read the Problem and All Related Information

In addition to carefully reading the word problem itself, also read all information related to the data display. This includes titles, axis labels, the scale, and the key, if included. Since time is of the essence, just take a quick look at the data to get a general overview of what is included. After you have determined what the question is asking, go back and carefully analyze and interpret the part of the display you will need to use to answer the question.

Step 2: Determine What Is Being Asked

Since graphs are often used to compare information, questions may ask you to compare information from two or more portions of a graph, or they may ask you to interpret the information in a data display and use it to solve a problem. Make sure you understand precisely what information the question is referring to and what you are being asked to do with that information. Once you are confident in what the question is asking, restate the question in your own words.

Step 3: Identify Pertinent Information and Key Words

A question may not require you to use all of the information included in a table or graph. Figure out what information you will need and mark it. Consider drawing a star beside the bars you will use on a bar graph, underlining the necessary data in a table, or circling the points referred to on a line graph. Make sure to check the labels on both axes of tables, bar graphs, and line graphs to ensure that you have selected the correct data.

Step 4: Make a Plan

How will you use all of the identified information to answer the question? Data analysis questions may require several steps. Think about what steps and operations you will use to solve the problem, and make a plan.

Step 5: Solve the Problem

Now use your plan from Step 4 to find the correct answer. Make sure you are using the correct information from the data display, and work carefully to perform any necessary operations.

Step 6: Check Your Work

Once you have found the answer, take another look at the graph or table. Use estimation to determine whether your answer is reasonable according to the data displayed. For example, take another look at the circle graph about the student population. The problem stated that the total number of students was 960. Since the freshman class is 30% of the total, we can estimate that the number of freshmen is about ⅓ of 960, or around 300. Make sure that your answer is in that neighborhood.

Examples

Now let's use what we have reviewed about data analysis to answer a couple of sample questions.

The graph shows Colleen's monthly expenses. According to the graph, what is the ratio of her rent and car expenses to her total budget?

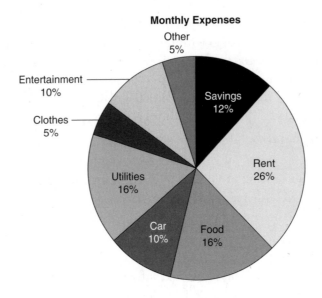

Monthly Expenses

1. ¹⁄₁₀
2. ¹⁄₂₆
3. ⁵⁄₁₃
4. ⁹⁄₂₅
5. ¹³⁄₅₀

Step 1: Read the Problem and All Related Information

Step 2: Determine What Is Being Asked

What is the ratio of the sum of the car and rent expenses to the total?

Step 3: Identify Pertinent Information and Key Words

Car = 10%

Rent = 26%

Total = 100%

Step 4: Make a Plan

Find the sum of the car and rent expenses. Form a ratio with this sum as the numerator and the total as the denominator. Simplify the ratio.

Step 5: Solve the Problem

Car + Rent = 10 + 26 = 36

$^{36}/_{100}$

$^{9}/_{25}$

Step 6: Check Your Work

Now it's your turn. Use the same circle graph to answer the following question. We'll give you the steps you will need to practice the process.

If Colleen makes $4,500 per month, what are her annual rent expenses?

1. $1,170
2. $2,600
3. $11,700
4. $14,040
5. $26,000

Step 1: Read the Problem and All Related Information

Step 2: Determine What Is Being Asked

_____

_____

Step 3: Identify Pertinent Information and Key Words

_____

_____

Step 4: Make a Plan

_____

_____

Step 5: Solve the Problem

_____

_____

Step 6: Check Your Work

The correct answer is 4.

DATA ANALYSIS DRILLS

Fill in the blanks for question 1. For each of the subsequent questions, choose the best answer.

1. **What are the steps for data analysis questions?**

   Step 1: _____

   Step 2: _____

   Step 3: _____

   Step 4: _____

   Step 5: _____

   Step 6: _____

Problems 2–4 refer to the following graph.

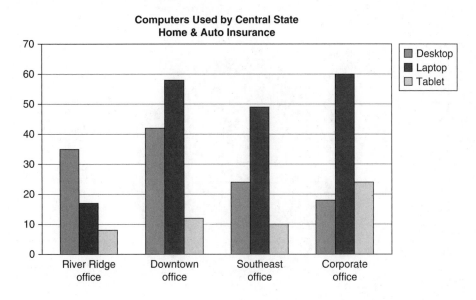

2. **Approximately what percent of the computers in the River Ridge office are laptops?**
   A. 8%
   B. 17%
   C. 30%
   D. 40%
   E. 60%

3. **About how many more tablets are in the corporate office than in the southeast office?**

   A. 6
   B. 10
   C. 14
   D. 20
   E. 24

4. **About how many desktop computers are in use throughout the company?**

   A. 50
   B. 120
   C. 180
   D. 350
   E. 300

Problems 5 and 6 refer to the following graph.

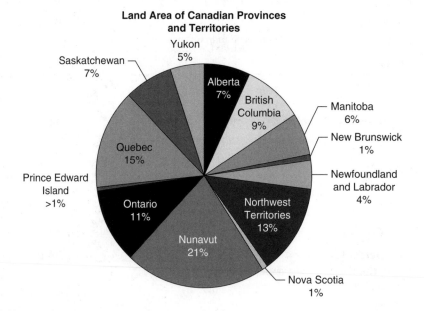

Land Area of Canadian Provinces and Territories

5. **The total land area of Canada is approximately 9,984,670 square kilometers. How many square kilometers larger is the area of Nunavut than Quebec?**

   A. 0.6 million
   B. 1.5 million
   C. 2.1 million
   D. 6 million
   E. 15 million

6. **Which provinces or territories combined equal approximately one-fourth of the land area of Canada?**
   A. Newfoundland and Labrador
   B. Nunavut, Ontario, and Quebec
   C. Northwest Territories and Alberta
   D. Saskatchewan, Ontario, and Nunavut
   E. Nunavut, Newfoundland, and Labrador

Problems 7 and 8 refer to the following information.

During the first month in operation, a new car dealership recorded how each customer learned of the business.

	Week 1	Week 2	Week 3	Week 4
Television	20	22	18	34
Internet	15	19	26	28
Newspaper	12	35	32	29
Mail	9	12	23	16
Other	14	17	30	41

7. **During the first month, how many customers learned of the car dealership from the Internet?**
   A. 15
   B. 28
   C. 70
   D. 88
   E. 94

8. **What percent of the customers learned of the company from the newspaper during the third week of business?**
   A. 33.3%
   B. 24.8%
   C. 20.2%
   D. 19.7%
   E. 17.8%

Problems 9 and 10 refer to the following graph.

Countryside Computer Services went into business during 2004. The graph shows the company's annual profits during its first few years in operation.

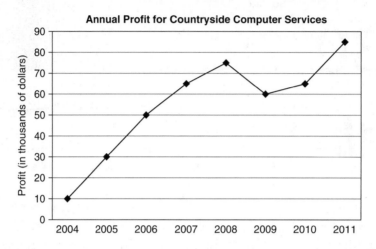

Annual Profit for Countryside Computer Services

9. **By how much did the profits increase between 2005 and 2006?**
   A. $2,000
   B. $5,000
   C. $20,000
   D. $30,000
   E. $50,000

10. **What was the company's mean annual profit during this period?**
   A. $55,000
   B. $65,000
   C. $70,000
   D. $75,000
   E. $85,000

chapter 30

Algebra

So far, the math skills we have reviewed have all involved numbers. In this chapter, we will go over what you will need to know about algebra. This is the area of mathematics in which the 123s meet the ABCs. Algebra is the strand of math that involves unknown values, which are often represented by letters. When working to determine the values of these letters, we will use many of the skills we have gone over in previous chapters, including operations, fractions, exponents, and decimals.

Words to Know

Before we get started, let's go over a few words related to algebra.

Variable

When you were younger, unknown values in math were probably represented by an empty box, a blank line, or a question mark, such as we see in $5 + ? = 8$. Well, algebra moves beyond the blank line stage to a more sophisticated method of representing missing values. The letters or symbols that represent unknown values are called **variables**. So the question mark in $5 + ? = 8$ could be replaced by the letter x, making the equation $5 + x = 8$. At times, more than one variable may be used in a given problem. In this case, each variable represents a different value.

$$4m - 3t + 7 = 16$$

In this example, m and t are variables, and each represents an unknown value.

Constant

The numbers or values that are known are called **constants**. Constants and variables often appear together.

$$4m - 3t + 7 = 16$$

In this example, 7 and 16 are constants. So what about the other numbers in this example? Great question!

Coefficients

When a number and a variable appear beside each other without an operating symbol between them, they are multiplied together. For example, $3t$ really means 3 *multiplied by* t. The number part of a term containing a number and a variable is the **coefficient**.

$$4m - 3t + 7 = 16$$

In this example, 4 and 3 are coefficients.

Algebraic Terms

Any variable, constant, or multiplication or division of a number with a variable is known as an **algebraic term**.

$8y$

$125z$

$9k^2$

Algebraic Expressions

An *expression* is a mathematical phrase that combines numbers and operations— and sometimes variables. An **algebraic expression** combines numbers, operations, and at least one variable.

$$5cd + 7 - a/2$$

In an algebraic expression, the terms are separated by plus or minus signs. This example has three terms. The first is $5cd$, the second is 7, and the third is $a/2$.

Working with Variables

Now that we know what variables are, what do we do with them? Let's find out.

Evaluating Algebraic Expressions

Each variable in an algebraic expression represents an unknown value. When we **evaluate algebraic expressions**, we replace each variable with its numeric value and then evaluate the numerical expression. Basically, we substitute the value for each variable and then find the value of the expression.

Evaluate $7s + 9t - 3a^2$ when s is 5, t is 4, and a is 2.

$$7(5) + 9(4) - 3(2)^2 =$$
$$35 + 36 - 3(4) =$$
$$35 + 36 - 12 =$$
$$71 - 12 = 59$$
$$59$$

Simplifying Algebraic Expressions

To **simplify** an expression means to combine like terms. That means, you combine terms that have the same variable and combine any constants.

Simplify $6a + 7 - a + 5$.

First, rearrange the terms so that like terms are together. Keep the term with the addition or subtraction sign that precedes it.

$$6a + 7 - a + 5$$
$$6a - a + 7 + 5$$
$$5a + 12$$

Keep in Mind

Keep in mind that when a variable does not include the coefficient, it is the same as the coefficient being 1. So x is the same as $1x$.

To combine terms, the variables must be exactly the same.

Simplify $5a + 3ab + 2a + 3$.

$$5a + 2a + 3ab + 3$$
$$7a + 3ab + 3$$

To simplify an expression that contains parentheses, use the distributive property first and then combine the terms.

$$4x + 7(x + 5)$$
$$4x + 7x + 35$$
$$11x + 35$$

Solving Equations

An **equation** is different than an expression in that it includes an equal sign. Basically, an equation states that two amounts are equal to each other.

$$5y = 15$$
$$4 + 7b = 25$$
$$3x + 12 = 28 - x$$

The **solution** of the equation is the value for the variable that makes the equation true. Take a look at the first example here, $5y = 15$. We already know that $5y$ really means $5 \times y$. We also already know that $5 \times 3 = 15$. That tells us that the value of y in the equation is 3. So the solution is $y = 3$, since this makes the equation true.

$$5y = 15$$
$$5(3) = 15$$
$$y = 3$$

When we solve an equation, we find the solution, or value, of each variable. To do this, we must isolate the variable, which means getting the variable alone on one side of the equal sign.

Keep in mind that the expressions on either side of the equation are equal. So whenever we make any change to one side of the equation to isolate the variable, we must do exactly the same thing to the other side for the sides to remain equal.

To solve an equation that involves only one operation, use the inverse operation on both sides. Remember, inverse operations are opposites; addition and subtraction are inverse operations, as are multiplication and division.

$$t - 8 = 2$$

The example involves subtraction, so we will perform addition on both sides of the equation.

$$t - 8 = 2$$
$$t - 8 + 8 = 2 + 8$$
$$t = 10$$

The solution is $t = 10$.

Equations often involve more than one operation. In this case, perform any addition or subtraction first, then perform any multiplication or division. Take a look at the following example.

$$6x + 12 = 42$$

We need to isolate the x in order to solve the equation. Notice that the first term involves multiplication, and the second term is added. To isolate the variable, we will use opposite operations. Remember, division is the opposite of multiplication, and subtraction is the opposite of addition. Let's start by subtracting the term that is added.

$$6x + 12 - 12 = 42 - 12$$
$$6x = 30$$

Since we subtracted 12 from both sides, both sides are still equal, and the equation remains true. Now let's use division to "undo" the multiplication.

$$6x \div 6 = 30 \div 6$$
$$x = 5$$

The solution of the equation is $x = 5$. To check your work, substitute the value of the variable in the original equation and make sure it is true.

$$6x + 12 = 42$$
$$6(5) + 12 = 42$$
$$30 + 12 = 42$$
$$42 = 42$$

Perfect!

What happens when there are variables on both sides of the equation? First, combine like terms by moving the variables to the same side. Then solve the equation as always.

$$7 + 4s = s + 22$$

First, move the variable s to the left side of the equation by subtracting it from both sides. Next, group the constants on the right side of the equation by subtracting 7 from both sides.

$$7 + 4s = s + 22$$
$$7 + 4s - s = s + 22 - s$$
$$7 + 3s = 22$$
$$7 - 7 + 3s = 22 - 7$$
$$3s = 15$$
$$3s/3 = 15/3$$
$$s = 5$$

Keep in Mind

Keep in mind that it may be easier to group variables on the side of the equation that contains the variable with the greatest coefficient. That way, you can avoid working with negative numbers.

Solving Inequalities

Inequalities are statements that tell us two amounts are not equal. They include one of the following symbols rather than an equal sign.

> is greater than

< is less than

≥ is greater than or equal to

≤ is less than or equal to

Inequalities are solved in the same way as equations, with one exception. When an inequality is divided by a negative number, the symbol is reversed. That means, if we have to divide both sides of an inequality by –2, for example, the *less than* sign becomes a *greater than* sign and vice versa.

$$4g - 6 > 14$$
$$4g - 6 + 6 > 14 + 6$$
$$4g > 20$$
$$4g/4 > 20/4$$
$$g > 5$$

So the value of *g* is greater than 5.

Now take a look at the next example. Notice that the sign is reversed when dividing by a negative number.

$$-3h - 8 \le 16$$
$$-3h - 8 + 8 \le 16 + 8$$
$$-3h \le 16 + 8$$
$$-3h \le 24$$
$$-3h/-3 \le 24/-3$$
$$h \ge -8$$

Solving Word Problems

To solve some word problems, it is necessary to translate the information into an algebraic expression. To do this, select a variable to represent the unknown value. Then look for key words that indicate the operation you need to use.

The square of a number decreased by 6 is greater than 4.

Let's use x as the variable. The phrase *the square of a number* tells us that we will use x^2. *Decreased by* 6 indicates subtraction. *Is greater than* indicates that this is an inequality.

$$x^2 - 6 > 4$$

Now we can solve the inequality.

$$x^2 - 6 > 4$$
$$x^2 - 6 + 6 > 4 + 6$$
$$x^2 > 10$$
$$\sqrt{x^2} > \sqrt{10}$$
$$x > \sqrt{10}$$

Multiplying Algebraic Expressions

To multiply algebraic expressions, multiply the coefficients first and then multiply the variables.

$$5d \times 7e = 35de$$

When the expressions being multiplied contain exponents, add the exponents of like terms.

$$3a^2 \times 2ac = 12a^3c$$

As you know, some expressions contain more than one term. When multiplying a one-term expression by an expression with two or more terms, be sure to multiply the single term by each of the terms in the second expression.

$$4x(6x^2 + 3xy + 8) = 24x^3 + 12x^2y + 32x$$

When both expressions contain two terms, we must multiply both terms in the first expression by both terms in the second. To do this, we use the FOIL method.

Multiply:

F   First × First

O   Outside × Outside

I   Inside × Inside

L   Last × Last

After multiplying, combine like terms. Let's try it.

$$(q + 3)(q - 6)$$
$$(q \times q)(q \times -6)(3 \times q)(3 \times -6) =$$
$$q^2 - 6q + 3q - 18 =$$
$$q^2 - 3q + 18$$

Factoring

In multiplication, factors are the terms that are multiplied. When we factor an expression, we separate the numbers or terms that have been multiplied. Factoring is one way of solving some kinds of algebraic equations and expressions.

One way to factor is to find the greatest common factor among the terms in the expression. The first step is to look for any common factors. Next, separate those factors from the expression.

Factor $6m^3 - 21m$.

Since 3 is a factor of both coefficients, we will separate this from the expression. And since m is a factor of both terms, we will separate this variable. We write the factors that have been separated outside of the parentheses and write the remaining values inside.

$$6m^3 - 21m = 3m(2m^2 - 7)$$

Take a look at the answer, $3m(2m^2 - 7)$. Notice that if we multiplied the terms together, the result would be the original expression, $6m^3 - 21m$.

Sometimes you will need to factor an expression that has four or more terms. To do this, you factor by grouping pairs of terms that contain common factors. Then you factor out the common factors from each of the pairs and place the common factor in front of the term in parentheses.

Factor $y^2 + 5y + 4y + 20$.

First, separate the terms into pairs.

$$y^2 + 5y + 4y + 20 = (y^2 + 5y) + (4y + 20)$$

Next, separate any common factors from both pairs.

$$(y^2 + 5y) + (4y + 20) = y(y + 5) + 4(y + 5)$$

Finally, write the common factor $(y + 5)$ first, followed by the terms that you factored out of each pair.

$$y(y + 5) + 4(y + 5) = (y + 5)(y + 4)$$

Another way to factor is to reverse the FOIL method used to multiply. This is used with expressions containing two or three terms that begin with a squared term and end with a constant, such as $x^2 + 6x - 2$.

Begin by determining which factors multiply together to result in the first term, or the term with the exponent. Then find two factors that are multiplied together to produce the final term and added together to produce the middle term. Pay close attention to the signs.

Factor $k^2 + 3k - 10$.

Since $k \times k = k^2$, this will be the first term in each set of parentheses.

$$(k)(k)$$

Now, determine what factors of -10 (the constant) can be added or subtracted to equal 3 (the coefficient of the middle term). Since $-2 \times 5 = -10$ and $-2 + 5 = 3$, write these values in the parentheses.

$$(k - 2)(k + 5)$$

What to Do

Now that you know the ABCs of algebra, let's go over the six steps you will use to answer these questions on the GED Math Test.

Algebra Steps

Step 1: Read the Problem
Step 2: Determine What Is Being Asked
Step 3: Identify Pertinent Information and Key Words
Step 4: Make a Plan
Step 5: Solve the Problem
Step 6: Check Your Work

Step 1: Read the Problem

First, read the problem carefully. Some questions may require using algebra to solve problems in other areas of math or in real-life situations. Make sure you understand the information given and know exactly what the problem states.

Step 2: Determine What Is Being Asked

Determine what the question is asking you to do or what problem you will need to solve. Are you being asked to evaluate, simplify, or solve? Are you supposed to substitute given values into an expression or find the value of the variable on your own? Once you are confident in what the question is asking, restate it in your own words.

Step 3: Identify Pertinent Information and Key Words

Once you have read the problem and understand the question, go back and locate any important information, numbers, and key words. In word problems, look for clues to indicate which operation or operations are necessary. Also pay attention to any operation signs or other symbols given in problems. Overlooking these can impact the result of your work.

Step 4: Make a Plan

Now determine which steps you will need to solve the problem. Keep in mind that inverse operations are used to solve equations. Also keep in mind that some of the questions will require several steps to find the correct answer. For example, using the FOIL method for multiplying expressions will require four multiplication problems, followed by combining like terms. Make sure you identify each step you will use.

Step 5: Solve the Problem

Now use your plan from Step 4 to find the correct answer to the problem. Work carefully and follow each step. Be patient. Due to the number of steps needed to solve some algebra problems, they can require more time than other types of questions. Take your time and pay close attention to exponents, negative signs, and variables as you work.

Step 6: Check Your Work

Always go back and check your work to be sure the answer you found is correct. Remember, just because your answer is among the choices listed does not mean it is the right one. The incorrect answer choices are based on common mistakes and misconceptions. Take the extra time to substitute the value of a variable back into the original equation, multiply problems that have been factored, and recheck any negative signs. You are working with a time limit on the test, but checking your work is a wise use of the time given.

Examples

Now let's work through a few examples of algebra questions.

Which of the following is NOT a value of x for the inequality $16x - 8 \geq 10x + 28$?

1. 2
2. 6
3. 8
4. 14
5. 18

Step 1: Read the Problem

Step 2: Determine What Is Being Asked

All but one of the answers is a possible solution. Which is not true in the inequality?

Step 3: Identify Pertinent Information and Key Words

The word <u>NOT</u> and the greater than or equal to symbol are important.

Step 4: Make a Plan

First, subtract 10x from both sides to move the variables to the left of the inequality. Then add 8 to both sides. After that, divide both sides to isolate the variable.

Step 5: Solve the Problem

$16x - 8 \geq 10x + 28$

$16x - 8 - 10x \geq 10x + 28 - 10x$

$6x - 8 \geq 28$

$$6x - 8 + 8 \geq 28 + 8$$

$$6x \geq 36$$

$$\frac{6x}{6} \geq \frac{36}{6}$$

$$x \geq 6$$

Step 6: Check Your Work

Now it's your turn. Take a look at the following example. We'll give you the steps you will need to practice the process.

Which shows that 12 less than 9 times a number is the same as 28 more than 4 times the same number?

1. $9 - 12x = 28x + 4$

2. $9x - 12 = 4x + 28$

3. $9x - 12 = 28x + 4$

4. $12 - 9x = 4x + 28$

5. $12x - 9 = 28 + 4x$

Step 1: Read the Problem

Step 2: Determine What Is Being Asked

_____

_____

Step 3: Identify Pertinent Information and Key Words

_____

_____

Step 4: Make a Plan

_____

_____

Step 5: Solve the Problem

_____

_____

_____

_____

Step 6: Check Your Work

The correct answer is 2.

ALGEBRA DRILLS

Fill in the blanks for question 1. For each of the subsequent questions, choose the best answer.

1. What are the steps for solving algebra problems?

    Step 1: _____

    Step 2: _____

    Step 3: _____

    Step 4: _____

    Step 5: _____

    Step 6: _____

2. Solve for y in the equation $8y - 7 = 3y + 13$.

    A. $y = 4$
    B. $y = 5$
    C. $y = 6$
    D. $y = 16$
    E. $y = 20$

3. During a yard sale, Alana earned three times as much money as Douglas. Roxana made $10 more than twice what Alana made. Together, they made $150. How many dollars did Alana make?

    A. 14
    B. 15
    C. 42
    D. 84
    E. 94

4. Factor $c^2 - 11 + 18$.

    A. $(c^2 - 2)(c - 9)$
    B. $(c + 2)(c + 9)$
    C. $(c^2 - 9)(c - 2)$
    D. $(c + 9)(c - 2)$
    E. $(c - 9)(c - 2)$

5. Eli bought two adult tickets and three children's tickets to the zoo for a total of $66. Caroline bought six adult tickets for $108. What is the cost of each children's ticket?

    A. $10
    B. $15

    C. $16

    D. $18

    E. $22

6. **Evaluate $12y^2 - 4z + 7$ when $y = 3$ and $z = -2$.**

    A. 43

    B. 51

    C. 87

    D. 107

    E. 123

7. **Simplify $7(r + 5) - 3(r - 8)$.**

    A. $4r + 11$

    B. $4r + 27$

    C. $4r + 59$

    D. $10r + 11$

    E. $10r + 59$

8. **Multiply $(v - 4)(v + 6)$.**

    A. $v^2 + 2v - 2$

    B. $v^2 + 2v - 24$

    C. $v^2 - 2v - 24$

    D. $v^2 + 10v - 24$

    E. $v^2 - 10v - 2$

chapter 31

Measurements

Think about the numbers you use every day. The half-gallon of milk in the fridge, the 10-pound dumbbells you lifted in the gym, and the three miles you drove to work. All of these involve measurement. Some of the questions on the GED Math Test will involve measurement too.

In this chapter, we will review both standard and metric units of measure, as well as conversions within each system. We will review measurements used for length, weight, capacity, and time.

Standard Units

In the United States, the measurements we use most commonly are known as **standard units**, which may also be referred to as **customary units**. These include inches, feet, ounces, cups, pounds, and gallons. Let's take a look at standard units of measure and how they relate to one another.

Length

To measure length or distance with standard units, we use **inches**, **feet**, **yards**, and **miles**.

> 12 inches = 1 foot
>
> 3 feet = 1 yard
>
> 1,760 yards = 1 mile

Capacity

Capacity measures volume, or how much something can hold. We measure capacity using **ounces**, **cups**, **pints**, **quarts**, and **gallons**.

8 ounces = 1 cup

2 cups = 1 pint

2 pints = 1 quart

4 quarts = 1 gallon

Keep in Mind

Keep in mind that measurement conversions will not be listed on the test or on the formula sheet. That means you will need to memorize how many ounces in a cup, how many yards in a mile, and the other common conversions given in this section.

Weight

Weight measures mass. The standard units we use to measure weight are **ounces**, **pounds**, and **tons**.

16 ounces = 1 pound

2,000 pounds = 1 ton

Time

We measure time in **seconds, minutes, hours, days, weeks, months,** and **years.**

60 seconds = 1 minute

60 minutes = 1 hour

24 hours = 1 day

7 days = 1 week

52 weeks = 1 year

12 months = 1 year

365 days = 1 year

Converting Standard Units

Converting units means to change from one unit of measure to another. For example, to find out how many ounces are in 2 pounds, you would use conversion. To find how many feet are in 10 miles, you would use conversion.

To convert a large unit to a smaller unit, multiply by the number of small units in the larger unit.

Convert 6 feet into inches.

Since feet are larger than inches, we will multiply the number of inches in one foot by the number of feet.

6 feet = 6 × 12 inches
6 feet = 72 inches

To convert a smaller unit to a larger unit, divide by the number of small units in the larger unit.

Convert 56 ounces into cups.

Since ounces are smaller than cups, we will divide the number of ounces by the number of ounces in one cup.

56 ounces ÷ 8 ounces = 7 cups

Operations with Measurement

At times, it is necessary to add, subtract, multiply, or divide measurements. Let's go over how to perform these operations.

Addition

To add measurements, first add the like units. Then convert the units to the simplest form.

Add 4 pounds 12 ounces and 5 pounds 9 ounces.

$$
\begin{array}{r}
4 \text{ pounds } 12 \text{ ounces} \\
+\ 5 \text{ pounds }\ \ 9 \text{ ounces} \\
\hline
9 \text{ pounds } 23 \text{ ounces}
\end{array}
$$

Now convert 23 ounces to pounds.

23 ÷ 16 = 1 pound 7 ounces

Write the sum of the weights in the simplest form.

9 pounds 23 ounces = 9 pounds + 1 pound 7 ounces = 10 pounds 7 ounces

Subtraction

To subtract measurements, subtract the like units, regrouping as needed. Then convert the units to the simplest form.

Subtract 3 feet 10 inches from 5 feet 7 inches.

$$
\begin{array}{r}
5 \text{ feet} \quad 7 \text{ inches} \\
- 3 \text{ feet} \ 10 \text{ inches} \\
\hline
\end{array}
$$

Since we cannot subtract 10 inches from 7 inches, regroup one foot into inches.

5 feet 7 inches = 4 feet 19 inches

Now subtract like units.

$$
\begin{array}{r}
4 \text{ feet} \ 19 \text{ inches} \\
- 3 \text{ feet} \ 10 \text{ inches} \\
\hline
1 \text{ foot} \ \ 9 \text{ inches}
\end{array}
$$

Multiplication

To multiply measurements, multiply each unit and then convert the units to the simplest form.

Multiply 4¾ cups by 5.

$$
\begin{array}{r}
4 \text{ cups} \ 6 \text{ ounces} \\
\times 5 \\
\hline
20 \text{ cups} \ 30 \text{ ounces}
\end{array}
$$

Now convert 30 ounces to cups, since this would be the simplest form.

30 ounces ÷ 8 ounces = 3 cups 6 ounces

Write the answer in the simplest form.

20 cups 30 ounces = 20 cups + 3 cups 6 ounces = 23 cups 6 ounces

Division

To divide measurements, it is easiest to convert everything to the same unit of measure and then divide. For example, to divide 7 pounds 8 ounces by 6, you could either convert the measurement entirely to pounds or entirely to ounces. Remember, 1 pound is 16 ounces. That means in this case it would be pretty ease to convert to pounds, because 7 pounds 8 ounces could also be called 7.5 pounds. But usually it is easier to break everything down into the smallest common unit of measure. Since 16 ounces are in a pound, that means 7 pounds is 7 time 16, or 112. Then add 8 to 112. So 7 pounds 8 ounces converts to 120 ounces total. Now you are ready for your division problem Let's work through the example together.

Divide 7 pounds 8 ounces by 6.

$7 \times 16 = 112$

$112 + 8 = 120$

$$\begin{array}{r} 20 \\ 6\overline{)120} \text{ ounces} \\ \underline{-12} \\ 00 \\ \underline{-0} \\ 0 \end{array}$$

The correct answer is 20 ounces.

Metric Units

Metric units are a decimal-based measuring system that works in powers of 10; each unit of measure is 10 times larger than the next smaller unit of measure and 10 times smaller than the next larger unit of measure. Take a centimeter for example. A centimeter (which means one hundredth of a meter, by the way) is larger than a millimeter, the next smallest unit of measure for length. How much larger? Ten times larger. There are 10 millimeters in every centimeter.

The next largest unit of measure of length after a centimeter is a decimeter (which means one-tenth of a meter). How much larger is a decimeter than a centimeter? Ten times larger. There are 10 centimeters in a decimeter. We will talk more about many different units of measure later in this chapter. First, let's go over the most common units of metric measurement.

Length

Meters are used to measure length or distance with metric units. One meter is slightly longer than one yard.

1 meter = about 39 inches

Capacity

Liters are used to measure liquid capacity. One liter is slightly larger than one quart.

1 liter = a little more than 1 quart

Weight

Grams are very small units that are used to measure weight. A paper clip weighs approximately 1 gram.

30 grams = 1 ounce

Meters, Liters, and Grams

Metric measurement is based on meters, liters, and grams. Prefixes attached to each of these units tell how many. Take a look at the list of prefixes.

Kilo (k) = 1,000 of the base unit

Hecto (h) = 100 of the base unit

Deka (dk) = 10 of the base unit

Base unit (meter, liter, gram)

Deci (d) = $^1/_{10}$ of the base unit

Centi (c) = $^1/_{100}$ of the base unit

Milli (m) = $^1/_{1,000}$ of the base unit

Take a look at the value associated with each prefix. Kilo, for example, is 1,000. That means, when this prefix is added to a unit, such as a meter, the unit is multiplied by 1,000. So a kilometer is the same as 1,000 meters. A centimeter is $\frac{1}{100}$ of a meter.

1 kilometer = 1,000 meters

1 meter = 100 centimeters

1 kilogram = 1,000 grams

1 liter = 1,000 milliliters

Converting Metric Measurements

Converting metric measurements involves moving a decimal point. The key to converting metric measurements is knowing how many places—and in which direction—to move the decimal. Converting larger units to smaller units is the same as multiplying by 10; converting smaller units to larger units is the same as dividing by 10.

To change from a larger unit to a smaller one, move the decimal point to the right. To change from a smaller unit to a larger one, move the decimal point to the left.

Take a look at the following chart.

kilo	hecto	deka	Unit (meter, liter, gram)	deci	centi	milli

Find the prefix of the original unit, then count how many places to move to get to the new unit. Move the decimal point that number of spaces in the same direction.

Convert 1,500 centimeters to meters.

Start at *centi* on the chart, since the original unit is centimeters. Count the number of spaces to the new unit, which is *meters*.

kilo	hecto	deka	Unit (meter, liter, gram)	deci	**centi**	milli

Since moving from centimeters to meters involves moving two spaces to the left, move the decimal point two places to the left.

1,500 cm = 15 meters

Another way to convert the base units to other metric units is to use multiplication. Take a look at the chart we discussed earlier.

Kilo (k) = 1,000 of the base unit

Hecto (h) = 100 of the base unit

Deka (dk) = 10 of the base unit

Base unit (meter, liter, gram)

Deci (d) = $\frac{1}{10}$ of the base unit

Centi (c) = $\frac{1}{100}$ of the base unit

Millli (m) = $\frac{1}{1,000}$ of the base unit

Convert 5 liters to milliliters.

According to the chart, one milliliter is $\frac{1}{1,000}$ of a meter, so to change from the larger unit to the smaller one, we will multiply by 1,000.

$5 \times 1,000 = 5,000$

$5 \text{ L} = 5,000 \text{ mL}$

What to Do

Now that we have reviewed the measurement concepts you will need to do well on the GED Math Test, let's go over the steps you will use to solve these problems.

Measurement Steps

Step 1: Read the Problem
Step 2: Determine What Is Being Asked
Step 3: Identify Pertinent Information and Key Words
Step 4: Make a Plan
Step 5: Solve the Problem
Step 6: Check Your Work

Step 1: Read the Problem

Always begin by carefully reading the problem. Since some of the problems involve measurement units you may not use on a regular basis, make sure to read slowly and precisely enough to understand all of the information clearly. Mistaking dekameters for decimeters would make a big difference.

Step 2: Determine What Is Being Asked

Look back at the problem and find out exactly what you are being asked to do. It is imperative to understand what measurement unit is being used and to know whether to convert centimeters to kilometers or to convert kilometers to centimeters. Once you have decided what the question is asking, restate it in your own words.

Step 3: Identify Pertinent Information and Key Words

Information that will be important to identify in measurement questions will include all units of measure, the quantity of each unit, and what conversions (if any) are required. Once you locate this information, underline it in the problem. If extra information is included, consider crossing it off to avoid confusion.

Step 4: Make a Plan

Determine what steps will be required to answer the question you restated in Step 2. When planning a strategy for converting standard measurements, think about whether you will need to multiply or divide. When planning for metric units, think about which direction to move the decimal point.

Step 5: Solve the Problem

Carry out the plan you devised in the previous step. Work carefully. Pay close attention to the placement of the decimal point when working with metric measures. Double-check to be sure that you are using the correct number of units for standard measurements, such as 2 cups in 1 pint, and 4 quarts in 1 gallon.

Step 6: Check Your Work

Look over your work in Step 5 before marking your answer to the question. Make sure you performed each operation and every step precisely. Think about the size of each unit of measure, and consider whether or not the answer makes sense. For example, since you know there are 16 ounces in 1 pound, it would not make sense for 2 pounds to equal 320 ounces.

Examples

Let's look at some sample measurement questions.

The entrance to Jackson & Jackson Law Offices is 660 feet from the mailbox at the corner post office. What fraction of a mile is the front door from the mailbox?

1. ¼
2. ⅛
3. 1/12
4. ¾
5. ⅜

Step 1: Read the Problem

Step 2: Determine What Is Being Asked

What fraction of a mile is 660 feet?

Step 3: Identify Pertinent Information and Key Words

Underline <u>660 feet</u> and <u>fraction of a mile</u>.

Step 4: Make a Plan

Divide 660 by the total number of feet in a mile. Then convert the answer to a fraction.

Step 5: Solve the Problem

660 feet ÷ 5280 = 0.125

0.125 = 12.5/100 = ⅛

Step 6: Check Your Work

Now it's your turn. Take a look at the example. We will give you the steps you will need to practice the process.

Mrs. Chen cooked a beef roast weighing 3.5 kilograms. Her family ate a total of 750 grams of the roast for dinner, and she used 300 grams of the roast to make sandwiches the next day. What is the weight of the remaining roast, in grams?

1. 3,500
2. 3,350

3. 3,200

4. 2,750

5. 2,450

Step 1: Read the Problem

Step 2: Determine What Is Being Asked

_____

_____

Step 3: Identify Pertinent Information and Key Words

_____

_____

Step 4: Make a Plan

_____

_____

Step 5: Solve the Problem

_____

_____

Step 6: Check Your Work

The correct answer is 5.

MEASUREMENT DRILLS

Fill in the blanks for question 1. For each of the subsequent questions, choose the best answer.

1. What are the steps for measurement problems?

   Step 1: _____

   Step 2: _____

   Step 3: _____

   Step 4: _____

   Step 5: _____

   Step 6: _____

2. The length of the sign in front of Dr. O'Malley's office is 75 inches. What is the length of the sign in feet?

   A. 6.25
   B. 6.5
   C. 6.75
   D. 7.25
   E. 7.5

3. Amar bought apples weighing a total of 88 ounces. The cost of the apples was $1.90 per pound. How much did he pay for the apples?

   A. $9.28
   B. $10.45
   C. $13.93
   D. $16.72
   E. $20.90

4. A punch recipe calls for 750 milliliters of pineapple juice, 875 milliliters of cranberry juice, 625 milliliters of orange juice, and 3 liters of ginger ale. How many liters of punch will the recipe make?

   A. 2.25
   B. 2.55
   C. 3.25
   D. 5.25
   E. 5.75

5. Franklin spent 2 hours watching a movie on TV. During that time, there were 42 minutes of commercials. What percent of the time did Franklin spend watching commercials?

   A. 17.5 percent
   B. 21 percent
   C. 24 percent
   D. 28.5 percent
   E. 35 percent

6. To paint the interior of his house, Logan bought 3 gallons of yellow paint, 2 quarts of tan paint, and 3 quarts of white paint. He used a total of 7 quarts to paint the bedrooms. How much paint does he have left?

   A. 1 gallon 1 quart
   B. 1 gallon 3 quarts
   C. 2 gallons 1 quart
   D. 2 gallons 2 quarts
   E. 2 gallons 3 quarts

7. The length of a map in Carmen's geography book is 12 centimeters. What is the length of the map in millimeters?

   A. 0.12 mm
   B. 1.2 mm
   C. 120 mm
   D. 1,200 mm
   E. 12,000 mm

8. To make each costume for a play, a seamstress uses 3 yards 10 inches of fabric. How much fabric will she use to make 9 identical costumes?

   A. 27 yards 10 inches
   B. 27 yards 19 inches
   C. 28.75 yards
   D. 29.5 yards
   E. 30 yards

chapter 32

Geometry

Geometry is the area of math that deals with lines, angles, and shapes. Not only will you need to recognize each of these, but you will also need to understand how they relate to one another and how to measure various aspects of them. In this chapter, we will review the geometry skills you will need for the GED Math test. Let's get started and get your geometry skills in tip-top shape.

Lines

A **point** is a specific location in space and has no length or width. In geometry, points are labeled with letters. A **line** is a collection of points that continues forever in both directions. It is often labeled by naming two of the points through which it passes.

A ———————————————————————— B
                                          k

Notice that the ends of the lines contain arrows. This shows that the line continues in both directions. Since this line passes through point A and point B, it can be named line AB, or simply AB. It can also be named line *k*, because of the label at the end of the line.

Line Segments

Line segments have two definite endpoints. The ends of a line segment are indicated with a point.

This is line segment JK, or simply JK.

Rays

A **ray** has a specific beginning point and continues indefinitely in the opposite direction. The beginning is indicated by a point, and the other end has an arrow, showing that it continues forever in that direction, as shown in ray XY, or XY.

Parallel Lines

Lines that are **parallel** remain the same distance apart at all points. In other words, they never cross.

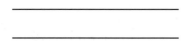

Intersecting Lines

Intersecting lines cross at a common point.

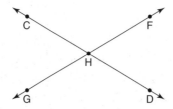

In the drawing, line CD and line FG intersect at point H.

Perpendicular Lines

Perpendicular lines intersect to form a 90-degree angle, which is the shape of the letter L. In the following example, lines QR and ST are perpendicular.

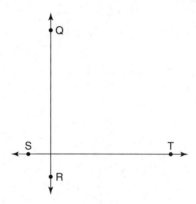

 Keep in Mind

Keep in mind that just like lines, line segments and rays can also be parallel, perpendicular, or intersecting.

Angles

An **angle** is formed when two lines, line segments, or rays intersect. The point of intersection is called the **vertex**. Take a look at the following angle.

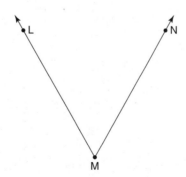

Rays LM and MN intersect at point M, so point M is the vertex. This can be labeled angle LMN or angle M. Using the symbol for angles, it would be ∠LMN or ∠M.

Angles are measured in degrees. A circle measures 360 degrees, and angles are measured according to which portion of a circle they represent. For example, a straight line is 180 degrees, since it would be half of a circle. A quarter of a circle is a 90-degree angle.

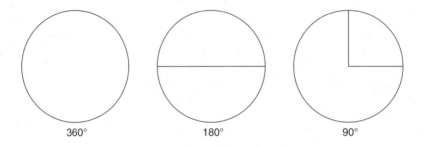

Right Angles

A 90-degree angle, which is the shape of the letter L, is called a **right angle**. The small square symbol indicates that the angle measures 90 degrees.

Acute Angles

Acute angles are those that measure less than 90 degrees. Notice that an acute angle is narrower than a right angle.

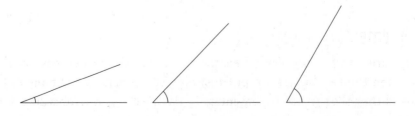

Obtuse Angles

Obtuse angles are those that measure greater than 90 degrees. Notice that obtuse angles are wider than right angles.

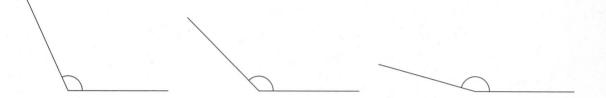

Reflex Angles

Reflex angles are those whose measures are greater than 180 degrees. In other words, they are greater than a straight line.

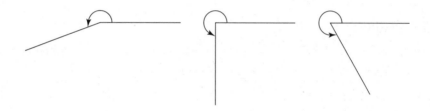

Adjacent Angles

Angles that share a common side are **adjacent angles**. In the following figure, angles M and N are adjacent.

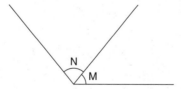

Complementary Angles

Angles are **complementary** when their sum equals 90 degrees, meaning that when the two angles are put together, they create a right angle. Take a look at the following complementary angles. Angle A measures 20 degrees, and angle B measures 70 degrees. Since 20 + 70 = 90, these angles are complementary.

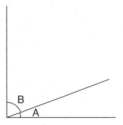

Supplementary Angles

Angles are **supplementary** when their sum equals 180 degrees, meaning that when the two angles are put together, they create a straight line. Take a look at the following supplementary angles. Angle C measures 145 degrees and angle D measures 35 degrees. Since 145 + 35 = 180, these angles are supplementary.

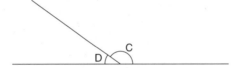

Vertical Angles

When two lines intersect, they form angles. The angles that are opposite each other are **vertical angles**. They have equal measurements.

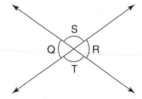

In this example, angle Q and angle R are vertical angles. Both of them measure 70 degrees. Likewise, angles S and T are vertical, because they both measure 110 degrees.

Corresponding Angles

Two angles that are in the same relative position are called **corresponding angles** and have equal measurements. Suppose a pair of lines is cut by a third line, known as a **transversal**. The angles that are in the same position relative to the transversal are corresponding.

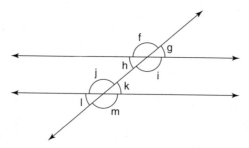

In this figure, angles f and i are corresponding, since they are in the same position relative to the transversal. Thus, they have equal measurements. Likewise, angles g and k are corresponding, as are angles h and j.

Two-Dimensional Figures

Two-dimensional figures are formed by combining points, lines, and angles. Many two-dimensional figures are **polygons**, which are closed geometric figures with straight sides. Let's go over several examples of polygons.

Triangles

Triangles are polygons with three sides and three angles. The sum of the interior angles of any triangle is 180 degrees.

An **equilateral triangle** has three equal sides and three angles measuring 60 degrees each. The little line across each side indicates that the lengths of the sides are equal.

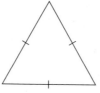

An **isosceles triangle** has two equal sides and two equal angles.

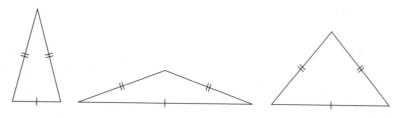

A **scalene triangle** has no equal sides and no equal angles.

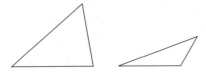

Right triangles have one right angle. The side opposite the right angle is called the **hypotenuse**. It is the longest side of the triangle.

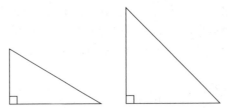

All angles of an **acute triangle** are less than 90 degrees. Equilateral triangles are acute since all of the angles measure 60 degrees.

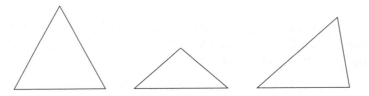

An **obtuse triangle** has one obtuse angle.

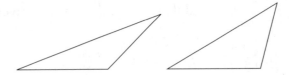

Quadrilaterals

Polygons with four sides and four angles are **quadrilaterals**. The sum of the interior angles of any quadrilateral is 360 degrees. Let's review a few examples.

A **parallelogram** is a quadrilateral that has opposite parallel sides and opposite equal angles.

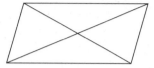

A **rectangle** is a quadrilateral with equal opposite sides and four right angles. Rectangles are a type of parallelogram.

A **square** is a quadrilateral with four equal sides and four right angles. Squares are examples of both rectangles and parallelograms.

A **rhombus** is a quadrilateral with four equal sides. Since a square also has four equal sides, it is an example of a rhombus.

A **trapezoid** is a quadrilateral that has exactly one pair of parallel sides.

Other Polygons

Triangles and quadrilaterals are the most common types of polygons found on the GED Math test; however, there are a few others with which you should be familiar. Polygons with five sides and five angles are **pentagons**. Those with six sides and angles are **hexagons**, and those with eight are **octagons**.

Pentagon   Hexagon   Octagon

Circles

Circles are also two-dimensional figures, but unlike triangles and quadrilaterals, they are not polygons because they have no straight sides. By definition, a circle is a plane figure with all points an equal distance from the center.

The distance from the center to any point on the circle is the **radius**. The **distance** from one side of the circle to the other, passing through the center, is the **diameter**. Take a look at the following circles. Line segment AB is a radius; line segment CD is a diameter. The diameter is twice the length of the radius.

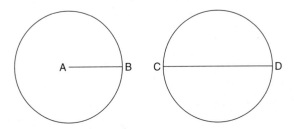

Similarity and Congruence

Figures that are the same shape but different sizes are **similar**. Take a look at the following right triangles. The corresponding angles, or those in the same positions, have the same measurements. The second triangle is smaller than the first; however, the lengths of the sides are proportional. These are examples of similar figures.

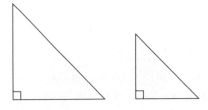

The corresponding sides of the figures can be written as a proportion to determine unknown measurements.

Figures that are the same shape and the same size are **congruent**. Since the following parallelograms have equal angle measurements and equal side lengths, they are congruent.

The figures may be turned in different directions and still be congruent.

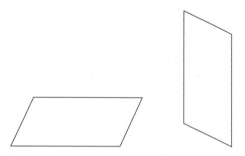

Three-Dimensional Figures

Three-dimensional geometric figures are known as **solids**. Some solids have flat sides that are called **faces**. Let's go over a few of the most common geometric solids.

Rectangular Solid

A **rectangular solid** has six faces, each in the shape of a rectangle. A shoe box is an example of a rectangular solid.

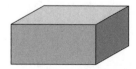

Cube

A **cube** has six square faces, all of which are equal. A six-sided die is an example of this solid.

Square Pyramid

A **square pyramid** has a base in the shape of a square and four triangle-shaped faces.

Cylinder

A **cylinder** has two parallel bases, both of which are circles. The curved sides are perpendicular to the bases. A soup can is an example of a cylinder.

Cone

A **cone** has one circular base; the sides are formed by a curved surface that connects to the vertex. As you can see, an ice cream cone and a pointed birthday hat are examples of cones.

What to Do

Now that you are in good shape to answer the geometry questions on the GED Math Test, let's go over the six steps you will use to solve these problems.

> ### *Geometry Steps*
> **Step 1:** Read the Problem
> **Step 2:** Determine What Is Being Asked
> **Step 3:** Identify Pertinent Information and Key Words
> **Step 4:** Make a Plan
> **Step 5:** Solve the Problem
> **Step 6:** Check Your Work

Step 1: Read the Problem

In addition to reading any information given in the problem, take a close look at any figures or diagrams given in geometry questions. Many of the questions assessing the skills covered in this chapter will include some sort of visual. Notice any measurements or information naming angles, lines, or rays.

Step 2: Determine What Is Being Asked

After reading the problem, make sure you understand what is being asked. Do you need to determine the measurement of an angle? Are you supposed to find the measurement of an angle that is complementary or supplementary to a given angle? Is the question asking which angles are adjacent to a given angle? Whatever the case, make sure you have a clear understanding of the question and then restate it in your own words.

Step 3: Identify Pertinent Information and Key Words

Before trying to answer the question, find and underline any important information in the text and in the visual. Look for angle measurements, the names of lines or rays, and vocabulary such as *complementary, supplementary, adjacent, parallel, perpendicular,* or any of the other words found in boldface throughout this chapter. Underline or circle this information in the figures as well as in the question.

It may be helpful to make notes on the illustration. For example, if the problem gives the measurements of any angles, write the information on the illustration. Label the diagram with any facts, measurements, or details that will be useful in solving the problem.

Step 4: Make a Plan

Now that you know what the question is asking and have identified the important information, map out the strategy you will use to solve the problem. For example, if a question asks you to find the measure of an angle that is supplementary to ∠S, you will first find the measure of ∠S and then subtract this measure from 180 degrees.

Step 5: Solve the Problem

Now follow the strategies laid out in Step 4 to solve the problem. Work carefully. It can be helpful to show your work in writing rather than completing the steps mentally. This makes it easier to identify and correct any errors when you check your work.

Step 6: Check Your Work

Look over your work one last time before marking your answer. Use estimation when possible, and make sure the answer is logical. For example, picture a benchmark angle in your mind, such as 45 or 90 degrees. Use this to estimate whether an angle measurement is accurate.

Examples

Let's look at some sample geometry questions.

Look at the diagram.

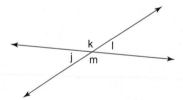

The measure of angle j is 37.5 degrees. What is the measure of angle k?

   A. 37.5 degrees

   B. 52.5 degrees

   C. 142.5 degrees

   D. 152.5 degrees

   E. 322.5 degrees

Step 1: Read the Problem

Step 2: Determine What Is Being Asked

What is the measure of the supplementary angle?

Step 3: Identify Pertinent Information and Key Words

The measure of angle j is 37.5 degrees. Since we need to know the location of angles j and k on the diagram, circle both of these.

Step 4: Make a Plan

To find supplementary angles, subtract the measure of angle j from 180.

Step 5: Solve the Problem

180 – 37.5 = 142.5 degrees

Step 6: Check Your Work

Now it's your turn. Take a look at the following example. We'll give you the steps you will need to practice the process.

A right triangle has one angle that measures 63 degrees. What is the measure of the third angle?

1. 27
2. 54
3. 63
4. 117
5. 207

Step 1: Read the Problem

Step 2: Determine What Is Being Asked

_____

_____

Step 3: Identify Pertinent Information and Key Words

_____

_____

Step 4: Make a Plan

_____

_____

Step 5: Solve the Problem

_____

_____

Step 6: Check Your Work

The correct answer is 1.

GEOMETRY DRILLS

Fill in the blanks for question 1. For each of the subsequent questions, choose the best answer.

1. **What are the steps for geometry questions?**
    Step 1: _____
    Step 2: _____
    Step 3: _____
    Step 4: _____
    Step 5: _____
    Step 6: _____

2. **What is the complement of a 75-degree angle?**
    A. 15 degrees
    B. 75 degrees
    C. 90 degrees
    D. 165 degrees
    E. 285 degrees

3. **The measure of $\angle$Y is 60 degrees. If $\angle$Z and $\angle$Y are vertical angles, what is the measure of $\angle$Z?**
    A. 30 degrees
    B. 60 degrees
    C. 90 degrees
    D. 120 degrees
    E. 180 degrees

4. **Look at the illustration. The measure of $\angle$c is 65 degrees.**

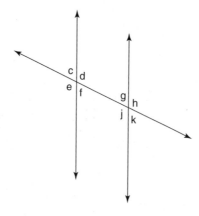

Which is true?

A. ∠d = 65 degrees
B. ∠h = 65 degrees
C. ∠j = 115 degrees
D. ∠k = 115 degrees
E. ∠e = 125 degrees

5. The design on Malia's business cards shows a parallelogram.

What is the measure of angle F?

A. 40 degrees
B. 80 degrees
C. 90 degrees
D. 100 degrees
E. 260 degrees

6. The two sails on Jackson's boat are similar triangles, as shown below.

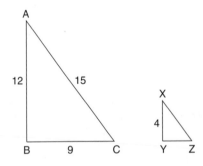

What is the length of XZ?

A. 3
B. 5
C. 7
D. 12
E. 15

Use the following information to answer questions 7 and 8.

In the figure shown, line segment ST is a diameter of the circle, and line segment QR is a radius. Line segment RU is also a radius. The measure of ∠QRS is 62 degrees.

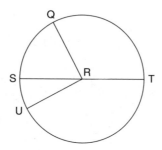

7. **What is the measure of ∠QRT?**
    A. 28 degrees
    B. 90 degrees
    C. 118 degrees
    D. 128 degrees
    E. 180 degrees

8. **In the diagram, ∠QRU is a right angle. What is the measure of ∠SRU?**
    A. 118 degrees
    B. 90 degrees
    C. 31 degrees
    D. 28 degrees
    E. 18 degrees

chapter 33

Formulas

As we have mentioned throughout this book, you will be given a list of mathematical formulas to use on the GED Math Test. The list will include formulas for determining area, perimeter, volume, measures of central tendency, and simple interest. There is no need to memorize these formulas, but you will need to understand when and how to use each of them.

In this chapter, we will introduce and review the formulas that will be provided to you on test day. Using them will involve many of the math skills previously discussed, including whole numbers, operations, fractions, geometry, and statistics.

Area

Area refers to the number of square units needed to cover a surface. Take a look at the following rectangle. The area of the figure is 12 square units, since it takes this number of units to cover the entire rectangle.

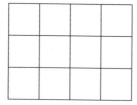

Here, we can easily count the number of squares to find the area, but this is not always possible. Let's go over the formulas that are used to find the area of several geometric shapes.

Area of a Square

$$\text{Area} = \text{Side}^2$$

To find the area of a square, multiply the lengths of two sides. Since the sides are all equal, this is the same as finding the square of the length of any side.

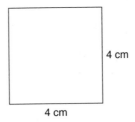

$$\text{Area} = 4^2$$
$$\text{Area} = 16 \text{ cm}^2$$

The area of the square is 16 square centimeters, or 16 cm².

Area of a Rectangle

$$\text{Area} = \text{Length} \times \text{Width}$$

To find the area of a rectangle, multiply the length and the width of the figure.

$$\text{Area} = 3 \text{ in.} \times 7 \text{ in.}$$

$$\text{Area} = 21 \text{ in.}^2$$

Area of a Parallelogram

$$\text{Area} = \text{Base} \times \text{Height}$$

To find the area of a parallelogram, multiply the length of the base by the height of the figure. Notice the dotted line in the illustration. It shows the height of the figure, not the length of the side.

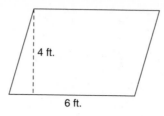

$$\text{Area} = 6 \text{ ft.} \times 4 \text{ ft.}$$
$$\text{Area} = 24 \text{ ft.}^2$$

Keep in Mind

Keep in mind that problems may give measurements you will not need to include in the formula to find area. For example, a diagram of a parallelogram may include measurements of the base, length, and height. Be careful to use the correct numbers in the formula and ignore any extra information.

Area of a Triangle

$$\text{Area} = \frac{1}{2} \times \text{Base} \times \text{Height}$$

To find the area of a triangle, multiply ½ by the base and the height of the figure. Notice the dotted line in the illustration. It shows the height of the triangle.

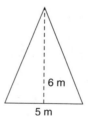

$$\text{Area} = \frac{1}{2} \times 5 \text{ m} \times 6 \text{ m}$$
$$\text{Area} = \frac{1}{2} (30) \text{ m}^2$$
$$\text{Area} = 15 \text{ m}^2$$

Area of a Trapezoid

$$\text{Area} = \tfrac{1}{2} \times (\text{Base}_1 + \text{Base}_2) \times \text{Height}$$

A trapezoid has two bases. These are the sides of the figure that are parallel to one another. The formula for finding the area of a trapezoid calls one of these parallel sides *base₁* and the other *base₂*. It does not matter which of the sides is called which.

To find the area of a trapezoid, multiply ½ by the sum of $base_1$ and $base_2$; then multiply by the height of the figure.

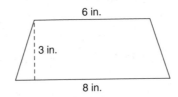

$$\text{Area} = \tfrac{1}{2} \times (6 \text{ in.} + 8 \text{ in.}) \times 3 \text{ in.}$$

$$\text{Area} = \tfrac{1}{2} \times (14 \text{ in.}) \times 3 \text{ in.}$$

$$\text{Area} = 7 \text{ in.} \times 3 \text{ in.}^2$$

$$\text{Area} = 21 \text{ in.}^2$$

Area of a Circle

$$\text{Area} = \pi \times \text{Radius}^2$$

Finding the area of a circle involves the symbol for **pi**. This symbol (π) represents the ratio of the circumference, or distance around, a circle, to its diameter. Pi is equal to approximately 3.14.

The formula for finding the area of a circle is Area = $\pi \times \text{Radius}^2$, although the shorthand version may sound more familiar: πr^2. To use the formula, multiply 3.14 by the square of the radius. As you know, the radius is the distance from the midpoint of the circle to the outside.

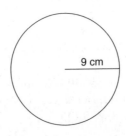

$$\text{Area} = \pi \times 9^2$$

$$\text{Area} = \pi \times 81$$

$$\text{Area} = 3.14 \times 81$$

$$\text{Area} = 254.34 \text{ cm}^2$$

Perimeter

Perimeter is the distance around a figure. Think of putting a fence around your yard. The length of the fence would be the perimeter. Basically, this measurement is the sum of the length of the sides of the figure. Here are the formulas that will help you determine this measurement.

Perimeter of a Square

$$\text{Perimeter} = 4 \times \text{Side}$$

Since the sides of a square are equal in length, we can multiply the length of one side by 4 to find the perimeter, or distance around the square.

5 ft.

$$\text{Perimeter} = 4 \times 5 \text{ ft.}$$

$$\text{Perimeter} = 20 \text{ ft.}$$

Perimeter of a Rectangle

$$\text{Perimeter} = 2 \times \text{Length} + 2 \times \text{Width}$$

To find the perimeter of a rectangle, multiply the length and width by 2, then add the products together. Remember that according to the order of operations, multiplication is performed before addition.

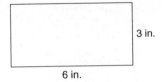

$$\text{Perimeter} = 2 \times 3 \text{ in.} + 2 \times 6 \text{ in.}$$
$$\text{Perimeter} = 6 \text{ in.} + 12 \text{ in.}$$
$$\text{Perimeter} = 18 \text{ in.}$$

A shortcut way to use the formula is to multiply the sum of the length and width by 2.

$$\text{Perimeter} = 2(\text{Length} + \text{Width})$$
$$\text{Perimeter} = 2(3 \text{ in.} + 6 \text{ in.})$$
$$\text{Perimeter} = 2(9 \text{ in.})$$
$$\text{Perimeter} = 18 \text{ in.}$$

Perimeter of a Triangle

$$\text{Perimeter} = \text{Side}_1 + \text{Side}_2 + \text{Side}_3$$

To find the perimeter of a triangle, add the lengths of the sides.

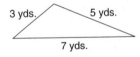

$$\text{Perimeter} = 7 \text{ yds.} + 3 \text{ yds.} + 5 \text{ yds.}$$
$$\text{Perimeter} = 15 \text{ yds.}$$

Circumference of a Circle

$$\text{Circumference} = \pi \times \text{Diameter}$$

The distance around a circle is called the *circumference* rather than the perimeter. To find the circumference, we will again use π, which is approximately 3.14.

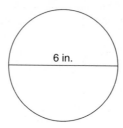

$$\text{Circumference} = \pi \times 6 \text{ in.}$$
$$\text{Circumference} = 3.14 \times 6 \text{ in.}$$
$$\text{Circumference} = 18.84 \text{ in.}$$

Volume

Volume measures capacity; it tells how much a solid is able to hold and is measured in cubic units. Take a look at the following solid.

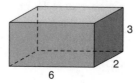

As you can see, the solid is 6 cubic units long, 2 cubic units wide, and 3 cubic units high. If we could count all of the cubic units, we would find that the solid has a capacity of 36. Since it is not possible to do this for most solids, let's go over the formulas you can use to determine this measurement.

Volume of a Cube

$$\text{Volume} = \text{Edge}^3$$

All of the sides of a cube are equal, so we can multiply this measurement by itself three times to find the volume.

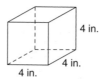

$$\text{Volume} = 4^3 \text{ in.}$$
$$\text{Volume} = 64 \text{ in.}^3$$

Volume of a Rectangular Solid

$$\text{Volume} = \text{Length} \times \text{Width} \times \text{Height}$$

As you know, multiplying length times width gives the area of the base. By multiplying this by the height, we are able to find the volume. Let's take another look at the rectangular solid we used earlier.

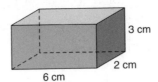

By counting the cubes, we found that the solid has a volume of 36 cubic units. Now let's use the formula to determine the volume.

$$\text{Volume} = 6 \text{ cm} \times 2 \text{ cm} \times 3 \text{ cm}$$
$$\text{Volume} = 36 \text{ cm}^3$$

Volume of a Square Pyramid

$$\text{Volume} = \frac{1}{3} \times (\text{Base edge})^2 \times \text{Height}$$

The base of a square pyramid is a square. Finding the square of the base edge is the same as finding the area of the base. This measurement is multiplied by $\frac{1}{3}$ and then by the height.

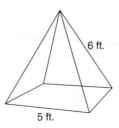

$$\text{Volume} = \frac{1}{3} \times (5 \text{ ft.})^2 \times 6 \text{ ft.}$$
$$\text{Volume} = \frac{1}{3} \times 25 \text{ ft.} \times 6 \text{ ft.}$$
$$\text{Volume} = 50 \text{ ft.}^3$$

Volume of a Cylinder

$$\text{Volume} = \pi \times \text{Radius}^2 \times \text{Height}$$

Since the base of a cylinder is a circle, the formula for finding the volume of this solid includes $\pi \times \text{Radius}^2$, which gives the area of the circle. We then multiply the area of the base by the height.

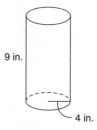

$$\text{Volume} = \pi \times 4^2 \text{ in.} \times 9 \text{ in.}$$
$$\text{Volume} = 3.14 \times 16 \text{ in.} \times 9 \text{ in.}$$
$$\text{Volume} = 452.16 \text{ in.}^3$$

Volume of a Cone

$$\text{Volume} = \tfrac{1}{3} \times \pi \times \text{Radius}^2 \times \text{Height}$$

Notice that the only difference between this formula and the one for finding the area of a cylinder is that we multiply by $\tfrac{1}{3}$ when finding the volume of a cone.

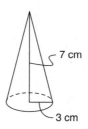

$$\text{Volume} = \tfrac{1}{3} \times \pi \times 3^2 \text{ cm} \times 7 \text{ cm}$$
$$\text{Volume} = \tfrac{1}{3} \times 3.14 \times 9 \text{ cm} \times 7 \text{ cm}$$
$$\text{Volume} = 65.94 \text{ cm}^3$$

Coordinate Geometry

Coordinate geometry involves points that are plotted on a coordinate plane. The coordinates are the numbers that indicate the location of a point on the plane. The first coordinate, known as the *x*-coordinate, tells how many spaces to the left or right from 0 the point is along the horizontal axis. The second coordinate, known as the *y*-coordinate, tells how many spaces above or below 0 the point along the vertical axis. So the coordinates (3, 2) identify a point that is 3 spaces to the left of 0 and 2 spaces above it.

Distance Between Points

$$\text{Distance between points} = \sqrt{(x_2 - x_1)^2 + (y_2 - y_1)^2}$$

In this formula, (x_1, y_1) and (x_2, y_2) are points in a plane. Take a look at the coordinate plane shown.

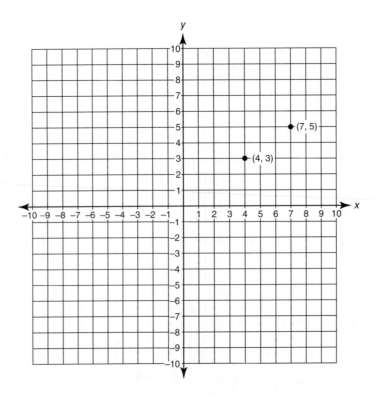

The first point marked is (4, 3) and the second is (7, 5). We can use the formula to find the distance between these points. The ordered pair (4, 3) will be (x_1, y_1) and (7, 5) will be (x_2, y_2).

$$\text{Distance between points} = \sqrt{(x_2 - x_1)^2 + (y_2 - y_1)^2}$$
$$\text{Distance between points} = \sqrt{(7 - 4)^2 + (5 - 3)^2}$$
$$\text{Distance between points} = \sqrt{(3)^2 + (2)^2}$$
$$\text{Distance between points} = \sqrt{9 + 4}$$
$$\text{Distance between points} = \sqrt{13}$$
$$\text{Distance between points} = 3.6$$

Slope of a Line

$$\text{Slope of a line} = \frac{y_2 - y_1}{x_2 - x_1}$$

In this formula, (x_1, y_1) and (x_2, y_2) are two points on the line. Let's take another look at the coordinate plane we used previously and find the slope of the line that runs through the points (7, 5) and (4, 3).

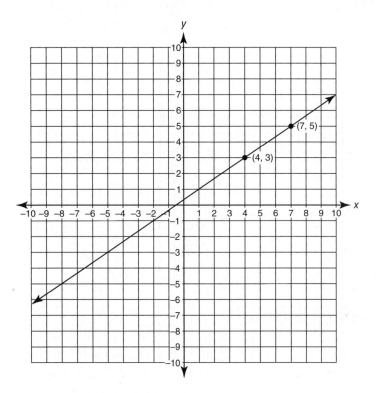

The first point marked is (4, 3) and the second is (7, 5). Again, the ordered pair (4, 3) will be (x_1, y_1) and (7, 5) will be (x_2, y_2). Let's use the formula to find the slope.

$$\text{Slope of a line} = \frac{y_2 - y_1}{x_2 - x_1}$$

$$\text{Slope of a line} = \frac{5 - 3}{7 - 4}$$

$$\text{Slope of a line} = \frac{2}{3}$$

Pythagorean Relationship

$$a^2 + b^2 = c^2$$

In this formula, a and b are the legs of a right triangle. The legs are the sides that meet to form the right angle. The hypotenuse, which is the side opposite the right angle, is represented by c. The formula for the Pythagorean relationship, also known as the Pythagorean theorem, is used to find the length of one side of a right triangle when the other two sides are given.

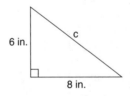

$$6^2 + 8^2 = c^2$$

$$36 + 64 = c^2$$

$$100 = c^2$$

$$\sqrt{100} = \sqrt{c^2}$$

$$10 = c$$

So the length of the hypotenuse is 10 inches.

Measures of Central Tendency

In Chapter 26, we reviewed the fact that measures of central tendency are ways to report the values at the center of a data set. These include mean, median, and mode. The formulas for mean and median will be included on the formula page for the GED Math Test. Let's take a look at these.

Mean

$$\text{Mean} = \frac{x_1 + x_2 + \cdots x_n}{n}$$

To find the mean of a set of numbers, first find the sum of all the numbers in the set. Then divide the sum by the number of items.

Find the mean of 12, 18, 24, 15, and 31.

$$\text{Mean} = \frac{12 + 18 + 24 + 15 + 31}{5}$$

$$\text{Mean} = \frac{100}{5}$$

$$\text{Mean} = 20$$

Median

Median = The middle value of an odd number of *ordered* scores, and halfway between the two middle values of an even number of *ordered* scores

To find the median of a set of numbers, first arrange the numbers in sequential order. Then find the middle value, if the set contains an odd number of scores.

Find the median of 12, 18, 24, 15, and 31.

12, 15, <u>18</u>, 24, 31

The median of the set is 18.

If the set contains an even number of scores, add the two middle values and divide the sum by 2. Take a look at the following example. There are six values in the set, so we'll have to add the middle values and divide by 2 to find the median.

Find the median of 12, 18, 24, 15, 31, and 40.

12, 15, <u>18, 24</u>, 31, 40

(18 + 24) ÷ 2 =

42 ÷ 2 = 21

The median of the set is 21.

Simple Interest

$$\text{Interest} = \text{Principle} \times \text{Rate} \times \text{Time}$$

Interest is another topic we discussed previously (Chapter 27), but we will review the formula here as well. *Principal* is the amount of the loan or the amount of money in an account. *Rate* is the percent of interest. *Time* is how long the principal is saved or borrowed, and it is generally reported in years.

Manuel opened a savings account with $5,000 at 3.5 percent interest. How much interest will he earn in the first month, if he makes no other deposits or withdrawals?

$$\text{Interest} = 5,000 \times 0.035 \times \tfrac{1}{12} = 14.58$$

He will earn $14.58 in interest during the first month.

Keep in Mind

Keep in mind that the formula for simple interest reports time in terms of years. If the length of time is less than one year, use a fraction representing the portion of the year that is being discussed.

Distance

$$\text{Distance} = \text{Rate} \times \text{Time}$$

To determine distance, multiply the rate, or speed, travelled by the length of time. Jenna is training for a marathon. Today, she ran at an average speed of 4.2 miles per hour for 3 hours and 30 minutes. How far did she run?

$$\text{Distance} = 4.2 \times 3.5$$
$$\text{Distance} = 14.7 \text{ miles}$$

Total Cost

$$\text{Total cost} = \text{Number of units} \times \text{Price per unit}$$

The formula for finding the total cost involves multiplying the number or units or items by the cost for each.

A bakery purchased 550 pounds of flour at a cost of $0.86 per pound. What was the total cost?

$$\text{Total cost} = 550 \times 0.86$$
$$\text{Total cost} = \$473$$

What to Do

Now that we have reviewed how to use the formulas that will be provided for the GED Math Test, let's go over the six steps you will use to solve these problems.

Formula Steps

Step 1: Read the Problem
Step 2: Determine What Is Being Asked
Step 3: Identify Pertinent Information and Key Words
Step 4: Make a Plan
Step 5: Solve the Problem
Step 6: Check Your Work

Step 1: Read the Problem

As you know, the formulas will be given, but it will be up to you to decide when to use each one. The only way to determine what formula should be used to solve a problem is to clearly understand the problem itself. What's the only surefire way to figure this out? Read each problem carefully and think about the scenario, if one is included.

Step 2: Determine What Is Being Asked

Now that you have read the problem, decide what the question is asking you to do. Are you being asked to find the total cost of a shipment or to find the mean price of each of the items? Do you need to find the volume of a rectangular solid or determine the area of its base? Figure out exactly what the question is asking, then restate it in your own words.

Step 3: Identify Pertinent Information and Key Words

Once you know what you are being asked to find or what problem you need to solve, look for any important information, facts, figures, and key words. Underline these in the problem. If measurements and other pertinent information are included in a diagram, table, or chart, be sure to circle or underline this information here as well. The goal is to be able to locate the data quickly when it is time to actually solve the problem.

Step 4: Make a Plan

Once you know what the question is asking, you can determine which formula you require to find the answer. Although you may have some of the formulas memorized, take advantage of the fact that they are right in front of you on the list. Copy the formula from the page, paying close attention to what information you will need.

Step 5: Solve the Problem

Once you have selected which formula to use, apply it to solve the problem. Plug the correct data into the formula, and follow the steps to find the answer.

Step 6: Check Your Work

Make sure to double-check your work before marking an answer. Use estimation to determine whether or not your answer is reasonable. For example, to find total cost, round the number of units and the price per unit to the nearest ten or hundred. Then multiply to determine about what the cost should be.

Also, think about whether or not your answer makes sense. For example, the mean of a data set should not be greater than the largest number in the set. The hypotenuse of a right triangle should be longer than the length of either leg. The amount of interest earned is not likely to be greater than the principal.

If you determine that your answer is unlikely or unreasonable, take another look at the formula to be sure you copied it correctly. Then check to be sure you put the correct values into the formula. Finally, check your math; make sure you completed the multiplication correctly, performed the right operations, and accurately applied exponents.

Examples

Let's look at a few sample questions involving some of the formulas we've reviewed.

The round ice-skating rink in the center of town has a diameter of 140 feet. What is the area of the rink?

1. 15,386 feet^3
2. 21,980 feet^3
3. 43,960 feet^3
4. 61,544 feet^3
5. 87,920 feet^3

Step 1: Read the Problem

Step 2: Determine What Is Being Asked

What is the area of a circle that has a diameter of 140 feet?

Step 3: Identify Pertinent Information and Key Words

The important information is <u>diameter of 140 feet</u>.

Step 4: Make a Plan

We will use the formula for the area of a circle, which is $\pi \times Radius^2$. The problem states the diameter but not the radius. To find the radius, we will divide the diameter by 2.

Step 5: Solve the Problem

Area = $\pi \times Radius^2$

Radius = Diameter ÷ 2

Radius = 140 ft. ÷ 2 = 70 ft.

Area = $3.14 \times 70^2 = 3.14 \times 4,900 = 15,386$ ft.^{2}

Step 6: Check Your Work

Now it's your turn. Take a look at the following example. We will give you the steps you will need to practice the process.

Morgan wants to photograph an eagle sitting on the roof of her office building. She stands 64 feet from the building, and the distance between her and the bird is 80 feet. What is the height of the building?

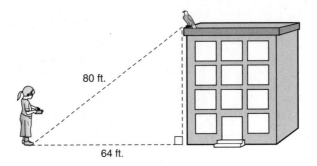

80 ft.

64 ft.

1. 12 feet
2. 32 feet
3. 48 feet
4. 64 feet
5. 102.4 feet

Step 1: Read the Problem

Step 2: Determine What Is Being Asked

_____

_____

Step 3: Identify Pertinent Information and Key Words

_____

_____

Step 4: Make a Plan

_____

_____

Step 5: Solve the Problem

_____

_____

Step 6: Check Your Work

The correct answer is 3.

FORMULA DRILLS

Fill in the blanks for question 1. For each of the subsequent questions, choose the best answer.

1. What are the steps for questions using mathematical formulas?

    Step 1: _____

    Step 2: _____

    Step 3: _____

    Step 4: _____

    Step 5: _____

    Step 6: _____

2. The rectangular flower bed in front of the public library is 35 feet long and 12 feet wide. What is the distance around the flower bed, in yards?
    A. 37
    B. 47
    C. 94
    D. 188
    E. 420

3. Andre is filling his cooler with ice water. If 1 gallon is approximately 231 cubic inches, about how many gallons of water does the cooler hold?

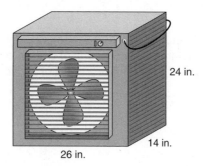

24 in.

14 in.

26 in.

    A. 12
    B. 19
    C. 38
    D. 76
    E. 87

4. The area of a square rug is 289 square feet. What is its perimeter?
   A. 17 feet
   B. 34 feet
   C. 68 feet
   D. 72.25 feet
   E. 96.33 feet

5. Lakeisha has two storage containers. One is cylindrical, and the other is cubical. What is the difference in the capacity of the containers, in cubic centimeters?

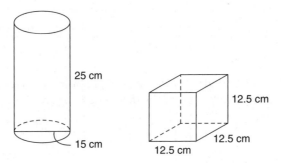

25 cm

15 cm

12.5 cm

12.5 cm

12.5 cm

   A. 1,953.13
   B. 2,462.5
   C. 4,415.63
   D. 15,709.37
   E. 17,662.5

6. On a business trip, Coleton traveled 218 miles before lunch and 184 miles after lunch. If his actual driving time was a total of 6 hours and 45 minutes, what was his average rate of speed to the nearest tenth of a mile per hour?
   A. 40.1
   B. 57.4
   C. 58.1
   D. 59.6
   E. 62.3

Use the following grid to answer questions 7 and 8.

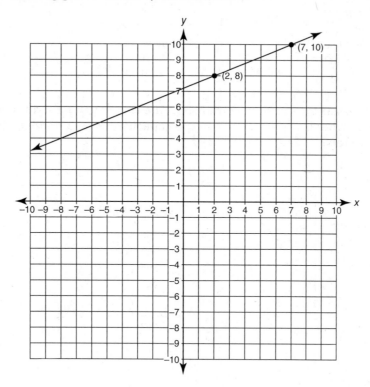

7. **What is the distance between the points on the coordinate plane, rounded to the nearest tenth?**

   A. 2.6
   B. 3.7
   C. 5.2
   D. 5.4
   E. 6.7

8. **What is the slope of the line?**

   A. ⁵⁄₂
   B. ⅖
   C. ½
   D. ¼
   E. ⅛

Part VII

Diagnostic Tests

chapter 34

GED Practice Test 1

LANGUAGE ARTS, WRITING, PART I

Choose the best answer to each question.

Questions 1–8 refer to the following article.

Diggers Hotline

(A)

(1) April is national safe digging month. (2) With the approach of spring, the snow begins to disappear. (3) Homeowners want to get started on outdoor projects and are hoping to get them done quickly. (4) It's understandable.

(B)

(5) Before starting on any project that require digging, all homeowners and contractors must call the Diggers Hotline at the toll-free number: (800) DIGGERS. (6) According to state law, anyone digging must contact the hotline at least three business days before starting work. (7) They must provide information on the type of work the location, and the type of equipment to be used. (8) Diggers Hotline contacts the utility company. (9) The utility company then sent out technicians. (10) They mark the underground cables or pipes with spray paint and colored flags. (11) After that, the digging can proceed safely.

(C)

(12) Diggers Hotline helps avoid damaging homes. (13) Basically ensures that neighborhoods will not be without gas or electricity for long periods of time. (14) Nationally, every year their are more than 200,000 accidents that occur when excavating work is performed. (15) These could be prevented but that's why it is important to call before you dig.

1. Sentence 1: **April is <u>national safe digging month</u>.**

    Which is the best way to write the underlined portion of this sentence? If the original is the best way, choose option (A).

    (A) national safe digging month
    (B) National Safe digging Month
    (C) national safe digging Month
    (D) National safe digging month
    (E) National Safe Digging Month

2. Sentence 3: **Homeowners want to get started on outdoor projects and are hoping to get them done quickly.**

    Which correction should be made to sentence 3?

    (A) change <u>want</u> to <u>wanted</u>
    (B) change <u>them</u> to <u>it</u>
    (C) insert a comma after <u>hoping</u>
    (D) change <u>are hoping</u> to <u>hope</u>
    (E) no correction is necessary

3. Sentence 5: **Before starting on any project that <u>require</u> digging, all home-owners and contractors must call the Diggers Hotline at the toll-free number: (800) DIGGERS.**

    Which is the best way to write the underlined portion of this sentence? If the original is the best way, choose option (A).

    (A) require
    (B) requires
    (C) requiring
    (D) required
    (E) had required

4. Sentence 7: **They must provide information on <u>the type of work the location, and the type of equipment</u> to be used.**

    Which is the best way to write the underlined portion of this sentence? If the original is the best way, choose option (A).

    (A) the type of work the location, and the type of equipment
    (B) the type of work. The location, and the type of equipment

(C) the type of work, the location, and the type of equipment
(D) the type of work, the location and the type of equipment
(E) the type of work; the location, and the type of equipment

5. Sentence 9: **The utility company then sent out technicians.**

Which correction should be made to sentence 9?

(A) change <u>utility</u> to <u>Utility</u>
(B) insert a comma after <u>company</u>
(C) change <u>sent</u> to <u>sends</u>
(D) change <u>sent</u> to <u>was sending</u>
(E) no correction is necessary

6. Sentence 13: <u>**Basically, ensures**</u> **that neighborhoods will not be without gas or electricity for long periods of time.**

Which is the best way to write the underlined portion of this sentence? If the original is the best way, choose option (A).

(A) Basically, ensures
(B) Basically ensures
(C) Basically, they ensures
(D) Basically, one ensures
(E) Basically, it ensures

7. Sentence 14: **Nationally, every year their are more than 200,000 accidents that occur when excavating work is performed.**

Which correction should be made to sentence 14?

(A) change <u>their</u> to <u>there</u>
(B) change <u>than</u> to <u>then</u>
(C) change <u>occur</u> to <u>occurs</u>
(D) insert a comma after <u>occur</u>
(E) no correction is necessary

8. Sentence 15: **These could be prevented but that's why it is important to call before you dig.**

Which correction should be made to sentence 15?

(A) change <u>could</u> to <u>would</u>
(B) insert a comma after <u>prevented</u>

(C) change <u>that's</u> to <u>thats</u>

(D) move <u>before</u> to after <u>dig</u>

(E) no correction is necessary

Questions 9–16 refer to the following article.

History of Video Gaming

(A)

(1) In the 1950s and 1960s there were engineers that, in their spare time, designed games to be played on mainframe computers. (2) They worked at universities and research facilities. (3) The general public didn't have access. (4) The father of video gaming was Ralph Baer. (5) In 1972 he invented the Odyssey console. (6) It was sold by magnavox and came with a cartridge that had 12 games.

(B)

(7) During the 1970s and 1980s other console systems were introduced. (8) The most notable was the Atari 2600. (9) In 1981 Nintendo released Donkey Kong. (10) It was the first game to have for levels of difficulty. (11) More and more games was released, including classics like Flight Simulator, SimCity, and Street Fighter 2. (12) Consoles became larger and graphics became more complex. (13) In 1995 Sony introduced Playstation, featuring games on CDs with 3D graphics. (14) Two million were sold the first year alone.

(C)

(15) Today's consoles use motion control for the gamer to control the figures. (16) Nintendo's Wii, the Sony Playstation 3, and Microsoft's Xbox 360 allow players access to long-running series hit games like Super Mario Brothers, Halo, Grand Theft, and Legend of Zelda. (17) Cloud gaming where the game is stored on a server and streamed into a computer, is gaining in popularity. (18) And video gaming isn't just for kids anymore. (19) First-generation gamers had entered their thirties and forties.

9. Sentence 1: **In the 1950s and 1960s, there were engineers that, in their spare time, designed games to be played on mainframe computers.**

Which correction should be made to sentence 1?

(A) change <u>were</u> to <u>was</u>
(B) remove the comma after <u>that</u>
(C) change <u>that</u> to <u>who</u>
(D) change <u>played</u> to <u>playing</u>
(E) no correction is necessary

10. Sentence 3: **The general public didn't have access.**

The most effective revision of sentence 3 would begin with which group of words?

(A) Not having access
(B) As a result, the public
(C) Instead of this, the public
(D) No public access
(E) For example, no access

11. Sentence 6: **It was sold by magnavox and came with a cartridge that had 12 games.**

Which correction should be made to sentence 6?

(A) change <u>was</u> to <u>is</u>
(B) change <u>magnavox</u> to <u>Magnavox</u>
(C) change <u>that</u> to <u>who</u>
(D) insert a comma after <u>cartridge</u>
(E) no correction is necessary

12. Sentences 7 and 8: **During the 1970s and 1980s other console systems were introduced. The most notable was the Atari 2600.**

The most effective combination of sentences 7 and 8 would include which group of words?

(A) introduced, but the most notable
(B) introduced and the most notable could be
(C) introduced, yet the most notable
(D) introduced, however, the most notable
(E) introduced, the most notable being

13. Sentence 10: **It was the first game to have for levels of difficulty.**

   Which correction should be made to sentence 10?

   (A) change <u>was</u> to <u>were</u>
   (B) insert a comma after <u>first</u>
   (C) change <u>for</u> to <u>four</u>
   (D) change <u>difficulty</u> to <u>difficulties'</u>
   (E) no correction is necessary

14. Sentence 11: **More and more games <u>was</u> released, including classics like Flight Simulator, SimCity, and Street Fighter 2.**

   Which is the best way to write the underlined portion of this sentence? If the original is the best way, choose option (A).

   (A) was
   (B) is
   (C) are
   (D) were
   (E) was being

15. Sentence 17: **Cloud gaming where the game is stored on a server and streamed into a computer, is gaining in popularity.**

   Which correction should be made to sentence 17?

   (A) insert a comma after <u>gaming</u>
   (B) change <u>is</u> to <u>are</u>
   (C) remove the comma after <u>computer</u>
   (D) change <u>is gaining</u> to <u>was gaining</u>
   (E) no correction is necessary

16. Sentence 19: **First-generation gamers had entered their thirties and forties.**

   Which correction should be made to sentence 19?

   (A) insert a comma after <u>generation</u>
   (B) change <u>gamers</u> to <u>Gamers</u>
   (C) change <u>had entered</u> to <u>are entering</u>
   (D) change <u>thirties</u> to <u>thirties'</u>
   (E) no correction is necessary

Questions 17–24 refer to the following letter.

39 Lucas Ave.
Stillwater, AL 32100
dmays@gmail.org
July 6, 2011

Mr. Joe Menot
Pegasus Tool & Die Co.
3211 Hwy. 65 S
Stillwater, AL 32100

Dear Mr. Menot:

(A)

(1) Please accept my application, which was posted in Monday's *Post Star*, for the position of apprentice machinist. (2) I would very much like to apply for that job. (3) I graduated from Stillwater High School in June. (4) While at the school, I took Shop my first year and I loved it. (5) I went to elementary school in Stillwater too.

(B)

(6) I learned more in Shop than I did in any other class. (7) My project was to build a miniature steam engine. (8) I completed it by the end of the school year with the help of Mr. Mylecrane. (9) He is my teacher. (10) I having always enjoyed working with my hands and I learn very quickly. (11) I especially liked working on the lathe Mr. Mylecrane said he would write a letter of recommendation for me if it would help.

(C)

(12) I am enclosing a resume. (13) At the end of the week, will call you and see if I can arrange a visit. (14) I would very much like to see how things is done at Pegasus and what kinds of things you manufacture. (15) Thank you for your time. (16) I look forward to hour meeting.

Sincerely yours,
David Mays

17. Sentence 1: **Please accept my application, which was posted in Monday's *Post Star*, for the position of apprentice machinist.**

    Which correction should be made to sentence 1?

    (A) insert a comma after <u>Please</u>
    (B) change <u>accept</u> to <u>accepts</u>
    (C) move <u>which was posted in Monday's</u> *Post Star* after <u>machinist</u>
    (D) change <u>Monday's *Post Star*</u> to *Monday's Post Star*
    (E) no correction is necessary

18. Which revision should be made to paragraph A?

    (A) remove sentence 1
    (B) move sentence 3 to the end of the paragraph
    (C) begin a new paragraph after sentence 4
    (D) remove sentence 5
    (E) no revision is necessary

19. Sentences 8 and 9: **I completed it by the end of the school year with the help of Mr. Mylecrane. He is my teacher.**

    The most effective combination of sentences 8 and 9 would include which group of words?

    (A) Mr. Mylecrane, being
    (B) Mr. Mylecrane, which is
    (C) Mr. Mylecrane, and he is
    (D) Mr. Mylecrane, as he is
    (E) Mr. Mylecrane, my

20. Sentence 10: **I <u>having always enjoyed working</u> with my hands and I learn very quickly.**

    Which is the best way to write the underlined portion of this sentence? If the original is the best way, choose option (A).

    (A) having always enjoyed
    (B) was always enjoying
    (C) were always enjoying
    (D) have always enjoyed
    (E) had always enjoyed

21. Sentence 11: I especially liked working on the <u>lathe Mr. Mylecrane</u> said he would write a letter of recommendation for me if it would help.

Which is the best way to write the underlined portion of this sentence? If the original is the best way, choose option (A).

(A) lathe Mr. Mylecrane
(B) lathe, Mr. Mylecrane
(C) lathe, though Mr. Mylecrane
(D) lathe. Mr. Mylecrane
(E) lathe, but Mr. Mylecrane

22. Sentence 13: At the end of the week, will call you and see if I can arrange a visit.

Which correction should be made to sentence 13?

(A) remove the comma after <u>week</u>
(B) insert <u>I</u> before <u>will</u>
(C) change <u>you</u> to <u>them</u>
(D) change <u>can</u> to <u>cans</u>
(E) no correction is necessary

23. Sentence 14: I would very much like to see how things is done at Pegasus and what kinds of things you manufacture.

Which correction should be made to sentence 14?

(A) change <u>much</u> to <u>mostly</u>
(B) insert a comma after <u>like</u>
(C) change <u>is</u> to <u>are</u>
(D) change <u>Pegasus</u> to <u>pegasus</u>
(E) no correction is necessary

24. Sentence 16: I look forward to <u>hour</u> meeting.

Which is the best way to write the underlined portion of this sentence? If the original is the best way, choose option (A).

(A) hour
(B) your
(C) its
(D) our
(E) we

Questions 25–33 refer to the following article.

Jets: Then and Now

(A)

(1) Jet aircraft are different from propeller planes, they use the exhaust from a gas turbine for propulsion. (2) The first jet airplane, a Heinkel He 178, flew in 1939 in Germany. (3) The Germans developed other jets during world war II, but they were never used extensively in the war or mass-produced. (4) The first jet airliner was the de Havilland Comet. (5) Its maiden flight was in 1952. (6) The plane seated 78 passengers and had a top speed of 500 mph.

(B)

(7) In 1958, Boeing introduced the 707. (8) It had four wing-mounted jet engines and had a speed of 550 MPH. (9) The aircraft was 128 feet long. (10) With a wingspan of 130 feet and seating for 140 people. (11) The early 707s had a range of 3,500 miles. (12) Boeing also produced the Tri-jet in the 1960s. (13) The plane having three jet engines mounted in the rear and was used extensively for shorter flights.

(C)

(14) Today, both Boeing and Airbus are developing a new generation of wide body craft. (15) Boeing has the 787 and Airbus the A-380. (16) Seating up to 575 passengers, the planes will be 20 feet wide, will fly at 650 MPH. (17) It will have a range of more than 8,000 miles. (18) Jets truly have come a long way in a short time.

(D)

(19) Another company, Airbus, rolled out its first of a new generation of jet aircraft, in 1972, called wide body jets. (20) Called the A-300, the plane had too wing mounted engines, with a fuselage of 177 feet and a wing span of 147 feet. (21) The plane seated 250, was cruising at 567 MPH, and had a range of 4,150 miles.

25. Sentence 1: Jet aircraft are different from propeller planes, they use the exhaust from a gas turbine for propulsion.

Which correction should be made to sentence 1?

(A) remove <u>are</u>
(B) insert a comma after <u>different</u>
(C) replace the comma with <u>because</u>
(D) remove the comma
(E) no correction is necessary

26. Sentence 3: The Germans developed other jets during world war II, but they were never used extensively in the war or mass-produced.

Which correction should be made to sentence 2?

(A) change <u>Germans</u> to <u>Germans'</u>
(B) change <u>world war</u> to <u>World War</u>
(C) remove the comma after <u>II</u>
(D) insert a comma after <u>extensively</u>
(E) no correction is necessary

27. Sentences 9 and 10: The aircraft was 128 feet <u>long. With</u> a wingspan of 130 feet and seating for 140 people.

Which is the best way to write the underlined portion of these sentences? If the original is the best way, choose option (A).

(A) long. With
(B) long; with
(C) long: with
(D) long. Having
(E) long with

28. Which sentence would be most effective if inserted at the beginning of paragraph A?

(A) The history of jet travel is as exciting as it is rich.
(B) Propeller planes are smaller than jet planes and cost less too.
(C) Traveling in a jet takes less time than traveling in a propeller plane.
(D) Planes are a great hobby.
(E) Traveling by plane is a lot nicer now that there are jets.

29. Sentence 13: **The plane <u>having</u> three jet engines mounted in the rear and was used extensively for shorter flights.**

    Which is the best way to write the underlined portion of this sentence? If the original is the best way, choose option (A).

    (A) having
    (B) had
    (C) have had
    (D) is having
    (E) was having

30. Sentences 16 and 17: **Seating up to 575 passengers, the planes will be 20 feet wide, will fly at 650 mph. It will have a range of more than 8,000 miles.**

    The most effective combination of sentences 16 and 17 would include which group of words?

    (A) and had a range
    (B) and having a range
    (C) and will have a range
    (D) as to having a range
    (E) yet will have a range

31. Sentence 19: **Another company, Airbus, rolled out its first of a new generation of jet aircraft, in 1972, called wide-body jets.**

    Which correction should be made to sentence 19?

    (A) move <u>called wide-body jets</u> after <u>aircraft</u>
    (B) change <u>Airbus</u> to <u>airbus</u>
    (C) change <u>its</u> to <u>it's</u>
    (D) insert a comma after <u>generation</u>
    (E) no correction is necessary

32. Sentence 21: **The plane seated 250, <u>was cruising</u> at 567 MPH, and had a range of 4,150 miles.**

    Which is the best way to write the underlined portion of this sentence? If the original is the best way, choose option (A).

    (A) was cruising
    (B) were cruising

(C) cruising

(D) cruised

(E) will cruise

33. Which revision would improve the effectiveness of the article?

(A) join paragraphs A and B

(B) join paragraphs C and D

(C) begin a new paragraph at sentence 16

(D) move paragraph C after paragraph D

(E) no revision is necessary

Questions 34–41 refer to the following article.

Watch Out for Telemarketing Fraud

(A)

(1) Every year hundreds of million dollars are losing by consumers due to telemarketing fraud. (2) People are duped on the phone into sending money to someone. (3) We end up getting nothing in return. (4) Here are some warning signs of telephone fraud to watch out for.

(B)

(5) If a person calls you and says that you have to act right away or the offer will expire that is a sign that something is wrong. (6) Or, if he says you can't afford to miss out on a high profit opportunity, that is another sign of fraud. (7) You should never giving a credit card number or bank account number to anybody over the phone.

(C)

(8) When someone calls you to sell you something, ask for a website address for the business so you can look to see if they is legitimate. (9) Ask for references from other people who were called by the telemarketer. (10) Whatever the situation, make sure you get something in writing before you agree to spend any money. (11) A reputable telemarketer will have no problem agreeing to your requests. (12) To summarize, be alert to the warning signs when a

caller tries to sell you something over the phone. (13) If the offer is for reel, then you can be confident in proceeding. (14) If you feel that you have been a victim of fraud, make sure you call the authorities at once.

34. Sentence 1: **Every year hundreds of million dollars are losing by consumers due to telemarketing fraud.**

    Which correction should be made to sentence 1?

    (A) insert a comma after <u>Every</u>
    (B) change <u>consumers</u> to <u>consumers'</u>
    (C) change <u>losing</u> to <u>lost</u>
    (D) capitalize <u>telemarketing</u>
    (E) no correction is necessary

35. Sentence 3: <u>**We**</u> **end up getting nothing in return.**

    Which is the best way to write the underlined portion of this sentence? If the original is the best way, choose option (A).

    (A) We
    (B) She
    (C) Them
    (D) They
    (E) Our

36. Sentence 5: **If a person calls you and says that you have to act right away or the offer will** <u>**expire that**</u> **is a sign that something is wrong.**

    Which is the best way to write the underlined portion of this sentence? If the original is the best way, choose option (A).

    (A) expire that
    (B) expire, that
    (C) expiring, that
    (D) expire; that
    (E) expire: that

37. Sentence 7: **You <u>should never giving</u> a credit card number or bank account number to anybody over the phone.**

    Which is the best way to write the underlined portion of this sentence? If the original is the best way, choose option (A).

    (A) should never giving
    (B) would never giving
    (C) should never given
    (D) might never given
    (E) should never give

38. Which sentence would be most effective if inserted at the beginning of paragraph C?

    (A) It is best to deal only with people who have been recommended by a friend.
    (B) Never give out personal information about yourself unless you are completely sure the person is legitimate.
    (C) Telephone fraud is one of the most devious crimes that exist in today's world.
    (D) There are other steps you can take to prevent yourself from being a victim of fraud as well.
    (E) If you ever have been a victim of fraud you know how terrible it is.

39. Sentence 8: **When someone calls you to sell you something, ask for a website address for the business so you can look to see if <u>they</u> is legitimate.**

    Which is the best way to write the underlined portion of this sentence? If the original is the best way, choose option (A).

    (A) they
    (B) those
    (C) it
    (D) its
    (E) he

40. Sentence 13: **If the offer is for reel, then you can be confident in proceeding.**

Which correction should be made to sentence 13?

(A) remove the comma after <u>reel</u>
(B) change <u>reel</u> to <u>real</u>
(C) change <u>be</u> to <u>being</u>
(D) insert a comma after <u>confident</u>
(E) no correction is necessary

41. Which revision would improve the effectiveness of paragraph C?
(A) move sentence 8 after sentence 9
(B) remove sentence 12
(C) move sentence 13 to the beginning of the paragraph
(D) begin a new paragraph with sentence 12
(E) remove sentence 14

Questions 42–50 refer to the following e-mail.

E-mail

To: customerservice@bigboxappliance.com
Subject: Warranty Coverage
Dear Sir/Madam:

(A)

(1) I bought a laptop computer at your store on February 12, 2009. (2) It was a New World computer. (3) At the same time I purchased a two-year extended warranty for $129. (4) I took the computer back to the store about six months later because the DVD drive would not work properly. (5) An associate sent the computer to your repair facility, and 10 days or so later, the laptop was returned in working order. (6) There was no charge to me.

(B)

(7) Then yesterday, the computer would not turn on. (8) I brought the computer into the store. (9) The computer was diagnosed as having a defective screen. (10) I was told the cost to replace them

would be $319 plus tax. (11) I replied that I had purchased the extended warranty but the associate showed me on his computer that the warranty had expired six days ago.

(C)

(12) Obviously I was outraged. (13) Your circular last Sunday advertise a brand-new laptop for $399, which is practically what I would have to pay to fix my computer. (14) I was never notified that my warranty would expire and was never offering the opportunity to extend it. (15) I believes Big Box should take the responsibility and repair the computer at no charge. (16) I have been a good customer and made many purchases at your store. (17) I hope to hear from you soon. (18) Luckily my friend let me use his computer so I could send this.

Andrea Fox
Cell: (654) 123-4567
foxyg@aol.net

42. Sentences 1 and 2: **I bought a laptop computer at your store on February 12, 2009. It was a New World computer.**

The most effective combination of sentences 1 and 2 would include which group of words?

(A) which was
(B) which was just made
(C) a New World laptop computer
(D) a computer made by New World
(E) manufactured by New World

43. Sentence 3: **At the same <u>time I</u> purchased a two-year extended warranty for $129.**

Which is the best way to write the underlined portion of this sentence? If the original is the best way, choose option (A).

(A) time I
(B) time; I
(C) time, I
(D) time and I
(E) time: I

44. Sentence 10: **I was told the cost to replace them would be $319 plus tax.**

Which correction should be made to sentence 10?

(A) change <u>told</u> to <u>tell</u>
(B) change <u>replace</u> to <u>replacing</u>
(C) change <u>them</u> to <u>it</u>
(D) insert a comma after <u>$319</u>
(E) no correction is necessary

45. Sentence 11: **I replied that I had purchased the extended warranty but the associate showed me on his computer that the warranty had expired six days ago.**

Which correction should be made to sentence 11?

(A) change <u>replied</u> to <u>replies</u>
(B) change <u>extended</u> to <u>extend</u>
(C) insert a comma after <u>warranty</u>
(D) change <u>had</u> to <u>have</u>
(E) no correction is necessary

46. Sentence 13: **Your circular last Sunday <u>advertise</u> a brand-new laptop for $399, which is practically what I would have to pay to fix my computer.**

Which is the best way to write the underlined portion of this sentence? If the original is the best way, choose option (A).

(A) advertise
(B) advertising
(C) was having advertised
(D) will advertise
(E) advertised

47. Sentence 14: **I was never notified that my warranty would expire and was never offering the opportunity to extend it.**

Which correction should be made to sentence 14?

(A) change <u>notified</u> to <u>notifies</u>
(B) insert a comma after <u>warranty</u>
(C) insert a semicolon after <u>expire</u>
(D) change <u>offering</u> to <u>offered</u>
(E) no correction is necessary

48. Sentence 15: **I believes Big Box should take the responsibility and repair the computer at no charge.**

Which correction should be made to sentence 15?

(A) change <u>believes</u> to <u>believe</u>
(B) change <u>take</u> to <u>be taking</u>
(C) insert a comma after <u>responsibility</u>
(D) move <u>no charge</u> to before <u>responsibility</u>
(E) no correction is necessary

49. Sentence 17: **I hope to hear from <u>you</u> soon.**

Which is the best way to write the underlined portion of this sentence? If the original is the best way, choose option (A).

(A) you
(B) them
(C) it
(D) him
(E) her

50. Which revision would improve the effectiveness of paragraph C?
(A) remove sentence 15
(B) place sentence 13 at the end of the paragraph
(C) move sentence 12 after sentence 13
(D) remove sentence 18
(E) place sentence 18 at the beginning of the paragraph

ANSWERS: LANGUAGE ARTS, WRITING, PART I

1. **(E)** Option (E) is correct because it capitalizes all the words that make up the proper name. Option (A) is not correct because it does not capitalize any of the words that make up the proper name. Options (B), (C), and (D) are wrong because they do not capitalize all of the words that make up the proper name.

2. **(D)** Option (D) is correct because the verb *hope* is parallel to the preceding verb, *want*. Option (A) is wrong because the verb *wanted* is in the past tense, while the action is in the present. Option (B) is incorrect because *them* is a plural pronoun that agrees with its antecedent *projects*. Option (C) inserts an unnecessary comma. Option (E) is incorrect because the verbs are not in parallel structure.

3. **(B)** Option (B) is correct. The subject, *project*, is singular, so it needs a singular verb. Option (A) is incorrect because it is a plural verb and the subject is singular. Option (C) is wrong because the present participle *requiring* doesn't make sense. Options (D) and (E) are incorrect because the past tense does not agree with the action, which takes place in the present.

4. **(C)** Option (C) is correct because it places a comma between all the items in a series. Options (A) and (D) are incorrect because they do not place commas between all the items in a series. Option (B) incorrectly places a period after *work*, making the next sentence a fragment. Option (E) incorrectly places a semicolon after the first item.

5. **(C)** Option (C) is correct because sentence 9 refers to the information in the previous sentence, which is in the present tense (*contacts*). Option (A) is incorrect; *utility* does not need to be capitalized. Option (B) is incorrect because a comma is unnecessary. Options (D) and (E) are wrong because the verb tenses do not agree with sentence 8.

6. **(E)** Option (E) is correct because it adds the singular subject *it*, referring to the hotline in sentence 12 and making it a complete sentence. Option (A) is incorrect because there is no subject in the sentence. Option (B) removes a necessary comma but still has no subject. Options (C) and (D) are both wrong because the subjects that are added do not agree with the antecedent, *Diggers Hotline*, in the previous sentence.

7. **(A)** Option (A) is correct because it replaces the incorrect possessive pronoun *their* with the correct pronoun *there*. Option (B) is incorrect because the sentence would not make sense. Option (C) changes the plural verb *occur* to a singular form; this is wrong because the verb refers to a plural subject—*accidents*. Option (D) would insert an unnecessary comma. Option (E) is wrong because the possessive pronoun *their* does not belong.

8. **(B)** Option (B) is the correct choice because it places a necessary comma between the two clauses in the compound sentence. Option (A) is incorrect; the resulting sentence does not make sense in terms of the subject. Option (C) misspells the contraction for <u>that is</u>. Option (D) is incorrect; the result would make no sense. Option (E) is wrong because the comma is needed to separate the two clauses in the sentence.

9. **(C)** Option (C) is correct because it replaces a pronoun that refers to a thing with a pronoun that refers to people—in this case, *engineers*. Option (A) changes a correct verb to one that does not agree with the subject. Option (B) would remove a necessary comma. Option (D) changes a correct verb form to an incorrect one. Option (E) is incorrect because *that* should not be used to refer to people.

10. **(B)** Option (B) is correct; the transition phrase indicates the cause-and-effect relationship that exists here. Option (A) is incorrect because the resulting sentence would be a fragment. Option (C) is wrong because the transition phrase indicates a relationship that does not exist. Option (D) would result in an incomplete sentence. Option (E) indicates that an example will follow, which is not the case.

11. **(B)** Option (B) correctly capitalizes the name of the company, Magnavox. Option (A) changes a verb from the past tense to the present tense; however, the action occurred in the past. Option (C) changes the correct pronoun, which refers to a thing or things, to a pronoun that refers to a person. Option (D) inserts a comma where none is needed. Option (E) is incorrect because the name of the company should be capitalized.

12. **(E)** Option (E) combines the two sentences in the most succinct method, making the second one an appositive. Option (A) uses a transition word, the conjunction *but*; however, this does not make sense in the context of

the sentence. Option (B) is extremely wordy. Option (C) combines the sentence using an inappropriate conjunction. Option (D) creates a comma splice.

13. **(C)** Option (C) substitutes the correct homonym (the number) for the incorrect one (in favor of). Option (A) changes the correct past tense, singular verb to an incorrect plural form. Option (B) inserts an unnecessary comma. Option (D) uses a possessive form where none is called for. Option (E) has an incorrect homonym.

14. **(D)** Option (D) is correct because it changes a verb in singular form to one in plural form so that it agrees with the subject, *games*. Option (A) is incorrect because the verb is singular and does not agree with the subject. Option (B) is wrong because the verb is singular and in the present tense, whereas the action is in the past tense. Option (C) is incorrect because the verb, although plural, is in the present tense. Option (E) is an incorrect verb form.

15. **(A)** Option (A) is correct because it inserts a necessary comma at the beginning of the phrase that modifies *Cloud gaming*. Option (B) is incorrect because it replaces a correct singular verb with a plural form. Option (C) would remove the necessary comma at the end of the modifying phrase. Option (D) is wrong because it changes the verb to a past tense, but the action is in the present. Option (E) is incorrect because it lacks the comma at the start of the modifying phrase.

16. **(C)** Option (C) is correct because it changes a verb in the past tense to one in the active present tense, since the action is on going now. Option (A) inserts an unnecessary comma. Option (B) capitalizes a noun that is not a proper name. Option (D) incorrectly makes *thirties* possessive. Option (E) has a verb in the wrong tense.

17. **(C)** Option (C) is correct because it moves the phrase next to what it modifies, *machinist*, rather than having it modify *my application*. Option (A) inserts an unnecessary comma. Option (B) changes a correct verb form to an incorrect one. Option (D) incorrectly italicizes *Monday* as though it were part of the newspaper's name. Option (E) is incorrect because the phrase *which was posted in Monday's Post Star* is not next to the noun that it modifies.

18. **(D)** Option (D) correctly eliminates a sentence that does not support the main idea. Option (A) removes the topic sentence for the paragraph. Option (B) does not make sense. Option (C) is wrong; no new paragraph should start there. Option (E) is incorrect because sentence 5 is clearly not related to the purpose of the paragraph.

19. **(E)** Option (E) is correct because it uses an appositive to combine the two ideas in the sentences. Option (A) uses a participle where none belongs. Option (B) uses unnecessary words and also incorrectly uses *which* rather than *who*. Option (C) is wordy. Option (D) changes the meaning slightly and is wordy.

20. **(D)** Option (D) is correct because the verb is in the correct tense and form. Option (A) uses a participle where none is needed. Option (B) is in the wrong tense. Option (C) is in the wrong tense and is plural rather than singular. Option (E) is incorrect because it is in the past perfect tense.

21. **(D)** Option (D) correctly separates the run-on sentence, which consists of two complete ideas, with a period. Option (A) is a run-on sentence, so it is wrong. Option (B) is a comma splice. Option (C) inserts an inappropriate conjunction. Option (E) inserts a transition word that changes the meaning.

22. **(B)** Option (B) completes the fragment by inserting a subject, *I*. Option (A) removes a necessary comma after the introductory clause. Option (C) replaces a correct pronoun with an incorrect one. Option (D) creates an incorrect verb form. Option (E) is wrong because the sentence has no subject.

23. **(C)** Option (C) is correct because it makes the singular verb plural to agree with the subject, *things*. Option (A) is incorrect because the sentence would make no sense. Option (B) inserts an unnecessary comma. Option (D) lowercases a proper name. Option (E) is wrong because the verb, *is*, does not agree with its subject, *things*.

24. **(D)** Option (D) is correct because it uses the correct homonym (the possessive pronoun for the second person plural) instead of the word *hour* (a unit of time). Option (A) uses the incorrect homonym.

25. **(C)** Option (C) adds an appropriate and necessary subordinating conjunction to join the two sentences. Option (A) creates a fragment by

removing the verb. Option (B) adds an unnecessary comma. Option (D) removes the comma but does not add the subordinating conjunction needed to separate the two clauses, making a run-on sentence. Option (E) is a comma splice.

26. **(B)** Option (B) is correct because a proper name—in this case, *World War II*—must be capitalized. Option (A) incorrectly makes *Germans* possessive. Option (C) removes a comma that is needed in the compound sentence. Option (D) inserts an unnecessary comma. Option (E) incorrectly has the name of the war lowercase.

27. **(E)** Option (E) joins the fragment with the complete sentence before it. Options (A) and (D) are sentence fragments. Options (B) and (C) incorrectly use a semicolon and a colon, respectively, to connect the fragment to the previous sentence.

28. **(A)** Option (A) is a topic sentence that introduces the information in paragraph A. Option (B) states details about propeller planes, but is not a good topic sentence. Option (C) also gives a detail about jet travel. Option (D) might be a possibility, but it is too generalized. Option (E) could be a topic sentence, but not of this paragraph.

29. **(B)** Option (B) corrects the verb by putting it in the past tense to agree with the verb in the previous sentence. Option (A) has an incorrect verb form. Options (C), (D), and (E) use incorrect verb tenses.

30. **(C)** Option (C) is correct because it combines the ideas using a conjunction and creating a parallel structure with the verb. Option (A) is incorrect because, even though it uses an appropriate conjunction, it has a verb that is in the past tense rather than the future tense. Option (B) also uses an appropriate conjunction but has an incorrect verb form. Option (D) is wrong because the transition words make no sense. Option (E) has an inappropriate conjunction, even though the verb form is correct.

31. **(A)** Option (A) is correct because the phrase modifies *jet aircraft* and *in 1972*. Option (B) is incorrect because the names of companies are capitalized. Option (C) changes the correct possessive pronoun to an incorrect contraction. Option (D) inserts an unnecessary comma. Option (E) is incorrect since the phrase is not placed next to what it modifies.

32. **(D)** Option (D) is correct because it creates parallel structure between the verbs in the sentence. Option (A) is incorrect because its verb is not parallel with the other two verbs. Option (B) uses a plural helping verb. Option (C) has an incorrect verb form. Option (E) uses a verb in the future tense, which is inappropriate since a past tense is needed here.

33. **(D)** Option (D) is correct because it moves the paragraph that talks about what is happening today to the end of the passage, which makes the passage flow logically. Option (A) is incorrect because these paragraphs have different main ideas. Option (B) is incorrect because the paragraphs do not belong together. Option (C) does not make sense. Option (E) is incorrect because paragraph C should clearly come after paragraph D.

34. **(C)** Option (C) is correct because it changes an improper verb form to a proper one. Option (A) inserts an unnecessary comma. Option (B) changes a plural noun to an unnecessary plural possessive. Option (D) is wrong because *telemarketing* does not need to be capitalized. Option (E) has an incorrect verb form in the sentence.

35. **(D)** Option (D) is correct; *they* is the correct pronoun because it agrees with its antecedent in the previous sentence, *people*. Options (A), (B), and (E) are wrong; they do not agree with the antecedent. Option (C) is an object pronoun, not a subject pronoun.

36. **(B)** Option (B) is correct because it inserts a comma after the opening clause of a compound sentence. Option (A) is incorrect because it has no comma. Option (C) has a comma but changes the verb to an incorrect form. Option (D) inserts a semicolon to set off the opening clause. Option (E) is wrong because the opening clause should not be set off with a colon.

37. **(E)** Option (E) is correct because it changes an improper verb form to a proper one. Option (A) has an incorrect verb form, as do options (B), (C), and (D).

38. **(D)** Option (D) is a topic sentence that tells what the paragraph is about, so it is most effective at the beginning of the paragraph. Option (A) is not effective. It is a detail, but it does not tell what the paragraph is about. Option (B) repeats information found in the previous paragraph. Option (C) is an opinion, but it does not tell what the paragraph is about. Option (E) is an opinion, not a topic sentence.

39. **(C)** Option (C) is correct because the pronoun *it* agrees with its antecedent, *business*. Option (A) is a plural pronoun and does not agree with the antecedent. Option (B) is not only plural, but it is a demonstrative pronoun. Option (D) is a possessive pronoun. Option (E) is incorrect because the pronoun should agree with *business* not *someone*.

40. **(B)** Option (B) is correct because it replaces the homonym *reel* (spool) with *real* (genuine). Option (A) is incorrect because the comma is needed. Option (C) inserts an incorrect verb form. Option (D) is incorrect; no comma is needed here. Option (E) uses a word that does not make sense in the sentence.

41. **(D)** Option (D) is correct because it splits the paragraph between two different topics: what to do when a person calls you and a summary. Option (A) makes no sense logically. Option (B) would remove the topic sentence for the paragraph. Option (C) would not make sense. Option (E) would remove important information.

42. **(C)** Option (C) is correct because the most effective combination of sentences 1 and 2 is *I bought a New World laptop computer at your store on February 12, 2009.* Option (A) would repeat the word *computer.* Options (B), (D), and (E) are too wordy.

43. **(C)** Option (C) is correct because a comma is needed after an opening clause. Option (A) does not have a comma after the clause. Option (B) incorrectly uses a semicolon. Option (D) inserts an unnecessary *and.* Option (E) incorrectly uses a colon to separate the clause.

44. **(C)** Option (C) is correct because *it* agrees with its antecedent in sentence 9, *computer.* Option (A) incorrectly changes the tense of the verb. Option (B) changes a correct verb form to an incorrect one. Option (D) inserts an unnecessary comma. Option (E) is incorrect because *them* is a plural pronoun, while the antecedent is singular.

45. **(C)** Option (C) is correct because a compound sentence needs a comma between its two clauses. Option (A) changes a correct verb tense to an incorrect one. Option (B) changes a correct adjective to an incorrect form. Option (D) changes a correct verb form to an incorrect one. Option (E) has no comma after the first clause.

46. **(E)** Option (E) is correct because it puts the verb in the past tense. Option (A) is incorrect because the action takes place in the past, not the present. Options (B) and (C) are incorrect verb forms. Option (D) is a future tense, but the action takes place in the past.

47. **(D)** Option (D) is correct because it changes the verb to agree with *notified* and creates parallel structure between them. Option (A) incorrectly changes a correct verb tense to the present. Option (B) inserts a comma where none is needed. Option (C) inserts a semicolon. Option (E) is incorrect because the verb *offering* is not parallel with *notified*.

48. **(A)** Option (A) is correct because it agrees with the subject of the sentence, *I*. Option (B) replaces a correct verb form with an incorrect one. Option (C) inserts a comma where none is required. Option (D) is incorrect because the change would make no sense. Option (E) is incorrect because the verb does not agree with the subject.

49. **(A)** Option (A) is correct because this is the correct pronoun; it refers to the company. None of the other options agree with the antecedent.

50. **(D)** Option (D) is correct because this sentence is the least related to the topic of the paragraph. Option (A) would remove an important sentence. Option (B) makes no sense. Option (C) would make the order of the paragraph strange. Option (E) is incorrect since this sentence does not belong in the paragraph.

LANGUAGE ARTS WRITING, PART II
Essay Directions and Topic

Look at the box on the next page. In the box are your assigned topic and the letter of that topic.

You must write on the assigned topic ONLY.

You will have 45 minutes to write on your assigned essay topic. You may return to the multiple-choice section after you complete your essay if you have time remaining in this test period. Do not return the Language Arts, Writing booklet until you finish both Parts I and II of the Language Arts, Writing Test.

Two evaluators will score your essay according to its overall effectiveness. Their evaluation will be based on the following features:
- Well-focused main points
- Clear organization
- Specific development of your ideas
- Control of sentence structure, punctuation, grammar, word choice, and spelling

REMEMBER, YOU MUST COMPLETE BOTH THE MULTIPLE-CHOICE QUESTIONS (PART I) AND THE ESSAY (PART II) TO RECEIVE A SCORE ON THE LANGUAGE ARTS, WRITING TEST. To avoid having to repeat both parts of the test, be sure to do the following:
- Do not leave the pages blank.
- Write legibly <u>in ink</u> so that the evaluators will be able to read your writing.
- Write on the assigned topic. If you write on a topic other than the one assigned, you will not receive a score for the Language Arts, Writing Test.
- Write your essay on the lined pages of the separate answer sheet booklet. Only the writing on these pages will be scored.

TOPIC A

Many people today are able to work at home.

Write an essay that tells the advantages or disadvantages of working at home. Give your opinion and support your view from your own personal observations and experiences.

Part II is a test to determine how well you can use written language to explain your ideas. In preparing your essay, you should take the following steps:

- Read the DIRECTIONS and the TOPIC carefully.
- Plan your essay before you write. Use the scratch paper provided to make any notes. These notes will be collected but not scored.
- Before you turn in your essay, reread what you have written and make any changes that will improve your essay.

Your essay should be long enough to develop the topic adequately.

ANSWERS: LANGUAGE ARTS, WRITING, PART II

All essays should be scored according to the GED essay rubric.

Examples of Excellent Topic Sentences

I think that working at home is a terrific convenience because you can have the best of both worlds.

I am totally against working at home because it means there is no separation between your private life and your career.

Examples of Using Varied Language and Details While Following the Rules of Edited American English (EAE)

For instance, you will be able to manage your time more effectively since you won't have to commute to a job site. It also means you will work more effectively since you will not be interrupted by situations that may arise in an office setting.

For example, you may end up spending more time working than you would if you worked in an office, and this may have a negative effect on your family life. Also, there would be little or no communication between you and your fellow workers.

- Organization should follow a clear, logical order.
- The essay should also have a closing that sums it up succinctly, such as:

These are some of the reasons that I think it is much better to work at home than in an office setting.

To sum up my feelings, I think that it is not a good move to work from home because of the added pressures you would experience.

SOCIAL STUDIES

Questions 1 and 2 are based on the following passage.

The Salem witch trials of 1692 in Massachusetts began when young girls from Salem village began to display strange behaviors such as screaming and twisting themselves into unnatural positions. The people of the town thought the girls were being harmed by witches.

More than 150 innocent people were arrested and imprisoned for witchcraft, and as a result of the subsequent trials, 19 people were hanged. In the years that followed, some of the accusers and jurors asked the community to pardon them for their actions. People who were convicted but not executed sent petitions demanding that their sentences be reversed. And centuries later, some descendants still seek to have the names of their ancestors cleared.

The events are an instance of mass hysteria, which occurs when one person exhibits symptoms, like nausea or headaches, and then others begin to show similar symptoms; the cause is psychological, not a contagion. The Salem witch trials are also frequently cited as an example of how things can go wrong in the legal system, such as when trials or interrogations occur based on false accusations. In fact, the term "witch hunt" is commonly used today to describe prosecutions fueled by panic and paranoia.

1. Which of the following is an opinion, rather than a fact, about the Salem witch trials?

   (A) People in the seventeenth century were more scared of witches than people are today.
   (B) The Salem witch trials took place during the colonial period.
   (C) Many more people were accused of witchcraft than were executed.
   (D) Mass hysteria is not caused by infection or disease.
   (E) The trials are regularly referred to as an example of a legal system failure.

2. Based on the passage, it can be assumed that

   (A) the people of Salem forgave the accusers and jurors
   (B) the events of 1692 have reverberated through the ages

(C) the young girls from Salem village did not know each other

(D) the Salem witch trials were a dangerous time in US history

(E) all of the wrongful convictions resulting from the witch trials were overturned

Question 3 is based on the following passage.

The Louisiana Purchase of 1803 was a contentious decision. On the one hand, the purchase was considered by some to be unconstitutional and an intrusion on states' rights. On the other hand, it would double the size of the United States. The territory that France offered to the United States stretched from the Gulf of Mexico in the south, north to Canada, west to the Rocky Mountains, and east to the Mississippi River. It would also provide crucial trade access for the United States through the port city of New Orleans. In the end, President Thomas Jefferson proceeded with the purchase, and it became a central moment in his presidency and for the United States.

3. The title that best expresses the main idea of this passage is:

(A) The Louisiana Purchase: The Expansion of US Territory in the Twentieth Century

(B) The Louisiana Purchase: The Turning Point of the US–French Alliance

(C) The Louisiana Purchase: How California Became Part of the United States

(D) The Louisiana Purchase: The End of States' Rights

(E) The Louisiana Purchase: A Pivotal yet Controversial Event in US History

Question 4 is based on the following passage.

The Lewis and Clark Expedition, which took place from 1804 to 1806, was led by Meriwether Lewis and William Clark. The explorers were given two goals. The first was to examine and document the plants, animals, and landscape they found during their journey. The second was to uncover the economic possibilities of the region— specifically, a water-based "Northwest Passage" for sailing from the East Coast of the United States to Asia for trade.

The explorers started in St. Louis, Missouri; crossed the Rocky Mountains; and made it to the area that is present-day Oregon in 1805. They then returned to the East Coast of the United States.

Although the explorers never found the Northwest Passage, the expedition was highly successful. Lewis and Clark brought back essential information in their personal journals about the people, land, plants, and animals they encountered during their travels. The maps they created—the first precise maps of the US Northwest Territory—led to great economic developments, further exploration, and the settlement of the land in the decades to come.

4. Which of the following sentences summarizes the passage preceding?

(A) After being unable to find the fabled Northwest Passage to Asia, the Lewis and Clark Expedition was deemed a failure and the group was ordered to return to Washington, DC.

(B) After crossing the Rocky Mountains, Lewis and Clark were surprised by an extremely harsh winter, so they settled in the region and lived among the indigenous people.

(C) Lewis and Clark effectively fulfilled the two goals of their expedition—to carefully document their journey and to open the West for economic development.

(D) The Lewis and Clark Expedition made it possible for the United States to take most territories in the West from Spain.

(E) The personal journals of Meriwether Lewis and William Clark are essential documents for gaining knowledge about US history.

Question 5 is based on the following cartoon.

5. This cartoon illustrates a foreign policy of the United States from the
    1800s known as the Monroe Doctrine. The people in the far right corner
    of the cartoon represent

    (A) Asian countries
    (B) US congressmen
    (C) European countries
    (D) US state governors
    (E) former US presidents

Questions 6 and 7 are based on the following cartoon.

LINCOLN'S LAST WARNING.

"Now, if you don't come down, I'll cut the Tree *from under you.*"

6. The person in the tree represents

    (A) settlers of the US West
    (B) Southern states
    (C) Mexico
    (D) Union soldiers
    (E) General Ulysses Grant

7. What is the subject of this cartoon?

    (A) President Lincoln's expertise with an ax
    (B) the execution of Army deserters during the Civil War
    (C) the tenacity of the Confederate army as an opponent
    (D) the Confederacy's refusal to voluntarily abolish slavery
    (E) Lincoln's battles with the US Congress

Question 8 is based on the following passage.

Dust storms caused major damage to the American Great Plains in the 1930s. This was the result of severe drought as well as many years of farming where precautions, such as crop rotation or cover crops, were not taken to prevent wind erosion. The natural grasses that normally kept the soil in place and trapped moisture—even during periods of drought and high winds—were lost. This caused winds to blow the soil into huge clouds that traveled as far away as New York and Washington, DC.

Because this natural disaster took place during the Great Depression, many people could not find other work to support their families. Hundreds of thousands of people fled the now-useless farmlands of Texas and Oklahoma and parts of New Mexico, Colorado, and Kansas—or "the Dust Bowl" as the region was then called—to other states such as California, hoping to find employment there. However, many were not successful. They often moved from one area to another, picking fruit or other crops on other people's farms for very low wages.

8. Which of these statements is accurate according to the information provided in the first paragraph?

(A) The Great Depression of the 1930s had a devastating effect on the American Great Plains.

(B) Essential crops could not be shipped to the rest of the country because of the dust storms.

(C) People from New York or Washington, DC, fled the dust storms, settling in the American Great Plains.

(D) Wind erosion was less severe in California than in Texas or Oklahoma.

(E) Proper farming techniques and natural vegetation are essential to maintaining healthy soil and renewable crops.

Questions 9 and 10 are based on the following poster.

9. This poster was used by the US government during which war?

    (A) World War I
    (B) the Civil War
    (C) World War II
    (D) the Korean War
    (E) the Spanish-American War

10. What is the main idea represented by this poster?

    (A) Women must return to the home when men come back from the war.
    (B) The homefront would be safer if there were fewer women in the workforce.

(C) The United States will single-handedly win the war.

(D) Women are capable of working the labor-intensive jobs that are crucial to the war effort.

(E) Wearing the proper attire is essential for safety in munitions factories.

Question 11 is based on the following passage.

The Montgomery Bus Boycott was a protest to oppose racial segregation on the public transit system in Montgomery, Alabama. At that time, African Americans were forced to sit at the back of the bus, and if the bus was full, they had to give up their seats to white people boarding the bus after them. The protest began in December 1955, after Rosa Parks, an African-American woman, was arrested for not giving up her seat. From that day forward, the city's African Americans stopped using the buses. People carpooled, took taxis, cycled, or simply walked. The protest was not short-lived, and since African Americans made up the majority of the system's customers, the city's bus system faced great financial hardship. This put pressure on city leaders to resolve the situation. In addition, the protest received a national audience after Martin Luther King's participation and subsequent arrest. The boycott finally ended in December 1956, after the US Supreme Court upheld an earlier ruling in July by a US district court that the bus system's segregation was unconstitutional.

11. Which statement is supported by the information in the passage?

(A) An important consequence of the protest was the considerable economic loss for the city transit system.

(B) People who could not walk or cycle were forced to hitchhike in order to get around the city.

(C) Many taxi drivers supported the protesters, even allowing them to pay less than the minimum fare.

(D) The protest was not supported by prominent civil rights leaders such as Martin Luther King

(E) African-American passengers were forced to pay double to ride the bus during the protests.

Question 12 is based on the following passage.

Although many languages were spoken throughout the lands conquered by the Romans, the official language of the Roman Empire was Latin. "Classical" Latin, as well as Greek, was used for literature and education. Classical Latin was both spoken and written, and it was taught in schools. It did not contain punctuation, lowercase letters, or even spacing between words. The "vulgar" Latin was commonly spoken in the western part of the empire but was rarely written down. In fact, it was written so infrequently that few examples of vulgar Latin exist today. However, vulgar Latin later evolved into the modern "romance" languages, such as Italian, French, Portuguese, and Spanish.

12. According to the information in this passage, which of the following statements is true?

   (A) Greek was banned in the Roman Empire.
   (B) All languages spoken today evolved from Latin.
   (C) The use of punctuation became customary after the fall of the Roman Empire.
   (D) Vulgar Latin was the preferred language of Roman soldiers.
   (E) The eastern part of the Roman Empire spoke mostly Greek.

Question 13 is based on the following passage.

In Western Europe during the Middle Ages, some peasants were known as serfs. The serfs lived on a piece of the land owned by a lord. On that land, the serfs could grow crops to provide for their families and sell the surplus produce for profit. In addition, the lord would protect the serfs' crops from robbers. In return, the serfs were expected to work the lord's fields. Serfs often had to pay the lord taxes or rent or give the lord produce from their parcel of land. Serfs also could not move away without the lord's permission. Serfdom began to decline in the fifteenth and sixteenth centuries. For some lords, it became more profitable to use all their land for their own crops and hire paid, temporary laborers instead.

13. The overall effect of serfdom was that the peasants were

(A) forced to grow crops instead of raising livestock
(B) legally and economically bound to a lord
(C) never able to provide surplus profits for the lord
(D) expected to hire temporary laborers to help them work the land
(E) protected from looters and thieves

Questions 14 and 15 are based on the following passage.

In 1532, when Francisco Pizarro arrived in South America from Spain, he found an Incan empire that was torn apart by civil war. By the mid-sixteenth century, the Incan Empire had expanded from present-day Peru to much of Bolivia, Argentina, Chile, Ecuador, and Colombia. But just a few years before Pizarro's arrival, the Incan emperor Huayna Capac died from smallpox while on a military campaign in Colombia. His death sparked a war of succession between his sons, Atahualpa and Huascar.

Atahualpa was not a legitimate heir to the throne, as his mother was not an Inca, but at the time of his father's death, Atahualpa was in the north with most of the empire's army, which was loyal to him. Huascar, the legitimate heir, was in the empire's capital city of Cuzco and quickly declared himself emperor. A bloody civil war then took place. Huascar was eventually captured in Cuzco by Atahualpa's trusted generals.

As Atahualpa traveled south from the city of Quito to Cuzco to formally take over the Incan empire, he came across Pizarro in the city of Cajamarca on November 15. The next day, after a brief meeting with Pizarro, the Spaniard's forces of less than 200 men captured Atahualpa.

While he was under guard, Atahualpa ordered his men to have Huascar killed. He also offered his captors a room filled with gold and silver so that Pizarro would spare his life. Although the treasure was given to Pizarro, Atahualpa was eventually charged by the Spaniards with several crimes, including the death of Huascar, and Atahualpa was executed in August 1533.

14. The author of this passage would believe which of the following statements about Pizarro?

    (A) Pizarro could not have defeated Atahualpa's army with just 200 men.
    (B) Pizarro's conquest of the Incan empire was helped by the devastating civil war.
    (C) Pizarro was responsible for the death of Huayna Capac.
    (D) Pizarro ordered the death of Huascar to end the civil war.
    (E) Pizarro had Atahualpa killed in order to take over the city of Quito.

15. Which of the following is an opinion, rather than a fact, about the Incan Empire?

    (A) The Incan Empire stretched across most of the western part of South America.
    (B) Atahualpa was not in Cuzco at the time of Pizarro's arrival in South America.
    (C) Huascar would have been emperor if Atahualpa's generals had not captured him.
    (D) Atahualpa was a prisoner under Pizarro for several months before he was executed.
    (E) The Incan emperors were likely merciless conquerors of tribes they encountered.

Question 16 is based on the following passage.

On the evening of December 16, 1773, a group of men boarded the three ships in Boston Harbor and dumped more than 300 chests of tea into the water. The event was part of a resistance movement against both the East India Company, which controlled all the tea that was brought to the colonies, as well as the Tea Act, which was passed by Parliament in England in 1773. Some British citizens living in the colonies objected to the Tea Act mostly because they felt these taxes were being imposed upon them by people they didn't elect to power. Parliament reacted to the Tea Party by closing Boston commerce until the costs of the destroyed tea had been repaid, which, in turn, sparked more protests from the colonists. Eventually this led to a more formal, well-organized act of sedition, in the form of the First Continental Congress and the beginning of the American Revolutionary War.

16. Based on the passage above, it can be assumed that

(A) the East India Company was never repaid for the damaged tea
(B) the Boston Tea Party was a significant moment for the American Revolution
(C) the First Continental Congress was a failure
(D) Parliament was unsuccessful in its attempts to close down Boston commerce
(E) the Tea Act of 1773 was quickly revoked

Questions 17 and 18 are based on the following cartoon.

17. What is the main idea of the cartoon?

(A) Children do not work enough hours in the day.
(B) All child labor employers are men.
(C) Girls did as much as work as boys in factories.
(D) Children should only do labor-intensive work before the age of 12.
(E) Child labor is oppressive and harmful to children.

18. The ring on the hand implies that

    (A) child labor only occurs in developed nations
    (B) these employers gain their wealth from the hard work of children
    (C) these children work in diamond mines
    (D) these children work in order to support their families
    (E) the parents of child laborers are rich

Questions 19 and 20 are based on the following cartoon.

THE GAP IN THE BRIDGE.

19. In this cartoon, the "Keystone USA" that Uncle Sam is leaning on means
    that US participation in the League of Nations is

    (A) negligible
    (B) comical
    (C) optional
    (D) crucial
    (E) distinguished

20. Uncle Sam's posture in the cartoon suggests that he

(A) does not care about the success of the League of Nations
(B) is enthusiastic about contributing in the League of Nations
(C) is concerned about the future of the League of Nations
(D) feels angry about the state of the League of Nations
(E) has an immense amount of pride in the League of Nations

Question 21 is based on the following table.

Country	Population in 2011	Population in 2001	% Growth 2001–2011
China	1,336,720,000	1,265,830,000	6%
India	1,210,200,000	1,008,730,000	20%
United States	313,230,000	281,420,000	11%
Indonesia	245,610,000	206,260,000	19%
Brazil	203,430,000	172,300,000	18%

21. According to the table, which of the following countries had the highest population growth rate for the 2001–2011 period?

(A) China
(B) India
(C) United States
(D) Indonesia
(E) Brazil

Question 22 is based on the following table.

Density of the Six Most Populated Us Cities	
City	Average # of People per Square Mile
New York City	27,000
San Francisco	18,000
Chicago	12,000
Los Angeles	6,500
Dallas	3,500
Houston	3,300

22. According to the table, the population density of Chicago is roughly double that of

    (A) New York City
    (B) Chicago
    (C) Los Angeles
    (D) Dallas
    (E) Houston

Question 23 is based on the following graph.

23. According to the graph, the US population reached a stable rate of growth in the years from

    (A) 1940 to 1945
    (B) 1945 to 1950
    (C) 1950 to 1960
    (D) 1960 to 1965
    (E) 1960 to 1970

Question 24 is based on the following passage.

The Deepwater Horizon oil spill—also known as the BP oil spill—began in the Gulf of Mexico on April 20, 2010, and is the largest accidental marine oil spill in history. A geyser of seawater caused an explosion at an offshore drilling platform, killing 11 people. Two days later, the drilling unit sank to the sea floor, and oil was discovered to be leaking from the wellhead. The leak continued for 87 days.

BP executives and US government officials scrambled to protect the US Gulf coast from the damaging effects of the spill. Oil washed up on hundreds of miles of coastline in states such as Louisiana, Mississippi, Alabama, and Florida. Thousands of species and sensitive ecological habitats such as marshlands and mangroves were physically covered by the oil. In addition, other toxic chemicals were released by the spill that could be consumed by animals or could reduce the oxygen supply in the US Gulf waters.

The terrible hidden and long-term effects of the oil spill are unknown. It is thought that it could take decades for the US Gulf to fully recover.

24. The author of the passage would likely agree with which of the following statements?

(A) The demand for energy to fuel our modern world is more important than the potential damage to the environment.

(B) The US government and BP company executives were not well prepared for the consequences of an offshore drilling platform accident of this magnitude.

(C) Most of the animals and habitats of the US Gulf coast were unaffected by the oil spill.

(D) The chemicals released by the oil spill were harmless and actually helped protect the animals and the environment from the oil.

(E) Other energy sources such as wind farms require the use of many acres of arable land and are dangerous to local birds.

Question 25 is based on the following passage.

Although coral reefs make up just a tiny portion of the surface of the world's oceans, they are one of the most diverse ecosystems on Earth. Reefs are created by corals—sea animals that secrete calcium carbonate, which forms the rigid structures of the reefs. The world's reefs provide a sanctuary for millions of creatures, from sharks and sea turtles to fish and crabs to clams, shrimp, and sponges. The world's reefs can be found in shallow, clear waters in warm climates, such as in the Caribbean and off the coasts of Hawaii and Australia.

Unfortunately, coral reefs are vulnerable to changes in the temperature of the ocean water. They are also in danger from overfishing and pollution, which often results in too much algae growing in and around the corals. Once destructive changes such as these occur, it is often impossible for the coral reefs to recover, and the reefs are permanently damaged.

25. Which statement appears to be the best summary of the passage preceding?

(A) Coral reefs are an important source of renewable energy.
(B) The world's coral reefs need to be protected from sea animals that secrete calcium carbonate.
(C) Global warming is defined as the rising of the average temperature of Earth's atmosphere and oceans.
(D) The only way to save coral reefs is to put an end to overfishing.
(E) While coral reefs can be teeming with life, they are also delicate ecosystems in great danger of being permanently damaged or lost forever.

Questions 26–28 are based on the following graphic.

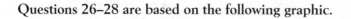

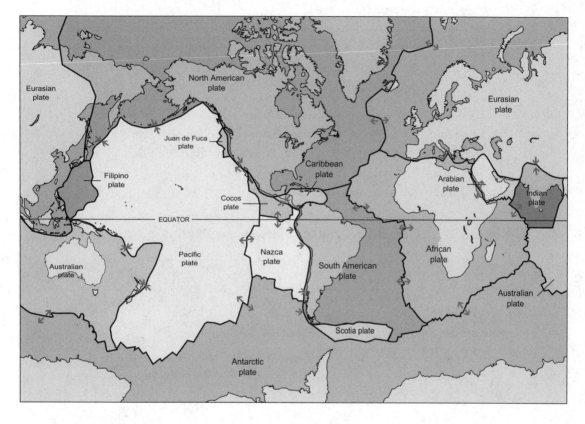

26. Earthquakes in countries such as Chile and Ecuador are the result of friction between which two plates?

   (A) the Nazca plate and South American plates
   (B) the Pacific and Australian plates
   (C) the North America and Eurasian plates
   (D) the African and South American plates
   (E) the Pacific and Antarctic plates

27. According to the arrows on the map, the North American plate and Eurasian plate are

   (A) moving in the same direction
   (B) sliding past each other
   (C) moving toward each other
   (D) moving away from each other
   (E) remaining still

28. A continental collision occurs when the two plates moving toward each other both contain continental crust. Instead of creating a subduction zone, where the less-dense oceanic crust is pushed beneath the more-dense continental crust, a continental collision can result in dramatic land formations, such as the Himalayan Mountains. According to the map, a continental collision can be seen where the

(A) Indian plate meets the Eurasian plate
(B) Pacific plate meets the Nazca plate
(C) African plate meets the South American plate
(D) Pacific plate meets the Antarctic plate
(E) North America plate meets the Eurasian plate

Questions 29 and 30 are based on the following graphic.

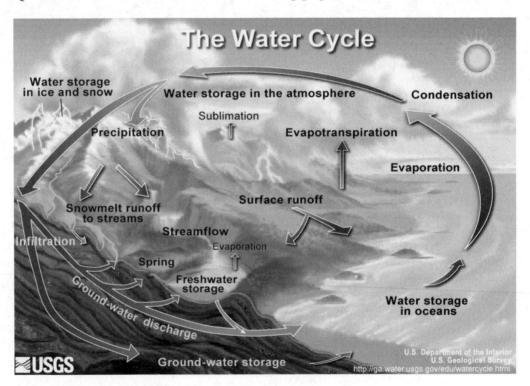

29. According to the map, water storage can occur

(A) in ice and snow
(B) in the ground
(C) in freshwater

    (D) in the atmosphere

    (E) all of the above

30. Precipitation occurs when water moves from

    (A) the ground to the atmosphere

    (B) the groundwater storage to the ocean

    (C) the ice and snow to the groundwater

    (D) the atmosphere to the ground

    (E) the groundwater to freshwater storage

31. All of the following government officials are elected to power by the citizens of the United States except

    (A) the president

    (B) a congressman

    (C) a Supreme Court justice

    (D) a senator

    (E) a state governor

32. As part of the federalist system, only the federal government can

    (A) levy taxes

    (B) declare war

    (C) establish schools

    (D) elect state governors

    (E) pass laws

33. As part of the checks and balances system, the US president can veto laws passed by

    (A) the Supreme Court

    (B) Great Britain and Canada

    (C) the United Nations

    (D) the US Congress

    (E) state governors

34. The government of the United States is a

    (A) democratic republic

    (B) constitutional monarchy

    (C) dictatorship

    (D) oligarchy

    (E) communist state

35. Which of the following amendments is not part of the Bill of Rights?

    (A) the right to a speedy trial

    (B) freedom from cruel or unusual punishment

    (C) the right to vote for women

    (D) freedom of speech

    (E) the right to trial by jury

36. Primary elections are held in order to

    (A) prohibit the viability of a third-party candidate

    (B) allow political parties to select a candidate for the party's nomination

    (C) remove a party from the political arena

    (D) allow voters to choose the location of the party convention

    (E) announce the results of exit polls

37. People who are in favor of maintaining the electoral college would disagree with which of the following statements?

    (A) The electoral college keeps a candidate from being elected president by winning only in heavily populated urban areas.

    (B) The electoral college encourages stability by maintaining the two-party system.

    (C) If a candidate were unable serve, the electoral college could choose a suitable replacement.

    (D) The electoral college neutralizes the effect of turnout disparities, which can be caused by inclement weather or when a highly contested issue is on the ballot.

    (E) The existence of the electoral college makes the national popular vote irrelevant.

38. Foreigners are allowed to live in the United States with government permission. All of the following are people with legal residency except

    (A) a person born of or adopted by a US citizen

    (B) a person with an expired student visa

    (C) a refugee fleeing warfare or prosecution

(D) a person with a valid residence card

(E) a person who has been nationalized

39. An authoritarian government is one in which political authority is concentrated in a small group of politicians. Power is maintained by the exclusion of potential political challengers through means such as violence and intimidation, as well as election rigging. Which of the following is the head of state of an authoritarian government?

(A) a governor

(B) a queen

(C) a colonel

(D) a dictator

(E) a prime minister

Question 40 is based on the following passage.

According to the US Census Bureau, about 131 million people reported voting in the 2008 US presidential election, an increase of 5 million from the 2004 elections. This increase included about 2 million more African-American voters, 2 million more Hispanic voters, and about 600,000 more Asian voters. In addition, voter turnout in the 18-to-24 age group increased to 49 percent in 2008 compared with 47 percent in 2004. However, the higher voter turnout in these groups was offset by unchanged or reduced turnout among other groups, such as non-Hispanic white voters. This caused the overall 2008 voter turnout to remain statistically unchanged—at 64 percent—from 2004.

40. Which statement is supported by information in the paragraph above?

(A) African-American women had the highest voter turnout rate in the 2008 election.

(B) Most of the increased voter turnout was seen in Midwest states.

(C) About 95 percent of all African-American voters cast a ballot for Barack Obama.

(D) The diversity of the voters seen in 2008 was the result of population growth.

(E) Voter participation of eligible voters among African Americans, Hispanics, and Asians all increased from 2004 to 2008.

41. All of the following are objects that can be a business's *capital* except

    (A) monetary investments
    (B) labor
    (C) computers and printers
    (D) farmland
    (E) a parking garage

42. A trade bloc is an agreement between governments where issues that could prohibit or impede trade or investments between nations are decreased or removed. Which of the following is an example of a trade bloc?

    (A) NAFTA
    (B) OPEC
    (C) NATO
    (D) the UN
    (E) WHO

43. When a new gaming console is released to the market, it often costs several hundreds of dollars and can be difficult to find in stores. This is also true of new video games, which can cost as much as $60. However, just a year or two after the release, these items can be found easily and often can be bought at half the price or less. This is an example of

    (A) sellers competing aggressively for market share
    (B) demand for a product outpacing supply
    (C) poor management of inventory
    (D) reduced prices due to increased supply and lower demand
    (E) product scarcity causing prices to go up

Questions 44–46 are based on the following passage.

In a capitalist economic system, all businesses are owned by individuals or groups of individuals (private), not by the government (public). Goods and services exist to generate profit, and prices are determined solely by supply and demand dynamics in the market. In a socialist economic system, goods and services exist for specific uses, not to generate revenue. Businesses are publicly owned, and price dynamics are centrally planned and controlled.

Many Western economies today combine elements of capitalism and socialism. While they are generally based on free-market capitalism, they also have socialist elements. These include industries that are owned and run by the government, such as transportation, infrastructure, education, and utilities. There are federal agencies in place to provide oversight on private businesses, which are also regulated by laws regarding the environment, labor, and product safety. Some industries are subsidized, meaning that the government sets prices for goods and services and disrupts the natural dynamics of price, supply, and demand in the free market. Many economies also include state-run, tax-funded programs such as welfare for the poor and social security for the aged.

44. Which of the following sentences summarizes the above passage?

(A) Most modern, Western economies can be described as "mixed" since they are not purely capitalist or socialist.

(B) Capitalism became the most prevalent economic system in the Western world in the nineteenth century.

(C) It is a mistake for Western countries to include state-run, tax-funded programs as part of their economic systems

(D) Federal agencies such as OSHA and the FDA are necessary to make sure citizens are healthy and safe.

(E) Free enterprise and competition are the backbone of the capitalist economy

45. Which of the following is not an example of a subsidy?

(A) Wheat farmers receive money from the government for exporting their product abroad.

(B) The price of gasoline is set at $2 per gallon at every gas station.

(C) Sugar is subject to sales tax at the supermarket.

(D) The minimum price of corn is guaranteed at $3.80 per bushel.

(E) Only two million foreign cars can be imported per year.

46. What do capitalism and socialism have in common?

(A) Prices are centrally planned and controlled.

(B) Both systems engage in producing goods and providing services.

(C) They are only found in modern Western countries.

(D) None of the revenue generated is taxed by the government.
(E) Neither provides social welfare programs.

Question 47 is based on the following graphic.

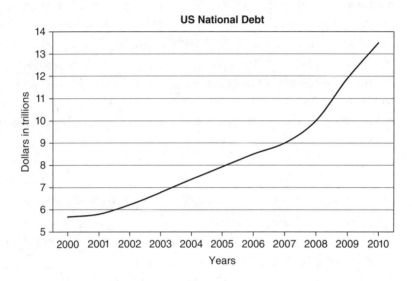

47. In which year did the US national debt reach at least $10 trillion?
(A) 2000
(B) 2002
(C) 2004
(D) 2008
(E) 2010

Questions 48 and 49 are based on the following passage.

The normal recession that occurred after the 1929 stock market crash turned into the Great Depression because of the actions—or lack of actions—by the Federal Reserve. After some large banks collapsed, people were afraid they would lose their savings. As a result, large groups descended on their local branches in panic, and there were runs on local banks, which subsequently collapsed. The supply of money in the US marketplace therefore shrank from 1929 to 1933. This lack of liquidity meant that businesses were unable to secure new loans or renew loans, which slowed down market investments and worsened the economy. The Federal Reserve could have taken steps to reverse this trend, such as buying government securities or providing emergency funds to the large banks. Instead, unemployment soared, production declined, consumer spending plummeted, and the nation fell into a dramatic and prolonged economic depression.

48. The author of this passage asserts that

   (A) the Federal Deposit Insurance Corporation, which guarantees the funds in personal accounts in case of bank failures, is a great achievement
   (B) the Federal Reserve was not able to increase the supply of money because of regulation and the gold standard
   (C) the Federal Reserve should have sold Treasury bonds to bring liquidity to the market
   (D) if the Federal Reserve had acted more aggressively to increase the supply of money, the Great Depression could have been avoided
   (E) efforts by the Federal Reserve to revive the US economy after the crash of 1929 were successful

49. Based on the information in the passage, a "run on the bank" occurs when

   (A) people withdraw their money, taking those funds out of circulation
   (B) the federal government buys government bonds
   (C) business cannot get or renew loans
   (D) prices of goods and services increases
   (E) the federal government provides emergency bailouts

50. Which of the following is an opinion, not a fact, about labor unions?

   (A) Labor unions use collective bargaining to negotiate for changes in wages and working conditions.
   (B) Labor strikes are detrimental to employers, consumers, and the economy.
   (C) The National Labor Relations Board steps in when companies and labor unions cannot come to an agreement.
   (D) Labor unions are required for all business by law.
   (E) A person who is a part of a labor union cannot be fired.

ANSWERS: SOCIAL STUDIES

1. **(A)** All the other statements are facts based on the date of the trials, the number of arrests that were made, the definition of *mass hysteria*, and the use of the witch trials as an example of the misuse of authority. There is no evidence in the passage that people in the 1600s feared witches more than people do today.

2. **(B)** The last sentence of the second paragraph, as well as the last sentence of the passage, illustrate how people have been affected by the trials, even hundreds of years later. Although the other answer choices may be true, they cannot be deduced from the information provided in the text.

3. **(E)** This answer most accurately reflects the central theme of the passage, which is that the Louisiana Purchase was controversial ("a contentious decision") but also fundamental ("a central moment") for the United States. The other options do not capture this idea. In addition, options (A), (C), and (D) are factually incorrect, and there is no indication in the passage about the effect of the Louisiana Purchase on US–French relations.

4. **(C)** The passage describes what the goals of the expedition were and how Lewis and Clark fulfilled those goals. Options (A) and (B) are factually incorrect, and options (D) and (E) do not summarize the passage as a whole. The topic is either outside the scope of the passage (option D) or the focus of the topic is too narrow (option E).

5. **(C)** The Monroe Doctrine stated that if European nations tried to colonize land or interfere with countries in North or South America, it would be seen as an act of aggression, and the United States would have to intervene.

6. **(B)** The date on which the cartoon was published (October 11, 1862) and the actions and words of President Lincoln in the image indicate that the man in the tree represents the Southern states.

7. **(D)** The tree in which the man sits symbolizes the institution of slavery. The president had informed the rebellious Southern states that if they did not rejoin the Union, he would free their slaves by executive order on January 1, 1863. The president essentially "cut the tree out from under" the South when the Emancipation Proclamation took effect on that day.

8. **(E)** The topic of the first paragraph is the cause of the severe dust storms that occurred in the 1930s, which is covered in option (E). Options (B) and (C) are not accurate statements. Options (A) and (D) are not based on the facts presented in the first paragraph, as the question states.

9. **(C)** This poster became the symbol of women laboring in manufacturing during World War II. The woman in the poster is commonly referred to as Rosie the Riveter.

10. **(D)** An able-bodied workforce was needed on the homefront to build planes and tanks and to work in munitions factories while millions of American men went to fight overseas in Europe and the Pacific region during World War II.

11. **(A)** Options (B), (C), and (E) cannot be deduced from the text of the passage, and option (D) states the opposite of the information presented in the passage about Martin Luther King. Option (A) is supported by the statement in paragraph 2 that "the city's bus system faced great financial hardship" because of the boycott.

12. **(C)** Since classical Latin was the only kind that was written and punctuation was not used, the practice of adding periods, commas, and other symbols must have evolved at a later time. Options (A) and (B) are inaccurate statements, and options (D) and (E) cannot be deduced from the information in the passage.

13. **(B)** The question asks you to describe the general consequence of serfdom on the peasants. Only option (B) encompasses the overall effect, which was that the peasants' lives were decisively connected to that of the lord. Options (A) and (C) cannot be deduced from the information in the passage; option (D) is untrue; and the scope of option (E) is too narrow.

14. **(B)** Several statements in the passage describe the Incan civil war and indicates that it doomed the empire. In the first sentence, the author says Pizarro found an empire "torn apart" by civil war. And at the end of the second paragraph, he describes the civil war as bloody. Options (C) and (D) are factually incorrect, and options (A) and (E) cannot be deduced from the information provided by the author.

15. **(E)** The passage does not provide evidence or explanations of how the Incans came to rule over those areas of South America. Options (A), (B), and (D) are facts, while option (C) cannot be deduced from the information provided by the author.

16. **(B)** More information is required to make the conclusions in options (A), (D), and (E). While possibly true, they cannot be deduced from the information provided in the text. Option (C) is outside the scope of the passage.

17. **(E)** By portraying the children as being crushed by the weight of the hand of their employer, the artist of the cartoon is implying that the children are being mistreated. Options (A) and (D) express ideas that are the opposite of the main idea of the cartoon. Options (B) and (C) cannot be deduced from the information provided in the text.

18. **(B)** The ring on the hand of the employer suggests that the employer is financially successful and, at the same time, exploits the children. The artist is implying that the success is possible because of child labor. The ring on the hand does not give any indication of the country where this child labor is taking place (option A), where these children work (option C), why these children work (option D), or whether their parents are prosperous (choice E).

19. **(D)** A keystone is a wedge-shaped stone that locks all the stones in an arch in place. Therefore, the artist of this cartoon is implying that the bridge, which represents the League of Nations, will collapse without the participation of the United States. This means that the United States plays an essential or "crucial" role. Options (A) and (C) suggest the opposite of what the artist is implying, and options (B) and (E) do not make sense in the context of the cartoon.

20. **(A)** Uncle Sam, as the personification of the United States, has a relaxed posture and therefore appears uninterested or indifferent about whether or not the League of Nations is successful. His posture does not imply that he is enthusiastic (option B), concerned (option C), angry (option D), or proud (option E).

21. **(B)** India showed a 20 percent growth in the years from 2001 to 2011, the highest among the five nations listed in the table.

22. **(C)** At 12,000, the average population density of Chicago is a little less than double the 6,500 average population density of Los Angeles.

23. **(C)** The graph shows a steady rate of growth, or plateau, that lasted from 1950 to 1955. During this time, the US population did not drastically increase or decrease. Options (A), (D), and (E) show steep declines in the US population. It was particularly dramatic in option (A)—from 1940 to 1945—since this was during World War II. Option (B) shows a steep increase, commonly referred to as the baby boom, since this was when Americans returned home from the war.

24. **(B)** Only option (B) matches the content and tone of the author's passage. Options (A), (C), and (D) express the opposite of the main idea of the passage and the author's point of view, while option (E) about wind farm energy is outside the scope of the passage.

25. **(E)** Option (A) is incorrect because the passage does not refer to coral reefs as a renewable energy source. Option (B) is factually inaccurate, as it is the corals themselves that secrete the calcium carbonate. Option (C) is outside the scope of the passage, while option (D) is too narrow in scope. Only option (E) accurately sums up the main ideas of the passage.

26. **(A)** Chile and Ecuador are on the west coast of the South American continent, which is found on the South American plate. According to the map, the Nazca plate pushes against the South American plate, which causes earthquakes in that part of the world.

27. **(D)** The arrows on the map show that the North American plate and Eurasian plate are moving away from each other.

28. **(A)** The map shows that where the Indian plate and the Eurasian plate collide, it is the convergence of continental crust. That is why the Himalayas, which contain the tallest mountain in the world, and the Tibetan plains are located there.

29. **(E)** Water can be stored as ice and snow, as water in the ground, and in rivers and lakes, as well as in clouds in the atmosphere.

30. **(D)** Option (A) is condensation, option (C) is infiltration, and options (B) and (E) are groundwater discharge.

31. **(C)** Supreme Court justices are nominated by the US president and are appointed after having been confirmed by the US Senate. The positions in the other options are all elected officials.

32. **(B)** Only the federal government can declare war. Both the state and federal governments can levy taxes (option A) and pass laws (option E). Only state governments can establish schools (option C), and the people of each state elect their governors (option D).

33. **(D)** Legislation that is passed by both the House of Representatives and the Senate is presented to the US president, who can then choose to veto the law. The president has no influence over laws passed by individual states (option E), other nations (option B), or international bodies like the United Nations (option C). The Supreme Court (option A) makes rulings; it does not pass laws.

34. **(A)** The United States is a democratic republic, which is a form of government in which the citizens of a nation choose the people who will run their government through elections of candidates from two or more political parties. In dictatorships (option C) and oligarchies (option D), a person or small group of people run the government but never step down or resign. In a constitutional monarchy (option B), a king or queen is the head of state, but he or she governs within the limits of a constitution and often works along with a parliament, which is similar to the US Congress. In a communist state (option E), the government is run by a single party.

35. **(C)** It describes the Nineteenth Amendment. The Bill of Rights is the first 10 amendments to the Constitution. Option (A) is the Sixth Amendment, option (B) is the eighth, option (D) is the first, and option (E) is the seventh.

36. **(B)** Primary elections are run by political parties. Candidates within the party hold debates and compete against each other to secure the nomination as the party's official candidate in the presidential general election.

37. **(E)** Those who want to reform or eliminate the electoral college often cite the 2000 presidential election. In general, electors cast their votes based on the tally of popular vote for the state as a whole, despite differences within the state counties. In the case of Florida, the popular vote was

split down the middle. The margin between Republican candidate George W. Bush and Democrat candidate Al Gore was just a few hundred votes. In the end, the Florida's 25 electoral votes went to Bush.

38. **(B)** Foreign visitors in the United States with student visas must renew their visas or return to their home country once the visa has expired.

39. **(D)** A dictator takes on exclusive and unlimited power without having inherited control through family connections the way option (B), a queen, might. A governor (option A) is a political official but not as high ranking as a head of state. A colonel (option C) is a high-ranking officer of the military, not of a government. And a prime minister (option E) is the head of state of a government with a parliamentary system, not an authoritarian state.

40. **(E)** More information is required to make the conclusions in options (A), (C), and (D). While possibly true, they cannot be deduced from the information provided in the text. Option (B) is outside the scope of the passage

41. **(B)** Businesses use capital to produce earnings or profits. Money (option A) can be used in various ways to help a company earn revenue, such as making investments or purchasing equipment. Computers and printers (option C) are examples of a business's equipment. Land (option D) and buildings (option E) are assets that can be rented or sold, also creating revenue for the business. Labor, however, is not capital. It is the actual work a person does. Through labor, a business can make goods or provide services, which in turn produce profits for the company.

42. **(A)** NAFTA stands for the North American Free Trade Agreement. It is a trade bloc between the United States, Mexico, and Canada. OPEC (option B) stands for Organization of Petroleum Exporting Countries and is an intergovernmental organization of 12 oil-producing countries. NATO (option C) stands for the North Atlantic Treaty Organization and is an intergovernmental military alliance. The UN (option D) stands for the United Nations, an international organization to foster cooperation and peace between nations. And WHO (option E) stands for the World Health Organization, a subsidiary agency of the UN that tries to prevent and treat outbreaks of infectious diseases.

43.   **(D)** When the gaming console or video game is no longer brand-new to the market, demand for the item goes down and the item is no longer scarce. This increases sellers' supply. To move inventory out of their stores, they lower the price.

44.   **(A)** It summarizes the main idea of the passage, which is that Western economies contain both capitalist and socialist elements. Option (B) cannot be deduced from the information provided in the text, and options (C), (D), and (E) are too narrow in scope to provide a summary of the passage.

45.   **(C)** Sales tax is not a government subsidy. It is a tax—collected by either the state or the federal government—that consumers pay at the point of purchase. The other options are examples of times when the government interferes with supply and demand dynamics.

46.   **(B)** In both capitalism and socialism, goods are produced and services are provided. Price controls (option A) are characteristic of socialism only. And options (C), (D), and (E) are factually incorrect.

47.   **(D)** According to the graph, the US national debt reached at least $10 trillion in 2008.

48.   **(D)** The author of the passage places the blame for the Great Depression on the Federal Reserve, providing details of how it failed to stop the recession and even worsened it into a depression. Options (A) and (B) cannot be deduced from the information provided in the text. Options (C) and (E) state the opposite of what the author asserts about treasury bonds and the efforts of the Federal Reserve.

49.   **(A)** A run on a bank is when a large number of people withdraw their funds from a bank all at once. As the passage states, "After some large banks collapsed, people were afraid they would lose their savings. As a result, large groups descended on their local branches in panic, and there were runs on local banks, which subsequently collapsed. Therefore, the supply of money in the US marketplace shrank from 1929 to 1933."

50.   **(B)** It does not truthfully describe labor strikes but instead provides an opinion on the effect that strikes can have. Options (A) and (C) are accurate statements about labor unions, while options (D) and (E) are factually incorrect.

SCIENCE

Choose the *one best answer* to each question.

1. A dog is lying on a scale. The weight of the dog is 13 pounds (58 newtons). What is the force that the scale is exerting upward on the dog?

   (A) 0 newtons
   (B) 13 newtons
   (C) 29 newtons
   (D) 58 newtons
   (E) 116 newtons

2. Which of the following statements provides evidence that visible light is made of electromagnetic waves rather than mechanical waves?

   (A) Sunlight can travel through window glass.
   (B) Sunlight can travel through a vacuum.
   (C) Sunlight can travel through clear plastic.
   (D) Sunlight can travel through Earth's atmosphere.
   (E) Sunlight can travel through seawater.

3. When a person touched a mug of tea, the person's hand felt warm. Which of the following statements gives the best explanation of this observation?

   (A) Thermal energy flowed from the person's hand to the mug.
   (B) Thermal energy flowed from the mug to the person's hand.
   (C) Thermal energy flowed in a continuous loop between the person's hand and the mug.
   (D) The person's hand was originally at the same temperature as the mug.
   (E) The person's hand was originally at a higher temperature than the mug.

4. Through which of the following materials does electricity travel most easily?

   (A) glass
   (B) plastic
   (C) rubber
   (D) plastic
   (E) metal

Questions 5 and 6 refer to the following diagram of a light ray hitting a flat surface of a transparent object.

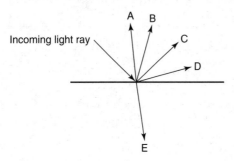

5. Which arrow shows the direction of the light ray that is reflected from the surface?

    (A) arrow A
    (B) arrow B
    (C) arrow C
    (D) arrow D
    (E) arrow E

6. Which arrow shows the direction of the light ray that is refracted by the object?

    (A) arrow A
    (B) arrow B
    (C) arrow C
    (D) arrow D
    (E) arrow E

7. A person is pushing a brick up a slanted wooden board. Which of the
    following statements gives the best comparison of the force required to
    cause the brick to begin moving and the force required to keep the brick
    moving?

    (A) More force is required to cause the brick to begin moving because
         the roughness of the surface of the brick and the board increase the
         friction that must be overcome for movement to begin.

    (B) More force is required to cause the brick to begin moving than to
         keep it moving because of the higher amount of potential energy in
         the board due to its greater mass.

    (C) The same amount of force is required to cause the brick to move and
         to keep it in motion because the potential energy of the brick does
         not change.

    (D) Less force is required to cause the brick to begin moving because
         there is less friction with the board than when the brick is already in
         motion.

    (E) Less force is required to cause the brick to begin moving than to
         keep it moving because of the higher amount of potential energy in
         the brick compared to the board.

8. The graph below shows the relationship between distance an object trav-
    eled and time. Which of the following is the best conclusion that can be
    made about the movement of the object?

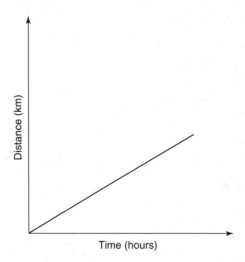

(A) The object moved at a constant positive speed.
(B) The object moved at a varying positive speed.
(C) The object remained stationary during the time interval shown.
(D) The object moved at a constant negative speed.
(E) The object moved at a varying negative speed.

9. In which of the following substances do the molecules have the highest average kinetic energy?

(A) water in a cup
(B) water vapor in the air within a house
(C) snowflakes falling to the ground
(D) ice cubes in a freezer
(E) water boiling in a teakettle

10. The diagram below shows a model of the structure of a lithium atom. Which of the following describes a type of particle in the nucleus of the atom?

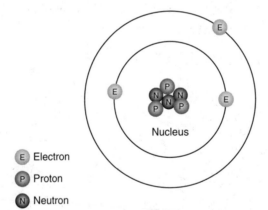

Nucleus

E Electron
P Proton
N Neutron

(A) uncharged protons
(B) positively charged protons
(C) negatively charged neutrons
(D) positively charged electrons
(E) negatively charged electrons

11. The diagram below shows models of neutral and electrically charged atoms. Which atom is a negative ion?

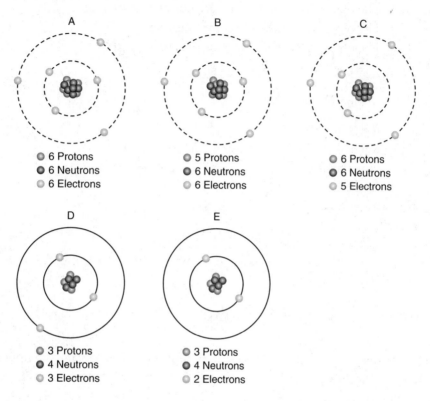

A
○ 6 Protons
● 6 Neutrons
○ 6 Electrons

B
○ 5 Protons
● 6 Neutrons
○ 6 Electrons

C
○ 6 Protons
● 6 Neutrons
○ 5 Electrons

D
○ 3 Protons
● 4 Neutrons
○ 3 Electrons

E
○ 3 Protons
● 4 Neutrons
○ 2 Electrons

(A) atom A
(B) atom B
(C) atom C
(D) atom D
(E) atom E

Questions 12–14 refer to the chart below, showing functional groups in compounds of organic substances.

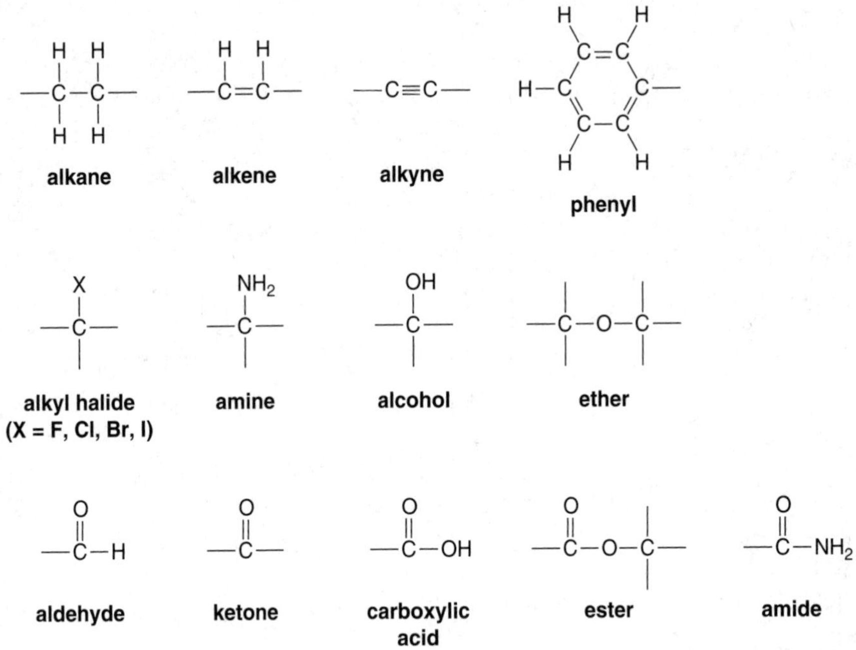

alkane   alkene   alkyne   phenyl

alkyl halide
(X = F, Cl, Br, I)   amine   alcohol   ether

aldehyde   ketone   carboxylic acid   ester   amide

12. The diagram below shows a structural model of an organic compound. According to the chart of functional groups, what type of compound does the diagram show?

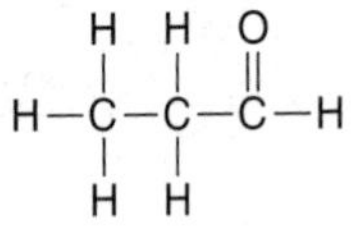

(A) alkane
(B) alcohol
(C) aldehyde
(D) carboxylic acid
(E) ether

13. In the chart of functional groups, a single line represents a single bond, a double line represents a double bond, and a triple line represents a triple bond. Which of the following compounds contain double bonds between carbon atoms?

(A) alkene compounds
(B) aldehyde compounds

(C) alkane and alkyl halide compounds

(D) ketone, carboxylic acid, and ester compounds

(E) aldehyde, ether, and amide compounds

14. Which of the following processes describes how a carboxylic acid compound might be changed to an amide compound?

(A) replace the C=O in carboxylic acid with –NH₂

(B) replace the –C– in carboxylic acid with =O

(C) replace the =O in carboxylic acid with an amine group

(D) replace the –OH in carboxylic acid with –NH₂

(E) replace the –C–OH in carboxylic acid with a phenyl group

15. A synthesis reaction is taking place in a closed system. The system has reached a dynamic equilibrium. What other type of chemical reaction must be taking place in the closed system?

(A) combustion reaction

(B) exothermic reaction

(C) endothermic reaction

(D) decomposition reaction

(E) displacement reaction

16. The diagram below shows a model of a water molecule. What type of chemical bond holds a water molecule together?

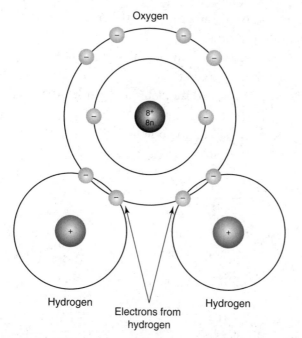

Oxygen

Hydrogen   Hydrogen

Electrons from hydrogen

(A) covalent
(B) ionic
(C) metallic
(D) van der Waals
(E) Lewis

17. Solid ammonium chloride, $NH_4Cl(s)$, dissolves in water. Why does a solution of $NH_4Cl(aq)$ have a pH that is less than 7.0?

(A) $NH_4^+(aq)$ ions react with water to form hydronium ions (H_3O^+).
(B) Ammonium chloride releases hydroxide ions (OH^-) into solution.
(C) Chloride ions (Cl^-) remove hydroxide ions (OH^-) from solution.
(D) Ammonium chloride absorbs hydronium ions (H_3O^+) from solution.
(E) Ammonium chloride absorbs hydroxide ions (OH^-) from solution.

18. The chemical equation below shows that the reaction of nitrogen dioxide produces nitrogen gas and oxygen gas and releases energy.

$$2NO_2(g) \rightarrow N_2(g) + 2O_2(g) + 66.4 \text{ kJ}$$

Which of the following statements best describes the reaction?

(A) The reaction is endothermic, and the potential energy of the reactant is greater than that of the products.
(B) The reaction is endothermic, and the potential energy of the reactant is less than that of the products.
(C) The reaction is exothermic, and the potential energy of the reactant is greater than that of the products.
(D) The reaction is exothermic, and the potential energy of the reactant equals that of the products.
(E) The reaction is exothermic, and the potential energy of the reactant is less than that of the products.

19. The diagram below shows characteristics of a woolly mammoth, African elephant, and Asian elephant.

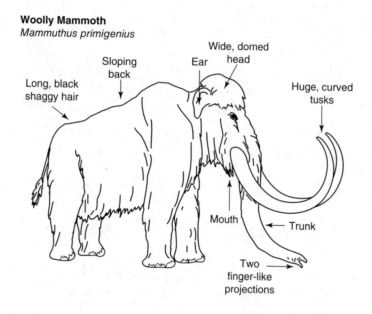

Woolly Mammoth
Mammuthus primigenius

Wide, domed head

Sloping back

Ear

Long, black shaggy hair

Huge, curved tusks

Mouth

Trunk

Two finger-like projections

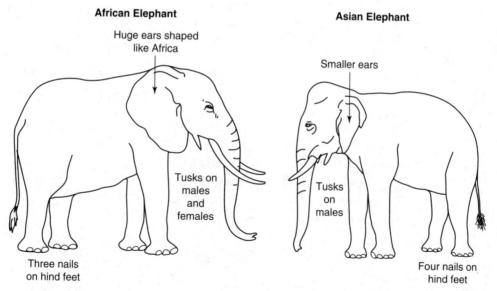

African Elephant

Huge ears shaped like Africa

Tusks on males and females

Three nails on hind feet

Asian Elephant

Smaller ears

Tusks on males

Four nails on hind feet

The frozen remains of woolly mammoths have been recovered from ice in Siberia. Analysis of DNA from the mammoths shows that they have many genetic similarities to modern elephants. The mammoth DNA is slightly more similar to that of Asian elephants than to that of African elephants. Which of the following conclusions is best supported by this DNA evidence?

(A) Woolly mammoths lived only in Asia.
(B) Woolly mammoths and modern elephants have a recent common ancestor.
(C) Woolly mammoths and Asian elephants belong to the same species.
(D) African elephants evolved from Asian elephants.
(E) Woolly mammoths ate the same plants as modern elephants do.

Questions 20–22 refer to the following diagram of an ocean food web.

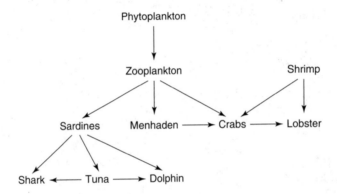

20. In the food web diagram, the arrows point from an organism to another organism that eats it. Which of the following is most likely to occur first if the menhaden population decreases?

(A) Sardines will have less competition for food.
(B) Crabs will not have a source of food.
(C) The population of shrimp will increase.
(D) Zooplankton will have more food available to them.
(E) The population of sharks will decrease.

21. According to the diagram, which of the following organisms consumes crabs?

(A) zooplankton
(B) menhaden
(C) shrimp
(D) sardines
(E) lobster

22. Which organism shown in the diagram obtains energy directly from the sun?

    (A) crabs
    (B) shrimp
    (C) phytoplankton
    (D) zooplankton
    (E) sardines

23. The diagram below shows the skulls of two types of animals. One of the animals ate plants, and the other ate other animals. Which of the following best describes how which skull provides evidence about the type of animal it belonged to?

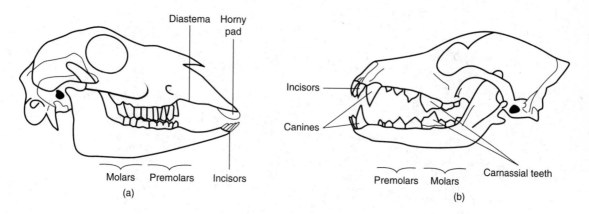

    (A) Skull A has flat molars suitable for crushing plants, so it belonged to a meat eater.
    (B) Skull A has incisors suitable for biting off plants, so it belonged to an herbivore.
    (C) Skull A has premolars suitable for cutting through flesh, so it belonged to a carnivore.
    (D) Skull B has canines suitable for stabbing and killing prey, so it belonged to a plant eater.
    (E) Skull B has premolars and molars suitable for grinding plants, so it belonged to a predator.

24. The figure shows a type of heron that lives in Africa and South Asia. Which characteristic of this bird supports the hypothesis that it spends a lot of time wading in bodies of water?

(A) the shape of its neck
(B) the size of its wings
(C) the position of its eyes
(D) the length of its legs
(E) the thickness of its beak

25. An organism's genes are made up of pairs of alleles that determine, among other characteristics, its physical appearance. An allele can be dominant or recessive. In pea plants, the allele (T) for a tall plant is dominant over the allele (t) for a short plant. A particular plant is tall. What conclusion can be made about its alleles for height?

(A) The allele pair could be Tt or TT.
(B) The allele pair must be TT.
(C) The allele pair could be Tt or tt.
(D) The allele pair must be tt.
(E) The allele pair could be TT or tt.

26. Which pair of organisms has the same type of ecological relationship as the one between an owl and a mouse?

    (A) tiger and cougar
    (B) squirrel and seeds
    (C) honeybee and flower
    (D) zebra and grass
    (E) wolf and rabbit

Questions 27 and 28 refer to the following diagram of the nitrogen cycle.

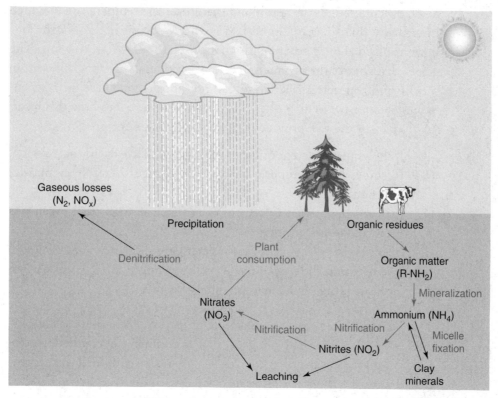

27. According to the diagram, which form of nitrogen is most likely to be taken up by plants?

    (A) N_2
    (B) $R\text{-}NH_2$
    (C) NO_3
    (D) NO_2
    (E) NH_4

28. Which of the following is directly involved in returning nitrogen (N_2) to the atmosphere?

    (A) plant consumption
    (B) leaching
    (C) precipitation
    (D) clay minerals
    (E) denitrification

29. The ocean around Antarctica, near the South Pole, is very cold. Fish die when their body fluids freeze. Some Antarctic fish have adapted by evolving compounds in their blood that lower the temperature at which their body fluids freeze. Some fish in the Arctic, near the North Pole, have evolved similar compounds that protect them from freezing. The genes that control the production of the compounds are very different in Arctic and Antarctic fish. These fish are not descended from a recent common ancestor. Which of the following best describes how this information about the fish provides evidence for evolution?

    (A) It shows that different organisms can adapt to live in the same region.
    (B) It shows that temperature is the strongest factor in natural selection.
    (C) It shows that a variety of genes can function to protect organisms from cold temperatures.
    (D) It shows that different organisms can have similar characteristics.
    (E) It shows that different organisms can adapt in similar ways when faced with the same environmental pressures.

30. The diagram below shows an example of recessive inheritance. The parents both carry a normal gene (N) that is dominant over the defective gene (n) they also carry that is recessive. Therefore, although the parents do not have the health disorder associated with the recessive gene, they are carriers for the disorder. The children of the parents can inherit two dominant N genes, a dominant N gene and a recessive n gene, or two recessive n genes. Which of the following statements always applies to the children of these parents?

Recessive Inheritance

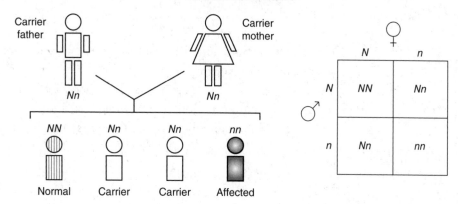

(A) All of the children will inherit at least one of the defective genes.
(B) Children who lack the dominant gene will have the genetically related health disorder.
(C) A child with two copies of the dominant gene can, in turn, have children with the genetically related health disorder.
(D) A child with two copies of the recessive gene cannot, in turn, have children.
(E) A child with one dominant gene and one recessive gene will, in turn, have children who are free of the genetically related health disorder.

31. Which of the following best describes how a producer in an ecosystem obtains energy?

(A) by using sunlight to make sugars during photosynthesis
(B) by breaking down organic matter to release nutrients
(C) by consuming plants
(D) by consuming other animals
(E) by living as a parasite on other organisms

32. In a type of small parrot called a budgerigar, the allele for green feathers (G) is dominant over the gene for blue feathers (g). A green bird with Gg alleles mates with another green bird with Gg alleles. What percentage of the baby birds would be expected to have green feathers?

(A) 0%
(B) 25%
(C) 50%

(D) 75%
(E) 100%

33. A student made three terrariums like the one shown in the photograph below. The student put each terrarium in sunlight for a different amount of time for a month. One terrarium received a short period of sunlight each day, one received a medium period, and one received a long period. To determine which period of sunlight is best to maintain the health of the terrarium, which of the following variables should be held constant?

(A) wavelengths of sunlight needed for photosynthesis
(B) length of time sunlight is received
(C) type of plants used
(D) color of the plants used
(E) growth rate of the plants used

34. Genetic engineering is being used to make crops more resistant to pests. A caterpillar called a corn borer can cause extensive damage to corn plants. Genes are being transferred to corn plants to see if the genetically modified plants can produce proteins that kill the caterpillar. How can scientists assess whether the genes are helping the plants become more resistant to damage by corn borers?

(A) by monitoring the reproductive cycle of the caterpillar in untreated corn
(B) by determining whether the caterpillar can be controlled with the use of chemicals sprayed on the plants
(C) by measuring the number of caterpillars affecting fields of untreated corn

(D) by comparing the number of caterpillars affecting similar fields of untreated corn and genetically modified corn

(E) by calculating the total mass of corn produced by the genetically modified corn

35. Which of the following is required for aerobic cellular respiration?

(A) chlorophyll
(B) sunlight
(C) oxygen
(D) carbon dioxide
(E) bacteria

36. The diagram below shows a flatworm. Flatworms are nonparasitic worms that can be found in freshwater and saltwater, and sometimes in soil. They use hairlike projections called cilia to move. Some students wanted to test how being in freshwater affected the movement of flatworms. The students put 20 flatworms in freshwater and then recorded their observations in detail. What was the most significant flaw in the students' experimental design?

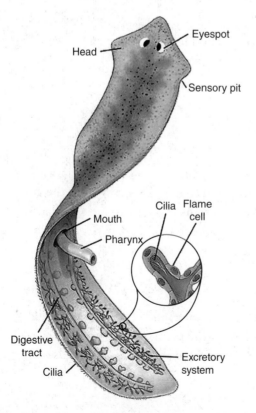

(A) There was no control group of flatworms for comparison.
(B) The number of flatworms used was too large.
(C) The students did not first develop a hypothesis.
(D) The experimental procedure had too many steps.
(E) The students did not collect enough data.

37. Why can the introduction of non-native animal or plant species damage an ecosystem?

(A) Non-native species lack natural predators, parasites, or diseases to control their population size.
(B) Non-native species provide excess food to native species.
(C) Non-native species adapt more quickly to environmental changes than do native species.
(D) Non-native species eat more food than native species.
(E) Non-native species reproduce more slowly than native species.

Questions 38 and 39 refer to the following diagram, which shows evolutionary relationships among several organisms.

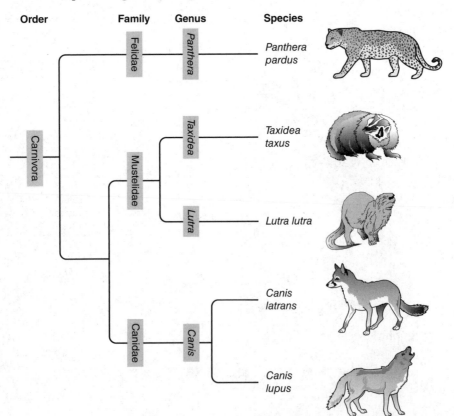

38. Which conclusion about the animals is supported by the diagram?

    (A) They are examples of the same species.
    (B) They are in the same family but are different species.
    (C) They are in the same genus and the same family.
    (D) They are in the same order but in different families.
    (E) They are in the same family and the same genus.

39. Which animal shown on the diagram is most closely related to *Lutra lutra*?

    (A) *Panthera pardus*
    (B) *Taxidea taxus*
    (C) *Canis latrans*
    (D) *Canis lupus*
    (E) They are all equally related.

40. The diagram below shows stages of growth of a broad-bean plant. What is this process called?

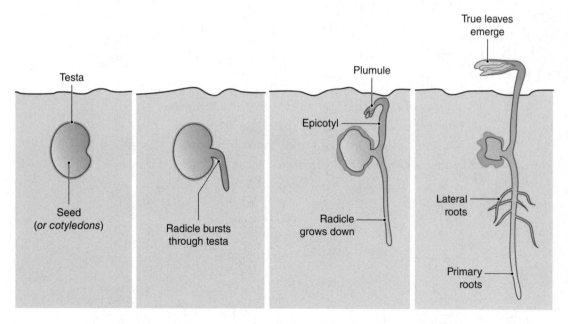

    (A) photosynthesis
    (B) germination
    (C) dispersal
    (D) reproduction
    (E) pollination

41. The chain-of-events chart below describes Earth's origin as part of the solar system. Which of the following statements belongs in the center oval of the chart?

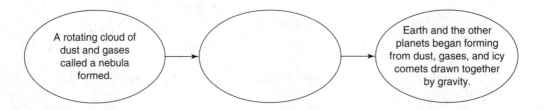

(A) A collision with another nebula provided energy for the solar system to begin to take form.

(B) The nebula moved from the center of the Milky Way galaxy to the Orion Arm.

(C) Gravity pulled most of the dust and gases into the center of the nebula, and the sun formed.

(D) Oceans formed as water vapor condensed and fell as rain throughout the nebular cloud.

(E) Asteroids and moons formed and then began orbiting the nebula.

42. Which of the following best explains the magnitude of an earthquake?

(A) depth at which the earthquake starts

(B) types of rocks that are affected by the earthquake

(C) extent of damage that the earthquake causes

(D) amount of energy that the earthquake releases

(E) amount of time that has passed since the last earthquake

43. The maps below show the positions of South America and Africa at two different times in Earth's history. Which of the following processes is most closely related to the change in position of the two continents?

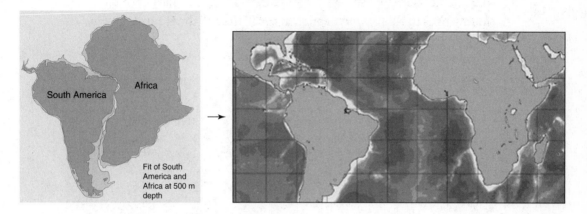

(A) reversals in the polarity of Earth's magnetic field
(B) flooding of continents caused by rising sea levels
(C) movements of Earth's tectonic plates
(D) volcanic eruptions along a deep-ocean trench
(E) erosion of sediments and bedrock

44. A person states that a full moon and a new moon always occur 14.75 days apart. Which of the following could be used to test the accuracy of the person's statement?
(A) hypothesis
(B) theory
(C) prediction
(D) observation
(E) conclusion

45. The map below shows part of the San Andreas fault system that marks the boundary between the Pacific plate and the North American plate. The arrows show how the plates are moving. Los Angeles is on the Pacific plate, and San Francisco is on the North American plate. Which of the following is most likely to happen at some time in the future if the movement of the plates remains the same?

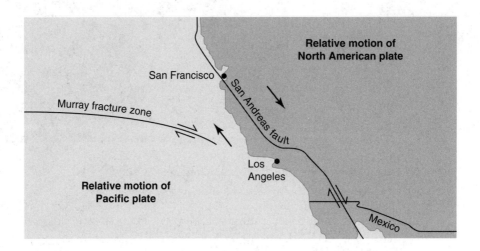

(A) Los Angeles will move to the same latitude as San Francisco.
(B) San Francisco will become an island in the Pacific Ocean.
(C) San Francisco will be pulled down into a subduction zone.
(D) Los Angeles will become part of the North American plate.
(E) Volcanic activity will begin along the fault between San Francisco and Los Angeles.

46. The diagram below shows Earth and the sun. What seasons do the Northern Hemisphere and Southern Hemisphere experience when Earth and the sun are in the positions shown?

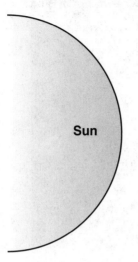

(A) Northern Hemisphere: summer; Southern Hemisphere: summer
(B) Northern Hemisphere: summer; Southern Hemisphere: winter
(C) Northern Hemisphere: spring equinox; Southern Hemisphere: fall equinox
(D) Northern Hemisphere: winter; Southern Hemisphere: winter
(E) Northern Hemisphere: winter; Southern Hemisphere: summer

47. Water moves among Earth's surface, shallow subsurface, and atmosphere by a set of processes called the water cycle. Through which process in the water cycle does most of the water that falls as precipitation on land enter streams and lakes?
(A) flow of groundwater
(B) surface runoff
(C) infiltration
(D) transpiration
(E) condensation

48. The diagram below shows a comet that is orbiting the sun. Why does the tail of a comet always point away from the sun?

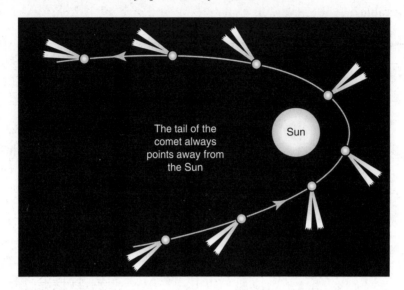

The tail of the comet always points away from the Sun

Sun

(A) The solar wind pushes the comet tail away from the sun.
(B) The comet tail is being repelled by the sun's gravity.
(C) The comet tail is being pulled toward a black hole in the Kuiper Belt.
(D) The comet tail points to the region of the Oort cloud from which the comet came.
(E) Only the part of the comet tail pointing away from the sun contains enough matter to reflect sunlight.

49. Earth's distance from the sun is ideal for the presence of life because it sets up conditions on the planet's surface that are unique in the solar system. Which of the following is unique to Earth?
(A) water in the solid, liquid, and gas phases
(B) volcanoes that produce igneous rocks
(C) methane gas in the atmosphere
(D) a moon that causes ocean tides
(E) a greenhouse effect

50. The table below shows Mohs scale of hardness for 10 minerals. A mineral with a higher Mohs scale number can scratch a mineral with a lower number. The graph below compares the relative hardness of the 10 minerals.

On the relative hardness scale, diamond is about 40 times harder than talc. Which of the following is the best conclusion that can be made using the table and the chart?

Mohs Scale

Hardness	1	2	3	4	5	6	7	8	9	10
Mineral	talc	gypsum	calcite	fluorite	apatite	orthoclase	quartz	topaz	corundum	diamond

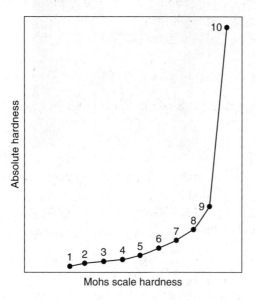

Mohs scale hardness

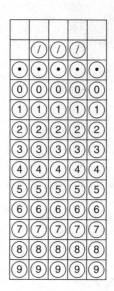

(A) The absolute hardness of quartz is less than the absolute hardness of corundum but greater than the absolute hardness of gypsum.

(B) A mineral that can be scratched by orthoclase can scratch gypsum and calcite.

(C) A mineral that can scratch apatite and be scratched by topaz is able to scratch corundum.

(D) The intervals between the numbers on the Mohs scale represent varying amounts of change in absolute hardness.

(E) The intervals between the numbers on the Mohs scale show that some minerals have negative values of absolute hardness.

ANSWERS: SCIENCE

1. **(D)** The surface supporting an object exerts an upward force on the object that is equal but opposite to the downward force of gravity on the object.

2. **(B)** Mechanical waves, such as sound waves, propagate through matter by actually causing an oscillation of the matter through which they are moving. Electromagnetic waves, such as visible light, can propagate through matter or through space that is devoid of matter.

3. **(B)** Thermal energy always flows from a warmer object to a cooler object.

4. **(E)** Electricity travels easily through a conductor; options (A), (B), (C), and (D) are insulators.

5. **(C)** A light ray reflects from a surface at the same angle it struck the surface. Arrow C forms the same angle to the surface as the incident ray.

6. **(E)** Only arrow E shows a light ray that enters the object and bends because the speed of light changes.

7. **(A)** The static friction between stationary objects with irregular surfaces is higher than the kinetic friction between those same objects moving relative to one another because of the resistance to movement caused by the interlocking surfaces.

8. **(A)** The line is straight, showing that the relationship between time and distance was constant, and the slope of the line is upward toward the right (positive).

9. **(E)** The average kinetic energy of the molecules of a substance increases as temperature increases. The water in option (E) has the highest temperature.

10. **(B)** The nucleus shows two types of particles: neutrons, which are neutral, and protons, which have a positive charge.

11. **(B)** A negative ion has more electrons than protons. Options (A), (C), (D), and (E) either have an equal number of electrons and protons or more protons than electrons.

12. **(C)** The compound contains a functional group made up of a carbon atom sharing a double bond with oxygen and a single bond with hydrogen, so the compound is an aldehyde.

13. **(A)** Alkenes contain a double bond between carbon atoms. (Phenyl compounds were not included in the answer choice because the bonds in a carbon ring are intermediate between single and double bonds.) The double bonds in options (B), (C), (D), and (E) are between carbon and oxygen.

14. **(D)** A carboxylic acid compound can be converted to an amide compound by chemically transforming the identity of the functional group. The process involves detaching the $-OH$ group and replacing it with $-NH_2$.

15. **(D)** A synthesis reaction involves combining elements or simpler compounds into a single, more complex compound. Its opposite is a decomposition reaction in which a single reactant breaks apart into elements or simpler compounds. A synthesis reaction must be balanced by a decomposition reaction for a system to achieve a dynamic equilibrium.

16. **(A)** The model shows that the oxygen atom shares an electron with each of the hydrogen atoms. Covalent bonds are characterized by the sharing of electrons.

17. **(A)** The pH of a solution is determined by the concentration of hydronium ions relative to hydroxide ions. When there is an excess of hydronium ions, the solution is acidic (pH less than 7.0). $NH_4Cl(aq) \rightarrow NH_4^+(aq) + Cl^-(aq)$; $NH_4^+ + H_2O \rightarrow H_3O^+ + NH_3$

18. **(C)** The reaction produces energy, so it is exothermic. In an exothermic reaction, the potential energy of the reactant is higher than that of the products.

19. **(B)** The similarities in DNA show that all three species have a recent common ancestor. The evidence cannot be used to determine the range of woolly mammoths or what types of plants they ate.

20. **(A)** Sardines, menhaden, and crabs all consume zooplankton. If the menhaden population decreases, sardines (and crabs) will have less competition for the zooplankton. With decreased availability of menhaden, crabs can still consume zooplankton and shrimp.

21. **(E)** An arrow points from crabs to lobsters, indicating that lobsters consume crabs.

22. **(C)** Phytoplankton are photosynthetic organisms, so they get energy to make food directly from the sun.

23. **(B)** The presence of incisors suitable for biting off plants indicates that skull A belonged to a plant-eating animal. Options (A), (C), (D), and (E) all have a mismatch between evidence from the teeth and the conclusion about the type of food eaten.

24. **(D)** Wading birds have evolved long legs to allow them to spend a lot of time standing in shallow water.

25. **(A)** Because the allele that codes for tallness is dominant, a tall plant could be heterozygous (Tt) or homozygous (TT). A tt plant would be short.

26. **(E)** An owl is a predator that consumes mice. A wolf is a predator that consumes rabbits. A tiger and a cougar do not interact in a natural food web. The squirrel and zebra consume plants, and a honeybee pollinates a flower when seeking nectar.

27. **(C)** The arrow indicating the uptake of nitrogen by plants extends from nitrates.

28. **(E)** The arrow indicating denitrification points to losses of nitrogen from the ground in the form of a gas that enters the atmosphere.

29. **(E)** The ocean environment at the poles is similar, and fish in both locations must adapt to withstand cold. The two fish populations are at opposite poles, and they do not share a recent common ancestor, but they have similar biochemical adaptations.

30. **(B)** The lack of the dominant allele allows the recessive trait (the genetically related health disorder) to be expressed. It is not possible to draw any conclusions about the future offspring of the children without knowing the genotype of the other parent.

31. **(A)** A producer is at the base of a food web. A producer makes its own food via photosynthesis or, much more rarely, chemosynthesis.

32. **(D)** The Punnett square for the cross is:

	G	**g**
G	*GG*	*Gg*
g	*Gg*	*Gg*

Therefore, 75 percent of the offspring would be expected to inherit at least one copy of the dominant allele from a parent. Because the dominant allele codes for green feathers, 75 percent of the offspring would be expected to be green.

33. **(C)** The terrariums should all have the same conditions except for the variable being tested. The same type of plants should be used in each terrarium, because different types of plants might have different growth requirements. The wavelengths of sunlight needed for photosynthesis (option A) is a property of a plant, not a variable to be manipulated. The length of time the terrariums receive sunlight (option B) is the variable being changed. Color and growth rates (options D and E) depend on the health of the plant.

34. **(D)** The caterpillar infestation rates for untreated corn and genetically modified corn must be compared to determine what effect, if any, the genetic modification has on the pest.

35. **(C)** Aerobic cellular respiration allows organisms to release energy stored in chemical bonds for use in metabolic processes. In the process, oxygen is combined with glucose to produce carbon dioxide, water, and energy.

36. **(A)** The lack of a control group gives no means of comparison as to how the flatworms might move differently in freshwater versus saltwater or soil.

37. **(A)** Non-native species, once established in an ecosystem, can outcompete native species because they have not coevolved with predators, parasites, or diseases that target them.

38. **(D)** The branches of the diagram show that all animals included belong to the order Carnivora but that they are in three different families.

39. **(B)** *Lutra lutra* and *Taxidea taxus* are the most closely related because they are in the same genus.

40. **(B)** The process by which a seed sprouts is called germination.

41. **(C)** Most of the mass of the nebula collected at the center and collapsed under the force of gravity until it became massive enough and hot enough for thermonuclear reactions to begin.

42. **(D)** The magnitude of an earthquake is a measure of the amount of energy released by the event.

43. **(C)** The continents were carried to different locations by the movement of the tectonic plates of which they are a part.

44. **(D)** The validity of a testable statement is determined by making observations that may support or contradict the statement.

45. **(A)** The map shows that the cities are on plates that meet along a transform boundary marked by the San Andreas fault. Relative plate motion is carrying Los Angeles north, so at some future time, the cities will be neighbors if the motion continues.

46. **(B)** The Northern Hemisphere is tilted toward the sun, so it is experiencing summer. The Southern Hemisphere is tilted away from the sun, so it is experiencing winter. At the equinox, neither hemisphere is tilted toward the sun.

47. **(B)** Most of the precipitation that falls on land runs over the surface of the ground before being channeled into rills and gullies that feed into streams, lakes, or other bodies of water.

48. **(A)** The charged particles of the solar wind sweep the ionized comet tail in the direction of the wind's movement (that is, away from the sun).

49. **(A)** Earth is the only planet in the solar system with a range of surface temperatures that allows large amounts of liquid water to be present.

50. **(D)** If the intervals between the numbers on the Mohs scale each represented the same amount of change in absolute hardness, then the graph would show a straight line rather than a curve.

LANGUAGE ARTS, READING

Questions 1–5 refer to the following excerpt from a novel.

Can This Man Survive?

The man flung a look back along the way he had come. The Yukon lay a mile wide and hidden under three feet of ice. On top of this ice were as many feet of snow. It was all pure white, rolling in gentle undulations where the ice-jams of the freeze-up had formed. North
(5) and south, as far as his eye could see, it was unbroken white, save for a dark hairline that curved and twisted from around the spruce-covered island to the south, and that curved and twisted away into the north, where it disappeared behind another spruce-covered island. This dark hairline was the trail—the main trail—that led south
(10) five hundred miles to the Chilcoot Pass, Dyea, and salt water; and that led north seventy miles to Dawson, and still on to the north a thousand miles to Nulato, and finally to St. Michael on Bering Sea, a thousand miles and a half thousand more.

But all this—the mysterious, far-reaching hairline trail, the absence of
(15) sun from the sky, the tremendous cold, and the strangeness and weirdness of it all—made no impression on the man. It was not because he was long used to it. He was a newcomer in the land, a cheechako, and this was his first winter. The trouble with him was that he was without imagination. He was quick and alert in the things
(20) of life, but only in things, not in the significances. Fifty degrees below zero meant eighty-odd degrees of frost. Such a fact impressed him as being cold and uncomfortable, an d that was all. It did not lead him to meditate on his frailty as a creature of temperature, and upon man's frailty in general, able only to live within certain narrow limits of heat
(25) and cold; and from there on it did not lead him to the conjectural field of immortality and man's place in the universe. Fifty degrees below zero stood for a bite of frost that hurt and that must be guarded against by the use of mittens, ear flaps, warm moccasins, and thick socks. Fifty degrees below zero was to him just precisely fifty
(30) degrees below zero. That there should be anything more to it than that was a thought that never entered his head.

—Adapted from "To Build a Fire," by Jack London, 1910

1. Which of the following phrases <u>best</u> describes what the man feels toward the cold?

   (A) hateful and bitter
   (B) vengeful and angry
   (C) oblivious and unconcerned
   (D) frightened but reasonable
   (E) aware but indifferent

2. What is the main effect of the author's description of the Yukon?

   (A) It impresses on the reader how vast, lonely, and cold it is.
   (B) It allows the reader to understand how beautiful it is.
   (C) It shows that the Yukon is an area like no other.
   (D) It mirrors the feelings the man has as he walks through the Yukon.
   (E) It suggests the likelihood of the man reaching his destination.

3. Which of the following <u>best</u> describes the mood created by this scene?

   (A) solemn
   (B) serene
   (C) sorrowful
   (D) abandoned
   (E) caring

4. Which of the following <u>best</u> expresses the main idea of the excerpt?

   (A) No one can survive the Yukon in the winter.
   (B) Life takes many turns, and often they are sudden.
   (C) Nature can be fickle at times.
   (D) Life is a complicated path for most people.
   (E) Man may not be aware of his own limitations.

5. Which of the following can you infer about the author of the excerpt?

   (A) He has walked the entire length of the trail.
   (B) He has experienced nearly dying from the cold.
   (C) He is worried that the man does not know where the path is.
   (D) He is very knowledgeable about the Yukon.
   (E) He knows the man in the excerpt.

Questions 6–12 refer to the following excerpt from a play.

Will the Storm Come?

Bertie: I don't think you should go out. Not now. The wind is rising and the dust may be bad.

Karl: I have to go and try to talk some sense into Larsen. He should know better than to try to plow the field when it's been so dry. It will only make the dust worse. What little cover there is over the ground will be gone.

Bertie: Please be careful. Take a lantern with you just in case.

Anna: Bye, Pa.

Karl: Bye, Anna. Don't worry, Bertie. I'll be back before dark.

[Karl leaves. Bertie goes over to the table and sits down next to Anna, who is reading a book. She begins knitting. They sit quietly together for a long time.]

Bertie: He will be all right. You'll see. As long as the wind doesn't pick up too much.

Anna: Yes, mama, I know. Why is Mr. Larson plowing? It hasn't rained in so many months. Doesn't he know it's better to leave the land alone?

Bertie: I reckon he is frustrated. He isn't thinking clearly. Oh, dear, Anna. Look out the window.

[Anna and Bertie both look out the window, horrified]

Bertie: It's the dust. It's coming. The wind must have picked up. Oh, Pa should never have gone. I told him so. What if he can't get back? What if he doesn't make it through the storm? [She starts to cry.]

Anna: He'll be all right. Mr. Larson's farm's not far. [She takes her mother's hand.] He'll be all right. Don't get yourself worked up. It is what it is.

[Anna hugs her mother]

Bertie: Keep looking. He has a lantern. He will turn it on and we will
(25) see him. I am sure of it.

Anna: Yes, mother. We will see him.

Bertie: Get me those old sheets. Wet them down. We will put them
under the doors. It will help keep the dust out.

[Anna goes to get the sheets. Bertie looks out the window again.]

Bertie: Hurry, it's coming. It's getting darker and darker.

[Anna hurries to push the sheets under the door.]

Bertie: (30) Do you hear it? Do you hear the sound of the wind?
How it moans.

[Anna peers out the window. She gasps.]

Anna: There's a little light I can see.

Bertie: [running to the window] It must be him. It must be . . .

6. Which of the following words <u>best</u> describes Bertie?

   (A) emotional
   (B) strong
   (C) powerful
   (D) cunning
   (E) colorful

7. Why is Bertie upset?

   (A) She thinks that Karl should not interfere in Larson's life.
   (B) She is worried about Karl losing his way in the dust storm.
   (C) She is worried that Karl and Larson will have a fight.
   (D) She believes that Karl is not strong enough.
   (E) She feels that Larson will lose his temper.

8. Based on the excerpt, what can be inferred about Karl's relationship with
   Larson?

   (A) Karl envies Larson's farming equipment.
   (B) They are competitive when it comes to farming.

(C) Larson likes Karl, but Karl is not sure about Larson.

(D) They are friends but do not see eye to eye.

(E) They don't get along at all well.

9. Which is the <u>most likely</u> reason that Anna takes her mother's hand?

(A) She is worried about her mother's health.

(B) She thinks that is what her mother wants.

(C) She wants to show her mother she is strong.

(D) She wants to calm her mother down.

(E) She is frightened of what may happen.

10. In which of the following ways are Bertie and Anna different?

(A) Anna has faced danger more than Bertie has.

(B) Bertie is judgmental while Anna is not.

(C) Anna is a romantic while Bertie is not.

(D) Anna is more impatient than Bertie.

(E) Anna is more realistic than Bertie.

11. Which of the following <u>best</u> describes what Anna means when she says, "It is what it is"?

(A) She is hoping her mother will comfort her.

(B) She is trying to help her mother stay realistic about the situation.

(C) She is telling her mother that the situation will change.

(D) She is explaining to her mother how difficult the situation is for them.

(E) She is trying to explain to her mother that her father will not return.

12. Which of the following <u>best</u> describes the mood created in this scene?

(A) harmonious

(B) sorrowful

(C) lighthearted

(D) suspenseful

(E) angry

Questions 13–17 refer to the following poem.

City Roofs
Charles Hanson Towne

Roof-tops, roof-tops, what do you cover?
Sad folk, bad folk, and many a glowing lover;
Wise people, simple people, children of despair—
Roof-tops, roof-tops, hiding pain and care.

(5) Roof-tops, roof-tops, O what sin you're knowing,
While above you in the sky the white clouds are blowing;
While beneath you, agony and dolor and grim strife
Fight the olden battle, the olden war of Life.

Roof-tops, roof-tops, cover up their shame—
(10) Wretched souls, prisoned souls too piteous to name;
Man himself hath built you all to hide away the stars—
Roof-tops, roof-tops, you hide ten million scars.

Roof-tops, roof-tops, well I know you cover
Many solemn tragedies and many a lonely lover;
(15) But ah, you hide the good that lives in the throbbing city—
Patient wives, and tenderness, forgiveness, faith, and pity.

Roof-tops, roof-tops, this is what I wonder:
You are thick as poisonous plants, thick the people under;
Yet roofless, and homeless, and shelterless they roam,
(20) The driftwood of the town who have no roof-top and no home!

13. Which of the following phrases <u>best</u> describes the overall mood of the poem?

   (A) calm and tranquil
   (B) tender and hopeful
   (C) humorous and cheerful
   (D) angry and bitter
   (E) carefree and fanciful

14. Which of the following is the <u>most likely</u> explanation of why the poet says that the rooftops "hide ten million scars" (line 12)?

   (A) The rooftops were built by man to keep people safe.
   (B) The rooftops keep the sadness in life from being seen.
   (C) The rooftops hurt the people who live under them.
   (D) The rooftops cannot keep everyone from hardship.
   (E) The rooftops give hope to people who are homeless.

15. Which is the <u>best</u> description of what the author thinks about the rooftops?

   (A) They are helpful in cold weather.
   (B) They keep people from doing what they want.
   (C) They keep the good from being seen.
   (D) They protect the homeless.
   (E) They are a necessary evil.

16. According to the poem, what effect do the rooftops have for the people under them?

   (A) They show people how wonderful life is.
   (B) They give the homeless a place to rest.
   (C) They keep people dry in wet weather.
   (D) They keep people from seeing the stars.
   (E) They make people angry.

17. Based on the poem what does the author hope will happen?

   (A) that life will improve with more openness
   (B) that the rooftops will be made stronger
   (C) that people will stop building rooftops
   (D) that people will move out of the city
   (E) that life will be dependent on the rooftops

Questions 18–21 refer to the following memo.

Will Day Care Help the Employees?

Memo: To All Employees

CHG Software is happy to announce that, after a six-month-long feasibility study, we have decided to offer an on-site day care facility for our employees. Realizing that our employees are our most valuable asset, and further realizing that employees appreciate being (5) cared for, we decided to implement a day care center beginning in two months.

The center will be located in the former small business accounting module, which has consolidated its operations with personal accounting. It will be in Building 3, A-6 North Wing, on the ground (10) floor. Construction workers have already started renovations.

HR has interviewed more than 75 applicants for day care employees. The center will be staffed with nine care providers. All workers will be certified in early childhood care and have an associate's degree in day care management. The day care center will have its own kitchen (15) facilities, which will provide a daily lunch as well as morning and afternoon snacks.

The center will be equipped with state-of the-art activity and art tables; each child will have his or her own cubby. There will be an outside play area also with state-of-the-art playground equipment.

(20) The center will be open Monday through Friday, from 8:00 A.M. to 6 P.M. Children from three months to age 12 are eligible. CHG Software has kept the cost to a minimum. Full-time day care will be provided for your children for only $580 per month, per child, with a 10 percent deduction for each additional child.

(25) Enrollment applications are available at HR. All children will need to have proof of vaccinations. We look forward to a new era here at CHG. Let us know how we are doing.

18. Based on the excerpt, which of the following can be inferred about the directors of CHG?

    (A) They do not take the idea of day care seriously.
    (B) They are charging too much for the day care service.
    (C) They are not committed to the idea of having a day care facility.
    (D) They are trying to make life easier for their employees.
    (E) They have not studied the idea of having day care thoroughly.

19. Which of the following <u>best</u> describes the style in which this memo is written?

    (A) detailed and technical
    (B) tentative
    (C) dry and clinical
    (D) straightforward and orderly
    (E) casual and chatty

20. Which of the following best restates the phrase "Realizing that our employees are our most valuable asset" (lines 3–4)?

    Realizing that

    (A) our employees are important to us
    (B) our employees are well paid by us
    (C) our employees are fortunate
    (D) our employees look for better treatment
    (E) our employees demand service

21. Which of the following <u>best</u> describes the way in which the memo is organized?

    (A) by listing information in order of importance
    (B) by listing information in a sequential order
    (C) in a cause-and-effect order
    (D) in an order that follows logically
    (E) by discussing familiar issues and then unfamiliar issues

Questions 22–28 refer to the following excerpt from a novel.

What Will the Reunion Be Like?

Cade settled into his seat on the plane. It was a long flight to Sierra
Leone, where he served as a Peace Corps volunteer so long ago. He
had wanted to return, but a civil war prevented it. As he landed, he
thought of his first visit. He remembered the long truck ride to Joru
(5) where he was to teach English. When he arrived, covered with dust,
the children ran up to him, shouting, "*Pumoi, pumoi* (white man)."

He was going back to Joru, but first he was going to see Kandeh
Massaquoi, his best student. He wanted to see the rice harvester
which Kandeh had built with the help of groups in the United States
(10) and China. Kandeh had proudly written to Cade about it. It
allowed the farmers to get their rice to market faster. Kandeh was
always idealistic. He cared about his people. He was Cade's favorite.

The next morning Cade hired a car and driver for the trip. It didn't
take long to get there. When they arrived, Cade was surprised to see a
(15) large building. There was a Mercedes parked in front. Cade got
out of the car and the front door opened. Kandeh approached quickly,
holding out his arms. "Hello, my old friend," he said, grinning broadly.
His hair was graying, and there was a long scar on his right arm.

They went inside. The room was large and well furnished. Kandeh
(20) motioned for Cade to sit in a black leather chair, while he sat on
an equally impressive sofa. Cade had expected something different.
"Does the house belong to you?" he asked.

Kandeh sighed. "There is much you do not know. In 1993 I returned
to my village, Baiama. The rebels were in control. They were holding
(25) my family hostage. I had no choice but to join them. They armed
me; we attacked neighboring villages, stole weapons and money. I did
it to stay alive. When the U.N. troops came, I hid the money and fled
to Liberia."

Incredulously, Cade asked him about the rice harvester. "It was
(30) destroyed years ago," Kandeh said. "Now I am a businessman."
Cade felt depressed. This wasn't what he imagined their reunion
would be like.

Cade got up awkwardly. "I must go. I want to get to Joru before nightfall and it's a long trip," he said. They shook hands and then (35) Cade walked out of the house to the waiting car.

—Adapted from *Peace Corps* by Charles Houston

22. Which of the following <u>best</u> describes the overall mood of the excerpt?

    (A) expectant
    (B) frightened
    (C) confident
    (D) humorous
    (E) satirical

23. Which of the following <u>best</u> describes Cade's feelings toward Kandeh at the end of the scene?

    (A) compassion
    (B) bitterness
    (C) hatred
    (D) confusion
    (E) relief

24. Based on the excerpt, when does this scene <u>most likely</u> take place?

    (A) late afternoon
    (B) just after lunch
    (C) middle of the night
    (D) midmorning
    (E) at dawn

25. Based on the excerpt, what will probably happen in the future?

    (A) Cade will send Kandeh another rice harvester.
    (B) Cade and Kandeh will stay good friends.
    (C) Cade and Kandeh will go into business together.
    (D) Cade will not contact Kandeh as much as before.
    (E) Cade will not go to Joru.

26. Which of the following phrases <u>best</u> describes Kandeh?

    (A) cunning and sly
    (B) nervous and shy

(C) afraid of the future
(D) proud of his accomplishments
(E) realistic about what he has done

27. Which of the following best describes why Cade "got up awkwardly" (line 33)?

(A) He felt hurt by Kandeh's lack of interest in his life.
(B) He realized that Kandeh did not want him to visit.
(C) He realized that Kandeh was a dangerous man.
(D) He felt badly about leaving so early to go to Joru.
(E) He was taken aback by what Kandeh told him.

28. Based on the information in this excerpt, Cade would most likely participate in which of the following activities?

(A) learn to fly
(B) work with a peace effort group
(C) take up painting as a hobby
(D) take classes in owning a business
(E) travel to tropical paradises

Questions 29–35 refer to the following excerpt from a short story.

"And so you go back to the office on Monday, do you, Jonathan?" asked Linda.

"On Monday the cage door opens and clangs to upon the victim for another eleven months and a week," answered Jonathan.

(5) Linda swung a little. "It must be awful," she said slowly.

"Would ye have me laugh, my fair sister? Would ye have me weep?"

Linda was so accustomed to Jonathan's way of talking that she paid no attention to it.

"I suppose," she said vaguely, "one gets used to it. One gets used to (10) anything."

"Does one? Hum!" The "Hum" was so deep it seemed to boom from underneath the ground. "I wonder how it's done," brooded Jonathan. "I've never managed it."

. . .

(15) "It seems to me just as imbecile, just as awful, to have to go to the office on Monday," said Jonathan, "as it always has done and always will do. To spend all the best years of one's life sitting on a stool from nine to five, scratching in somebody's ledger! It's a strange use to make of one's . . . one and only life, isn't it? Or do I fondly dream?" (20) He rolled over on the grass and looked up at Linda. "Tell me, what is the difference between my life and that of an ordinary prisoner. The only difference I can see is that I put myself in jail and nobody's ever going to let me out. That's a more intolerable situation than the other. For if I'd been—pushed in, against my will—kicking, even—once the (25) door was locked, or at any rate in five years or so, I might have accepted the fact and begun to take an interest in the flight of flies or counting the warden's steps along the passage with particular attention to variations of tread and so on. But as it is, I'm like an insect that's flown into a room of its own accord. I dash against the (30) walls, dash against the windows, flop against the ceiling, do everything, in fact, except fly out again. And all the while I'm thinking, like that moth, or that butterfly, or whatever it is, 'The shortness of life! The shortness of life!' I've only one night or one day, and there's this vast dangerous garden, waiting out there, (35) undiscovered, unexplored."

—Adapted from *The Garden Party and Other Stories*
by Katherine Mansfield

29. Why is Jonathan upset?

    (A) He wants to get a raise.
    (B) He cannot express himself.
    (C) He does not enjoy his job.
    (D) He does not have a job.
    (E) He wants to move to another city.

30. Which of the following words <u>best</u> describes what Linda feels toward Jonathan?

    (A) She thinks he talks too much.
    (B) She is worried he will quit his job.
    (C) She cares about him.
    (D) She wishes he were stronger.
    (E) She wants him to stop complaining.

31. Based on the excerpt, which description <u>best</u> characterizes the relationship between Linda and Jonathan?

    (A) They put up with each other's complaints.
    (B) They rarely talk to one another.
    (C) They like to tell each other secrets.
    (D) They can tell each other anything.
    (E) They do not understand one another.

32. Why does Jonathan liken his situation to being in jail?

    (A) He feels he should be punished.
    (B) He spent time in jail when he was younger.
    (C) He feels stuck in his situation.
    (D) He thinks he has too many restrictions.
    (E) He thinks he has done something very wrong.

33. Based on the excerpt, what is Jonathan <u>most likely</u> to do in the future?

    (A) insult Linda
    (B) run away
    (C) turn to another for help
    (D) continue to work at his job
    (E) start a new life

34. Based on the excerpt, which of the following words would the narrator <u>most likely</u> use to describe Jonathan?

    (A) dramatic but ineffectual
    (B) competitive but understanding
    (C) lighthearted but practical
    (D) indifferent but innocent
    (E) saddened but caring

35. Which of the following <u>best</u> describes the mood of the excerpt?

    (A) life-threatening
    (B) ironic
    (C) fanciful
    (D) theatrical
    (E) tranquil

Questions 36–40 refer to the following review.

What Does the Critic Think of the Movie?

Director Richard Moore has another blockbuster hit with *The Uranium Factor*. George Terry, played perfectly by Richard Burns, is a brilliant but somewhat eccentric (he sleeps in a Himalayan Dome Tent in his dorm room at MIT) college student. Bored with his (5) courses, George designs and builds a time machine in the basement. On a cold, snowy January evening, he sets the time dial to 2150. With the push of a button, he is hurtled forward in time. Scenes rush by faster and faster until he passes out.

George wakens in a crater. Predictably, the dormitory is gone. He (10) covers the time machine with a camouflage net. As he walks through the streets of Cambridge, there are destroyed buildings everywhere; there also don't seem to be any people. Rounding a corner, he sees a huge spaceship, guarded by armed robots more than eight feet tall. One fires at him, and a laser beam blasts the paving beneath him. (15) George falls, only to be whisked away by a rider on a motorcycle, which can also fly.

They go far from town to a cabin in the woods. Over coffee in a bare room lit by a kerosene lamp, Anna (Violet Ritter) tells the story. They came in 2141. People fought back, but they were no match for the (20) robots. Their masters never come out of the spaceships, which are all over the planet. The robots call themselves Zorons. They have been rounding up humans, taking them to uranium mines in Russia, Australia, and Canada.

George learns the aliens came from the Centaurus Galaxy, nearly (25) 12 light-years away. Their own planet ran out of uranium; they traveled to Earth, rich with the ore, enslaving humans to work in the mines and load the space freighters. George and Anna are going to take on the Zorons.

I won't give the ending away, but the special effects are definitely (30) Oscar winning. The camera work is stunning too, and the performances by Burns and Ritter are first-rate. It is the first role for both of them. The script, also by a newcomer, Alex Brandeis, is taut and suspenseful; however, the plot does seem to be a bit familiar. It's a story

(35) that seems to occur in the movies from time to time. Even so, this movie will leave you clutching your seat the whole time.

36. Which of the following is the main idea of the review?

    The author

    (A) thinks the movie should not have been produced
    (B) likes aspects of the film in spite of some faults
    (C) feels the movie is too overwhelming
    (D) believes the acting could have been crisper
    (E) would like to see the movie over before judging it

37. Which of the following best describes the tone of this review?

    (A) informative
    (B) worried
    (C) overwhelmed
    (D) indifferent
    (E) humorous

38. Why does the reviewer say, "Predictably, the dormitory is gone" (line 9)?

    (A) to show that the movie was terrible
    (B) to suggest that this is what happens every day
    (C) to show that the movie was funny
    (D) to suggest that the story line has been used before
    (E) to suggest that the acting was poor

39. Which of the following best expresses the reviewer's opinion of the special effects?

    (A) There were too many special effects.
    (B) The special effects were too sentimental.
    (C) The special effects showed promise but were amateurish.
    (D) They were exciting, but they interfered with the plot.
    (E) The special effects were first-rate.

40. Which of the following <u>best</u> describes the style in which this review is written?

    (A) breezy and humorous
    (B) biased
    (C) encouraging but critical
    (D) methodical and clear
    (E) floral but honest

ANSWERS: LANGUAGE ARTS, READING

1. **(E)** The narrator makes it clear that the man is aware of the cold but does not respond to it in any way other than factually. There is no evidence for options (A), (B), or (D). In option (C), while the man does not seem concerned, it is clear that he is not oblivious to the cold.

2. **(A)** The description of the Yukon shows how large and cold and lonely it is. The author may think that the Yukon is beautiful, but that is not the primary effect of the description, so option (B) is incorrect. Option (C) may be true, but this is not the effect of the description of the Yukon. Neither option (D) nor option (E) is correct; the description does not mirror the man, and there is no suggestion that the man will reach his destination.

3. **(A)** The mood of the scene is very solemn; a man may be facing death because of the cold. The Yukon may seem serene, but that is not the mood of the scene, so option (B) is incorrect. Options (C), (D), and (E) do not describe the mood.

4. **(E)** The man does not realize that he is in danger of dying. Option (E) is the best expression of the main idea. Option (A) is not actually true and certainly not the main idea of the excerpt. Option (B) and (C) could be main ideas but not of this excerpt. Option (D) is likely true but, again, not the main idea of this excerpt.

5. **(D)** Option (D) is something you can figure out about the author because of the way he writes about the Yukon. There is nothing to suggest that options (A) and (B) are true. Option (C) does not seem to be the author's concern. There is no way of knowing if option (E) is correct.

6. **(A)** Option (A) describes Bertie best. While she could be strong, she seems to be falling apart, so option (B) is incorrect. She doesn't seem particularly powerful, nor does she seem cunning or colorful, so options (C), (D), and (E) are also incorrect.

7. **(B)** Option (B) states the reason that Bertie is upset. Option (A) does not seem to be the reason. There is no evidence that she believes option (C) to be true nor that option (D) or option (E) is true.

8. **(D)** Option (D) is the best answer since it reflects the fact that they seem to be friends but do not agree on everything, such as plowing when it is so dry. There is no basis for options (A) and (B). Option (C) cannot be verified either. Option (E) does not seem likely; there is no hint that they don't get along at all.

9. **(D)** Option (D) seems the most likely reason. There is no evidence that Anna is concerned about her mother's health. Option (B) does not seem likely. Option (C) does not make sense; she is strong. Option (E) might be an answer but not the most likely reason for her action.

10. **(E)** It seems that Anna has a better grip on reality, so option (E) is the best choice. There is no way of knowing whether option (A) is correct. There is no mention of either one being judgmental, so option (B) cannot be correct. Options (C) and (D) are not evident either.

11. **(B)** Option (B) is the most reasonable answer. Option (A) doesn't seem likely, since the mother is in no condition to comfort her. Option (C) is incorrect; this is not hinted at. Options (D) and (E) are not reasonable.

12. **(D)** Option (D) is the best description of the mood. No one knows if Karl will make it back. The mood is suspenseful. Option (A) and (C) are clearly incorrect. Although Bertie is crying, the overall mood is not sorrowful, so option (B) is wrong. Option (E) does not fit with the story line.

13. **(D)** The poet seems quite angry about the situation as it is. Option (A) does not describe the mood of the poem, nor do options (B) and (C). And there is nothing carefree or fanciful about the poem, so option (E) is incorrect also.

14. **(B)** Option (B) best explains what the phrase means. Option (A) is not true. The poet does not say that the rooftops hurt the people who live under them, only that there is misery under them, so option (C) is incorrect. Options (D) and (E) do not explain the meaning of the phrase either.

15. **(C)** Option (C) is correct. This is what the author says about the rooftops. There is no mention of them in bad weather, nor does the poet say that they keep people from doing what they want, so options (A) and (B) are incorrect. The poet says that the homeless have no rooftops, so option (D) is wrong. There is no indication that option (E) is correct.

16.   **(D)** Option (D) is what the poem says the rooftops do. They certainly don't show how wonderful life is, nor do they give the homeless a place to rest as options (A) and (B) say; in fact, they do the opposite. The poem says nothing about what happens when it rains, nor does it say that the rooftops make people angry (they do make the poet angry), so options (C) and (E) are incorrect.

17.   **(A)** Option (A) seems to be what the author most likely hopes will happen. Options (B) and (C) are not mentioned or hinted at, nor are options (D) and (E) suggested as likely.

18.   **(D)** Option (D) is the correct answer; you can figure this out from the information in the memo. Option (A) is not plausible; they have studied having a day care center and are implementing it. They are taking the idea very seriously. Option (B) cannot be verified, so it cannot be the correct choice. Option (C) is contrary to what the memo says; they are instituting a day care facility, so they are committed to the idea. Option (E) is incorrect; it seems they have researched the concept thoroughly.

19.   **(D)** Option (D) is the best description of the style in which the memo is written. It is not technical or overly detailed, nor is it tentative; it is very direct. So options (A) and (B) are incorrect. The memo does not seem dry or clinical, and it certainly is not chatty, so options (C) and (E) are also incorrect.

20.   **(A)** Option (A) is a restatement of the phrase. Option (B) is incorrect because there is nothing said about how the employees are paid. Option (C) does not carry the same meaning; in fact, it is the opposite of the phrase. Options (D) and (E) do not restate the phrase correctly either.

21.   **(D)** Option (D) best describes the way in which the memo is organized. The information it contains follows a logical order. Options (A) and (B) are incorrect; the information is not listed in the order of importance nor is it in a sequential order. While there might be a cause-and-effect issue about the day care, it doesn't exist in the memo, so option (C) is incorrect. Option (E) is also incorrect.

22.   **(A)** Option A is correct. There is a feeling of expectancy throughout most of the excerpt. There is nothing to suggest that options (B) and (C) are correct. The excerpt is not humorous or satirical, so options (D) and (E) are wrong.

23.   **(D)** Cade feels confused after meeting with Kandeh; the meeting was not what he expected, so option (D) is correct. Cade does not express compassion toward Kandeh nor is he bitter, so options (A) and (B) are incorrect. There is no hint that option (C) is correct, nor is there a suggestion that option (E) is true.

24.   **(D)** The excerpt says that Cade left to see Kandeh in the morning and that it didn't take long to get to his place, so it stands to reason that the meeting took place during midmorning. Option (A) is unlikely since he left in the morning and it was only a short trip to Kandeh's place. Option (B) is not the correct answer since it would mean it was a rather long trip to Kandeh's home. Neither option (C) or (E) makes sense.

25.   **(D)** Option (D) would most likely happen. Cade realizes that Kandeh is not the same person he knew; they probably would not be in contact as much as before when Cade was excited about the rice harvester. It is unlikely that Cade would send another rice harvester (option A). While Cade and Kandeh might stay good friends, the ending of the excerpt did not foretell this happening. Option (C) is definitely not likely to happen. Option (E) does not seem likely, since Cade took the long trip to Africa to return to Joru.

26.   **(E)** Option (E) seems to be the best answer. Kandeh accepts what has happened to him in a realistic way. While hiding the money and running away might be considered cunning (option A), this is not the best description of Kandeh, who was forced to join the rebels. Option (B) and (C) certainly do not describe him. Option (D) does not seem to fit either. While he talks about what has happened, there is no sense that he was proud of what he did.

27.   **(E)** Option (E) makes the most sense. Cade expected Kandeh to be the same as when he saw him last. What Kandeh told him upset him. There is no sign that option (A) is true. Kandeh was very friendly to Cade, so option (B) is wrong. While Kandeh had fought with the rebels, option (C) is not why Cade got up awkwardly; he was not afraid of him. Option (D) is very unlikely.

28.   **(B)** Option (B) seems to be the most logical choice. Cade seems idealistic, so this activity would probably appeal the most. There doesn't seem to be any reason that he would want to learn to fly or take up painting,

so options (A) and (C) are incorrect. There is nothing in the excerpt to suggest that he would want to own a business or travel to tropical paradises, so options (D) and (E) are incorrect as well.

29. **(C)** Option (C) is correct. Jonathan's words supply this information. There is no evidence in the excerpt for options (A), (B), (D), and (E).

30. **(C)** The dialogue between Jonathan and Linda shows that Linda cares about Jonathan, so option (C) is correct. There is no support for option (A). She may worry that he will quit his job, but that is not indicated in the excerpt, so option (B) is wrong. Options (D) and (E) may be true, but there is nothing to indicate this.

31. **(D)** Option (D) is correct; the fact that Linda is "so accustomed to Jonathan's way of talking" shows they are completely open with each other. Option (A) might be true, but this is not the best characterization of their relationship. There is no evidence in the excerpt for options (B). Options (C) and (E) do not seem to be indicated.

32. **(C)** Option (C) is correct. His words indicate that he feels there is no solution to his situation. Options (A), (B), and (E) are incorrect because there is no mention of punishment, wrongdoing, or spending time in jail. Option (D) could be something Jonathan is feeling, but it is not indicated in words.

33. **(D)** Option (D) is correct. He may be resigned ("another eleven months and a week"), but he will continue. Options (A), (B), (C), and (E) have no support in the excerpt. There does not seem to be anyone else Jonathan would turn to, and he says himself that he cannot get out of his situation.

34. **(A)** Option (A) is correct. Jonathan certainly is dramatic, but at the same time he has no alternatives; he must return to work. He is not competitive, so option (B) is not correct. His attitude cannot be described as lighthearted or indifferent, so options (C) and (D) are incorrect. He may be saddened, but he doesn't care for his job, so option (E) is incorrect.

35. **(D)** The references to prison and insects dashed against the wall give a theatrical tone to the excerpt; Jonathan doesn't really believe that. Option (A) is incorrect; brother and sister are lying on the grass, so there

is nothing life-threatening about the excerpt. Option (B) is incorrect; there is no irony in his words. Option (C) cannot be correct because he is portraying the reality of his job. Although there may be tranquility in lying on the grass, his words do not convey that sense, so option (E) is incorrect.

36. **(B)** Option (B) best sums up the main idea of the review. Option (A) is definitely not what the reviewer says or suggests. Neither option (C) nor (D) is suggested by the review. There is no mention of having to see the movie again, so option (E) is wrong.

37. **(A)** Option (A) describes the tone of the review the best. The tone is definitely not worried or overwhelmed, so options (B) and (C) are wrong. The reviewer does not seem indifferent, and while there may be some lighthearted parts, the overall tone is not humorous. Thus, options (D) and (E) are incorrect as well.

38. **(D)** This is the meaning of the reviewer's statement. The statement does not mean that the movie was terrible or that such a thing happens every day, so options (A) and (B) are incorrect. The meaning has nothing to do with the movie being funny or the acting being poor, so both options (C) and (E) are incorrect as well.

39. **(E)** The reviewer says that the special effects were Oscar quality, so option (E) is correct. The reviewer did not say that there were too many special effects or that they were sentimental or amateurish, so options (A), (B), and (C) are incorrect. The reviewer did say the special effects were exciting, but not that they interfered with the plot, making option (D) wrong as well.

40. **(C)** Option (C) seems to be the best description of the way in which the review is written. It does not seem breezy or humorous, so option (A) is incorrect. There is no sense that the review is biased, so option (B) is wrong. Neither *methodical* nor *floral* would not be a good word to describe the review, so options (D) and (E) are wrong also.

MATH
PART 1 (calculators allowed)

1. If Bobby can run 8 miles in an hour, how many miles can he run in 15 minutes?

   (A) 1
   (B) 2
   (C) 4
   (D) 7
   (E) 120

2. If $5x + y = 27$, and $y = 2$, then $x =$

3. Four people went to a restaurant and each paid separately. Their individual bills were \$15, \$17, \$14, and \$19. What was the average bill, in dollars?

   (A) \$14.50
   (B) \$15.65
   (C) \$16.25
   (D) \$17.00
   (E) \$19.10

4. A group contains 4 men and 20 women. If 1 person is selected, what is the probability the person is a man?

   (A) ¼
   (B) ⅕
   (C) ⅙
   (D) ⅘
   (E) ⅚

5. A rectangular region has sides of 8 and 10. What is the perimeter of this region?

   (A) 2
   (B) 18
   (C) 26
   (D) 28
   (E) 36

6. A T-shirt costs n dollars to purchase, and a jacket costs m dollars to purchase. Before tax, which of the following represents the cost to purchase the T-shirt and the jacket?

   (A) nm
   (B) $\dfrac{n}{m}$
   (C) $n+m$
   (D) $\dfrac{m}{n}$
   (E) $n-m$

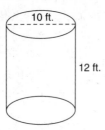

7. The diagram represents the dimensions of a cylindrical storage silo. If the silo already contains 100 cubic feet of grain, what is the maximum whole number of cubic feet of grain that can be added to the silo?

    (A) 20
    (B) 842
    (C) 1,100
    (D) 1,340
    (E) 3,668

8. A secretary can type 65 words per minute. If she spends 3 hours a day typing, how many words will she type in 5 days?

    (A) 58,500
    (B) 54,000
    (C) 31,200
    (D) 1,875
    (E) 975

9. What percent of 650 is 78?

    (A) 4%
    (B) 8.33%
    (C) 12%
    (D) 31%
    (E) 57.2%

10. The number of birds sighted by a bird-watcher is directly proportional to the amount of time he spends in the park. If the bird-watcher sights 30 birds when he spends 2 hours in the park, how many birds will he sight if he spends 5 hours in the park?

    (A) 60
    (B) 75

(C) 80
(D) 90
(E) 150

11. If ⅔x = 6, then x =

(A) 1
(B) 1½
(C) 4
(D) 5⅓
(E) 9

12. A box of pancake mix measures 11 inches tall, 5 inches long, and 3 inches wide. Shipments from the factory come in a single large box containing 20 boxes of pancake mix. In cubic inches, what is the smallest possible volume of the large box?

(A) 165
(B) 300
(C) 1,100
(D) 2,200
(E) 3,300

13. Jacob purchased a $13,000 car with a 5 percent down payment. In dollars, how much was his down payment?

(A) 2,600
(B) 1,300
(C) 1,050
(D) 800
(E) 650

14. Which of the following is a solution of $1 - 3x < 0$?

(A) 3
(B) 0
(C) –1
(D) –2
(E) –5

15. A portion of a kitchen floor measuring 60 inches long by 96 inches wide will be tiled. How many 6-inch-square tiles would be required to cover this portion of the floor?

    (A) 26
    (B) 52
    (C) 156
    (D) 160
    (E) 210

16. Two angles of a triangle have a sum of 150 degrees. What is the measure, in degrees, of the remaining angle?

    (A) 20
    (B) 30
    (C) 45
    (D) 60
    (E) 90

17. Sam invested $500 in a CD (certificate of deposit) that earned 1.5 percent interest per year. After two years, how much interest had Sam earned?

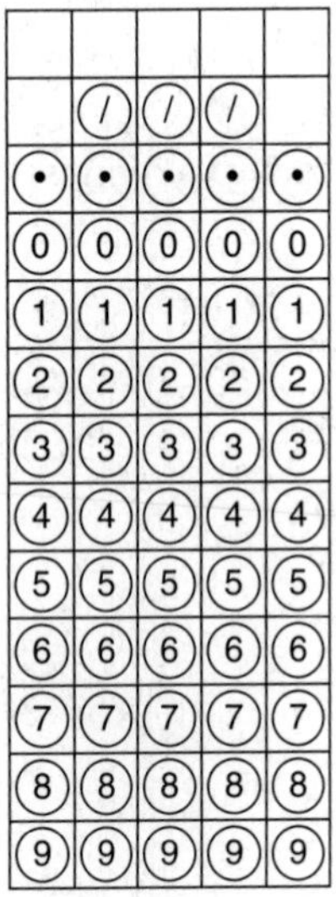

18. The monthly cost of a cell phone plan is $35 plus 3 cents for every minute after a total of 500 minutes has been used. In dollars, what will Geri's bill be if she uses 800 minutes in a single month?

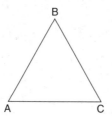

19. The triangle in the figure above is an equilateral triangle with a perimeter of 18. What is the length of side AB?

(A) 18
(B) 9
(C) 6
(D) 3
(E) 1

20. A jar contains red and blue marbles. The probability that a randomly selected marble is red is ¼. If 27 of the marbles are blue, how many marbles are in the jar?

(A) 6
(B) 9
(C) 24
(D) 31
(E) 36

21. At the beginning of the week, the balance of Cindy's bank account was $1,273. On Tuesday, she wrote a check for rent ($750) and a check for her electric bill ($60). On Wednesday, she wrote a check for groceries and other supplies ($81.96). Finally, on Friday, she used an ATM to take out $40 in cash. Assuming all of the checks went through on the same day they were written, what was her bank balance after these transactions?

22. Josh and Terry both collect coins. Together they have a total of 46 coins. If Josh has 12 more coins than Terry, how many coins does Josh have in his collection?

    (A) 15
    (B) 17
    (C) 29
    (D) 34
    (E) 40

23. Frank's company reimburses him 52 cents for every mile he drives while on company business. Last week, he drove a total of 400 miles, and half of these miles were on company business. How much will Frank be reimbursed?

    (A) $52
    (B) $104
    (C) $152
    (D) $208
    (E) $452

24. The average of four numbers is 8. If the sum of three of the numbers is 22, what is the value of the remaining number?

    (A) 8
    (B) 10
    (C) 12
    (D) 22
    (E) 32

25. Which of the following is the sum of $3x$, x, $2y$, and $-5y$?

    (A) x
    (B) $-30xy$
    (C) $4x - 3y$
    (D) $3x - 10y$

Part 2 (no calculators)

Questions 26–28 refer to the graph below.

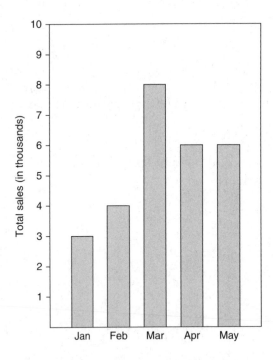

26. What were the total sales in January?

    (A) 3
    (B) 30
    (C) 3,000
    (D) 30,000
    (E) 3,000,000

27. What were the total sales in January through May?

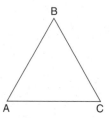

28. Between which two months was there the biggest change in total sales?

(A) January to February
(B) February to March
(C) March to April
(D) April to May
(E) this cannot be determined from the graph

29. Sides AB and AC in the triangle above have the same length. If the measure of angle B is 80 degrees, what is the measure of angle A, in degrees?

(A) 30
(B) 40
(C) 50
(D) 80
(E) 100

30. After getting a ride from a taxi, Harold decides to leave a 20 percent tip on a \$30 fare. In dollars, how much is his total cost for the taxi ride?

(A) 6
(B) 25
(C) 32
(D) 36
(E) 50

31. On the graph of $y = 3x - 5$, what is the x-coordinate of the point that has a y-coordinate of 22?

(A) 6
(B) 9
(C) 20
(D) 61
(E) 71

32. In a small office, secretaries earn \$14 an hour, while data entry specialists earn \$12 an hour. If there are a secretaries and b data entry specialists in the office, which of the following represents their total hourly pay, in dollars?

(A) $a + b$
(B) $14a + 12b$
(C) $12a + 14b$
(D) $26ab$
(E) $26(a + b)$

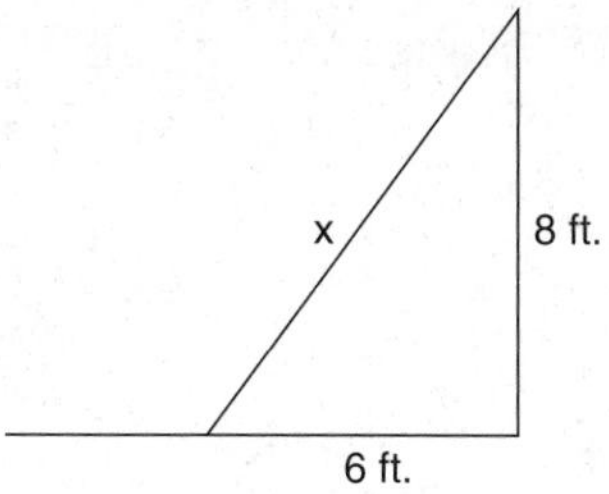

33. The diagram above shows a ladder of length x leaning against a wall. Which of the following expressions represents the value of x, in feet?

(A) $6^2 + 8^2$

(B) $\sqrt{6^2 + 8^2}$

(C) $6^2 - 8^2$

(D) $8^2 - 6^2$

(E) $\sqrt{8^2 - 6^2}$

34. What is the slope of the line that passes through the points $(2,2)$ and $(5,6)$?

(A) $-\frac{4}{3}$

(B) $-\frac{3}{4}$

(C) 1

(D) $\frac{3}{4}$

(E) $\frac{4}{3}$

35. Which of the following is equivalent to $3x^4 - 6x^2$?

(A) $3x^2$
(B) $3x^2(x^2)$
(C) $3x^2(5x^2)$
(D) $3x^2(x^2 - 6)$
(E) $3x^2(x^2 - 2)$

Age	Number of Students
18	2
19	4
20	1
Over 20	6

36. The table above shows the ages of students enrolled in a cooking class. What is the median age of the students?

37. Rectangle A has a length of ℓ and a width of w. Rectangle B has a length of ℓ and a width of $2w$. Which of the following statements is true?

(A) The area of rectangle A is twice the area of rectangle B.
(B) The perimeter of rectangle A is 2 less than the perimeter of rectangle B.

(C) The area of rectangle A is half the area of rectangle B.

(D) The perimeter of rectangle A is 4 less than the perimeter of rectangle B.

(E) The area of rectangle A is a fourth of the area of rectangle B.

38. On a bookshelf, there are x science books, y math books, and z history books. Which of the following expressions represents the percentage of history books on the shelf?

(A) $\dfrac{z}{100(x+y+z)}\%$

(B) $\dfrac{100z}{x+y}\%$

(C) $\dfrac{100z}{x+y+z}\%$

(D) $\dfrac{z}{100}\%$

(E) $100z\%$

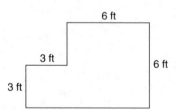

39. A vegetable garden is to be built by following the diagram above. How many feet of fencing will be needed to completely enclose the perimeter of the garden?

(A) 6

(B) 18

(C) 27

(D) 30

(E) 36

40. The square root of 38 is between which of the following pairs of numbers?

(A) 5 and 10
(B) 10 and 15
(C) 15 and 20
(D) 20 and 25
(E) 25 and 30

41. A 16-ounce box of cereal costs $3.75. Which of the following expressions represents the cost of a single ounce of this cereal, in dollars?

(A) 3.75(16)

(B) 16−3.75

(C) $\dfrac{3.75}{16}$

(D) 16+3.75

(E) $\dfrac{16}{3.75}$

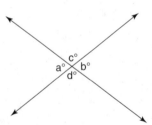

42. In the figure above $a = 80$. What is the value of $c + d$?

(A) 80
(B) 100
(C) 160
(D) 200
(E) 280

43. Which of the following is equivalent to $\dfrac{5}{1,000}$?

(A) 0.5
(B) 0.05
(C) 0.005

(D) 0.0005

(E) 0.00005

44. If $x = 3$ and $y = -2$, what is the value of $x^2 - y^2$?

(A) 2

(B) 4

(C) 5

(D) 10

(E) 13

Questions 45 and 46 use the graph below.

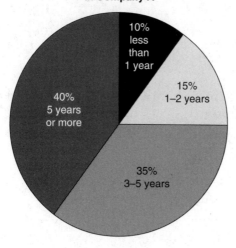

Years of Experience for Employees at Company A

45. Which of the following represents the fraction of employees with 3 or more years of experience?

(A) $\frac{1}{10}$

(B) $\frac{1}{4}$

(C) $\frac{2}{5}$

(D) $\frac{3}{4}$

(E) $\frac{9}{10}$

46. If there are 500 employees at the company, how many have 5 or more years of experience?

47. A custom piece of fabric can be made from a choice of 4 different colors, 3 different patterns, and 8 different types of stitching. How many combinations of colors, patterns, and stitching are possible?

(A) 15
(B) 20
(C) 56
(D) 72
(E) 96

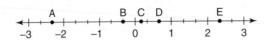

48. On the number line above, which of the following points represents ⅔?

(A) A
(B) B
(C) C
(D) D
(E) E

49. The area of the rectangle above is 24. What is the length?

(A) 2
(B) 4
(C) 6
(D) 12
(E) 20

50. Use the grid to plot the point on the graph of $y = x^2 + 1$ where $x = -1$.

ANSWERS: MATH

1. **(B)** $\dfrac{8 \text{ miles}}{1 \text{ hour}} = \dfrac{8 \text{ miles}}{60 \text{ minutes}} = \dfrac{\frac{1}{4}(8) \text{ miles}}{\frac{1}{4}(60) \text{ minutes}} = \dfrac{2 \text{ miles}}{15 \text{ minutes}}.$

2. $x = 5$ Plug the value of y into the equation and solve for x:

   $5x + y = 27$

   $5x + 5 = 27$

   $5x = 25$

   $x = 5$

3. **(C)** In general, to find the average, you find the sum of all the values and then divide by the number of values. In this case, there are four values so the average is $\dfrac{15 + 17 + 14 + 19}{4} = 16.25.$

4. **(C)** The probability that the person selected is a man can be found by dividing the total number of men by the total number of people in the group: $\frac{4}{24} = \frac{1}{6}.$

5. **(E)** The perimeter is the sum of the lengths of all the sides. The rectangle has two sides with lengths of 8 and two sides with lengths of 10. Therefore, the perimeter is $8 + 8 + 10 + 10 = 36.$

6. **(C)** The total cost would be the sum of the individual prices. In other words, the total cost is $n + m.$

7. **(B)** Essentially, this question is asking you to find the volume that remains if 100 cubic feet is already used. Before you can calculate this, you must find the total volume of the silo. Using the formula for the volume of a cylinder, the total available volume is $12 \times 3.14 \times 5^2 = 942.$ Since 100 cubic feet is already being used, 842 cubic feet of space is still available.

8. **(A)** In a single day, the secretary types for $3 \times 60 = 180$ minutes, and since she types 65 words a minute, she will type $65 \times 180 = 11{,}700$ words a day. Finally, she will type $5 \times 11{,}700 = 58{,}500$ words in 5 days.

9. **(C)** $\left(\dfrac{78}{650} \times 100\right)\% = 12\%$.

10. **(B)** If y is directly proportional to x, $y = kx$ for some number k. If you let the number of birds sighted be represented by n and the amount of time spent in the park be represented by t, you get the formula $n = kt$. Plugging in the initial information yields the equation $30 = 2k$, and solving this yields $k = 15$. Therefore, the formula is $n = 15t$. Finally, plugging in 5 for t yields $n = 15 \times 5 = 75$.

11. **(E)** Multiply both sides by $\frac{3}{2}$: $x = \frac{3}{2}(6) = 9$.

12. **(E)** The large box must be large enough to accommodate all 20 of the smaller boxes, which each have a volume of $11 \times 5 \times 3 = 165$ cubic inches. Thus, it must have a volume of at least $20 \times 165 = 3{,}300$ cubic inches.

13. **(E)** $\frac{5}{100} \times 13{,}000 = 650$.

14. **(A)** The key here is to solve for x while remembering that the direction of the inequality will switch when you divide or multiply by a negative number. The inequality $1 - 3x < 0$ is the same as $x > \frac{1}{3}$ and only option (1) is larger than $\frac{1}{3}$.

15. **(D)** The total area to be tiled is $60 \times 96 = 5{,}760$ square inches, and the tiles are $6 \times 6 = 36$ square inches each. Therefore, it will require $\frac{5{,}760}{36} = 160$ tiles to cover this portion of the floor.

16. **(B)** The sum of the measure of all the angles in a triangle is 180 degrees. Since you are given two angles, the remaining angle has a measure of $180 - 150 = 30$ degrees.

17. **$15** $500 \times \dfrac{1.5}{100} \times 2 = 15$.

18. **$44** Geri will be charged \$35 plus 3 cents for every minute over 500. In this case, she used 300 minutes over 500, so her bill will be $35 + 0.03 \times 300 = 44$.

19. **(C)** All three sides of an equilateral triangle have the same length, and the perimeter is the sum of these lengths. If the perimeter is 18, then the length of any side is 18 ÷ 3 = 6.

20. **(E)** Let x represent the number of red marbles. Since the probability that a marble is red is ¼, it must be that $\dfrac{x}{x+27} = $ ¼. When this is solved, you find that $x = 9$, and the total number of marbles is 27 + 9 = 36.

21. **$341.04** 1,273 − 750 − 60 − 81.96 − 40 = 341.04.

22. **(C)** Let x represent the number of coins in Josh's collection and y represent the number of coins in Terry's collection. Since there is a total of 46 coins, $x + y = 46$. Also, since Josh has 12 more coins than Terry, $x = y + 12$. Substituting this value for x in the original equation, $y + 12 + y = 46$, and $y = 17$. Since Josh has 12 more, the final answer is 12 + 17 = 29.

23. **(B)** Half of the 400 miles were on company business, so he will be reimbursed 200 × 0.52 = 104.

24. **(B)** Let x represent the unknown number. Since you know the average is 8, you know the sum of the numbers divided by 4 is 8. But you already know the sum of the first three numbers is 22. This gives you the equation $\dfrac{22+x}{4} = 8$, which has a solution of $x = 10$.

25. **(D)** $3x + x + 2y + (-5y) = (3+1)x + (2-5)y = 4x - 3y$.

26. **(C)** Total sales are in thousands, so multiply 3 by 1,000 to get 3,000.

27. **27,000** 3,000 + 4,000 + 8,000 + 6,000 + 6,000 = 27,000.

28. **(B)** The biggest height difference between bars on the graph is between the second and third bars.

29. **(C)** Since sides AB and AC have the same length, angles A and C have the same measure. In total, there are 180 degrees in the triangle, and 80 are accounted for with angle 2. Therefore, angle A will have a measure of $\dfrac{180-80}{2} = 50$ degrees.

30. **(D)** The tip was $^{20}\!/_{100} \times 30 = 6$ giving a total fare of $30 + 6 = \$36$.

31. **(B)** The x-coordinate can be found by replacing the value of y in the equation given to get $22 = 3x - 5$ and solving for y. The solution to this equation is $x = 9$.

32. **(B)** Each of the secretaries earns \$14 an hour, and the total paid to the secretaries is $14a$. Each of the data entry specialists earns \$12, and the total paid to them is $12b$. Finally, the overall total paid to both is $14a + 12b$.

33. **(B)** By the Pythgorean theorem, $x^2 = 6^2 + 8^2$ and $x = \sqrt{6^2 + 8^2}$.

34. **(E)** $m = \dfrac{6-2}{5-2} = \dfrac{4}{3}$.

35. **(E)** Factor out $3x^2$ from both terms.

36. **20** There is a total of 13 data values, and the median is the middle, or seventh value.

37. **(C)** The area of rectangle A is $\ell \times w$, while the area of rectangle B is $\ell \times 2w = 2\ell w$. Therefore, rectangle B has twice the area of A, or A has half the area of B.

38. **(C)** In general, you can think of finding a percentage as dividing the part you are interested in by the whole and then multiplying by 100. In this case, the part is the number of history books, z, and the whole is the total number of books, $z + x + y$.

39. **(D)** The perimeter is the sum of the lengths of all the sides. In this case, it is $3 + 3 + 3 + 6 + 6 + 9 = 30$.

40. **(A)** The square root of 36 is 6, and the square root of 49 is 7. Since 38 is between 36 and 49, the square root of 38 must be between 6 and 7.

41. **(C)** To find the unit price, divide the total price by the number of units (in this case, ounces).

42. **(D)** Since these lines meet at a single point, the sum $a + b + c + d = 360$. As opposite angles, $a = b = 80$ and $c + d = 360 - 2(80) = 200$.

43. **(C)** There are three zeros in 1,000, so starting with 5, move the decimal to the left three digits.

44. **(C)** $3^2 - (-2)^2 = 9 - 4 = 5$.

45. **(D)** Using the chart, $35\% + 40\% = 75\%$ of employees who have 3 or more years of experience. As a fraction, $75\% = {}^{75}/_{100} = {}^{3}/_{4}$.

46. **200** ${}^{40}/_{100} \times 500 = 200$.

47. **(E)** There are $4 \times 3 \times 8 = 96$ possible combinations.

48. **(D)** There are two tick marks between each whole number, each representing a third. Since D is on the second tick mark from zero, D represents the point ${}^{2}/_{3}$.

49. **(C)** The area of 24 is found by multiplying the length and the width of the rectangle. The width is the distance between –2 and 2, which is 4. The length will then be $24 \div 4 = 6$.

50. When $x = -1$, $y = 2$ and the plotted point will be $(-1, 2)$.

chapter 35

GED Practice Test 2

LANGUAGE ARTS, WRITING, PART I

Choose the best answer to each question.

Questions 1–8 refer to the following letter.

Shining Star Insurance Company
318 North 26th Street
Wilson, OK 61007

Dear Ms. Cruz:

(A)

(1) Thank you for choosing Shining Star to insure your home and it's possessions. (2) We are pleased to be of service to you and want to introduce you to the information you will need about our company. (3) We pride ourselves on our customer service who we believe is the most user-friendly in the industry. (4) Our customer service experts will help you settle any claim that you need to make speedily, with the least amount of inconvenience.

(B)

(5) We are enclosing a booklet that Shining Star sends to every new customer. (6) It is being packed with information on how to protect your home from theft and burglary. (7) There are blank pages at the back where you can make a record of your valuables. (8) The booklet also contain important facts about making sure your home does not have any situations which could increase the possibility of a fire. (9) It's a good idea to keep the booklet in a safe place.

(C)

(10) In addition to providing fast, worry-free claim service, Shining Star can also help you choose a contractor to perform any repairs needed after damage occurs in your home, or finding a person to oversee the repairs. (11) Just go to our website at www .shiningstarinsco.net, enter your zip code. (12) A list of qualified, approved contractors will appear.

(D)

(13) Our claims specialists are available seven days a week, from 7 A.M. to 9 P.M., central time. (14) If you have any questions, please don't hesitate to call us. (15) Every member of the team at Shining Star Insurance Company looks forward to serving your insurance needs for many years; we wanted to thank you again for choosing us.

Sincerely,
Shining Star Insurance Company

1. Sentence 1: **Thank you for choosing Shining Star to insure your home and it's possessions.**

   Which correction should be made to sentence 1?

   (A) change <u>you</u> to <u>your</u>
   (B) change <u>choosing</u> to <u>having chose</u>
   (C) insert a comma after <u>Star</u>
   (D) change <u>it's</u> to <u>its</u>
   (E) no correction is necessary

2. Sentence 3: **We pride ourselves on <u>our customer service who we believe is</u> the most user-friendly in the industry.**

   Which is the best way to write the underlined portion of this sentence? If the original is the best way, choose option (A).

   (A) our customer service who we believe is
   (B) our customer service, which we believe is
   (C) our customer service. Who we believe is
   (D) our customer service, who we are believing
   (E) our customer service that being

3. Sentence 6: **It is being packed with information on how to protect your home from theft and burglary.**

   Which correction should be made to sentence 6?

   (A) change <u>is being packed</u> to <u>is packed</u>
   (B) change <u>your</u> to <u>their</u>
   (C) insert a comma after <u>information</u>
   (D) change <u>to protect</u> to <u>protecting</u>
   (E) no correction is necessary

4. Sentence 8: **The booklet also contain important facts about making sure your home does not have any situations which could increase the possibility of a fire.**

   Which correction should be made to sentence 8?

   (A) insert a comma after <u>sure</u>
   (B) change <u>could increase</u> to <u>could increased</u>
   (C) change <u>contain</u> to <u>contains</u>
   (D) change <u>does not have</u> to <u>does not having</u>
   (E) no correction is necessary

5. Sentence 10: **In addition to providing fast, worry-free claim service, Shining Star can also help you choose a contractor to perform any repairs needed after damage occurs in your home, or finding a person to oversee the repairs.**

   Which correction should be made to sentence 10?

   (A) remove the comma after <u>service</u>
   (B) change <u>to perform</u> to <u>performing</u>
   (C) insert a comma after <u>occurs</u>
   (D) change <u>finding</u> to <u>find</u>
   (E) no correction is necessary

6. Sentences 11 and 12: **Just go to our website at www.shiningstarco.net, enter your zip code. A list of qualified, approved contractors will appear.**

   The most effective combination of sentences 11 and 12 would include which group of words?

   (A) code, however a list
   (B) code, yet a list
   (C) code and a list
   (D) code, and a list
   (E) code, but a list

7. Sentence 13: **Our claims specialists are available <u>seven days a week, from 7 A.M. to 9 P.M., central time</u>.**

   Which is the best way to write the underlined portion of this sentence? If the original is the best way, choose option (A).

   (A) seven days a week, from 7 A.M. to 9 P.M., central time
   (B) seven-days a week, from 7 A.M. to 9 P.M., central time

(C) seven days a week from 7 A.M. to 9 P.M. central time

(D) seven days, a week, from 7 A.M. to 9 P.M., Central Time

(E) seven days a week, from 7 A.M. to 9 P.M., Central Time

8. Sentence 15: **Every member of the team at Shining Star Insurance Company looks forward to serving your insurance <u>needs for many years; we wanted to thank you</u> again for choosing us.**

Which is the best way to write the underlined portion of this sentence? If the original is the best way, choose option (A).

(A) needs for many years; we wanted to thank you

(B) needs for many years, we want to thank you

(C) needs for many years we want to thank you

(D) needs for many years, we will want to thank you

(E) needs, for many years; we want to thank you

Questions 9–16 refer to the following article.

Gray Whales

(A)

(1) The gray whale is one of nature's most majestic creatures. (2) Its size is notable, a gray whale can reach as long as 45 feet in length and weigh more than 30 tons. (3) From April to November the gray whale lives in the Arctic waters of the Bering and Beaufort Seas. (4) The whale then travels to the warm waters off the coast of Baja California, Mexico, where they mate. (5) Their migration habits are unique as well.

(B)

(6) The females birth and nurse their young in Baja. (7) The baby whales, which are called calves, grew very quickly. (8) The whales return to the North, after the young have become strong, in late winter. (9) The round trip is more than 10,000 miles, making it the longest migration of any mammal on Earth.

(C)

(10) The whales swim in groups called pods, each pod can contain as many as 16 whales. (11) While migrating, the whales swimming

24 hours a day. (12) Gray whales can swim underwater for up to an hour. (13) Because they are mammals they must eventually come to the surface for air.

(D)

(14) When the whales surface, they exhale a powerful stream of air, vapor, and water called a blow. (15) The blow can reach as high as 15 feet. (16) The gray whale is truly an awesome animal, and whale watchers enjoy every opportunity to see them.

9.   Which revision should be made to paragraph A?

   (A)   move sentence 1 to the end of the paragraph
   (B)   remove sentence 2
   (C)   move sentence 5 after sentence 2
   (D)   move sentence 3 to the beginning of the paragraph
   (E)   no revision is necessary

10.   Sentence 2: **Its size is notable, a gray whale can reach as long as 45 feet in length and weigh more than 30 tons.**

   Which correction should be made to sentence 2?

   (A)   insert <u>and</u> after the comma
   (B)   remove the comma after <u>notable</u>
   (C)   insert <u>however</u> after the comma
   (D)   replace the comma with <u>because</u>
   (E)   no correction is necessary

11.   Sentence 6: **The <u>females birth</u> and nurse their young in Baja.**

   Which is the best way to write the underlined portion of sentence 6? If the original is the best way, choose option (A).

   (A)   females birth
   (B)   females give birth
   (C)   female birth
   (D)   females birthed
   (E)   females gave birth

12. Sentence 7: **The baby whales, which are called calves, grew very quickly.**

    Which correction should be made to sentence 7?

    (A) change <u>calves</u> to <u>calfs</u>
    (B) remove the comma after <u>whales</u>
    (C) change <u>grew</u> to <u>grow</u>
    (D) change <u>called</u> to <u>calling</u>
    (E) no correction is necessary

13. Sentence 8: **The whales return to the North, after the young have become strong, in late winter.**

    Which correction should be made to sentence 8?

    (A) remove the comma after <u>strong</u>
    (B) change <u>return</u> to <u>returning</u>
    (C) move <u>in late winter</u> after <u>North</u>
    (D) change <u>North</u> to <u>north</u>
    (E) no correction is necessary

14. Sentence 10: **The whales swim in groups called pods, each pod can contain as many as 16 whales.**

    Which correction should be made to sentence 10?

    (A) remove the comma after <u>pod</u>
    (B) change <u>each</u> to <u>every</u>
    (C) change <u>pods</u> to <u>pod</u>
    (D) insert <u>and</u> after the comma
    (E) no correction is necessary

15. Sentence 11: **While migrating, the whales <u>swimming</u> 24 hours a day.**

    Which is the best way to write the underlined part of the sentence? If no correction is necessary, choose option (A).

    (A) swimming
    (B) swims
    (C) having swam
    (D) have swum
    (E) swim

16. Which sentence would be most effective if inserted at the beginning of paragraph (D)?

   (A) The baby whales are very affectionate, and many times will allow humans to come up very close to them.
   (B) Every year, whale watchers up and down the California coast thrill to observe the gray whales on their long journey.
   (C) Baleen whales don't have teeth, they have plates that filter tiny fish and shrimp when water passes over them.
   (D) In addition to whales, dolphins and porpoises also belong to the order of cetaceans.
   (E) Whales inhabit all the oceans of the Earth and can be found in many different sizes.

Questions 17–25 refer to the following article.

How to Dress for a Job Interview

(A)

(1) Dressing correctly for a job interview is very important. (2) The first thing an interviewer will noticing is what you're wearing. (3) If the interviewer does not like how you are dressed. (4) Then you will already have a strike against you. (5) Is an old saying, "Dress for success," and it's very true when dressing for a job interview.

(B)

(6) Both men and women should dress conservatively. (7) Wear a solid-colored dark blue or gray suit, with a white shirt or blouse, or a shirt/blouse coordinated with the suit. (8) Make sure your shoes is polished. (9) Men should wear dark socks, and women should have a neutral or light colored panty hose. (10) Make sure you have a full tank of gasoline and a car that is working.

(C)

(11) Avoid using to much aftershave, cologne, or perfume. (12) Men shouldn't wear any jewelry, and women should go easy with the jewelry. (13) Men should select a conservative tie, and women should have chosen a skirt that is not too short. (14) Any tattoos should be

covered. (15) Finally, bringing a briefcase or portfolio will give you a professional touch. (16) Check yourself in a mirror one last time before you goes in.

17. Sentence 2: **The first thing an interviewer will noticing is what you're wearing.**

    Which correction should be made to sentence 2?

    (A) insert a comma after <u>interviewer</u>
    (B) change <u>will noticing</u> to <u>will notice</u>
    (C) change <u>you're</u> to <u>your</u>
    (D) change <u>wearing</u> to <u>worn</u>
    (E) no correction is necessary

18. Sentences 3 and 4: **If the interviewer does not like how you are dressed. Then you will already have a strike against you.**

    Which is the most effective combination of sentences 3 and 4?

    (A) Then, you will already have a strike against you, if the interviewer does not like how you are dressed.
    (B) You will already have a strike against you, then; if the interviewer does not like how you are dressed.
    (C) If the interviewer does not like how you are dressed, then you will already have a strike against you.
    (D) You will already have a strike against you, if the interviewer does not like how you are dressed then.
    (E) If the interviewer does not like how you are dressed, then you will already be having a strike against you.

19. Sentence 5: **Is an old saying, "Dress for success," and it's very true when dressing for a job interview.**

    What correction should be made to sentence 5?

    (A) remove the comma after <u>saying</u>
    (B) change <u>Dress</u> to dress
    (C) change <u>it's</u> to <u>its</u>
    (D) insert <u>There</u> before <u>Is</u>
    (E) no correction is necessary

20. Sentence 7: **Wear a solid-colored dark blue or gray suit with a white shirt or blouse, or a shirt/blouse coordinated with the suit.**

    Which correction should be made to sentence 7?

    (A) change <u>solid</u> to <u>Solid</u>
    (B) insert a comma after <u>colored</u>
    (C) change <u>wear</u> to <u>wearing</u>
    (D) change <u>coordinated</u> with <u>coordinate</u>
    (E) no correction is necessary

21. Sentence 8: **Make sure your shoes is polished.**

    Which correction should be made to sentence 8?

    (A) change <u>polished</u> to <u>polish</u>
    (B) change <u>make</u> to <u>making</u>
    (C) change <u>is</u> to <u>are</u>
    (D) insert a comma after <u>sure</u>
    (E) no correction is necessary

22. Which revision would improve the effectiveness of paragraph (B)?

    (A) remove sentence 6
    (B) move sentence 7 to the beginning of the paragraph
    (C) move sentence 8 to the end of the paragraph
    (D) move sentence 9 after sentence 6
    (E) remove sentence 10

23. Sentence 11: **Avoid using to much aftershave, cologne, or perfume.**

    Which correction should be made to sentence 11?

    (A) change <u>using</u> to <u>used</u>
    (B) change <u>to</u> to <u>too</u>
    (C) remove the comma after <u>aftershave</u>
    (D) change <u>perfume</u> to <u>perfumes</u>
    (E) no correction is necessary

24. Sentence 13: **Men should select a conservative tie, and women <u>should have chosen</u> a skirt that is not too short.**

Which is the best way to write the underlined portion of this sentence? If the original is the best way, choose option (A).

(A) should have chosen
(B) should be choosing
(C) choose
(D) should have chose
(E) should choose

25. Sentence 16: **Check yourself in a mirror one last time <u>before you goes in.</u>**

Which is the best way to write the underlined portion of the sentence? If the original is the best way, choose option (A).

(A) before you goes in
(B) before you go in
(C) before you going in
(D) before you did go in
(E) before go in

Questions 26–33 refer to the following article.

Riding Toy Recalled

(A)

(1) The Consumer Safety Bureau (CSB) announced today that it is recalling a children's riding toy called "Scurry n Go." (2) "Scurry n Go" was intended for children at least two years of age. (3) The manufacturer, kid fun, of Brooklyn, NY, said that it was taking back about 120,000 units that were sold. (4) The company said that consumers will receive the full purchase price. (5) Another 30,000 toys will be returned by department stores toy stores discount outlets and mail order firms.

(B)

(6) The CSB has found that children riding the toy can tip forward. (7) Children fall to the ground. (8) The danger of falling has been confirmed by reports of 20 incidents nationwide over the past four months. (9) There will be reports of four children receiving cuts on the chin severe enough to need stitches.

(C)

(10) Parents who need more information are encouraged to call the CSB at its recall hotline toll free number: 888-123-4567, or go to the website at www.csb.net. (11) "Scurry n Go" is made of yellow molded plastic with black wheels. (12) The riding toy is 20 inches long, 10 inches wide and 12 inches in height. (13) The toy's model number is 0318QS. (14) The model number can be found on the underside of the toy. (15) It is printed in black on a white Universal Product Code (UPC) sticker. (16) An aid for the CSB said the recall is proceeding smoothly.

26. Sentence 2: **"Scurry n Go" <u>was intending</u> for children at least two years of age.**

Which is the best way to write the underlined portion of the sentence? If the original is the best way, choose option (A).

(A) was intending
(B) was intend
(C) were intending
(D) was intended
(E) were intended

27. Sentence 3: **The manufacturer, kid fun, of Brooklyn, NY, said that it was taking back about 120,000 units that were sold.**

Which correction should be made to sentence 3?

(A) remove the comma after <u>NY</u>
(B) change <u>was taking</u> to <u>has been taken</u>
(C) change <u>kid fun</u> to <u>Kid Fun</u>
(D) replace <u>it</u> with <u>they</u>
(E) no correction is necessary

28. Sentence 5: **Another 30,000 toys will be returned by** <u>department stores</u> <u>toy stores discount outlets and mail order firms.</u>

    Which is the best way to write the underlined portion of this sentence? If the original is the best way, choose option (A).

    (A) department stores toy stores discount outlets and mail order firms.
    (B) department stores, toy stores discount outlets, and mail order firms.
    (C) department stores toy stores discount outlets, and mail order firms.
    (D) department stores, toy stores, discount outlets, and mail order firms.
    (E) department stores, toy stores, discount outlets, mail order firms.

29. Sentences 5 and 6: **The CSB has found that children riding the toy can tip forward. Children fall to the ground.**

    The most effective combination of sentences 6 and 7 would include which group of words?

    (A) forward, and, as a result, they can fall
    (B) forward, and, however, they can fall
    (C) forward, and one falls
    (D) forward, unless they fall
    (E) forward, and as a result they have fallen

30. Sentence 9: **There** <u>will be reports</u> **of four children receiving cuts on the chin severe enough to need stitches.**

    Which is the best way to write the underlined portion of the text? If the original is the best, choose option (A).

    (A) will be reports
    (B) was being reports
    (C) will have been reports
    (D) is reports
    (E) have been reports

31. Sentences 13 and 14: **The toy's model number is 0318QS. The model number can be found on the underside of the toy.**

    The most effective combination of sentences 13 and 14 would include which group of words?

    (A) and they can
    (B) and them can

(C)   and one there can
(D)   and then their can
(E)   and it can

32.   Sentence 16: **An aid for the CSB said the recall is actually proceeding smoothly.**

Which correction should be made to sentence 16?

(A)   change is to are
(B)   replace aid with aide
(C)   replace for with below
(D)   move actually to the end of the sentence
(E)   no change is necessary

33.   Which revision would improve the effectiveness of paragraph (C)?

(A)   move sentence 10 to the end of the paragraph
(B)   remove sentence 13
(C)   move sentence 15 to come after sentence 12
(D)   move sentence 11 to the end of the paragraph
(E)   remove sentence 16

Questions 34–42 refer to the following interoffice memo.

Date: 05/17/2012
To: All Employees
From: Paul Carson, CEO
Subject: ID Badges

(A)

(1) Security has notified me that there has been a large increase in the number of ID badges that have been reported lost or missing. (2) There have also been reports of employees loaning their badges to other employees when they go out to lunch. (3) While some may think these acts is minor, I cannot say how important it is to make sure that our customers' data are secure at all times.

(B)

(4) Beginning next Monday, the company will put in place a new security policy. (5) This policy will ensure the confidentiality of our

clients and is called Security Enforcement 5. (6) The policy is also known as "Be On Guard." (7) Any employee who reports a lost or misplaced ID badge will be issued a warning. (8) A second violation has resulted in the employee having the cost of the ID badge taken out of his or her paycheck. (9) A third violation will mean that the person will lose her or his rite to a pay raise for one year.

(C)

(10) This new policy will be strictly followed. (11) Any questions or comments can be directed to Mrs. May Head of Human Resources. (12) I thank all of you for your hard work and understanding but I know you understand the importance of this safeguard.

(D)

(13) Swiping your ID when you enter, and leave the building allows security to know who is and who isn't in the building at all times. (14) Without that information, it is impossible to know whether strangers are accessing our database with illegal goals. (15) Our first and foremost mission is to protect the information in our files from those who would use them for deceitful purposes.

34. Sentence 3: **While some may think these acts <u>is</u> minor, I cannot say how important it is to make sure that our customers' data are secure at all times.**

Which is the best way to write the underlined portion of this sentence? If the original is the best way, choose option (A).

(A) is
(B) are
(C) has been
(D) were
(E) being

35. Sentence 4: **Beginning next Monday, the company will put in place a new security policy.**

The most effective revision of sentence 4 would begin with which words?

(A) As a consequence, beginning
(B) For instance, beginning

(C) Even though, next

(D) However, next

(E) As a probability, beginning

36. Sentences 5 and 6: **This policy will ensure the confidentiality of our clients and is called Security Enforcement 5. The policy is also known as "Be on Guard."**

The most effective combination of sentences 5 and 6 would include which group of words?

(A) Security Enforcement 5, "Be on Guard"

(B) that is also called

(C) a confidential policy

(D) ("Be on Guard")

(E) policy, has ensured

37. Sentence 8: **A second violation <u>has resulted</u> in the employee having the cost of the ID badge taken out of his or her paycheck.**

Which is the best way to write the underlined portion of the sentence? If the original is the best way, choose option (A).

(A) has resulted

(B) resulted

(C) results

(D) will result

(E) been resulted

38. Sentence 9: **A third violation will mean that the person will lose her or his rite to a pay raise for one year.**

Which correction should be made to sentence 9?

(A) change <u>violation</u> to <u>Violation</u>

(B) change <u>mean</u> to <u>means</u>

(C) replace <u>that</u> with <u>which</u>

(D) change <u>rite</u> to <u>right</u>

(E) no correction is necessary

39. Sentence 11: **Any questions or comments can be directed to <u>Mrs. May Head of Human Resources.</u>**

    Which is the best way to write the underlined portion of the sentence? If the original is the best way, choose option (A).

    (A) Mrs. May Head of Human Resources
    (B) Mrs May, Head of Human Resources
    (C) Mrs. May, Head of Human Resources
    (D) Mrs. May head of human resources
    (E) Mrs. May; Head of Human Resources

40. Sentence 13: **Swiping your ID when you <u>enter, and leave</u> the building allows security to know who is and who isn't in the building at all times.**

    Which is the best way to write the underlined portion of the sentence? If the original is the best way, choose option (A).

    (A) enter, and leave
    (B) enter and leave
    (C) enter and can leave
    (D) enter, but leave
    (E) enter; and leave

41. Sentence 15: **Our first and foremost mission is to protect the information in our files from those who would use them for deceitful purposes.**

    Which correction should be made to sentence 15?

    (A) change <u>mission</u> to <u>missions</u>
    (B) change <u>our</u> to <u>your</u>
    (C) replace <u>them</u> with <u>it</u>
    (D) remove <u>to</u>
    (E) no correction is necessary

42. Which revision would improve the effectiveness of the memo?

    (A) join paragraphs A and B
    (B) join paragraphs B and C
    (C) move paragraph D after paragraph A
    (D) begin a new paragraph at sentence 7
    (E) no revision is necessary

Questions 43–50 refer to the following passage.

Quaker Cola Co. Annual Report

(A)

(1) Quaker Cola Company announced its annual report for 2011 on Friday. (2) Its annual sales increased 11 percent over 2011. (3) After taxes, its profits rose 14 percent, which is in large part the result of cost-cutting measures put in place by ceo Arthur Fletcher. (4) The company also announced plans to create an employee profit sharing plan. (5) Details will be on the company website within three months.

(B)

(6) You can hear about packaging and new fruit drinks. (7) New packaging for the cola products has been put in place. (8) The new design conveys a feeling of youthfulness and making our product more attractive to young people. (9) Quaker also introduced a new line of cranberry fruit juice drinks. (10) That represented 3 percent of sales for the year. (11) A new energy drink, with promising results, was test-marketed in California. (12) This year the test marketing will be done, and in eight additional western states.

(C)

(13) After several years of planning and research, Quaker launched your marketing plan in 2011 to establish a presence in the booming Southeast Asian market. (14) Forecasts predict that by 2015 the Asian market will grow. (15) To 15 percent of total revenue. (16) The company had planned to open a regional office in Ho Chi Minh City, Vietnam, in early 2013.

43. Sentence 3: **After taxes, its profits rose 14 percent, which is in large part the result of cost-cutting measures put in place by ceo Arthur Fletcher.**

Which correction should be made to sentence 3?

(A) remove the comma after <u>taxes</u>
(B) change <u>rose</u> to <u>rise</u>
(C) change <u>large</u> to <u>larger</u>
(D) change <u>ceo</u> to <u>CEO</u>
(E) no correction is necessary

44. Sentence 6: **You can hear about packaging and new fruit drinks.**

Which revision would improve the effectiveness of sentence 6?

(A) Quaker has done a great deal to expand its marketing.
(B) Packaging and new fruit drinks were added.
(C) Packaging was something that was changed.
(D) The new kind of drinks proved very successful.
(E) There are many ways the company can improve its image.

45. Sentence 8: **The new design conveys a feeling of youthfulness and <u>making our product</u> more attractive to young people.**

Which is the best way to write the underlined portion of this sentence? If the original is the best way, choose option (A).

(A) making our product
(B) are making our product
(C) makes our product
(D) were making our product
(E) will be making our product

46. Sentence 11: **A new energy drink, with promising results, was test-marketed in California.**

Which correction should be made to sentence 11?

(A) change <u>was</u> to <u>were</u>
(B) change <u>promising</u> to <u>promised</u>
(C) place <u>with promising results</u> after <u>California</u>
(D) remove the comma after <u>drink</u>
(E) no correction is necessary

47. Sentence 12: **This year the test marketing will be <u>done, and analyzed</u> in eight additional western states.**

Which is the best way to write the underlined portion of this sentence? If the original is the best way, choose option (A).

(A) done, and analyzed
(B) done and analyzed
(C) done, yet analyzed
(D) done, and also analyzed
(E) done, and might be analyzed

48. Sentence 13: **After several years of planning and research, Quaker launched your marketing plan in 2011 to establish a presence in the booming Southeast Asian market.**

    Which correction should be made to sentence 13?

    (A) remove the comma after <u>research</u>
    (B) change <u>launched</u> to <u>was launching</u>
    (C) change <u>your</u> to <u>its</u>
    (D) place <u>booming</u> before <u>presence</u>
    (E) no correction is necessary

49. Sentences 14 and 15: **Forecasts predict that by 2015 the Asian market <u>will grow. To 15 percent</u> of total revenue.**

    Which is the best way to write the underlined portion of this sentence? If the original is the best way, choose option (A).

    (A) will grow. To 15 percent
    (B) will grow, to 15 percent
    (C) will grow; to 15 percent
    (D) will grow: to 15 percent
    (E) will grow to 15 percent

50. Sentence 16: **The company <u>had planned</u> to open a regional office in Ho Chi Minh City, Vietnam, in early 2013.**

    Which is the best way to write the underlined portion of this sentence? If the original is the best way, choose option (A).

    (A) had planned
    (B) was planning
    (C) will plan
    (D) plans
    (E) have planned

ANSWERS: LANGUAGE ARTS, WRITING, PART I

1. **(D)** Option (D) is correct because it changes the contraction that means *it is* to the possession form of *it*, *its*. Option (A) changes the correct pronoun to a possessive pronoun. Option (B) is not correct because the verb form *having chose* is incorrect grammatically and does not make sense in the sentence. Option (C) inserts an unnecessary comma. Option (E) does not correct the spelling error.

2. **(B)** Option (B) is correct because it exchanges the relative pronoun *that* for *who* since it refers to *customer service*, which is not a human but a thing. Option (A) incorrectly puts commas around an incorrect relative pronoun. Option (C) makes an incomplete sentence from the clause. Option (D) uses an incorrect verb form. Option (E) uses *that* correctly but has an incorrect verb form.

3. **(A)** Option (A) is correct because it changes the incorrect verb form to a correct verb form. Option (B) incorrectly changes a correct possessive to an incorrect possessive pronoun. Option (C) is incorrect because it inserts a comma where none is needed. Options (D) and (E) are incorrect because they have incorrect verb forms.

4. **(C)** Option (C) is correct because this verb form agrees with the subject. Option (A) inserts a comma where none is needed. Options (B), (D), and (E) have incorrect verb forms.

5. **(D)** Option (D) is correct because the verb *find* agrees with the verb *choose*; they are parallel. Option (A) is incorrect because the comma is needed after *service*. Option (B) replaces a correct verb form with an incorrect one. Option (C) inserts a comma where none is needed. Option (E) is incorrect because the verb form is not parallel.

6. **(D)** Option (D) is correct because it combines the ideas of the two sentences clearly, and it correctly uses a comma to join them. Option (A) is incorrect because the conjunction *however* does not make sense. Option (B) is incorrect because *yet* doesn't make sense. Option (C) has the correct conjunction but incorrectly omits the comma. Option (E) also uses an incorrect conjunction.

7. **(E)** Option (E) is correct because it capitalizes the proper name *Central Time* and has correct comma usage. Option (A) does not correct capitalize *Central Time*. Option (B) incorrectly hyphenates *seven days*. Option

(C) removes necessary commas. Although option (D) does capitalize *Central Time* correctly, it inserts an unnecessary comma after *days*.

8. **(A)** Option (A) is correct because it uses a semicolon to join two complete ideas. Option (B) is incorrect because a comma is not used to join two complete ideas. Option (C) creates a run-on sentence. Option (D) uses a verb in the future tense rather than the present tense. While option (E) uses a semicolon correctly, it incorrectly inserts a comma that is not needed.

9. **(C)** Option (C) correctly rearranges the paragraph so that it has a cohesive train of thought. Option (A) moves the topic sentence to the end, which is incorrect. Option (B) would leave out a key idea of the paragraph. Option (D) would break up the coherence of the paragraph. Option (E) would not result in a clear continuity of thought.

10. **(D)** Option (D) is correct because it adds an appropriate and necessary subordinating conjunction to join the two sentences. Option (A) doesn't correctly connect the two ideas. Option (B) creates a run-on sentence. Option (C) incorrectly uses the conjunction *however*, which does not make sense in the sentence. Option (E) does not connect the two ideas correctly.

11. **(B)** Option (B) is correct because the verb *give* is necessary to complete the thought. The present tense is used to agree with *nurse*. Option (A) is incorrect because *birth* is a noun. Option (C) is wrong because the writer is talking about more than one whale, and *birth* is not a verb. Option (D) is incorrect because *birthed* is not standard usage; in any case, the tense does not agree with the second verb. Option (E) is also incorrect because it uses the past tense.

12. **(C)** Option (C) is correct because the present tense, *grow*, should follow the present tense of the preceding verb, *are*. Option (A) is incorrect; the plural of *calf* is *calves*. Option (B) removes a necessary comma. Option (D) changes the verb to an incorrect form. Option (E) has verbs in the present tense and past tense in the same sentence.

13. **(C)** Option (C) is correct because the adverbial phrase modifies the verb phrase *return to the North*. Option (A) unnecessarily removes a comma. Option (B) is an incorrect verb form. Option (D) is incorrect because when a direction is used as a locality and not a direction, it is capitalized. Option (E) is incorrect because the sentence does not read well.

14. **(D)** Option (D) is correct because the conjunction *and* makes the comma splice a compound sentence. Option (A) would make a run-on

sentence. Option (B) is incorrect since *each* indicates individuality. Option (C) is wrong because *pods* refers to *groups* and should be plural. Option (E) is a comma splice.

15. **(E)** Option (E) is correct because the present tense agrees with the present participle, *migrating*. Option (A) has an incorrect verb form. Option (B) incorrectly uses the singular verb with the plural noun *whales*. Option (C) puts the idea in the past, as does option (D).

16. **(B)** Option (B) is correct because it best introduces the information given in the rest of the paragraph. Option (A) belongs with paragraph (B). Options (C) and (D) don't have anything to do with the information in paragraph (D). Option (E) is too general to be a topic sentence.

17. **(B)** Option (B) is correct because the verb form is correct. Option (A) is wrong because there is no need for a comma. Option (C) incorrectly uses a possessive pronoun rather than the contraction for *you are*. Option (D) uses an incorrect verb form. The same is true of option (E).

18. **(C)** Option (C) is correct because it combines sentences 3 and 4 in a logical compound sentence. Options (A) and (D) do not make sense. Option (B) incorrectly uses a semicolon to join a dependant and independent clause. The verb tenses do not agree in option (E).

19. **(D)** Option (D) is correct as it creates a complete sentence with a subject. In option (A), a comma precedes the use of quotation marks. Option (B) is incorrect because the first word in a quote is always capitalized. Option (C) incorrectly changes the contraction *it's* to the possessive *its*. Option (E) is an incomplete sentence without a subject.

20. **(B)** Option (B) is correct because items in a list are separated by commas. Option (A) is incorrect; there is no reason to capitalize *solid*. Option (C) makes no sense because it uses the present participle *wearing*. Option (D) incorrectly changes an adjective verb form to a present tense verb. Option (E) is incorrect because the list would not be correctly punctuated.

21. **(C)** Option (C) is correct because the plural verb *are* agrees with the plural subject *shoes*. Option (A) is incorrect because the past participle, *polished*, is the object of the verb. Option (B) does not make sense. There is no grammatical reason to install a comma after *sure* as in option (D). In option (E), the plural subject does not agree with the singular verb.

22. **(E)** Option (E) is correct because sentence 10 does not relate to the subject of the paragraph. Option (A) is the topic sentence. Option (B) would put a sentence that is not a topic sentence at the start of the paragraph. Option (C) is incorrect because this sentence belongs with the following sentence. Option (D) is wrong because logically the sentence does not belong there.

23. **(B)** Option (B) is correct; *too*, meaning *also*, is needed in the context of the sentence. Option (A) replaces a correct verb form with an incorrect one. Option (C) incorrectly removes a necessary comma. Option (D) creates a plural noun where a singular is preferred. Option (E) uses the preposition *to*, which is incorrect in the context of the sentence.

24. **(E)** Option (E) is correct because *should choose* agrees with the previous verb *should select* and is parallel. Options (A), (B), and (C) are incorrect because, in each case, the second verb is not parallel with the first verb. Option (D) is incorrect grammatically; *have chose* is not a past participle.

25. **(B)** Option (B) is correct because the singular verb *go* agrees with the singular subject *you*. Option (A) is incorrect because *goes* is plural and does not agree with *you*. Options (C) and (D) have a different tense than the first verb *check*. Option (E) has no subject for the verb *go*.

26. **(D)** Option (D) is correct because it uses a correct verb form. Option (A) is incorrect because *was intending* is not the verb form that is needed here; it changes the meaning of the sentence. Option (B) has a grammatically incorrect verb. Option (C) is plural when it should be singular and is also an incorrect verb form. Option (E) is plural and the subject is singular.

27. **(C)** Option (C) is correct because *Kid Fun* is the name of a specific company and should be capitalized. Option (A) removes a necessary comma. Option (B) is incorrect because the verb tense does not make sense. Option (D) is wrong because *manufacturer* is singular, so a pronoun referring to it should be singular as well. Option (E) is incorrect because *kid fun* is a proper name and should be capitalized.

28. **(D)** Option (D) is correct because it places commas between all the words in a series. Option (A) does not insert a comma after *discount outlets*. Option (B) does not have a comma after *toy stores*. Option (C) is wrong because there should be commas after *department stores* and *toy stores*. Although the commas are correctly placed in option (E), there is no *and* to complete the series.

29. **(A)** Option (A) is correct because it combines the two sentences using a conjunction that makes sense in the context of the sentence and has the correct pronoun. Option (B) uses an incorrect conjunction; it does not make sense. Option (C) uses an incorrect pronoun for the antecedent *children*. Option (D) uses an incorrect conjunction. Option (E) has an incorrect verb tense and doesn't make sense.

30. **(E)** Option (E) is correct because the action took place in the past not in the future. Options (A) and (C) are incorrect because the future tense *will be* and *will have been* do not follow the tense of the previous sentence and make no sense. Option (B) is incorrect because *was being* is an incorrect verb form. Option (D) is wrong because the verb is singular and the subject *reports* is plural.

31. **(E)** Option (E) is correct because *The toy's model number is 0318QS, and it can be found on the underside of the toy* is the most straightforward. Option (A) is incorrect because *model number* is singular while *they* is plural. Options (B), (C), and (D) use an incorrect pronoun as well as unnecessary words.

32. **(B)** Option (B) is correct because it replaces the homonym *aid* (to help) with *aide* (assistant). Option (A) is incorrect because the subject, *recall*, is singular and *are* is plural. Option (C) would not make sense. Option (D) is not correct because the adverb *actually* should be next to the verb it modifies. Option (E) is not correct because the word *aid* does not make sense in the sentence.

33. **(A)** Option (A) is correct because it makes an effective closing statement. Options (B) and (E) are incorrect because they present supporting details. Options (C) and (D) create an illogical sequence of ideas. Option (E) removes an important detail.

34. **(B)** Option (B) is correct because *are* agrees with the plural subject, *acts*. Options (A) and (C) are singular verbs. Option (D) is plural but the wrong tense. Option (E) is not a complete verb.

35. **(A)** Option (A) is correct because it shows a causality relationship between what has happened and what will happen. Option (B) is incorrect because it suggests an example where none exists. Options (C) and (D) suggest relationships that do not exist in the sentence. Option (E) changes the meaning of the sentence.

36. **(A)** Option (A) is correct because it uses an appositive to combine the ideas in the two sentences. Option (B) repeats words unnecessarily.

Option (C) changes the idea of the original sentences. Option (D) is incorrect because the parentheses are unnecessary. Option (E) has the wrong tense and does not make sense.

37. **(D)** Option (D) is correct because the future is implied in the context of the sentence. Options (A), (B), and (C) have verb tenses that are inconsistent with the idea of the sentence. Option (E) is not a grammatically correct verb form.

38. **(D)** Option (D) is correct because it correctly changes *rite* to *right*. Option (A) is incorrect; there is no reason to capitalize *violation*. Option (B) is wrong because the future tense does not require an *s* added to the verb. Option (C) makes no sense. Option (E) is an incorrect verb form.

39. **(C)** Option (C) is correct because it uses a comma to set off an appositive phrase. Option (A) omits the comma. Option (B) has the comma, but it omits the period after *Mrs.* Option (D) has no comma, and the title is lowercase. Option (E) uses a semicolon rather than a comma to set off the title.

40. **(B)** Option (B) is correct because the subject of the sentence, *you*, has two verbs, *enter* and *leave*. Option (A) is incorrect because no comma is needed between the verb phrases. Options (C) and (D) do not make sense. Option (E) incorrectly adds a semicolon.

41. **(C)** Option (C) is correct because the pronoun *it* agrees with its antecedent *information*. Options (A) and (B) are incorrect because the sentence would make no sense. Option (D) would result in an incorrect verb form. Option (E) is incorrect because *them* does not agree with *information*, its antecedent.

42. **(C)** Option (C) is correct because paragraph (D) continues the discussion of missing ID badges. Options (A) and (B) are incorrect because the paragraphs discuss different subjects. Option (D) is wrong because sentence 7 does not begin a new subject. Option (E) is incorrect because the paragraphs are not in logical order.

43. **(D)** Option (D) is correct because it capitalizes the title CEO. Option (A) removes a comma where one is needed. Option (B) changes the proper verb form to an incorrect one. Option (C) incorrectly changes a correct adjective to a comparative form. Option (E) does not correct the capitalization error.

44. **(A)** Option (A) is the best choice because it is a topic sentence that covers the entire paragraph. While option (B) talks about what was done, it is not broad enough to be a topic sentence. Option (C) just repeats the information in the following sentence. Option (D) talks about only one

of the changes, so it is not a good topic sentence. Option (E) has little to do with the information that follows.

45. **(C)** Option (C) is correct since it creates a parallel structure between the verbs *conveys* and *makes*. Option (A) is incorrect since the verb form is not parallel to *conveys*. Option (B) is an incorrect verb form and not parallel. Options (D) and (E) are incorrect since they are not correct verb forms (one is in the past and the other in the future), nor are they parallel with *conveys*.

46. **(C)** Option (C) is correct because it moves the phrase *with promising results* after the phrase that it modifies, *was test-marketed in California.* Option (A) changes a correct verb form to an incorrect one, since the subject is singular. Option (B) substitutes an incorrect form of the adjective *promising*. Option (D) removes a necessary comma. Option (E) has the phrase incorrectly modifying *energy drink*.

47. **(B)** Option (B) is correct because the subject of the sentence, *test marketing*, has two verbs—*will be done* and *analyzed*—and no comma is needed between them. Option (A) is incorrect because of the comma separating the verb phrases. Option (C) keeps the unnecessary comma and adds a conjunction, *yet*, which does not make sense in the sentence. Option (D) is wrong because *also* repeats the same idea as *and* and is not needed. Option (E) changes the verb *analyzed* to *might be analyzed*, which changes the meaning of the sentence.

48. **(C)** Option (C) is correct because it replaces an incorrect possessive pronoun with the correct form. Option (A) removes a necessary comma. Option (B) replaces the correct verb with an incorrect verb form. Option (D) changes the meaning of the sentence. Option (E) is incorrect because the possessive pronoun *your* does not agree with its antecedent, *Quaker.*

49. **(E)** Option (E) is correct because it correctly joins the fragment *to 15 percent of total revenue* to the main clause of the sentence. Option (A) is incorrect because the prepositional phrase is an incomplete sentence. Option (B) is wrong because no comma is needed between the prepositional phrase and the main clause of the sentence. Options (C) and (D) are similarly incorrect since neither a semicolon nor a colon is required between the phrase and the main clause of the sentence.

50. **(D)** Option (D) is correct because present tense is the correct verb form. Option (A) is in the past tense and makes no sense in the sentence; this is also true of option (B). The plan is already in place, so option (C) is incorrect. Option (E) is incorrectly in the past tense.

LANGUAGE ARTS, WRITING, PART II
Essay Directions and Topic

Look at the box on the next page. In the box are your assigned topic and the letter of that topic.

You must write on the assigned topic ONLY.

You will have 45 minutes to write on your assigned essay topic. You may return to the multiple-choice section after you complete your essay if you have time remaining in this test period. Do not return the Language Arts, Writing booklet until you finish both Parts I and II of the Language Arts, Writing Test.

Two evaluators will score your essay according to its overall effectiveness. Their evaluation will be based on the following features:

- Well-focused main points
- Clear organization
- Specific development of your ideas
- Control of sentence structure, punctuation, grammar, word choice, and spelling

REMEMBER, YOU MUST COMPLETE BOTH THE MULTIPLE-CHOICE QUESTIONS (PART I) AND THE ESSAY (PART II) TO RECEIVE A SCORE ON THE LANGUAGE ARTS, WRITING TEST. To avoid having to repeat both parts of the test, be sure to do the following:

- Do not leave the pages blank.
- Write legibly <u>in ink</u> so that the evaluators will be able to read your writing.
- Write on the assigned topic. If you write on a topic other than the one assigned, you will not receive a score for the Language Arts, Writing Test.
- Write your essay on the lined pages of the separate answer sheet booklet. Only the writing on these pages will be scored.

TOPIC A

Many schools are adopting a uniform code.

Write an essay that tells whether you think required uniforms are a good idea or a bad idea. Give your opinion and support your view from your own personal observations and experiences.

Part II is a test to determine how well you can use written language to explain your ideas. In preparing your essay, you should take the following steps:

- Read the DIRECTIONS and the TOPIC carefully.
- Plan your essay before you write. Use the scratch paper provided to make any notes. These notes will be collected but not scored.
- Before you turn in your essay, reread what you have written and make any changes that will improve your essay.

Your essay should be long enough to develop the topic adequately.

ANSWERS: LANGUAGE ARTS, WRITING, PART II

All essays will be scored according to the GED essay rubric.

Example of Excellent Topic Sentences

I believe that requiring uniforms in school is a good idea because it makes every student look the same rather than having clothing that announces who a student thinks he or she is.

I am totally against having students wear uniforms because it invades the private choices of students, and there are very few choices left in schools.

Examples of Paragraphs Using Varied Language and Details While Following the Rules of Edited American English (EAE)

For instance, I have seen students with very strange outfits that really made me nervous. I know that people who dress dramatically are trying to draw attention to themselves, but when they do so, I think it takes away from an atmosphere where people can be serious and learn.

For example, requiring uniforms means that everyone will look the same, which means no one will be able to be creative in their choice of clothing. I don't mean that clothes that are too revealing or weird should be allowed. There can be some kind of dress code, but uniforms are too restrictive.

- Organization should follow a clear, logical order.
- The essay should also have a closing that sums up it up succinctly, such as:

These are some of the reasons that I believe that uniforms should be required in schools so that the school can have a better atmosphere that helps students learn.

To sum up my feelings, I think that it goes too far to require students to dress in uniforms because it steals their right to express themselves.

SOCIAL STUDIES

Questions 1–3 refer to the quotation below.

We hold these truths to be self-evident: that all men and women are created equal; that they are endowed by their Creator with certain inalienable rights; that among these are life, liberty, and the pursuit of happiness; that to secure these rights governments are instituted, deriving their just powers from the consent of the governed. . . . The history of mankind is a history of repeated injuries and usurpations on the part of man toward woman, having in direct object the establishment of an absolute tyranny over her.

1. The document from which this quotation is taken is modeled after which of the following founding documents of the United States?

    (A) The Mayflower Compact (1620)
    (B) The Fundamental Orders of Connecticut (1639)
    (C) The Declaration of Independence (1776)
    (D) The Virginia Statute for Religious Freedom (1786)
    (E) The United States Constitution (1787)

2. The authors of this quotation were early advocates of

    (A) prohibition
    (B) religious freedom and toleration
    (C) separation of church and state
    (D) states' rights
    (E) women's rights

3. The concept that governments derive "their just powers from the consent of the governed" is known in American political thought as

    (A) popular sovereignty
    (B) checks and balances
    (C) civil rights
    (D) the Establishment Clause
    (E) separation of powers

Questions 4 and 5 refer to the quotation below.

> . . . we may hear without surprise or scandal that the introduction, or at least the abuse of Christianity, had some influence on the decline and fall of the Roman empire . . . the active virtues of society were discouraged; and the last remains of military spirit were buried . . . a large portion of public and private wealth was consecrated to the . . . demands of charity and devotion.

—*The History of the Decline and Fall of the Roman Empire* (1776), ch. 39

4. In this excerpt, historian Edward Gibbon discusses the influence of which of the following on the decline of the Roman Empire?

(A) the Protestant Reformation
(B) the overextension of the Roman military
(C) burdensome taxation policies
(D) the early Catholic church
(E) incursions of barbarians on the German frontier

5. Gibbon's contention that "a large portion of public and private wealth was consecrated to the . . . demands of charity and devotion" most likely refers to

(A) the cost of public games, like chariot races, in the Roman Empire
(B) the large sums of money spent by early Christians to support the Church
(C) the rising cost of the imperial military establishment
(D) the growing cost of providing social services to Roman citizens
(E) the administrative costs of the empire

Questions 6–8 refer to the chart below.

Persons Obtaining Legal Permanent Resident Status in the United States					
Year		**Year**		**Year**	
1950	249,187	1987	601,516	2008	1,107,126
1967	361,972	1997	797,847	2009	1,130,818
1977	462,315	2007	1,052,415	2010	1,042,625

Source: US Department of Homeland Security, Persons Obtaining Legal Permanent Resident Status: Fiscal Years 1820 to 2010.

6. Which of the following might account for the steady rise in immigrants gaining legal permanent resident status over the period covered in the chart?

    (A) the rapid growth of illegal immigration over the last 75 years
    (B) the increase in available unskilled factory jobs in the United States since 1967
    (C) the abolition of restrictive immigration quotas with the passage of the Immigration and Nationality Act of 1965
    (D) new immigration policies implemented in the United States following the September 11 attacks
    (E) the closing of the Ellis Island immigration facility in 1954

7. Which of the following two areas represent the most common places of origin of the immigrants to the United States referenced in the chart?

    (A) northern and western Europe
    (B) the former Soviet Union and the Balkans
    (C) Latin America and Asia
    (D) Africa and the Middle East
    (E) southern and eastern Europe

8. Which of the following was a major pull factor for immigration to the United States in the period covered in the chart?

    (A) wars in Europe and Asia
    (B) economic opportunity in the growing US economy
    (C) religious persecution
    (D) oppressive totalitarian regimes in various parts of the world
    (E) famine and disease outbreaks

Questions 9–11 refer to the graph below.

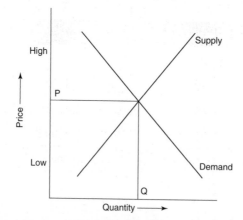

9. According to this graph, which of the following is a likely outcome if the quantity of a good available to the public, represented by the horizontal axis of the graph, is INCREASED?

    (A) Nothing will happen, as the graph demonstrates that quantity and price are not related.
    (B) Supply of the good will decrease.
    (C) Demand for the product will decrease.
    (D) The price of the good will decrease.
    (E) The graph does not provide enough information to determine the effect of increasing the quantity of the good available.

10. According to this graph, which of the following would likely happen to the price of a good if demand remains unchanged and supply DECREASES?

    (A) Prices never change in relation to supply.
    (B) Only inflation can raise prices in any appreciable way.
    (C) Because demand remains constant, the effect on price cannot be determined.
    (D) The graph does not provide enough information to determine the effect on price given these conditions.
    (E) The price of the good will increase.

11. According to this graph, if supply of a good increased dramatically and demand for that good fell sharply, what would be the effect on the price of the good?

    (A) The price would increase sharply.
    (B) The price would increase but only slightly.
    (C) The price would decrease sharply.
    (D) The price would decrease but only slightly.
    (E) The graph does not provide enough information to determine the effect on price given those conditions.

Questions 12–14 refer to the quotation below.

> The most stringent protection of free speech would not protect a man in falsely shouting fire in a theatre and causing a panic. [. . .] The question in every case is whether the words used are used in such circumstances and are of such a nature as to create a clear and present danger that they will bring about the substantive evils that Congress has a right to prevent.

12. The quotation above, taken from the majority opinion in a 1919 Supreme Court case, relates to which of the following constitutional amendments?

    (A) First Amendment
    (B) Second Amendment
    (C) Fifth Amendment
    (D) Eighth Amendment
    (E) Fourteenth Amendment

13. In what way does this opinion help to define a right guaranteed to the American people under the Constitution?

    (A) It affirms the right of Americans to protect themselves by carrying weapons in public.
    (B) It further strengthens protections against cruel and unusual punishment.
    (C) It articulates a "right to privacy" by reinforcing Americans' right to see whatever films they choose in a theater.
    (D) It places limits on free speech by defining a category of speech that is not protected.
    (E) It clarifies an American's protection against self-incrimination.

14. The law that gave rise to this Supreme Court case, the Sedition Act of 1918, was passed due to American involvement in which war?

    (A) the American Revolution
    (B) the War of 1812
    (C) the Spanish-American War
    (D) World War I
    (E) World War II

Questions 15–17 refer to the document below.

NO Freeman shall be taken or imprisoned, or be disseized of his Freehold, or Liberties, or free Customs, or be outlawed, or exiled, or any other wise destroyed; nor will We not pass upon him, nor condemn him, but by lawful judgment of his Peers, or by the Law of the land. We will sell to no man, we will not deny or defer to any man either Justice or Right.

15. This excerpt, from the Magna Carta of 1297 and still a statute today, helped to establish one of the fundamental principles of

    (A) international trade and finance
    (B) English Common Law
    (C) the French Revolution
    (D) Spanish control of its North American colonies
    (E) rights and freedoms of citizens of the Roman Empire

16. The principle outlined in this provision of the Magna Carta is associated with which of the following freedoms or rights?

    (A) freedom of religion
    (B) freedom of speech
    (C) right to petition the government for redress of grievances
    (D) protection from cruel and unusual punishment
    (E) right to due process of law

17. According to Thomas Jefferson, violations of the right established in clause 29 of the Magna Carta of 1297 were responsible in part for causing what war between the United States and Great Britain?

    (A) Queen Anne's War
    (B) King George's War
    (C) the French and Indian War
    (D) the American Revolution
    (E) the War of 1812

Questions 18–21 refer to the illustration below.

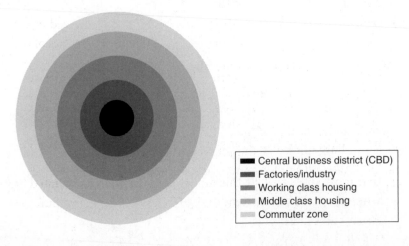

	Central business district (CBD)
	Factories/industry
	Working class housing
	Middle class housing
	Commuter zone

18. The illustration above, called the Concentric Zone Model, is used by geographers as one possible explanation for

    (A) the distribution of social groups within urban areas
    (B) the placement of urban centers near natural resources
    (C) the existence of zones of gentrification in inner-city areas
    (D) the reliance of major American cities on extensive public transportation systems
    (E) the influence of physical features on the development of cities

19. In the Concentric Zone Model, poor urban dwellers and factory workers would be most likely to live in the zone labeled

    (A) Central Business District
    (B) Factory Zone
    (C) Working Class Zone
    (D) Residential Zone
    (E) Commuter Zone

20. Under this model, why would the wealthiest residents of cities most likely move to the outermost rings of the city?

    (A) to be nearer to entertainment and cultural options, which would also be located on the outskirts of the city
    (B) to escape the pollution and poverty of some of the inner rings of the city
    (C) to be closer to their places of employment, which would be located near the outside of the Residential Zone
    (D) because only the outer rings of the city have housing units, and none exist in the inner rings of the city
    (E) because wealthier residents are more likely to be engaged in agricultural activities, which can only take place in the outer rings of the city

21. Some criticisms of the Concentric Zone Model might include

    (A) its inability to account for physical features that might impede or change growth patterns in a city
    (B) its inability to account for gentrification and urban renewal in inner cities
    (C) that most cities that fit this model are located in the United States, where inner-city areas tend to be poorer, unlike many European or Asian cities

(D) the effects of urban politics and municipal laws on urban development

(E) all of the above are legitimate criticisms of the Concentric Zone Model

Questions 22–25 refer to the graph below.

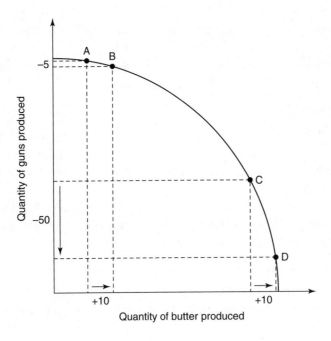

22. The production possibilities curve illustrates which of the following concepts in economics?

(A) that certain commodities can never be produced at the same time in a given economy

(B) the combination of two commodities that can be produced simultaneously in a given period of time and their effect on each other

(C) that goods are generally produced independently from each other in a given economy

(D) that the resources needed to produce guns are in chronically short supply

(E) that an increase or decrease of the production of butter will have no effect on the production of guns

23. In economics, the sacrifice in production of one good to increase production of another good is referred to as

    (A) means of production
    (B) human capital
    (C) opportunity cost
    (D) purchasing power parity
    (E) gross domestic product

24. One of the assumptions made by this graph is that

    (A) the factors of production needed to produce the two goods are roughly equivalent
    (B) the raw materials needed to produce the two goods must be the same
    (C) the two goods are made side by side in the same factory
    (D) both goods are equally significant to the overall national economy
    (E) production of one good has no effect on the production of the other

25. The "guns or butter" argument was used by Lyndon Johnson during his second term to illustrate the difficulties of spending money on both social programs and the

    (A) New Deal
    (B) Federal Aid Highway Act
    (C) Strategic Defense Initiative
    (D) Vietnam War
    (E) Berlin Airlift

Questions 26 and 27 refer to the passage below

With malice toward none; with charity for all; with firmness in the right, as God gives us to see the right, let us strive on to finish the work we are in; to bind up the nation's wounds; to care for him who shall have borne the battle, and for his widow, and his orphan—to do all which may achieve and cherish a just and lasting peace among ourselves, and with all nations.

26. This excerpt, from the Second Inaugural Address of Abraham Lincoln, was given within weeks of what major event?

    (A) the fall of Fort Sumter
    (B) the issuance of the Emancipation Proclamation

(C)   the conclusion of the Battle of Gettysburg

(D)   the surrender of Robert E. Lee's army to Ulysses Grant

(E)   the readmission of Louisiana to the Union

27.   Which of the following statements most accurately summarizes Lincoln's views toward the South as stated in the passage?

(A)   The Union should surrender to the South so the war can come to a quick end.

(B)   Although the Union has won the war, the government intends to treat the South with respect and to bring the nation back together.

(C)   The Union, with God's help, has defeated the South, and the South should be harshly punished.

(D)   The South should pay heavy war reparations to care for orphans and widows from the Union army.

(E)   The Union should bear the costs of caring for both Northern and Southern war veterans in order to placate the South.

Questions 28–30 refer to the quotation below.

A good person will resist an evil system with his whole soul.
Disobedience of the laws of an evil state is therefore a duty.

28.   The quotation above, from Mohandas K. Gandhi, relates to the efforts of

(A)   Gandhi to end segregation in South Africa, where he was employed as an attorney

(B)   African Americans to gain civil rights in 1950s and 1960s America

(C)   the Muslim minority in what is now Pakistan to gain independence from India

(D)   people across the world to resist the spread of Soviet Communism

(E)   India to gain its independence from Great Britain

29.   Mohandas Gandhi was an advocate of which of the following philosophies?

(A)   anarchism

(B)   nonviolent resistance

(C)   accommodationism

(D)   apartheid

(E)   segregation

30. The quotation above, written by Gandhi in the 1930s, was heavily influenced by the writings and philosophies of which of the following?

    (A) American transcendentalist author Henry David Thoreau
    (B) American civil rights leader Martin Luther King, Jr.
    (C) German leader Adolf Hitler
    (D) Soviet leader Vladimir Lenin
    (E) English philosopher John Locke

Questions 31–34 refer to the quotation below.

> The interpretation of the laws is the proper and peculiar province of the courts. A constitution is, in fact, and must be regarded by the judges, as a fundamental law. It therefore belongs to them to ascertain its meaning, as well as the meaning of any particular act proceeding from the legislative body. If there should happen to be an irreconcilable variance between the two, that which has the superior obligation and validity ought, of course, to be preferred; or, in other words, the Constitution ought to be preferred to the statute, the intention of the people to the intention of their agents. . . .

31. The quotation above, from Federalist No. 78, lays the groundwork for which of the following powers that the Supreme Court would gain in the 1803 case of *Marbury v. Madison*?

    (A) the ability to suspend the writ of habeas corpus
    (B) impeachment
    (C) judicial review
    (D) regulation of interstate commerce
    (E) taxation

32. According to the passage, "interpretation of the laws is the peculiar province of the courts." This statement is an example of what doctrine essential to the American constitutional system?

    (A) direct democracy
    (B) proportional representation
    (C) separation of powers
    (D) term limits
    (E) executive privilege

33. The statement that "the Constitution ought to be preferred to the statute," advocates the position that the Constitution is

    (A) the supreme law of the land
    (B) unable to be amended
    (C) able to be changed or affected by state laws
    (D) not subject to interpretation
    (E) a hindrance to majority rule

34. Federalist No. 78, along with the other Federalist Papers, were published between 1787 and 1788 in support of

    (A) protests against the Stamp Act
    (B) the start of the American Revolution
    (C) the ratification of the Treaty of Paris
    (D) the ratification of the Constitution
    (E) government response to the Whiskey Rebellion

Questions 35–37 refer to the chart below.

GDP Components–United States($ Billions)						
		2009	2009	2009	2009	2010
	Line	I	II	III	IV	I
C	1	**Gross domestic product**	**14,178.0**	**14,151.2**	**14,242.1**	**14,453.8**	**14,601.4**
	2	**Personal consumption expenditures**	**9,987.7**	**9,999.3**	**10,132.9**	**10,236.4**	**10,362.3**
	3	Goods	3,197.7	3,193.8	3,292.3	3,337.1	3,406.6
		Durable goods	1,025.2	1,011.5	1,051.3	1,052.0	1,072.8
	5	Nondurable goods	2,172.4	2,182.2	2,241.0	2,285.1	2,333.8
	6	Services	6,790.0	6,805.6	6,840.6	6,899.3	6,955.8
I	7	**Gross private domestic investment**	**1,689.9**	**1,561.5**	**1,556.1**	**1,707.8**	**1,763.8**
	8	Fixed investment	1,817.2	1,737.7	1,712.6	1,731.4	1,726.9
	9	Nonresidential	1,442.6	1,391.8	1,353.9	1,366.9	1,371.3
	10	Structures	533.1	494.8	457.9	434.1	417.5
	11	Equipment and software	909.5	897.0	895.9	932.8	953.9

GDP Components–United States($ Billions) *(Continued)*		2009	2009	2009	2009	2010
Line		I	II	III	IV	I
12	Residential	374.6	345.9	358.8	364.5	355.5
13	Change in private inventories	−127.4	−176.2	−156.5	−23.6	36.9
14 X-M	**Net exports of goods and services**	**−378.5**	**−339.1**	**−402.2**	**−449.5**	**−499.4**
15	Exports	1,509.3	1,493.7	1,573.8	1,680.1	1,729.3
16	Goods	989.5	978.1	1,045.2	1,140.6	1,180.0
17	Services	519.8	515.6	528.5	539.6	549.3
18	Imports	1,887.9	1,832.8	1,976.0	2,129.7	2,228.7
19	Goods	1,508.2	1,461.1	1,592.8	1,739.4	1,827.8
20	Services	379.6	371.7	383.1	390.3	400.9
21 G	**Government consumption expenditures and gross investment**	**2,879.0**	**2,929.4**	**2,955.4**	**2,959.2**	**2,974.7**
22	Federal	1,106.7	1,138.3	1,164.3	1,170.1	1,186.4
23	National defense	750.7	776.2	795.8	793.5	805.6
24	Nondefense	356.0	362.1	368.5	376.7	380.7
25	State and local	1,772.3	1,791.2	1,791.1	1,789.0	1,788.3

Source: US Bureau of Economic Analysis

35. Gross domestic product, an important measure of a country's economic well-being and standard of living, encompasses which of the following?

(A) the potential number of goods and services a country can produce within a given time period

(B) the final market value of all goods and services produced within a country in a given time period

(C) the amount of goods and services people of a country can buy under the right conditions

(D) only a comparison of net imports and exports

(E) a measure of how government expenditures create jobs in an economy

36. The chart above, listing the components of the gross domestic product of the United States, shows which of the following?

(A) that investment in nonresidential structures, like office buildings, has fallen from the first quarter of 2009 to the first quarter of 2010

(B) that the country is importing more each quarter than it exports

(C) that government investment in the American economy rose each quarter

(D) that the GDP of the United States contacted in the second quarter of 2009

(E) all of the above are true

37. Federal government expenditures, listed as one of the components of GDP, were used by the federal government to combat the Great Depression. Advocacy of using federal government expenditures to alleviate economic downturns is most closely associated with which of the following economists?

(A) Adam Smith

(B) Milton Friedman

(C) David Ricardo

(D) Karl Marx

(E) John Maynard Keynes

38. The Human Development Index (HDI), which until 2010 used gross domestic product as one component of its measure of quality of life, is an important tool used by geographers and economists to track human development. Given this information, which of the following is likely true of the Human Development Index?

(A) African countries, due to their generally high GDP figures, would likely rank high in the HDI.

(B) The countries with the highest HDI scores in North America are all likely to be Latin American countries.

(C) Of the 45 countries in the Low Human Development category of the HDI, nearly all of them are from South America.

(D) Countries in the European Union are likely to score very high on the HDI scale.

(E) Countries in sub-Saharan Africa would likely score higher on the HDI than countries in the Middle East.

Questions 39 and 40 refer to the quotations below.

Article I, Section 8, Clause 1. The Congress shall have Power to lay and collect Taxes, Duties, Imposts and Excises, to pay the Debts and provide for the common Defense and general Welfare of the United States; but all Duties, Imposts and Excises shall be uniform throughout the United States.

Amendment XVI. The Congress shall have power to lay and collect taxes on incomes, from whatever source derived, without apportionment among the several States, and without regard to any census or enumeration.

39. The quotations above, from the US Constitution and the Sixteenth Amendment to the Constitution, define in part the federal government's power of taxation. In what way does the Sixteenth Amendment change the original language of Article I, Section 8?

   (A) It allows the federal government to impose taxes that do not provide for the common defense or general welfare.
   (B) It allows the federal government to levy taxes, like income taxes, that are not equally imposed on all states.
   (C) It mandates that the federal government take a census and enumerate the people of a given state before imposing an income tax.
   (D) It places the power of taxation with the president, while Article I, Section 8, gives that power to Congress.
   (E) It calls for a reapportionment of Congressional representation based upon the income tax.

40. Article I, Section 8, allows for the collection of "Taxes, Duties, Imposts and Excises" by the federal government. Given that an impost is a type of tax levied on imports, which of the following most likely defines an excise tax?

   (A) a tax levied on property owned by an individual
   (B) a tax on inheritances or gifts from deceased relatives
   (C) a tax levied on goods manufactured within the United States
   (D) a tax on profits made from investments
   (E) a tax on timber cut from American forests

41. The Sixteenth Amendment, ratified in 1913, was one of four amendments, including those dealing with women's suffrage and Prohibition, that are associated with which political movement in America?

(A) Reconstruction
(B) the Great Society
(C) civil rights
(D) Progressivism
(E) strict construction

Questions 42 and 43 refer to the cartoon below.

42. The above cartoon, which appeared in Benjamin Franklin's *Philadelphia Gazette* in 1754, most likely originally called for the American colonists to do which of the following?

(A) become members of a mutual defense pact against the French in the upcoming French and Indian War
(B) protest against the Intolerable Acts
(C) join with the British to defend Georgia against an invasion from Spanish Florida
(D) draft the Articles of Confederation
(E) resist the Newburgh Conspiracy, hatched by a group of Continental Army officers

43. What is the most likely reason for this cartoon becoming such an important symbol during the American Revolution?

(A) Patriots were drawn to the biblical connotations of the snake as a force in opposition to power.

(B) Benjamin Franklin was the leading political figure in the American colonies and demanded his cartoon be used.

(C) Colonists intended to exclude colonies like Georgia and Delaware, not pictured in the cartoon, from the new American nation.

(D) Only united could the colonies hope to defeat the British Empire, which was much stronger, wealthier, and better equipped.

(E) The colonists felt that only a strong federal system of government would enable them to survive.

Questions 44–46 refer to the cartoon below.

44. The above cartoon, from a French newspaper in 1898, depicts which of the following?

    (A) economic competition between the European powers and Japan in China at the turn of the century
    (B) European rivalries during the height of imperialism
    (C) Chinese indignation at the interference of Europe and Japan in its affairs
    (D) the European colonial powers and the Japanese partitioning China over Chinese objections
    (E) all of the above are correct interpretations

45. The British monarch depicted in this cartoon, seated on the far left, is a representation of

    (A) Queen Elizabeth I
    (B) Queen Mary
    (C) Queen Victoria
    (D) Queen Anne
    (E) Queen Elizabeth II

46. The competition over China, Africa, and other areas of the world in the late nineteenth century was one of the major causes of

    (A) the Great Depression
    (B) the rise of Soviet Communism
    (C) the Crimean War
    (D) World War I
    (E) the creation of Israel

Questions 47–50 refer to the quotation below.

> That they will view this as seizing the rights of the states, and consolidating them in the hands of the general government, with a power assumed to bind the states, not merely in cases made federal, but in all cases whatsoever, by laws made, not with their consent, but by others against their consent; that this would be to surrender the form of government we have chosen, and live under one deriving its powers from its own will, and not from our authority; and that the co-states, recurring to their natural rights not made federal, will concur in declaring these void and of no force, and will each unite with this commonwealth in requesting their repeal at the next session of Congress.

> —The Kentucky Resolution of 1798

47. The quotation above, from a document written by Thomas Jefferson in 1798, advocates what position with regard to the US Constitution?

    (A) a position of federal government sovereignty
    (B) a position of states' rights over national authority
    (C) a position of minority rule over the majority
    (D) a position that the legislative power of the Congress should be paramount
    (E) a position that the courts should interpret the laws made by Congress

48. This resolution, along with a companion resolution in Virginia, was written in response to which of the following acts of the federal government under John Adams?

    (A) the "undeclared war" with France
    (B) the "Citizen Genet" affair
    (C) Jay's Treaty
    (D) the Alien and Sedition Acts
    (E) the appointment of the "Midnight Judges"

49. The Virginia and Kentucky Resolutions became the basis for what constitutional theory, that would allow states to strike down acts of the federal government they found unconstitutional and would be revived again by the South in the 1820s and 1830s?

    (A) judicial review
    (B) nullification
    (C) majority rule
    (D) popular sovereignty
    (E) checks and balances

50. In the Declaration of Independence, Thomas Jefferson articulated his vision of the "natural rights" mentioned in the passage. Which of the following was the phrase Jefferson used to define these natural rights?

    (A) self-evident truths
    (B) life, liberty, and the pursuit of happiness
    (C) all men are created equal
    (D) deriving their just powers from the consent of the governed
    (E) in the course of human events

ANSWERS: SOCIAL STUDIES

1. **(C)** This excerpt—from the Declaration of Sentiments, drafted at the Women's Rights Convention in Seneca Falls, New York, in 1848—is very closely modeled on the Declaration of Independence. The Declaration of Sentiments replaces key sections of Jefferson's original document with references to women and women's rights.

2. **(E)** This analysis question requires that you notice key portions of the text, including "all men and women are created equal," and "on the part of man over woman." These portions of the excerpt reveal the advocacy of women's rights intended by the authors of the document.

3. **(A)** This question tests your knowledge of significant principles of American constitutional government. The concept of popular sovereignty is one of the founding governmental principles of the United States and has been articulated on numerous occasions, including in the Declaration of Independence.

4. **(D)** This passage discusses the profound effect of the early Catholic Church on the Roman Empire and is one of the main contentions of Gibbon's seminal work.

5. **(B)** This question requires you to interpret Gibbon's argument and determine which of the options best applies to that argument. In this case, the economic impact of the early church and its effect on the empire is the crux of the argument.

6. **(C)** The passage of the Immigration and Nationality Act of 1965, which ended the immigration quota system established in the early 1920s, is the main reason for the upsurge.

7. **(C)** The majority of the immigrants coming into the United States since 1965 have been from Latin America and Asia. The majority came from countries such as Mexico, China, the Philippines, and India.

8. **(B)** Pull factors are those positive factors that attract immigrants to their new area. Of the options, only option (B) is a pull factor. All the others, including wars and persecution, are push factors, which are negative factors that cause immigrants to leave their old area to seek better living conditions.

9. **(D)** According to the graph, and the law of supply and demand, increasing the supply of a good will result in a decrease in price.

10. **(E)** The law of supply and demand states that if supply deceases while demand remains unchanged, prices in the market will increase. Only option (E) correctly accounts for these forces.

11. **(C)** As both an increase in supply and a decrease in demand will serve to lower prices, the combination of the two would lower the price of the good significantly.

12. **(A)** This question asks you to interpret a passage from the majority opinion in *Schenck v. United States* and to connect its limitations on freedom of speech with the rights granted under the First Amendment to the US Constitution. The "clear and present danger" test was one of the standards for free speech protections in the United States until the 1960s.

13. **(D)** For this question, you need to determine the intent of the justices in the majority opinion in the case and to connect that opinion to a fundamental constitutional right guaranteed to Americans.

14. **(D)** This question asks about the chronology of major American military engagements and the relation of the stated opinion to those engagements. Information provided in the question gives you some reference point to help answer this question.

15. **(B)** The year 1297 predates the French Revolution and the Spanish colonial period, and it is far too late to relate to the Roman Empire. This eliminates options (A), (C), (D), and (E).

16. **(E)** This question asks you to interpret the meaning of the passage and connect that meaning to the rights and freedoms fundamental to both Great Britain and the United States.

17. **(D)** In the Declaration of Independence, Jefferson claims that King George III of Great Britain has "obstructed the Administration of Justice," a reference to the violation of due process in the colonies. Jefferson's connection to the American Revolution and authorship of the Declaration of Independence leads you to option (D).

18. **(A)** Reading the key to the chart should provide enough information to eliminate options (B) and (E), which deal with physical features. The chart does not provide information about options (C) or (D), leaving option (A).

19. **(C)** This question requires you to interpret the information on the chart to determine where poor workers would live in the Concentric Zone Model.

20. **(B)** Since the Concentric Zone Model places industry and lower-class housing toward the middle of the city, it is most likely under this model that wealthier residents would move away from the city center to escape the pollution of the factories and the poverty of the lower-class neighborhoods.

21. **(E)** The Concentric Zone Model does not account for factors like physical geography, municipal politics, gentrification, or the inapplicability of the model to many major cities, especially those outside the United States. Thus, option (E) is the correct answer.

22. **(B)** The graph illustrates the interconnection of two seemingly unrelated items being produced over a period of time and how the production of one good necessarily affects the other.

23. **(C)** In economics, the opportunity cost is the sacrifice in production of one good for increased production of another. The production possibilities curve helps to illustrate the opportunity cost for production of the goods depicted on the graph.

24. **(A)** The factors of production—the materials, labor, and resources needed to produce a given good—must be roughly equivalent for the principles illustrated by the graph to hold true.

25. **(D)** Lyndon Johnson used the "guns or butter" example to illustrate the difficulty of maintaining spending on the social programs of his Great Society and on the rapidly escalating Vietnam War.

26. **(D)** Lincoln's Second Inaugural Address, given in March 1865, gave a brief summary of his views on the end of the Civil War, which was rapidly drawing to a close. The speech took place about two weeks before Robert E. Lee surrendered his forces to Ulysses S. Grant at Appomattox Court House, Virginia, and less than a month before Lincoln's assassination.

27. **(B)** Lincoln famously and eloquently outlines his views on the coming period of Reconstruction, namely that the South should be welcomed back to the Union without the retribution and punishment demanded by many in the North.

28. **(E)** Mohandas Gandhi, the most significant leader of the Indian independence movement, wrote this quotation during his country's struggle to gain its independence from the British Empire. Gandhi wrote and spoke extensively on the subject of Indian independence during the early twentieth century.

29. **(B)** The quotation advocates nonviolent civil disobedience, which was the core philosophy of Gandhi's Indian independence movement.

30. **(A)** Gandhi was heavily influenced, as was Martin Luther King, Jr., by the writings of American Transcendentalist author Henry David Thoreau. Thoreau's treatise *On the Duty of Civil Disobedience* helped form much of Gandhi's own philosophy of satyagraha.

31. **(C)** This quotation, examining the powers of the federal courts in relation to the legislative branch, lays the groundwork for the majority opinion in *Marbury v. Madison* by articulating the responsibility of the courts to resolve conflicts between acts of the legislature and the Constitution. This power, known as judicial review, allows the Supreme Court to determine the constitutionality of federal laws.

32. **(C)** The fundamental principle of the separation of powers is the division of the various mechanisms and functions of government among the three branches to ensure that no one branch will become too powerful.

33. **(A)** This question requires a close reading of the text and a knowledge of American federalism to eliminate options (B), (C), (D), and (E).

34. **(D)** Given the years 1787–1788, the first three options can be eliminated, as they all happened before that period. Given the quotation and the time period, option (D), the ratification of the Constitution, makes the most sense.

35. **(B)** In economics, one definition of gross domestic product is the final market value of all goods and services produced within a country in a given time period.

36. **(E)** The information in the chart shows that all of the choices are true.

37. **(E)** John Maynard Keynes, whose work on employment and monetary policy was one of the theoretical underpinnings of the New Deal, advocated government spending to alleviate bad economic conditions within a given country.

38. **(D)** Africa, due to its high number of poor and underdeveloped nations, has the largest concentration of "low human development" countries, eliminating options (A) and (C). Also, the Middle East, with its relatively high GDP figures, fares much better on the HDI than sub-Saharan Africa. The United States and Canada (options B and E) are the highest-ranked HDI countries in North America, leaving only option (D).

39. **(B)** The Sixteenth Amendment allows the federal government to legally levy an income tax on American citizens.

40. **(C)** Excise taxes, which were a very important source of revenue for the US government before the Sixteenth Amendment, are taxes on goods manufactured within the country in which they are levied.

41. **(D)** The Sixteenth, Seventeenth (direct election of US Senators), Eighteenth (Prohibition), and Nineteenth (women's suffrage) Amendments are known collectively as the Progressive Amendments due to their close ties to that political movement of the early twentieth century.

42. **(A)** The "Join, or Die" cartoon, published at the beginning of what would become the French and Indian War, called for the American colonists to join a mutual defense pact against the French and their Native American allies.

43. **(D)** The colonies used the "Join, or Die" cartoon in various forms, including one labeled "Unite, or Die" as a symbol to encourage colonial unity during the Revolution against the much more powerful British.

44. **(E)** This cartoon represents the European powers (Britain, France, Germany, and Russia) and Japan competing for economic gains and territory in China near the end of the Chinese imperial period. China, whose imperial government was increasingly weak near the end of the nineteenth century, was powerless to stop the growing "spheres of influence" of these powers.

45. **(C)** This is a depiction of Queen Victoria, who reigned over the height of the British Empire at the end of the nineteenth century.

46. **(D)** The competition among the European powers over territory in several parts of the world, including China, is often cited by historians as one of the major causes of World War I, in which the competing European alliances of the day drew most of the world into a protracted and bloody conflict between 1914 and 1918.

47. **(B)** The Kentucky Resolution was one of the strongest statements of states' rights in the early republic. It was the basis for many of the states' rights arguments used by the South in the antebellum period.

48. **(D)** The Virginia and Kentucky Resolutions were written as a direct response to the Alien and Sedition Acts, which Jefferson's Democratic Republicans felt were unconstitutional. As there was no mechanism in 1798 for laws to be declared unconstitutional, Jefferson advanced this theory to dispose of the laws.

49. **(B)** The theory of nullification was the name given to the proposed ability of the states to declare laws unconstitutional. This theory was revived by South Carolina during the so-called Nullification Crisis in the late 1820s and 1830s.

50. **(B)** Jefferson used the phrase *life, liberty and the pursuit of happiness* to articulate his vision of the natural rights to which all men were entitled.

SCIENCE

Choose the *one best answer* to each question.

1. Which of the following statements describes the transfer of heat mainly by convection?

   (A) Ceramic floor tiles feel cold to a barefoot person.
   (B) Air in contact with the warm ground rises higher into the atmosphere.
   (C) When one end of an iron nail is put into a candle flame, the other end becomes warm.
   (D) The handle of a metal spoon resting in a bowl of ice cubes becomes cold.
   (E) Popcorn heated in a microwave oven becomes hot.

2. The diagram below shows the forces acting on a rock resting motionless on the ground.

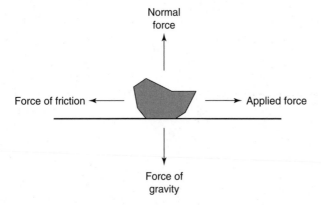

Why is the rock not moving in response to the applied force acting on it?

   (A) The applied force is less than or equal to the force of friction.
   (B) The force of gravity is less than the normal force.
   (C) The normal force is greater than the force of friction.
   (D) The force of gravity is greater than the applied force.
   (E) The force of friction is equal to the force of gravity.

3. A sample of nitrogen gas has a temperature of 25°C and a pressure of 0.1 MPa.

    Which of the following would cause the temperature of the gas to increase?

    (A) decreasing the mass of the gas while keeping the pressure constant
    (B) increasing the rate of diffusion of the gas
    (C) increasing the specific heat capacity of the gas
    (D) insulating the gas from its surroundings
    (E) increasing the pressure of the gas by decreasing its volume

4. The diagram below shows a wave.

    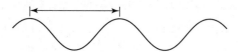

    What does the arrow indicate?

    (A) amplitude
    (B) frequency
    (C) wavelength
    (D) period
    (E) hertz

5. The diagram below shows a ball on a string traveling in a circle. The arrow shows the direction the ball is moving in.

    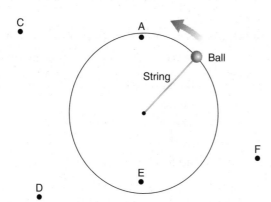

If the string breaks when the ball is at point A, at which point is the ball most likely to land?

(A) point B
(B) point C
(C) point D
(D) point E
(E) point F

6. A recreational boat traveled at an average speed of 14 meters per second for 200 seconds.

Which of the following can be determined using this information?

(A) distance traveled
(B) acceleration
(C) inertia
(D) instantaneous speed
(E) initial velocity

7. A flash of lightning can be seen before the thunder associated with it can be heard.

Which of the following statements best explains this observation?

(A) A thunderstorm produces electromagnetic waves more quickly than mechanical waves.
(B) Electromagnetic waves are diffracted more than mechanical waves when traveling through air.
(C) The amplitude of electromagnetic waves is lower than that of mechanical waves.
(D) The frequency of electromagnetic waves is higher than that of mechanical waves.
(E) The speed of electromagnetic waves traveling through air is faster than that of mechanical waves.

8. The graph below shows the relationship between the distance an object traveled and time.

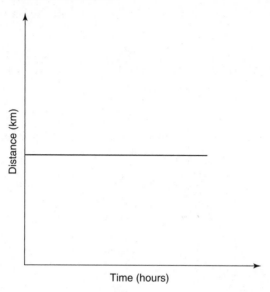

Time (hours)

Which of the following is the best conclusion that can be made about the movement of the object?

(A) The object moved at a constant positive speed.
(B) The object moved at a varying positive speed.
(C) The object remained stationary during the time interval shown.
(D) The object moved at a constant negative speed.
(E) The object moved at a varying negative speed.

9. Electrical forces are able to act between electrically charged particles that are not in contact. The strength of the electrical force is greatly affected by the distance between the particles. The electrical force can be attractive, causing the particles to move together, or repulsive, causing the particles to move apart.

Which of the following statements is the best description of the electrical force between two oppositely charged particles?

(A) The strength of the electrical force decreases as the particles move closer together.
(B) The repulsive force and the attractive force balance one another when the particles touch.
(C) The repulsive force changes to an attractive force as the particles move farther apart.

(D) The attractive force increases as the distance between the particles decreases.

(E) The attractive force changes to a repulsive force when the particles are close together.

10. The diagram below shows a model of a single water molecule and a group of water molecules connected by hydrogen bonds.

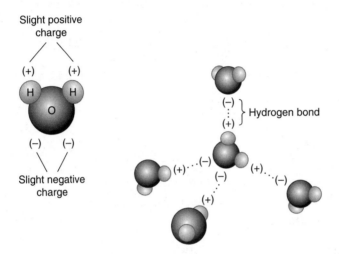

Why are hydrogen bonds able to form between water molecules?

(A) Some water molecules have a positive electrical charge, and some have a negative electrical charge.

(B) Although a water molecule is electrically neutral, the distribution of electrons causes one end to be negative and the other to be positive.

(C) The negative charge of one water molecule attracts the negative charges of other water molecules.

(D) The electrical charges between water molecules are stronger than the covalent bonds within the molecules.

(E) A water molecule with a stronger electrical charge pulls a hydrogen atom from a water molecule with a weaker electrical charge.

Questions 11–13 refer to the following skeleton equation for a chemical reaction:

$$C_6H_{14}(l) + O_2(g) \rightarrow CO_2(g) + CO(g) + C(s) + H_2O(g)$$

11. Which of the following shows the correctly balanced equation?

    (A) $2C_6H_{14}(l) + 5O_2(g) \rightarrow CO_2(g) + CO(g) + 8C(s) + 7H_2O(g)$
    (B) $2C_6H_{14}(l) + 4O_2(g) \rightarrow CO_2(g) + 4CO(g) + C(s) + 14H_2O(g)$
    (C) $C_6H_{14}(l) + 6O_2(g) \rightarrow 2CO_2(g) + 2CO(g) + 2C(s) + 6H_2O(g)$
    (D) $2C_6H_{14}(l) + 3O_2(g) \rightarrow 5CO_2(g) + 3CO(g) + 4C(s) + H_2O(g)$
    (E) $C_6H_{14}(l) + 5O_2(g) \rightarrow CO_2(g) + CO(g) + 4C(s) + 7H_2O(g)$

12. Which of the following reactants or products is in either the liquid or the solid state?

    (A) CO_2, H_2O
    (B) C, O_2
    (C) C_6H_{14}, C
    (D) O_2, CO_2
    (E) C_6H_{14}, H_2O

13. What type of chemical reaction does the equation represent?

    (A) combustion
    (B) synthesis
    (C) decomposition
    (D) single replacement (single displacement)
    (E) double replacement (double displacement)

14. The diagram below shows a model of an atom.

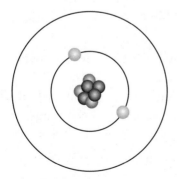

● 3 Protons
● 4 Neutrons
○ 2 Electrons

Which of the following is the best description of the atom?

(A) negative ion
(B) positive ion
(C) radioactive ion
(D) catalyst atom
(E) neutral atom

15. The chart below shows the reactivity series of metals.

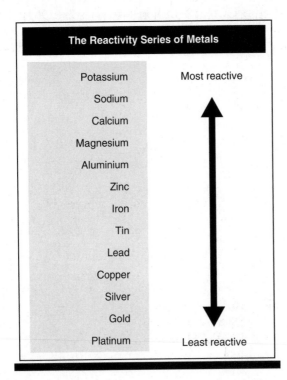

According to the chart, which of the following results in a chemical reaction taking place?

(A) Copper metal is placed in an aqueous solution of a silver compound.
(B) Gold metal is placed in an aqueous solution of a zinc compound.
(C) Magnesium metal is placed in an aqueous solution of a sodium compound.
(D) Iron metal is placed in an aqueous solution of a calcium compound.
(E) Lead metal is placed in an aqueous solution of an aluminum compound.

16. Which of the following is the best description of an ionic bond?

    (A) Ions with opposite charges are attracted to one another.
    (B) Ions with similar charges are attracted to one another.
    (C) Two atoms share valence electrons.
    (D) Two ions share protons.
    (E) Two atoms share neutrons.

17. The table below gives the specific heat capacity of various substances.

Substance	Specific Heat Capacity J/(kg • K)
Aluminum	900
Glass	670
Granite	840
Platinum	130
Silver	230
Water	4,186
Wood	1,700

    If the same amount of heat is transferred to 1 kilogram of each of the following substances, which substance will have the greatest increase in temperature?

    (A) water
    (B) aluminum
    (C) silver
    (D) wood
    (E) granite

18. The element iron (Fe) has 26 protons.

    What is a conclusion that can be made using this information?

    (A) Iron contains no neutrons.
    (B) Iron contains 26 electrons.
    (C) Iron contains 13 neutrons and 13 electrons.
    (D) Iron contains a total of 56 neutrons and electrons.
    (E) Iron contains a total of 78 protons, neutrons, and electrons.

19. The diagram below shows the components of an animal cell and a plant cell.

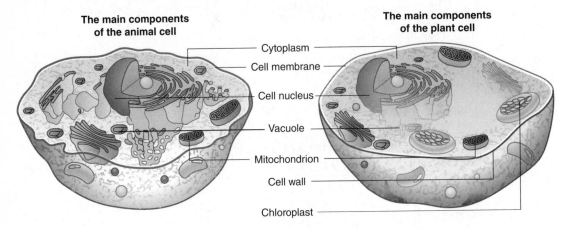

The main components of the animal cell

The main components of the plant cell

Cytoplasm
Cell membrane
Cell nucleus
Vacuole
Mitochondrion
Cell wall
Chloroplast

A person is using a microscope to examine some cells.

The presence of which features would indicate that the cells are from a plant?

(A) vacuoles and mitochondria
(B) nuclei and cytoplasm
(C) cell membrane and vacuoles
(D) cell walls and chloroplasts
(E) cytoplasm and mitochondria

20. Before Europeans settled in Illinois, the dominant species of trees in the forests were oaks that were fire-tolerant. Large fires were common, and many were set by Native Americans when they were hunting. When the Europeans arrived, they suppressed fires, so fires became much less common. Oak trees need high levels of light for growth. Fires cleared out shrubs that would otherwise shade young oak trees. After the fires were suppressed, the number of shade-tolerant trees such as sugar maples increased dramatically, and the number of oaks greatly decreased.

Why has the balance shifted between oak trees and sugar maple trees?

(A) The suppression of fire affected the thickness of soil in the forests.
(B) The suppression of fire decreased the amount of light needed by the sugar maple trees.
(C) The suppression of fire altered the rate of photosynthesis of forest trees.

(D) The suppression of fire increased the rate of leaf production by sugar maple trees.

(E) The suppression of fire changed the pattern of succession in the forests.

21. The diagram below shows a fern fossil.

In what type of environment did this fossil most likely form?

(A) desert
(B) coral reef
(C) deep ocean
(D) forest
(E) Arctic island

Questions 22–24 refer to the following food web diagram.

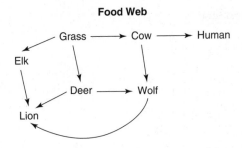

22. In the food web diagram, the arrows point from an organism to another organism that eats it.

    Which two organisms compete for prey?

    (A) elk and deer
    (B) deer and lion
    (C) wolf and cow
    (D) grass and human
    (E) lion and wolf

23. According to the diagram, which of the following organisms is a carnivore?

    (A) elk
    (B) lion
    (C) deer
    (D) cow
    (E) grass

24. According to the diagram, if the wolf population increases, the population of which of the following organisms would be most likely to decrease first?

    (A) elk and human
    (B) cow and lion
    (C) deer and cow
    (D) grass and elk
    (E) human and lion

25. The diagram below shows a representation of the carbon cycle.

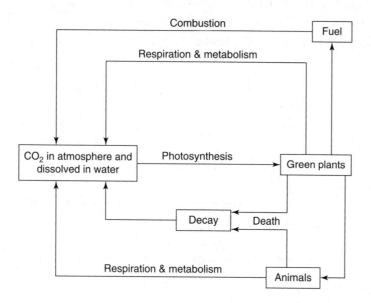

The carbon cycle describes how carbon moves among the atmosphere, Earth's surface, and living organisms.

Which process in the carbon cycle is likely to be affected the most by human activity?

(A) photosynthesis by green plants
(B) respiration and metabolism of animals
(C) combustion of fuel
(D) respiration and metabolism of green plants
(E) death and decay of animals and green plants

26. Why do bacteria adapt more quickly to environmental changes than whales do?

(A) Bacteria are much smaller than whales.
(B) Bacteria live in many more types of ecosystems than whales do.
(C) There are many more bacteria than there are whales.
(D) Bacteria reproduce much more rapidly than whales do.
(E) Bacteria are more complex than whales.

27. Genes are made up of pairs of alleles. An allele can be dominant or recessive. In humans, the allele for dimples is dominant, and the allele for no dimples is recessive. If a person has one dominant allele and one recessive allele for dimples, which of the following would be true for this person's child?

(A) The child will inherit the dominant allele for dimples.
(B) The child will inherit the recessive allele for dimples.
(C) The child has an equal chance of inheriting the dominant allele or the recessive allele for dimples.
(D) The child has a greater chance of inheriting the dominant allele for dimples.
(E) The child has a greater chance of inheriting the recessive allele for dimples.

28. Which pair of organisms has the same type of ecological relationship as the one between a panda and bamboo?

(A) giraffe and tree leaves
(B) mouse and owl
(C) alligator and fish
(D) bison and sheep
(E) polar bear and seal

29. Which of the following is required for photosynthesis by green plants?

(A) glucose
(B) oxygen
(C) hydrogen sulfide
(D) bacteria
(E) chlorophyll

30. Which of the following is a characteristic shared by all mammals?

(A) producing milk for their young
(B) having sharp claws
(C) having large, sensitive eyes
(D) being able to hibernate
(E) using dens or caves for shelter

31. The diagram below shows an example of dominant inheritance.

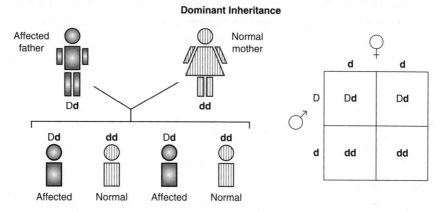

Dominant Inheritance

The father carries a defective gene (D) that is dominant over the recessive gene (d) he carries that is normal. Therefore, the father has the health disorder associated with the dominant gene. The mother has two copies of the normal recessive gene. The children of the parents can inherit a dominant D gene and a recessive d gene, or two recessive d genes.

Which of the following statements always apply to the children of these parents?

(A) All of the children will inherit the defective gene from the father.
(B) Children without the dominant gene will have the genetically related health disorder.
(C) A child with two copies of the recessive gene cannot in turn have children with the genetically related health disorder.
(D) A child with two copies of the recessive gene is not at risk of having the genetically related health disorder.
(E) A child with one dominant gene and one recessive gene will in turn have children who all will be affected by the genetically related health disorder.

32. Which of the following best describes how a carnivore in an ecosystem obtains energy?

(A) by consuming plants
(B) by consuming other animals
(C) by living as a parasite on other organisms
(D) by breaking down organic matter to release nutrients
(E) by using sunlight to make sugars during photosynthesis

33. In a type of squirrel called the Eastern gray squirrel, the allele for gray fur (G) is dominant over the gene for brown feathers (g). A squirrel with GG alleles mates with a squirrel with gg alleles.

    What percentage of the baby squirrels would be expected to have gray fur?

    (A) 0 percent
    (B) 25 percent
    (C) 50 percent
    (D) 75 percent
    (E) 100 percent

34. The diagram below shows the spectrum of visible light. Each color of visible light has a particular wavelength in nanometers. For example, green light has wavelengths around 550 nanometers.

    A student is conducting an experiment on the growth rate of algae in response to wavelengths of light. The student's hypothesis is that red algae will grow fastest when exposed to red light.

    Which variable should be manipulated to test the hypothesis?

    (A) rate of cellular respiration in the algae
    (B) color of light to which the algae are exposed
    (C) time of day that the algae are exposed to light
    (D) color of the algae used
    (E) wavelength of red light used

35. Which of the following is most likely to lead to ecological succession?

    (A) Leaves drop from trees as the seasons change from fall to winter.
    (B) A developer builds a road through a forest.
    (C) Two wolves fight to establish which one is dominant.
    (D) Existing organisms are disturbed or removed by a powerful flood affecting a large area.
    (E) Gray whales migrate along the Pacific coast from Mexico to the Arctic.

36. The table below shows when some forms of life first appeared in the geologic record or when they became extinct.

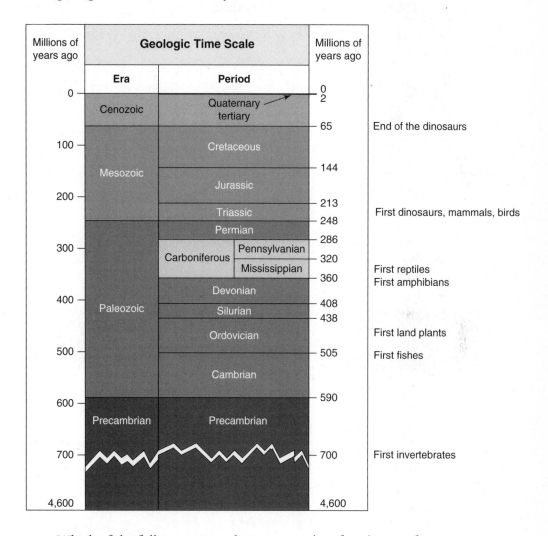

Which of the following gives the correct order of evolution of organisms, from oldest to youngest?

(A) dinosaurs, reptiles, land plants, invertebrates
(B) fishes, land plants, amphibians, birds
(C) invertebrates, amphibians, mammals, reptiles
(D) land plants, reptiles, fishes, dinosaurs
(E) dinosaurs, mammals, birds, reptiles, amphibians

37. The diagram below shows a joint in the human body.

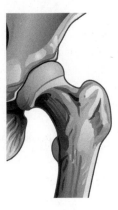

Where in the body is this joint located?

(A) elbow
(B) wrist
(C) spine
(D) hip
(E) skull

Questions 38 and 39 refer to the following diagram, which shows evolutionary relationships among several types of birds.

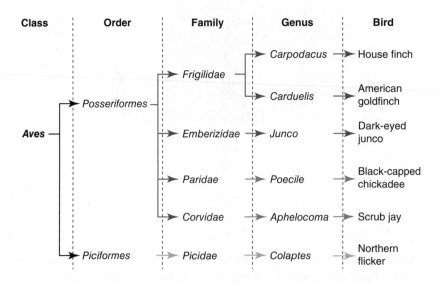

38. What conclusion can be made regarding the dark-eyed junco and the scrub jay?

    (A) They are in the same class and in the same family.
    (B) They are in the same family and in the same genus.
    (C) They are in the same class but in different orders.
    (D) They are in the same genus but in different classes.
    (E) They are in the same order but in different families.

39. Which bird shown on the diagram is least closely related to the American goldfinch?

    (A) house finch
    (B) dark-eyed junco
    (C) black-capped chickadee
    (D) scrub jay
    (E) northern flicker

40. The diagram below shows the structure of a plant leaf.

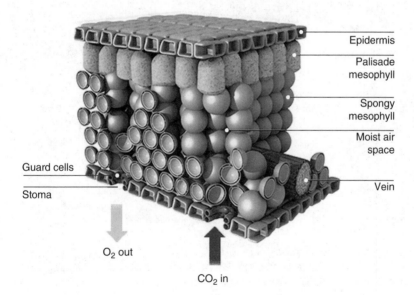

Which of the following is a function of the stoma?

    (A) They allow gas exchange between the plant and the surrounding air.
    (B) They provide support that helps keep the plant upright.
    (C) They contain chloroplasts where photosynthesis takes place.

(D) They transport water and dissolved food throughout the plant.

(E) They protect the plant against the absorption of pesticides and other harmful substances.

41. Which of the following factors is most important in causing Earth's seasons?

(A) tilt of Earth's axis

(B) speed of Earth's rotation

(C) convection cells in the atmosphere

(D) distance from the sun during the year

(E) wavelength of solar radiation received at Earth's surface

42. The map below shows the locations of earthquakes that occurred over a 15-year period.

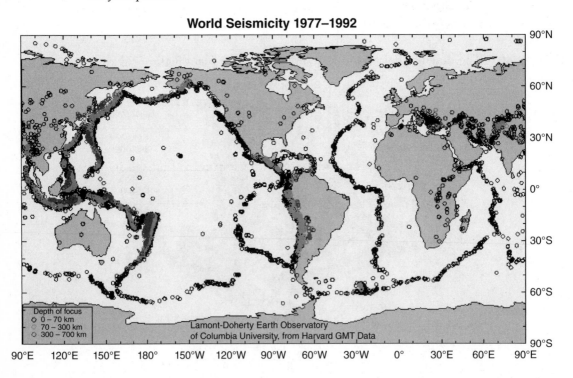

World Seismicity 1977–1992

Which of the following most closely corresponds to the earthquake locations?

(A) locations of hydrothermal vents

(B) locations of oceanic spreading centers

(C) locations of tectonic plate boundaries

(D) locations of mantle plumes and hotspots

(E) locations of boundaries between continental and oceanic crust

43. Hurricanes are powerful tropical cyclones.

What is the source of energy that powers hurricanes?

(A) heavy rainfall caused by changes in land elevation

(B) the collision of a warm air mass and a cold air mass along a frontal boundary

(C) differences in climate due to seasonal changes that occur in the tropics and subtropics

(D) strong winds that are produced as atmospheric high-pressure systems cross the equator

(E) the release of stored heat into the atmosphere as water vapor condensing in rising air

44. Which of the following is mainly caused by the gravitational attraction between Earth and the moon?

(A) eclipses of the moon

(B) mountains and valleys on the moon's surface

(C) ocean tides on Earth

(D) aurora displays (Northern and Southern Lights) in Earth's atmosphere

(E) Earth's magnetic field

Questions 45 and 46 refer to the following diagram showing the distribution of water on Earth.

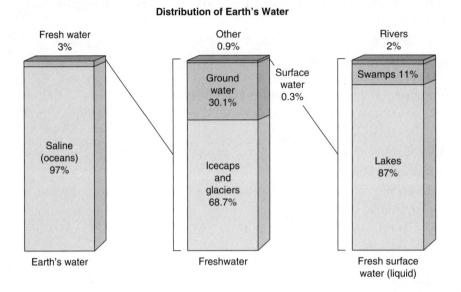

Distribution of Earth's Water

45. About how much of Earth's total water is contained in rivers?

(A) less than 0.3 percent
(B) 2 percent
(C) between 11 percent and 38.6 percent
(D) 17 percent
(E) about 25 percent

46. Where is most of Earth's freshwater located?
(A) groundwater
(B) icecaps and glaciers
(C) rivers
(D) swamps
(E) lakes

47. Geologists study sedimentary rock layers to determine what conditions were like on Earth's surface long ago.

Which of the following ideas are the geologists' conclusions based on?

(A) The rate at which rocks change is constant over time.
(B) The processes operating at Earth's surface today are the same as the ones in the past.

(C) Chemical reactions affecting rocks were slower in the past than they are today.

(D) The types of minerals making up Earth's crust have changed steadily over time.

(E) Sedimentary rocks are unaffected by processes taking place in the atmosphere.

48.   The diagram below shows processes in the rock cycle.

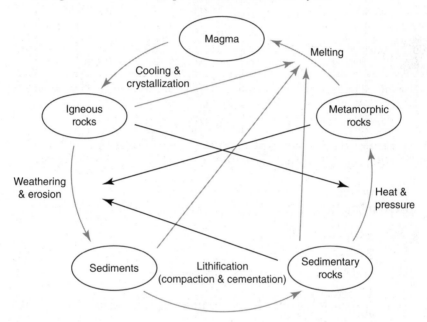

According to the diagram, what is a major source of the sediments that make up sedimentary rocks?

(A) minerals that form as magma cools and crystallizes into solid rock

(B) evaporation of water that leaves behind minerals that had been dissolved in it

(C) compaction and cementation of particles into new rocks

(D) particles derived from metamorphic rocks as they break apart

(E) heat and pressure that change the types of minerals in igneous rock

Questions 49 and 50 refer to the following table of characteristics of planets in the solar system.

Characteristic	Mercury	Venus	Earth	Mars	Jupiter	Saturn	Uranus	Neptune
Diameter (km)	4,878	12,104	12,756	6,787	142,800	120,000	51,118	49,528
Orbital period (Earth years)	0.24	0.62	1	1.88	11.86	29.46	84.01	164.8
Rotation period (in Earth days)	58.65	−243*	1	1.03	0.41	0.44	−0.72*	0.72
Inclination of axis (degrees)	0.0	177.4	23.45	23.98	3.08	26.73	97.92	28.8

*A negative value for the rotation period shows that the direction of rotation of the planet is opposite to the direction in which it orbits the sun.

49. Which of the following planets takes the shortest time to complete one rotation on its axis?

(A) Mercury
(B) Venus
(C) Earth
(D) Mars
(E) Saturn

50. Which of the following planets completes an orbit around the sun in less time than Earth does?

(A) Venus
(B) Jupiter
(C) Saturn
(D) Uranus
(E) Neptune

ANSWERS: SCIENCE

1. **(B)** Convection is heat transfer by the movement of matter; it takes place in liquids and gases. Conduction is heat transfer between objects that are in direct contact. Radiation is energy transfer by electromagnetic waves.

2. **(A)** An applied force must be greater than the force of friction for an object to move across a surface with which it is in contact.

3. **(E)** The temperature and pressure of a gas are directly proportional to each other. If one increases, the other increases.

4. **(C)** Wavelength is the distance between identical points on neighboring cycles of a waveform.

5. **(B)** When the string breaks, the centripetal force that was pulling the ball inward is removed. The ball continues in its direction of movement in a straight line.

6. **(A)** Distance can be determined when the average speed and elapsed time are known. Distance equals speed multiplied by time.

7. **(E)** Mechanical waves are produced by vibrations of particles in a medium. They have a much slower speed than electromagnetic waves, which can travel through a vacuum.

8. **(C)** The line is straight, showing that the relationship between time and distance was constant, but the line has no slope, indicating that distance did not change over time.

9. **(D)** Electrical forces are extremely sensitive to distance. Decreasing the separation distance between particles with opposite charges greatly increases the force of attraction between them.

10. **(B)** Water is a polar molecule, so one end is slightly positive and the other is slightly negative, even though the overall charge of the molecule is neutral. Hydrogen bonds form as the negative end of one molecule is attracted to the positive end of another molecule.

11. **(E)** When properly balanced, the equation shows an equal number of each element on both sides—6 carbon atoms, 14 hydrogen atoms, and 10 oxygen atoms.

12. **(C)** The states of matter of the reactants and products are shown in the equation as being liquid (l), solid (s), or gas (g). The compound C_6H_{14} is in the liquid state, and the element C is in the solid state. In this reaction, H_2O is in the gas state.

13. **(C)** The reaction is a combustion reaction because oxygen reacts with another compound to form carbon dioxide and water. In this case, the combustion is incomplete (insufficient oxygen is available) because elemental carbon and carbon monoxide are also produced.

14. **(B)** A positive ion has more protons than electrons.

15. **(A)** An element that is higher in the activity series (more reactive) will displace an element that is lower in the activity series (less reactive). Copper is higher than silver in the series. Options (B), (C), (D), and (E) give metals that are lower in the series than the metal that might be displaced.

16. **(A)** Ionic bonds form because of the attractive electrostatic force between oppositely charged ions.

17. **(C)** Of the substances, silver has the lowest specific heat capacity. Therefore, the temperature of silver will rise fastest with the addition of thermal energy.

18. **(B)** An atom of an element has the same number of protons and electrons.

19. **(D)** A plant cell has a cell wall and chloroplasts, but an animal cell does not.

20. **(E)** The change in the environment (less frequent fires) made it possible for different types of trees to become dominant, thus changing the pattern of succession.

21. **(D)** Ferns thrive in moist, shady, warm conditions. They are likely to be found in a temperate or tropical forest.

22. **(E)** The diagram shows arrows pointing from deer to both lions and wolves. Both lions and wolves eat deer, so they are in competition for a food resource.

23. **(B)** Of the organisms given, only a lion eats meat.

24. **(C)** Wolves eat deer and cows, so an increase in the wolf population would put downward pressure on the populations of deer and cows first.

25. **(C)** The combustion of fuel, especially oil and coal, by humans greatly affects the concentration of carbon dioxide in the atmosphere. Although humans also affect the growth of plants and animals, these activities do not have as strong an impact on the carbon cycle as the burning of fuel.

26. **(D)** Generations of bacteria can be produced very rapidly, so their populations can adapt to environmental pressures in a fairly short time. Whales take years to reach maturity and produce only one calf at a time, so their reproduction rate is slow.

27. **(C)** The child will inherit one allele that codes for dimples from each parent. There is an equal chance for either the dominant or the recessive allele to be passed to the child.

28. **(A)** A panda is an herbivore (an animal that gets its food from plants) that eats bamboo. A giraffe is an herbivore that eats tree leaves.

29. **(E)** Chlorophyll is a green pigment that uses energy from sunlight to synthesize simple carbohydrates from carbon dioxide and water. Oxygen is a by-product.

30. **(A)** All mammals produce milk for their young. Not all mammals have claws, seek shelter in caves or dens, or have the ability to hibernate. Many marine and freshwater mammals have poor eyesight.

31. **(D)** The lack of the dominant allele allows the recessive trait (absence of the genetically related health disorder) to be expressed. It is not possible to draw any conclusions about the future offspring of the children without knowing the genotype of the other parent.

32. **(B)** A carnivore is an animal that gets its food by eating other animals.

33. **(E)** The Punnett square for the cross is

	g	g
G	Gg	Gg
G	Gg	Gg

Therefore, all of the offspring would inherit a dominant allele from the GG parent. Because the dominant allele codes for gray fur, 100 percent of the offspring would be gray.

34. **(B)** The color of light to which the algae are exposed must be varied among all the colors to test whether a particular color enhances the growth rate.

35. **(D)** Ecological succession is the natural change in the species structure of an ecosystem following a disturbance to the ecosystem (or in the initial colonization of a new habitat).

36. **(B)** The table shows that only option (B) lists organisms in order of their first appearance.

37. **(D)** A hip joint (option D) is a ball-and-socket joint. An elbow (option A) is a hinge joint. A wrist (option B) and spine (option C) have gliding joints. A skull (option E) has fibrous (unmoving) joints.

38. **(E)** The diagram shows that both birds are in the order *Passeriformes* but in different families.

39. **(E)** The northern flicker is least closely related to any of the other birds on the diagram because it is in a separate order from the others.

40. **(A)** The diagram shows carbon dioxide entering the leaf and oxygen exiting. Therefore, stoma allow gases to enter and leave the plant.

41. **(A)** The tilt of Earth's axis causes seasons because it allows for the uneven distribution of solar energy hitting the surface over the course of a year.

42. **(C)** Most earthquakes occur along tectonic plate boundaries.

43. **(E)** The release of latent heat by the condensation of water vapor provides fuel for further intensification of a tropical cyclone. The heated air expands and rises, causing surface air pressure to decrease further.

44. **(C)** Ocean tides are caused mainly by the gravitational attraction between Earth and the moon, with a smaller component being caused by the gravitational attraction between Earth and the sun. Eclipses (option A) are caused by the relative positions of Earth, the moon, and the sun.

45. **(A)** The diagram shows that about 3 percent of Earth's total water is freshwater. Of that, about 0.3 percent is surface water. Rivers account for only a small portion of surface water.

46. **(B)** Only 3 percent of Earth's total water is freshwater. Icecaps and glaciers contain 68.7 percent of the planet's freshwater.

47. **(B)** The principle of uniformitarianism is a basic underpinning of geology. It states that the processes shaping Earth are uniform through time. Therefore, processes that affect the formation of sedimentary rocks today can be used as models for processes that operated in the past.

48. **(D)** Weathering and erosion break down rocks. Sediments derived from existing rocks (sedimentary, igneous, or metamorphic) can be compacted and cemented to form new sedimentary rocks.

49. **(E)** The rotation period of a planet is the length of time required for one complete rotation about its axis. Of the planets listed, Saturn has the shortest rotation period.

50. **(A)** Earth requires one year to complete an orbit around the sun. Venus completes an orbit in about a quarter of the time (0.24 Earth year).

LANGUAGE ARTS, READING

Questions 1–6 refer to the following excerpt from a novel.

What Will His Future Be?

George came down the little incline from the New Willard House at seven o'clock. Tom Willard carried his bag. The son had become taller than the father.

On the station platform, everyone shook the young man's hand. More (5) than a dozen people waited about. George was embarrassed. Gertrude Wilmot, a tall thin woman of fifty who worked in the Winesburg post office, came along the station platform. She had never before paid any attention to George. Now she stopped and put out her hand. In two words she voiced what everyone felt. "Good (10) luck," she said sharply and then, turning, went on her way.

When the train came into the station, George felt relieved. He scampered hurriedly aboard. George glanced up and down the car to be sure no one was looking, then took out his pocket-book and counted his money. His mind was occupied with a desire not to (15) appear green. Almost the last words his father had said to him concerned the matter of his behavior when he got to the city. "Be a sharp one," Tom Willard had said. "Keep your eyes on your money. Be awake. That's the ticket. Don't let anyone think you're a greenhorn."

After George counted his money, he looked out of the window and (20) was surprised to see that the train was still in Winesburg.

The young man, going out of his town to meet the adventure of life, began to think but he did not think of anything very big or dramatic.

He thought of little things—Turk Smollet wheeling boards through the main street of his town in the morning, Butch Wheeler the lamp (25) lighter of Winesburg hurrying through the streets on a summer evening and holding a torch in his hand, Helen White standing by a window in the Winesburg post office and putting a stamp on an envelope.

The young man's mind was carried away by his growing passion for (30) dreams. One looking at him would not have thought him particularly sharp. With the recollection of little things occupying his mind, he closed his eyes and leaned back in the car seat. He stayed that way for a long time, and when he aroused himself and again looked out of the car window, the town of Winesburg had (35) disappeared and his life there had become but a background on which to paint the dreams of his manhood.

—Adapted from *Winesburg, Ohio* by Sherwood Anderson

1. Which of the following words *best* describes what George feels about leaving his hometown?

   (A) indifferent
   (B) frightened
   (C) eager
   (D) sad
   (E) rebellious

2. Why does George feel relieved when the train arrives at the station?

   (A) He can look out and remember what his town looks like.
   (B) He was worried the train would be cancelled.
   (C) He is able to finally get away from his father.
   (D) He can get away from the people who have come to say good-bye.
   (E) He knows that he will be able to get to his destination in time.

3. Which of the following *best* describes what Tom Willard means when he tells George, "Be a sharp one" (lines 16–17)?

   (A) Have a nasty tongue.
   (B) Watch out for your things.
   (C) Improve your mind.
   (D) Do not hurt anyone.
   (E) Keep your clothes neat.

4. Based on the excerpt, what description *best* characterizes the relationship between George and his father?

   (A) They have a strong bond.
   (B) They are both opinionated.
   (C) They have different views of society.
   (D) They both want to escape from their lives.
   (E) They have a distant relationship.

5. Based on the excerpt, what is George *most likely* to do in the future?

   (A) return home on the next train
   (B) fail to find himself
   (C) seek out adventure
   (D) call home immediately
   (E) apply for a job working on a train

6. Which of the following *best* describes the mood created in the excerpt?

   (A) anxious
   (B) dreamy
   (C) humorous
   (D) fanciful
   (E) tragic

Questions 7–12 refer to the following excerpt from a play.

Why Does She Want to Go to Washington?

Scene 1

Rebecca: (Hands her father a flyer) A representative from Girl's Brigade passed this out yesterday at school. She gave a short talk during assembly and answered questions. I want to go, Dad.

Father: Hmm. What's this? "You are invited to a March on Washington . . ." What is this, Rebecca?

Rebecca: A lot of organizations are mobilizing to march in Washington. There will be people coming from all over the country to demonstrate for decent housing and better education and jobs for black people. It's important. And Jamie's parents said she could go. I want to go with her. We can take the train and . . .

Father: Hold on there, young lady. You're telling me you want to go and demonstrate for black people?

Rebecca: Well, it's not just black people . . . it's for everyone. Equality for all people. It's called the March on Washington for Jobs and Freedom. It's the 100th anniversary of the Emancipation Proclamation. You, know. Abraham Lincoln's . . .

Father: (Sharply) I know what the Emancipation Proclamation is! I don't think this is a good idea. You are only 16 years old.)

To go off in a strange city full of people you don't know . . .
it's too dangerous. I don't care what Jamie's parents said,
you are not going.

Rebecca: But Dad, Rev. Davies said in his sermon last Sunday that
the march has the church's endorsement. Bob Dylan and
Joan Baez will be there. And a lot of other famous people.

Father: Bob who? I don't care who is going to be there, you won't.
Besides, it's on a school day. I don't want to talk about it
anymore.

Rebecca: You don't understand anything.

Scene 2

Father: Rebecca, I watched the March on Washington on TV.
Martin Luther King, Jr.'s "I have a dream" speech was very
moving. I liked the part about going back to the ghettos
and slums and changing things.

Rebecca: [sullenly] You wouldn't let me go.

Father: I know. You probably think that I am too stubborn. But I still
think you are too young to be on your own. Plus it was in the
middle of the week. School is important. Still, it would have
been something to be there . . .

Rebecca: [more animated] Maybe there is some group around here
that I can join. I want to help.

Father: That's a good idea. Let's ask Rev. Davies what we can do.

7. Which of the following *best* describes Rebecca?

(A) bitter and resentful
(B) friendly and warm
(C) intelligent and ambitious
(D) sneaky and manipulative
(E) idealistic and caring

8. Based on the information in this excerpt, Rebecca would *most likely*
participate in which of the following activities?

(A) cleaning up her room
(B) going to a baseball game
(C) collecting food for the needy
(D) visiting a veterans hospital
(E) attending a folk music concert

9. Which of the following is the *most likely* reason that Rebecca runs off?

   (A) She needs to get her books from school.
   (B) She was going to see a movie with Jamie.
   (C) She wanted to ask Rev. Davies something.
   (D) She did not like what her father said.
   (E) She smelled something burning in the oven.

10. Which of the following *best* describes the mood of Scene 1?

    (A) lighthearted
    (B) tense
    (C) suspenseful
    (D) harmonious
    (E) sorrowful

11. Which of the following *best* describes how the father felt at the beginning of Scene 2?

    (A) stubborn
    (B) embarrassed
    (C) saddened
    (D) bitter
    (E) vengeful

12. Based on the excerpt, which of the following phrases *best* describes the relationship between Rebecca and her father?

    (A) rebellious and agitated
    (B) distant and formal
    (C) judgmental and turbulent
    (D) close and loving
    (E) fragile and tenuous

Questions 13–17 refer to the following poem.

What Does She Remember About Her Mother?

My mother's hands are cool and fair,
They can do anything.
Delicate mercies hide them there
Like flowers in the spring.

(5) When I was small and could not sleep,
She used to come to me,
And with my cheek upon her hand
How sure my rest would be.

For everything she ever touched
(10) Of beautiful or fine,
Their memories living in her hands
Would warm that sleep of mine.

Her hands remember how they played
One time in meadow streams, —
(15) And all the flickering song and shade
Of water took my dreams.

Swift through her haunted fingers pass
Memories of garden things; —
I dipped my face in flowers and grass
(20) And sounds of hidden wings.

One time she touched the cloud that kissed
Brown pastures bleak and far; —
I leaned my cheek into a mist
And thought I was a star.

(25) All this was very long ago
And I am grown; but yet
The hand that lured my slumber so
I never can forget.

For still when drowsiness comes on
(30) It seems so soft and cool,
Shaped happily beneath my cheek,
Hollow and beautiful.

> —"Her Hands" from *Songs for My Mother*, by Anna Hempstead
> Branch, 1917

13. When does the first part of the poem *most likely* take place?

(A) during the spring
(B) when the child was in a pasture
(C) when the child was in a meadow

(D) when the child was going to sleep

(E) after the poet has grown up

14. Which of the following phrases *best* describes the overall mood of the poem?

(A) lighthearted

(B) nostalgic

(C) confused

(D) contrary

(E) confident

15. Which of the following is the most likely explanation of why the poet uses phrases such as "memories living in her hands" and "haunted fingers" (lines 11 and 17)?

(A) to show that her mother had worked hard in her lifetime

(B) to show that her mother's hands were unattractive

(C) to suggest that her mother's hands were old

(D) to show that her mother was unwell

(E) to suggest that her mother had many experiences

16. What can you infer about the poet's mother?

(A) She had little understanding of nature.

(B) She was a practical woman.

(C) She was always very formal.

(D) She enjoyed comforting her child.

(E) She wanted to travel to foreign lands.

17. If the poet could give advice to a friend about how to help her child go to sleep, which of the following would she be *most likely* to say?

(A) Sing to her.

(B) Tell her a story.

(C) Caress her.

(D) Leave her alone.

(E) Give her warm milk.

Questions 18–22 refer to the following memo.

Why Is Carpooling Important?

Memo: To All Employees

Because the company has grown so fast over the last 12 months, it has become evident that there is often not enough parking for everyone. Many times employees are forced to park on the grass, which, besides being unattractive, does damage to the ground. Adding (5) new parking spaces is expensive and environmentally unfriendly.

Management here at Solarama has therefore decided to take a proactive position regarding carpooling. There are many advantages to carpooling. It helps the environment; you will use less gas and cause fewer emissions. You will save money; by ride sharing, you will end (10) up purchasing less gasoline. It will resolve the company's parking problem. And carpooling will enhance the image of Solarama with our customers and with our community. Let's set an example and make the concept of driving alone a thing of the past!

To that end, we are setting up a system of incentives to reward those (15) who carpool, take a bus, bicycle, or walk to the office. Employees who carpool will be given preferred parking spaces. Those who ride the bus or subways will be given rebates toward the cost of the ticket. Bike racks will be installed in the front. We will start construction next week on locker room and shower facilities and should be (20) completed in two weeks.

In addition, all employees who participate and use alternate means to driving alone to commute to and from the office will receive a reward equal to 1 percent of their net biweekly income on each paycheck for as long as they continue to participate.

(25) Sign-up sheets are now available. A database will be set up so you can easily find those who live near you, and routes will be mapped. Existing bus routes and bike trails will also be mapped. We are very excited here at Solarama with our new carpooling program.

18. Which of the following *best* restates the phrase "To that end" (line 14)?

   (A) Since we have noticed
   (B) In order to solve the problem
   (C) Getting to the end
   (D) Because we want to change
   (E) Ending a phase

19. Based on the memo, what does Solarama *most likely* make?

   (A) children's toys
   (B) ski equipment
   (C) gasoline engines
   (D) photovoltaic panels
   (E) frozen food

20. Which of the following *best* describes the style in which this memo is written?

   (A) technical and dry
   (B) straightforward and detailed
   (C) amusing and humorous
   (D) scholarly and involved
   (E) challenging and overwhelming

21. Based on the memo, who would most likely benefit from the locker and shower facilities?

   (A) employees who ride buses to work
   (B) employees who carpool to work
   (C) employees who bike to work
   (D) employees who ride alone to work
   (E) employees who take public transportation to work

22. Which of the following best describes the way in which the memo is organized?

   (A) by comparing and contrasting information
   (B) by presenting a problem and suggesting a solution
   (C) by discussing familiar terms first, then going on to unfamiliar terms
   (D) by giving a sequence of events
   (E) in no particular order

Questions 23–28 refer to the following excerpt from a short story.

Will Josh's Team Win the Big Game?

Josh woke up early. Today was the big game with Rosentown High, their arch rival. Valley needed this win. The winner would go on to the division semi-finals. And Coach Murphy said Josh would be the closer. He had to pitch his best. He dressed quickly and did his
(5) morning workout routine. Driving to the field, Josh thought how remarkable it was that he would be graduating in just a few more weeks. He crossed his fingers and hoped that there would be some scouts in the bleachers.

As game time approached, Josh headed out to the bullpen. He was
(10) nervous; Rosentown had beaten them last year 5–1. Andy, the starting pitcher, was already warming up. Soon the game started.

The first five innings were a pitcher's duel and the game remained scoreless. During the sixth inning Valley's second baseman, Willie, drove in two runs with a solid home run. When Valley took the field
(15) at the bottom of the seventh inning it was clear that Andy was tiring. Coach Murphy motioned to the bullpen, and Josh began to warm up.

All of a sudden, the bases were loaded. There were no outs. Coach signaled, and Josh headed for the mound. "Throw with confidence," he said as he gave Josh the ball. "Focus on the potential positive of
(20) each pitch. Keep your wrist loose, and remember to follow through." Then he patted him on the back.

Josh fingered the ball in his glove, lining up the seams. He threw; the batter hit an infield pop fly. The next batter quickly took two called strikes. "I can do this," Josh told himself, but inside he was not so sure.
(25) The next pitch he threw was in the dirt. Then two more balls, and the count was full. He wiped the sweat from his forehead. His mouth was dry. His vision seemed blurred. He took a long, deep breath and focused. Coach's words echoed in his mind. "Throw with confidence," he heard his coach say. It was almost hypnotic.

(30) Josh positioned his middle finger and index finger on the ball, wound up, and threw as hard as he could. The batter swung wildly. "Strike three," called the umpire. Josh had thrown a magnificent slider. One out to go, he thought. Again, he heard Coach's voice. And he threw three strikes, all perfect sliders. Valley won 2–0!

23. Which of the following *best* describes the relationship between Josh and Coach Murphy?

    (A) easygoing but distant
    (B) cordial and pleasant
    (C) testy and competitive
    (D) indifferent and cool
    (E) friendly but disciplined

24. Which of the following *best* expresses the main idea of the excerpt?

    (A) A young pitcher could not overcome his nervousness about a big baseball game even though he won it.
    (B) A young pitcher performed well in front of baseball scouts.
    (C) A young pitcher was able to overcome his fears and throw the strikes he needed to win an important game.
    (D) A young pitcher doubted his ability to win an important game.
    (E) A young pitcher threw perfect sliders throughout an important game.

25. Which of the following is the *most likely* reason that the author says, "It was almost hypnotic" (line 29)?

    (A) to suggest that Coach's words were unclear
    (B) to suggest that Coach was not telling Josh the right advice
    (C) to suggest that Josh was feeling sleepy
    (D) to suggest that Coach's words had a deep effect on Josh
    (E) to suggest that Josh did not understand what Coach said

26. Based on the information in this excerpt, how would Josh *most likely* behave during a chess competition?

    He would

    (A) focus completely on each play
    (B) start to get more nervous with every play
    (C) forget the rules of the game
    (D) tell his opponent that he did not stand a chance
    (E) talk a lot during the game

27. Which of the following *best* describes Josh?

(A) a brilliant pitcher who is self-trained
(B) someone who will succeed in college
(C) a hard worker who is able to concentrate
(D) someone who is ambitious and driven
(E) a careful pitcher with little spark

28. Which of the following can you infer about Coach Murphy?

(A) He thinks that coaching is not challenging.
(B) He gets angry at players very easily.
(C) He is a helpful and effective coach.
(D) He does not enjoy coaching.
(E) He worries about whether to take another job.

Questions 29–35 refer to the following excerpt from a novel.

Who Will Get to Use the Car?

"Ted! Will you kindly not interrupt us when we're talking about serious matters!"

"Aw, punk," said Ted. "Ever since somebody slipped up and let you out of college, you've been pulling these nut conversations about
(5) what-nots and so-ons. Are you going to—I want to use the car tonight."

Babbitt, his father, wailed, "Oh, you do! I may want it myself!"
Verona protested, "Oh, you do, Mr. Smarty! I'm going to take it myself!" Tinka cried, "Oh, papa, you said maybe you'd drive us down to Rosedale!" and Mrs. Babbitt, "Careful, Tinka, your sleeve is in the
(10) butter." They glared, and Verona said, "Ted, you're a perfect pig about the car!"

"Course you're not! Not a-tall! You just want to grab it off, right after dinner, and leave it in front of some girl's house all evening while you sit and chat about the men you're going to marry—if only
(15) they'd propose!"

"Well, Dad oughtn't to NEVER let you have it! You and those beastly Jones boys drive like maniacs!"

"Aw, where do you get that stuff! You're so darn scared of the car that you drive uphill with the emergency brake on!"

"(20) I do not! And you—Always talking about how much you know about motors, and Eunice Littlefield told me you said the battery fed the generator!"

"You—why, my good woman, you don't know a generator from a battery." Not unreasonably was Ted lofty with her. He was a natural (25) mechanic, a maker and tinkerer of machines.

"That'll do now!" Babbitt flung in mechanically.

Ted negotiated: "Gee, honest, Rone, I don't want to take the old boat, but I promised a couple of girls in my class I'd drive them down to chorus rehearsal, and, gee, I don't want to, but a (30) gentleman's got to keep his social engagements."

"Well, upon my word! You and your social engagements! In high school!"

"Oh, aren't we select since we went to college! Let me tell you there isn't a private school in the state that's got as swell a bunch as we have."

(35) Somewhat later as it was getting dark, after diplomacies, Ted persuaded Verona to admit that she was merely going to the Armory that evening to see the dog and cat show. She was then, Ted planned, to park the car in front of the candy store across from the Armory and he would pick it up.

—Adapted from *Babbitt* by Sinclair Lewis

29. What is the overall mood of the excerpt?

  (A) congenial
  (B) depressed
  (C) contemplative
  (D) exciting
  (E) argumentative

30. Why is Verona upset?

  (A) She wants to visit her friends, and Ted wants to visit his too.
  (B) Ted thinks her friends are silly.
  (C) She thinks her father favors Ted over her.
  (D) She wants to use the car, and Ted wants to use it too.
  (E) She wants to annoy Ted, but it is not working.

31. Based on the excerpt, what does Ted *most likely* think about his sister?

    (A)   He thinks she should have more friends.
    (B)   He thinks that college ruined her.
    (C)   He believes that she is too ambitious.
    (D)   He wants to be friends, but she makes it difficult.
    (E)   He likes to tease her, but he cares about her.

32. When does the scene in this excerpt take place?

    (A)   right after breakfast
    (B)   late at night
    (C)   in the morning
    (D)   before lunch
    (E)   during dinner

33. Which phrase *best* describes Ted?

    (A)   emotionless and sad
    (B)   humorous but argumentative
    (C)   anxious and shy
    (D)   confused but forgiving
    (E)   careful and controlling

34. What is the most likely meaning of line 32, "Oh, aren't we select since we went to college!"?

    (A)   You chose to go to college, so you should be happier.
    (B)   You think you are perfect because you went to college.
    (C)   You became an outstanding student while at college.
    (D)   You think that college is more important than a social life.
    (E)   You became more socially aware because of college.

35. In which of the following ways are Ted and Verona alike?

    (A)   They are both irritable when they are hungry.
    (B)   They are both worried about their future.
    (C)   They are both worried about each other.
    (D)   They are both helpful and watch over each other.
    (E)   They are both stubborn and want their own way.

Questions 36–40 refer to the following review.

What Does the Critic Think of *Eighth Street*?

With the opening of his first play, *Eighth Street*, last night at the
Orpheum, Hector Clemente promises to be a rising new star on the
theatrical scene. Set in Miami's Little Havana along Calle Ocho, or
Eighth Street, the center of the bustling area that is home to many
(5) Cuban Americans, the play breaks down stereotypes about class
strictures and love.

Isabella, played by the beautiful Emily Garcia, is a student at the
university majoring in art. There she meets Santiago (Jack Bernardo),
a young attorney who also teaches an introductory course on
(10) constitutional law. Bernardo's magnetism radiates on stage, so
much so that young Emily at times blurts out her lines confusedly.

Santiago, the only son of a wealthy bond trader on Wall Street, is
immediately attracted to Isabella, and soon, it is evident they are
falling in love. Much of their dialogue is clichéd and certainly could
(15) be reworked in this reviewer's opinion, as they talk in a trendy
night club in South Beach, but his presence is undeniable.

Act Two opens in Isabella's home, a modest one-story bungalow off
Eighth Street. Her mother, Pilar (Natalie Rivera), has worked hard
her whole life as a hotel maid, raising her daughter by herself. They
(20) argue; Isabella wants to bring Santiago to dinner, but her mother
refuses. "Wasn't Raul good enough for you?" Pilar screams, referring to
Isabella's boyfriend before she went to college. Isabella runs crying
from the house.

The final act takes place in Domino Park. Amid the seated men
(25) playing chess, checkers, and dominoes, Pilar sits apprehensively.
Isabella and Santiago enter. The tension is thick, and the three
heatedly exchange accusations at each other, playing their Latin
temperaments to the hilt. Then Santiago goes down on his knees and
proposes to Isabella. Pilar softens and tears run down her cheeks. She
(30) realizes they are one family now.

Although flawed in some aspects, the play certainly kept the
audience's attention, and there were cheers at the end. I look forward
to Clemente's next play.

36. Which of the following *best* describes the tone of the review?

  (A) fresh and thoughtful
  (B) sarcastic and critical
  (C) humorous and lighthearted
  (D) clever but breezy
  (E) sobering and plodding

37. Which of the following *best* expresses the author's opinion of *Eighth Street?*

  (A) He liked the dialogue but not the plot.
  (B) He thought that Bernardo could have been better.
  (C) He wanted the playwright to make Pilar's role larger.
  (D) He thought it was absorbing.
  (E) He wanted the actors to be more forceful.

38. Which of the following *best* describes the style in which the review is written?

  (A) methodical and trying
  (B) ornate and flowery
  (C) economical and brief
  (D) detailed and professional
  (E) intellectual and technical

39. Based on the information in the review, what can you infer about what the author thinks of Jack Bernardo?

  (A) He thinks he overacts.
  (B) He thinks he has a future in acting.
  (C) He thinks he has great looks.
  (D) He thinks he has excellent communication skills.
  (E) He thinks he has been in a lot of plays.

40. Why does the author include the audience's response to the play?

  (A) to show that most people really liked the play
  (B) to show that the audience had mixed feelings about the play
  (C) to suggest that the audience was filled with friends of the actors
  (D) to suggest that the audience was new to theater
  (E) to show that the audience did not agree with him

ANSWERS: LANGUAGE ARTS, READING

1. **(C)** Option (C) is the best choice; George is relieved to get on the train and dreams of adulthood. Options (A) and (B) are incorrect; there is nothing in the passage that indicates indifference or fear. Option (D) is incorrect; he does not seem sad to be leaving. Option (E) is wrong because he does not appear to be rebellious in any way.

2. **(D)** Option (D) is correct. The excerpt clearly states the he "was embarrassed" by all the people who had come to say good-bye. There is no indication that option (A) is true. Options (B) and (C) cannot be correct because there is no mention of the train being cancelled or that he wants to get away from his father. And although the train may or may not arrive on time, this is not mentioned, so option (E) is incorrect.

3. **(B)** Option (B) is correct. In this context, *sharp* connotes being observant. Option (A) is incorrect because, although the word *sharp* can have this meaning, it makes no sense here. Options (C) and (E) could be possible connotations of *sharp*, but there is no evidence that this is what his father meant. Option (D) could be a possibility, but it is not the best answer in the context of the excerpt.

4. **(A)** Option (A) is correct. The father and son are clearly close to each other; the father offers advice and the son accepts without question. Father and son may be opinionated, but there is nothing in the passage to indicate that, so option (B) is incorrect. There is no mention of either's views of society (option C). While George may feel he is escaping from his life, option (D) is incorrect because there is no mention of his father's desire to do the same. Option (E) is incorrect because the passage clearly shows that there is a strong relationship between them.

5. **(C)** Option (C) is correct. George is setting out "to paint the dreams of his manhood." Option (A) cannot be correct as there is little likelihood that he will return anytime soon. Perhaps in the end he will fail to find himself, but there is nothing in the excerpt to support that conclusion (option B). Option (D) is wrong because there is no suggestion that he will call home immediately. And there is no mention of him wanting to work on a train; therefore, option (E) is incorrect.

6. **(B)** Option (B) is correct. The final paragraph confirms a dreamy mood. Option (A) is incorrect because George does not seem anxious, even

though he is nervous about his money. The passage might be considered slightly humorous, but this is not its mood, so option (C) is also incorrect. Option (D) is wrong because there is no suggestion of anything fanciful. And there is nothing to indicate a tone of tragedy in the passage, so option (E) cannot be correct.

7. **(E)** Option (E) is correct; her desire to participate in the march and her wish to help those who are less fortunate tell the reader that she is idealistic and caring. There is no evidence that she has any bitterness or resentment, so option (A) is incorrect. She may be friendly and warm, and intelligent and ambitious, but those traits are not shown in the excerpt, so options (B) and (C) cannot be correct. And there is nothing to suggest that she is sneaky (option D).

8. **(C)** Option (C) is correct. Rebecca says in Scene 2, "I want to help," so donating to the needy would most likely appeal to an idealistic person. Cleaning her room might be something she has to do but not something she want to do, so option (A) is incorrect. Option (B) is incorrect because going to a baseball game is not a selfless act. While visiting a hospital might be something a caring person would do, there is not enough evidence to conclude that, so option (D) is wrong. Although folk musicians are mentioned (option E), this is not the most likely choice.

9. **(D)** Option (D) is correct because Rebecca was upset her father would not let her go to the march. Option (A) is incorrect because nothing is mentioned about books at school. There is no evidence she was going to see a movie (option B). Although she talks about Rev. Davies, there is nothing to suggest she wanted to ask him a question (option C). Option (E) is incorrect because there is nothing in the excerpt about cooking.

10. **(B)** Option (B) is correct; Rebecca and her father are disagreeing, and the scene is full of conflict. Option (A) is wrong because there is nothing lighthearted in the exchange. Nor is there any suspense (option C). The mood of the scene is the opposite of harmonious, so option (D) is incorrect. And although Rebecca may be sorry she can't go to the march (option E), that is not the mood of the scene.

11. **(B)** Option (B) is correct because Rebecca's father admits that Martin Luther King, Jr., gave a "moving" speech, and he realizes it would have been a good experience for Rebecca to have gone to the march. Option (A) is incorrect because he was stubborn in Scene 1 but not in Scene 2. There is no evidence the father felt saddened (option C). Options (D) and (E) have no basis in the excerpt.

12. **(D)** Option (D) is correct; their dialogue shows a close and loving bond, especially in Scene 2. Option (A) is not correct; Rebecca may be rebellious when her father refuses to let her go to Washington, but she does obey him. They do not have a distant and formal relationship (option B). There also is no evidence of a judgmental or fragile relationship (options C and E).

13. **(D)** Option (D) is correct; the poet is remembering when she was "small and could not sleep." Option (A) is incorrect; the poet only compares the touch of her mother's hand to flowers in the spring. Options (B) and (C) are incorrect; meadows and pastures are used as metaphors to describe the child's dreams. Option (E) is incorrect because it is at the end of the poem that the child is grown up.

14. **(B)** Option (B) is correct because the poet talks of "Memories of garden things," which strongly suggests that she is nostalgic. Option (A) is wrong because there are no lines that suggest lightheartedness. Likewise, nothing in the poem indicates confusion (option C). Options (D) and (E) are incorrect because the poet is neither contrary nor confident in tone.

15. **(E)** The phrases in option (E) serve to reinforce the image that the poet's mother had experienced life to the fullest. Option (A) cannot be correct because there is no mention of her mother working. The poet never describes her mother's hands as either unattractive or old (options B and C). Option (D) is obviously wrong; if anything, the poem suggests that her mother was healthy and vibrant.

16. **(D)** Option (D) is correct; the entire poem describes the many ways the mother comforted her child. Contrary to option (A), it is evident that the mother had a great understanding of nature. Option (B) is incorrect because, although the poet's mother may have been practical, there is nothing in the poem that says this. Option (C) is incorrect because nothing in the poem shows the mother as formal. The mother could have wanted to travel to foreign lands (option E), but the poem only talks of her attention to her child.

17. **(C)** Option (C) is correct because the entire poem is about the mother's hands and how comforting they were. The poet's mother may also have sung to her, but it is not mentioned in the poem (option A). Similarly, the poem does not talk of her telling a story (option B) or giving her child warm milk (option E). Option (D) is incorrect because the mother is with her child in each stanza.

18. **(B)** Option (B) is correct; the phrase is a continuation of the company's decision from the previous paragraph: "to take a proactive position regarding carpooling." Option (A) doesn't logically follow the idea of the previous paragraph. Options (C) and (E) are incorrect; they don't make any sense in the context of the sentence. Option (D) is incorrect, because the idea is *to solve* and not *to change*.

19. **(D)** Option (D) is correct; because the company's name has *solar* in it, it follows that it would make solar photovoltaic panels. The name Solarama does not suggest either toys (option A) or ski equipment (option B). Option (C) is incorrect because it is illogical that a company that manufactures gasoline engines would be interested in saving gasoline through carpooling. Option (E) is also wrong; frozen food is not associated with anything solar.

20. **(B)** Option (B) is correct; the main idea is presented clearly, with detailed information. Option (A) is incorrect because no technical details are included. Option (C) is incorrect because the memo is not humorous but factual. Option (D) is wrong since nothing scholarly is presented, just easy-to-understand facts. And Option (E) is incorrect; there is nothing overwhelming or difficult to understand in the memo.

21. **(C)** Option (C) is correct; those who bike to work would need to freshen up and change clothes, especially in the warmer months. Employees who ride buses (option A) or carpool (option B) to work would not need to change clothes. Option (D) is incorrect; the main idea of the memo is to encourage carpooling, not to drive alone. Option (E) is incorrect because *public transportation* and *buses* are synonymous.

22. **(B)** Option (B) is correct; the problem is lack of parking, and the solution is carpooling, public transportation, biking, or walking. None of the other options correctly describe the organization of the excerpt.

23. **(E)** Option (E) is correct; the coach is friendly but keeps a professional attitude with Josh, and Josh takes his words to heart. Option (A) is incorrect; the relationship seems easygoing, but there is no distance between them. Option (B) could be a possible choice, but it misses the professional advice Coach gives Josh, so it is incorrect. Options (C) and (D) are wrong because there is no evidence of testiness or indifference in their relationship.

24. **(C)** Option (C) is correct; the pitcher was able to overcome his nervousness and come through with some big pitches. This is the main idea of the excerpt. Option (A) is incorrect because Josh overcame his nervousness and did not give in to it. Although scouts are mentioned, it is not clear whether there actually were scouts at the game (option B), and this is not the main idea. Although the pitcher did doubt if he could win (option D), this is not the main idea. Option (E) is incorrect because he did not throw perfect sliders all the time; some of his pitches were in the dirt or were balls.

25. **(D)** Option (D) is correct. The author uses the adjective *hypnotic* to reinforce the idea that Josh completely and unconsciously accepted Coach's words to throw confidently. Option (A) is incorrect because *hypnotic* is not synonymous with *unclear*. Option (B) is incorrect because it does not make sense. It is not logical that a pitcher would feel sleepy while pitching (option C). Option (E) is incorrect because *hypnotic* does not mean a lack of understanding.

26. **(A)** Option (A) is correct since Josh is portrayed as someone who concentrates deeply on what he is doing. Option (B) is incorrect because he did overcome his nervousness on the mound and would do the same if he were playing chess. There is no evidence in the excerpt that Josh would forget the rules of the game, so option (C) is incorrect. Josh does not challenge his opponent when he plays baseball (option D) and he is not talkative (option E), so he would most likely act the same way if he played chess.

27. **(C)** Option (C) is correct; Josh is portrayed as someone who works hard at pitching and can concentrate on getting the job done. While he may be a brilliant pitcher, there is no evidence in the passage that he is self-trained, so option (A) is incorrect. The reader has no way of knowing if he will succeed in college (option B). Josh may be ambitious, but he is not described as driven (option D) in the excerpt. Option (E) is incorrect because he has quite a bit of spark and energy.

28. **(C)** Option (C) is correct because the coach says the right things to Josh to calm him down. There is no evidence that he thinks coaching is not challenging (option A), and he does not display any anger in the excerpt (option B). Option (D) is incorrect because he is portrayed as a good and understanding coach. Option (E) is wrong because the excerpt never mentions that the coach might be thinking about taking another job.

29. **(E)** Option (E) is correct; the overall mood is combative as Ted and Verona argue over who will get the car that night. Option (A) is incorrect

because, while they may be congenial most of the time, there is no evidence that the family is congenial in the excerpt. The mood is not depressed because their words do not evoke depression (option B). Option (C) is incorrect, as there is no hint of contemplation. Although Ted seems somewhat excitable, the mood of the excerpt is not exciting (option D).

30. **(D)** Option (D) is correct because they both have plans to go out for the evening. Option (A) is incorrect because this is not the issue; who is going to get the car is the issue. Option (B) is wrong because, while Ted does somewhat insult her friends, he does it after they have started fighting, so this is not the reason she is upset. Option (C) is wrong; there is no evidence to suggest that Verona thinks her father favors Ted. Nor is she just trying to annoy Ted (option E); she wants to use the car.

31. **(E)** Option (E) is correct. Ted is definitely teasing his sister, with phrases like "you drive uphill with the emergency brake on!" Yet he obviously cares about her as well. Option (A) is incorrect; there is nothing in the passage to indicate he thinks she should have more friends. Option (B) is wrong; if anything, he is a little jealous of her going off to college. Option (C) is incorrect because there is no evidence that indicates he thinks she is too ambitious. Option (D) is also wrong; they *are* friends, and he is teasing her.

32. **(E)** Option (E) is correct; Mrs. Babbitt says to Verona's sister Trinka, "Your sleeve is in the butter." Later, the excerpt states that it was getting dark, which makes option (B) incorrect; they are talking about later that evening, not late at night. Options (C) and (D) are illogical; the time frame is right after dinner.

33. **(B)** Option (B) is correct; Ted is portrayed as having a sense of humor but also as being quarrelsome. He is certainly emotional, which negates option (A). Option (C) is incorrect because there is nothing shy about him. He does not seem confused (option D), and there is nothing in the excerpt to suggest that he is careful and controlling (option E).

34. **(B)** Option (B) is correct because the way in which *select* is used indicates superiority or perfection. Option (A) is incorrect; there nothing in the passage to indicate that Verona went to college to be happier. Although she may be an outstanding student (option C), there is nothing in the excerpt about that. There is also no evidence that Verona thinks college is more important than a social life (option D). Option (E) is incorrect because she does not talk about her life at college, so we cannot know how socially aware she is.

35. **(E)** Option (E) is correct because they fight over who will get to use the car and refuse to give up. Option (A) is incorrect because there is no evidence that they are irritable because they are hungry. Options (B) and (C) are wrong because no worry is expressed in the passage about either's future or that one is worried about the other. Perhaps they do watch over each other, but that is not indicated; they don't seem particularly helpful either, so option (D) is incorrect.

36. **(A)** This is the best description of the review. The reviewer seems very thoughtful about the play and the characters in it. The writing is not trite or used. Option (B) is not correct because, while the reviewer does criticize some aspects of the play, that is not the overall tone of his review, and the review is definitely not sarcastic. Option (C) does not seem correct; the tone is not lighthearted but rather serious. Neither option (D) nor option (E) is correct either; the review is not breezy or plodding.

37. **(D)** Option (D) is correct; the playwright says the play kept the audience's attention. Option (A) is wrong; the reviewer thought some of the dialogue was clichéd. He thought the opposite of option (B). He did not say anything about making Pilar's role larger, so option (C) is wrong. He also did not say or suggest the idea in option (E).

38. **(D)** The reviewer seems to know a lot about theater and is detailed in his review, so option (D) is correct. The review does not seem methodical or trying, and it is certainly not ornate or flowery, so options (A) and (B) are wrong. The review also does not seem brief, intellectual, or technical, so options (C) and (E) are both incorrect.

39. **(B)** The reviewer talks about Bernardo's magnetism. He certainly likes him as an actor, so option (B) is the most likely choice. While Bernardo has a strong magnetism, the reviewer does not think he overacts, so option (A) cannot be true. Option (C) might be true, but there is nothing in the review to suggest this. Neither option (D) nor option (E) is indicated by the review.

40. **(A)** Option (A) is the best answer. Option (B) is definitely incorrect; the audience liked the play. There is no suggestion that the audience was filled with friends of the actors, so option (C) is wrong. Option (D) is not indicated by the review, and option (E) is wrong as well since the reviewer liked the play in spite of some flaws.

MATH
PART 1 (calculators allowed)

1. A rectangular storage bin is 3 feet wide, 6 feet long, and 3 feet tall. If ⅔ of the bin is filled with animal feed, how many cubic feet of animal feed are stored in the container?

    (A) 9
    (B) 12
    (C) 18
    (D) 36
    (E) 54

2. A company charges a late fee as a percentage of the bill. If a customer's bill is $125 and the late fee is $3.75, what percentage does the company charge?

    (A) 3.00%
    (B) 3.75%
    (C) 4.00%
    (D) 7.50%
    (E) 35.75%

3. To rent a car, Cindy must pay $15 a day plus 5 cents for every mile she drives. In dollars, what is her final bill if she rents a car for 3 days and drives a total of 50 miles?

Age (in years)	Frequency of Attendance
Younger than 10	12
10 to 14	8
15 to 20	1
Older than 20	18

4. The table above represents the ages of people attending a child's birthday party. If a person is randomly selected from the group, what is the probability that the person is younger than 10 years old?

5. If $2x + 2y = 10$, then $x + y =$

(A) 2
(B) 5
(C) 6
(D) 8
(E) 12

6. Which of the following is a solution of $7 - 5x \leq 42$?

(A) −12
(B) −10

(C) –8
(D) –7
(E) –6

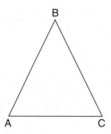

7.   In the diagram above, the measures of angle A and angle C are 60 degrees. If the length of AB is 12, what is the length of AC?

(A) 12
(B) 6
(C) 4
(D) 3
(E) 1

8.   A teacher has determined that, at most, only two students should share a computer at a time. If she has 21 students, what is the smallest number of computers she should have available to students?

9. A backyard pool measures 6 feet wide and 10 feet long. How many feet of safety fencing are required to surround the entire perimeter of the pool?

   (A) 16
   (B) 22
   (C) 26
   (D) 32
   (E) 60

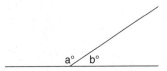

10. In the diagram above, angles a and b are along a straight line. If the measure of angle a is 130 degrees, what is the measure of angle b?

    (A) 30
    (B) 40
    (C) 50
    (D) 60
    (E) 80

11. At a company picnic, 25 percent of the people attending are managers. If there are 300 managers, how many people, in total, are attending the picnic?

    (A) 25
    (B) 75
    (C) 100
    (D) 120
    (E) 750

12. A train can travel 125 kilometers in 2½ hours. If the train maintains the same speed, how many hours will it take to travel 400 kilometers?

    (A) 20
    (B) 16
    (C) 8
    (D) 4
    (E) 2

13. Which of the following is equivalent to $9x^2 - 5x + 3x$?

    (A) $9x^2 - 2x$
    (B) $9x^2 - 8x$
    (C) $17x^2 - x$
    (D) $7x^2$
    (E) $17x^2$

14. Gary purchased 3 shirts that cost $9.99 each, 2 pairs of pants that cost $14.99 each, and 1 hat that cost $12.99. Assuming a 3 percent sales tax is charged on all items, what was the total cost of Gary's purchases?

15. Jacob plays chess regularly with his friends. On each of 5 days last week, he played 14, 15, 19, 20, and 25 games. What was the average number of games he played per day?

    (A) 17
    (B) 18.6
    (C) 23.3
    (D) 31
    (E) 93

16. The interest on a simple interest loan was $45. If the loan term was 6 months at 8%, how much, in dollars, was borrowed?

   (A) 2,160
   (B) 1,125
   (C) 1,080
   (D) 563
   (E) 360

17. Using the number line above, what is the value of A – B?

   (A) –2½
   (B) –2¼
   (C) –1¼
   (D) 1¼
   (E) 2¼

18. The average of 5 and x is 10. What is the value of x?

19. Amy is planning a wedding and has decided that she will provide each of her 38 guests with 2 small gift bags. If the gift bags are $10.50 each, how many dollars in total will she spend on the gift bags?

    (A) 398
    (B) 420
    (C) 475
    (D) 798
    (E) 855

20. Hank has a total of 58 sports cards in his collection. His collection consists of only football and baseball cards, and he has 14 more baseball cards than football cards. How many football cards are in Hank's collection?

    (A) 22
    (B) 36
    (C) 40
    (D) 44
    (E) 72

21. Last year, a newspaper reached 35,000 households a day. If circulation is down 20 percent, how many households a day does the newspaper currently reach?

    (A) 7,000
    (B) 17,500
    (C) 16,560
    (D) 28,000
    (E) 34,980

22. If $\frac{1}{4}x + 1 = 8$, then $x =$

    (A) 36
    (B) 32
    (C) 28
    (D) 18
    (E) 12

23. The value of a is directly proportional to the value of b. If $a = 21$ when $b = 3$, what is the value of a when $b = 5$?

    (A) 18
    (B) 23
    (C) 24
    (D) 29
    (E) 35

24. A business owner pays a graphic designer a flat fee of x dollars plus y dollars per hour to design her logo. If the designer takes t hours to complete the logo, which of the following represents the business owner's cost?

    (A) $t(x + y)$
    (B) $tx + y$
    (C) $x + ty$
    (D) $x + y$
    (E) $x + y + t$

25. While he is at work, Jackson receives 4 e-mails an hour from an automated monitoring service. If he works 8 hours a day, how many e-mails will he receive from this service in 6 work days?

    (A) 18
    (B) 24
    (C) 32
    (D) 192
    (E) 208

Part 2 (no calculators)

26. If $n = -5$, then $n^2 - 1 =$

    (A) –26
    (B) –11
    (C) 9
    (D) 10
    (E) 24

Questions 27 and 28 refer to the graph below, which represents the number of customers per week for the first five weeks a hardware store was open.

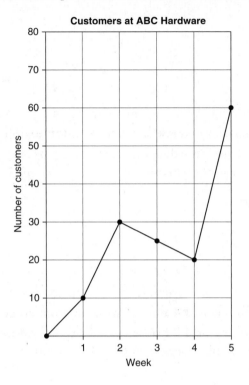

Customers at ABC Hardware

27. In total, how many customers did the store have in its first five weeks?

   (A) 80
   (B) 95
   (C) 140
   (D) 145
   (E) 310

28. In which week were there the fewest customers?

   (A) Week 1
   (B) Week 2
   (C) Week 3
   (D) Week 4
   (E) Week 5

29. Which of the following is equivalent to $(x + 5)(x - 5)$?

    (A) $x^2 - 25$
    (B) $x^2 - 10$
    (C) $x^2 + 10x - 25$
    (D) $x^2 + 10x - 10$
    (E) $x^2 - 10x - 10$

30. Crystal earns a $5 commission for every customer she refers to her bank. If she earned $65 in commissions last week, how many customers did she refer?

    (A) 11
    (B) 12
    (C) 13
    (D) 14
    (E) 15

31. A summer camp's policy states that there must be 3 camp counselors for every field trip. Additionally, there must be 2 assistants for every 10 campers on the trip. If c campers will be going on a field trip, which of the following represents the number of assistants that will be required?

    (A) $c/5$
    (B) $5c$
    (C) $10c + 2$
    (D) $2c + 10$
    (E) $5c + 2$

Total Entertainment Center Orders in the First Quarter			
	Model A	**Model B**	**Total**
Design 1	150	120	270
Design 2	200	30	230
Total	350	150	500

32. The table above represents the different types of entertainment centers ordered from a furniture company in the first quarter of the year. What fraction of orders was for Model A?

(A) ³⁄₁₀
(B) ²⁄₅
(C) ³⁄₅
(D) ⁷⁄₁₀
(E) ⁴⁄₅

33. Plot the point on the line $2x + 5y = 10$ where $x = 10$.

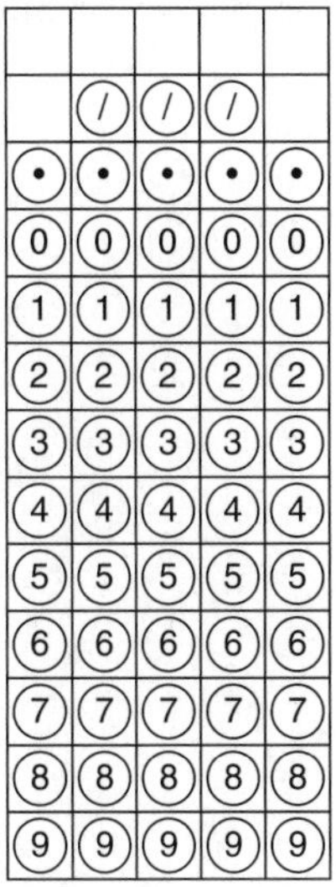

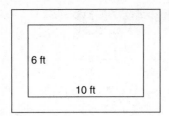

34. A concrete walkway will be installed around a garden with the measurements shown in the figure above. If the walkway will be *m* feet wide, which of the following expressions represents its area?

(A) $60 + 16m + m^2$
(B) $60 + 32m + 4m^2$
(C) $16m + m^2$
(D) $20m + m^2$
(E) $32m + 4m^2$

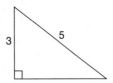

35. What is the area of the triangle pictured above?

36. The median of 4, 7, 10, 12, and x is 7. What is the largest possible value of x?

(A) 0
(B) 4
(C) 7
(D) 10
(E) 12

37. What is the x-coordinate of the point where $y = 3x - 9$ crosses the x-axis?

(A) –9
(B) –3
(C) 0
(D) 3
(E) 9

38. A restaurant's lunch special allows customers to pick from 3 soups, 6 sandwiches, and 4 desserts. How many soup, sandwich, and dessert combinations are possible?

(A) 13
(B) 22
(C) 25
(D) 68
(E) 72

39. What is the value of $\left(\frac{2}{3}\right)^3$?

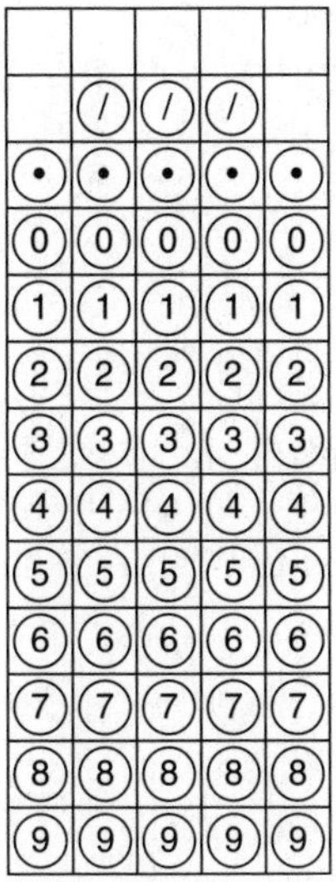

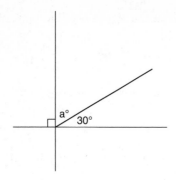

40. In the figure above, what is the value of *a*?

   (A) 30
   (B) 40
   (C) 45
   (D) 60
   (E) 90

41. Which of the following is equivalent to 5.1×10^{-3}?

   (A) 0.00051
   (B) 0.0051
   (C) 0.051
   (D) 5,100
   (E) 51,000

42. A 64-ounce bottle of soda costs $1.59. Which of the following represents the cost of a single ounce of this soda, in dollars?

   (A) 64(1.59)
   (B) 64 − 1.59
   (C) $^{1.59}\!/_{64}$
   (D) 64 + 1.59
   (E) $^{64}\!/_{1.59}$

43. The area of triangle A is 4. The height of triangle B is twice that of triangle A, and the length of the base of triangle B is the same as that of triangle A. What is the area of triangle B?

   (A) 2
   (B) 4

(C) 8

(D) 16

(E) 32

44. What is the slope of the line that passes through the points (0, 0) and (2, 5)?

(A) $-\frac{5}{2}$

(B) $-\frac{2}{5}$

(C) 0

(D) $\frac{2}{5}$

(E) $\frac{5}{2}$

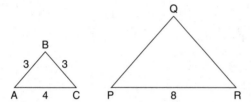

45. The triangles in the figure above are similar. What is the perimeter of triangle PQR?

(A) 10

(B) 14

(C) 16

(D) 20

(E) 48

46. Carey's washing machine required repair, and the bill was $150 plus an 8 percent restocking fee for parts the repairman had to use. What was the total repair bill, in dollars?

(A) 142

(B) 158

(C) 162

(D) 166

(E) 178

47. An exercise set comes with 10-pound and 25-pound weights. Which of the following represents the total weight of x 10-pound weights and y 25-pound weights?

(A) $35xy$
(B) $35(x+y)$
(C) $35x+y$
(D) $10x+25y$
(E) $x+y+35$

48. The longest side of a triangle is 10 units long and the shortest side is 6 units long. If the largest angle in the triangle is 90 degrees, what is the length of the remaining side of the triangle?

(A) 4
(B) 6
(C) 5
(D) 7
(E) 8

49. What is the product of $4x^2$ and $5x^4$?

(A) $9x^8$
(B) $20x^8$
(C) $9x^6$
(D) $20x^6$
(E) $9x^2$

50. If $\dfrac{x}{6} = \frac{1}{2}$, what is the value of x?

(A) 2
(B) 3
(C) 12
(D) 20
(E) 24

ANSWERS: MATH

1. **(D)** The volume of the entire bin is $3 \times 6 \times 3 = 54$ cubic feet. The two-thirds that are filled accounts for $\frac{2}{3} \times 54 = 36$ cubic feet of the storage.

2. **(A)** Let x represent the percentage the company charges. Translating the given information into an equation yields $125x = 3.75$. The solution is found by dividing both sides by 125.

3. **$47.50** The charge for the 3 days is $15 \times 3 = 45$, while the charge for the 50 miles is $0.05 \times 50 = 2.5$. Finally, the total is $45 + 2.5 = 47.5$.

4. **0.3077** The probability is found by dividing the frequency by the total. In this case, $\dfrac{12}{12+8+1+18} = 0.3077$.

5. **(B)** Both of the terms $2x$ and $2y$ share a factor of 2. When this is factored out, the equation becomes $2(x+y) = 10$. Dividing both sides by 2 yields the equation $x + y = 5$.

6. **(E)** When solving the inequality, remember that the direction will change if you divide or multiply by a negative number. The inequality $7 - 5x \leq 42$ is equivalent to the inequality $x \geq -6$. Only option (E) satisfies the resulting inequality.

7. **(A)** Since the measures of angles A and C are 60 degrees, the measure of angle B must be $180 - 60 - 60 = 60$. When all three angles in a triangle are equal, the lengths of all of the sides are also equal.

8. **11** $21 \div 2 = 10.5$, but it isn't possible to have half a computer. To make sure there are enough, round up to 11.

9. **(D)** The perimeter is the sum of the lengths of all the sides: $6 + 10 + 6 + 10 = 32$.

10. **(C)** Two angles along a straight line must have a sum of 180 degrees. The measure of angle b is $180 - 130 = 50$.

11. **(B)** $300 \times \frac{25}{100} = 75$.

12. **(C)** The train is traveling at a speed of $125 \div 2\frac{1}{2} = 125 \div 2.5 = 50$ kilometers per hour, and it will take the train $400 \div 50 = 8$ hours to travel 400 kilometers.

13. **(A)** Only terms with the same exponent and same variable can be combined. Thus, $9x^2 - 5x + 3x = 9x^2 + (-5 + 3)x = 9x^2 - 2x$.

14. **$75.13** Before tax, Gary's total was $3(9.99) + 2(14.99) + 12.99 = 72.94$. To find the value after tax, multiply 72.94 by 1.03 to get the final answer.

15. **(B)** The average is found by adding all of the values and dividing by the number of values: $\dfrac{14 + 15 + 19 + 20 + 25}{5} = 18.6$.

16. **(B)** The formula for the interest on a simple interest loan is $I = Prt$ where t is in years. In this case, $45 = P(0.08)(\frac{6}{12})$ where P represents the principal, or amount borrowed. Solving for P yields the final answer of 1,125.

17. **(B)** The space between 0 and 1 has 3 tick marks representing $\frac{1}{4}$, $\frac{1}{2}$, $\frac{3}{4}$, and the point B is on the tick mark representing $\frac{1}{4}$. The value of A − B is $-2 - \frac{1}{4} = -2\frac{1}{4}$.

18. **15** If the average of 5 and x is 10, then $\dfrac{x + 5}{2} = 10$. This equation has a solution of $x = 15$.

19. **(D)** Amy will need to buy a total of $38 \times 2 = 76$ gift bags for a total cost of $76 \times 10.5 = \$798$.

20. **(A)** Let f represent the number of football cards and b the number of baseball cards in Hank's collection. Since there is a total of 58 cards, $f + b = 58$. Also, since there are 14 more baseball cards than football cards, $b = 14 + f$. Substituting the second equation into the first yields the equation $f + 14 + f = 58$. In other words, $2f = 44$ and $f = 22$.

21. **(D)** The total reduction in circulation is $\frac{20}{100} \times 35,000 = 7,000$. Therefore, the current circulation is $35,000 - 7,000 = 28,000$.

22. **(C)** Subtract 1 from both sides of the equation to get $\frac{1}{4}x = 7$ and then multiply both sides of the equation by 4 to get $x = 28$.

23. **(E)** If a is directly proportional to b, there is a number k such that $a = bk$. You know that a is 21 when b is 3 and plugging this into the statement above will give you the value of k, which is 7. Therefore, $a = 7b$, and when b is 5, a is $5 \times 7 = 35$.

24. **(C)** Only y depends on the number of hours (t). The total hourly pay will be yt, and the total pay will include the flat fee of x dollars, giving a total fee of $x + yt$.

25. **(D)** Jackson receives $4 \times 8 = 32$ e-mails a day. Therefore, over 6 days, he will receive $6 \times 32 = 192$ e-mails.

26. **(E)** $(-5)^2 - 1 = 25 - 1 = 24$.

27. **(D)** $10 + 30 + 25 + 20 + 60 = 145$.

28. **(A)** Week 1 had only 10 customers.

29. **(A)** Use FOIL to multiply the two binomials: $(x + 5)(x - 5) = x^2 - 5x + 5x - 25 = x^2 - 25$.

30. **(C)** The total commission Crystal will earn is $5 for each customer, or 5 times the number of customers. Since you know her commission is $65, you can divide by 5 to find that the number of customers is 13.

31. **(A)** If x represents the number of assistants, the equation $\frac{2}{10} = \frac{x}{c}$ can represent the information we are given. Cross multiplying and solving for x yields:

$$2c = 10x$$

$$x = \frac{2c}{10} = \frac{c}{5}$$

32. **(D)** 350 of the 500 orders were for model A. As a fraction, this is $\frac{350}{500} = \frac{35}{50} = \frac{7}{10}$.

33. **(10, –2)** When $x = 10$, $2(10) + 5y = 10$ and $y = -2$. The point plotted should therefore be $(10, -2)$.

34. **(C)** The area of the larger rectangle is $(6 + m)(10 + m)$ and the area of the garden is $6 \times 10 = 60$ square feet. The area of the walkway is the area left over when the garden area is subtracted from the larger rectangular area: $(6 + m)(10 + m) - 60 = 60 + 16m + m^2 - 60 = 16m + m^2$.

35. **10** The area of any triangle is $\frac{1}{2}bh$ where b represents the length of the base and h represents the height. Here, you have the height but not the base. However, since the triangle is a right triangle, you can find the length of the base with the Pythagorean theorem: $3^2 + b^2 = 5^2$. Solving this, $b = 4$, and the area is $\frac{1}{2} \times 4 \times 5 = 10$.

36. **7** The median is the middle value when all of the values are put in order from least to greatest. Ignoring x and placing these numbers in order, you get the list: 4, 7, 10, 12. For 7 to be the median when x is placed in the list, 7 must be in the middle. This means the x must be to the left of 7 in the list. The largest possible value that will allow this to occur is if $x = 7$.

37. **(D)** When the line crosses the x-axis, the value of y is 0. Using this in the equation, you will find $0 = 3x - 9$ or $x = 3$.

38. **(E)** There are a total of $3 \times 6 \times 4$ combinations possible.

39. $$\left(\frac{2}{3}\right)^3 = \frac{2^3}{3^3} = \frac{2 \times 2 \times 2}{3 \times 3 \times 3} = \frac{8}{27}.$$

40. **(D)** The sum of $a + 30 = 90$ since the two combined are opposite a 90-degree angle. Therefore, $a = 90 - 30 = 60$.

41. **(B)** The -3 exponent on the 10 tells you to move the decimal to the left 3 digits to get 0.0051.

42. **(C)** To find the unit cost, divide the total cost by the number of ounces, 64.

43. **(C)** The area of triangle A is 4, so if we call the height of triangle A h and the base b, $\frac{1}{2}bh = 4$. Since the height of triangle B is twice the height of triangle A, and the length of the base is the same, the area of triangle B is $\frac{1}{2}b(2h) = bh = 8$.

44. **(E)** $m = \dfrac{5-0}{2-0}$.

45. **(D)** Since triangle ABC is similar to triangle PQR, there is a single number you can multiply each side of ABC by to get the length of the corresponding side in PQR. If you notice that AB has a length of 4 while PR has a length of 8, you can see that multiplier is 2. This means that the length of PQ and QR are both $3 \times 2 = 6$, and the perimeter is $6 + 6 + 8 = 20$.

46. **(C)** $150 + \frac{8}{100}(150) = 162$.

47. **(D)** If there are x 10-pound weights, they will weigh a total of $10x$ pounds. Similarly, if there are y 25-pound weights, they will weigh a total of $25y$ pounds. Therefore, the set will weigh a total of $10x + 25y$ pounds.

48. **(E)** A triangle with a 90-degree angle is called a right triangle, and the Pythagorean theorem will apply. The Pythagorean theorem states that $a^2 + b^2 = c^2$ where c is the longest side (the hypotenuse). Applying that to this problem: $6^2 + b^2 = 10^2$ and $b = 8$.

49. **(D)** The word *product* involves multiplication, and when you multiply two terms that have the same base, you add exponents. Therefore, $(4x^2)(5x^4) = 20x^{2+4} = 20x^6$.

50. **(B)** Cross multiply to get the equation $2x = 6$. Dividing both sides by 2 yields $x = 3$.

Answer Key

CHAPTER 3

Basic English Usage Drills

1. **Step 1:** Read the Sentence
   Step 2: Identify the Subject, Verb, and Pronouns
   Step 3: Determine Whether the Subject and Verb Agree
   Step 4: Determine Whether the Verb Tense Is Correct
   Step 5: Determine Whether the Pronoun Is Correct
   Step 6: Read Each Answer Choice

2. E	5. B	8. E	11. C	14. B
3. D	6. C	9. E	12. E	15. E
4. B	7. D	10. B	13. C	

CHAPTER 4

Sentence Structure Drills

1. **Step 1:** Read the Sentence
   Step 2: Determine Whether or Not the Sentence Is Complete
   Step 3: Determine Whether or Not the Ideas Are Expressed Clearly
   Step 4: Look for Parallelism
   Step 5: Decide How to Improve the Sentence
   Step 6: Read Each Answer Choice

2. E	5. C	8. A	11. B	14. A
3. D	6. D	9. C	12. E	15. A
4. D	7. B	10. D	13. E	

CHAPTER 5

Mechanics Drills

1. Step 1: Read the Sentence
   Step 2: Look at the Letters
   Step 3: Peruse the Punctuation
   Step 4: Scope Out the Spelling
   Step 5: Fix What You Found
   Step 6: Examine the Answers

2. D	5. A	8. A	11. A
3. E	6. D	9. B	12. B
4. D	7. D	10. E	13. A

CHAPTER 6

Organization Drills

1. Step 1: Read the Passage
   Step 2: Read the Question
   Step 3: Identify the Main Idea and Supporting Details
   Step 4: Identify the Organizational Pattern
   Step 5: Look for Transitions
   Step 6: Select the Best Revision

2. B	5. E	8. D
3. A	6. B	9. B
4. D	7. D	10. D

CHAPTER 8

World History Drills

1. Step 1: Read All the Information
   Step 2: Identify the Question
   Step 3: Underline Key Words and Phrases
   Step 4: Determine Meanings
   Step 5: Think About What You Already Know
   Step 6: Select the Best Answer

2. C	5. D	8. A
3. C	6. A	9. E
4. B	7. B	10. E

CHAPTER 9

US History Drills

1. **Step 1:** Read All the Information
   Step 2: Identify the Question
   Step 3: Underline Key Words and Phrases
   Step 4: Determine Meanings
   Step 5: Think About What You Already Know
   Step 6: Select the Best Answer

2. D	5. B	8. D
3. B	6. A	9. C
4. C	7. E	10. E

CHAPTER 10

Civics and Government Drills

1. **Step 1:** Read All the Information
   Step 2: Identify the Question
   Step 3: Underline Key Words and Phrases
   Step 4: Determine Meanings
   Step 5: Think About What You Already Know
   Step 6: Select the Best Answer

2. A	5. B	8. B
3. C	6. C	9. D
4. E	7. A	10. C

CHAPTER 11

Economics Drills

1. **Step 1:** Read All the Information
   Step 2: Identify the Question
   Step 3: Underline Key Words and Phrases
   Step 4: Determine Meanings
   Step 5: Think About What You Already Know
   Step 6: Select the Best Answer

2. D	5. E	8. B
3. B	6. D	9. C
4. E	7. D	10. D

CHAPTER 12

Geography Drills

1. **Step 1:** Read All the Information
   Step 2: Identify the Question
   Step 3: Underline Key Words and Phrases
   Step 4: Determine Meanings
   Step 5: Think About What You Already Know
   Step 6: Select the Best Answer

2. D	5. D	8. B	11. E
3. B	6. A	9. D	12. C
4. E	7. D	10. B	

CHAPTER 13

Life Science Drills

1. **Step 1:** Read All the Information
   Step 2: Identify the Question
   Step 3: Underline Key Words and Phrases
   Step 4: Determine Meanings
   Step 5: Think About What You Already Know
   Step 6: Select the Best Answer

2. E	5. D	8. A
3. B	6. E	9. E
4. D	7. B	10. E

CHAPTER 14

Earth and Space Science Drills

1. **Step 1:** Read All the Information
   Step 2: Identify the Question
   Step 3: Underline Key Words and Phrases
   Step 4: Determine Meanings
   Step 5: Think About What You Already Know
   Step 6: Select the Best Answer

2. D	5. D	8. D
3. A	6. D	9. A
4. B	7. A	10. C

CHAPTER 15

Chemistry Drills

1. **Step 1:** Read All the Information
   Step 2: Identify the Question
   Step 3: Underline Key Words and Phrases
   Step 4: Determine Meanings
   Step 5: Think About What You Already Know
   Step 6: Select the Best Answer

2. C	5. A	8. D	11. E
3. B	6. E	9. B	12. C
4. B	7. B	10. B	

CHAPTER 16

Physics Drills

1. **Step 1:** Read All the Information
   Step 2: Identify the Question
   Step 3: Underline Key Words and Phrases
   Step 4: Determine Meanings
   Step 5: Think About What You Already Know
   Step 6: Select the Best Answer

2. C	5. E	8. C
3. E	6. D	9. C
4. B	7. C	10. D

CHAPTER 17

Prose Fiction Reading Comprehension Drills

1. **Step 1:** Read the Purpose Question
   Step 2: Read All of the Multiple-Choice Questions
   Step 3: Read the Passage
   Step 4: Reread the Question You Are Preparing to Answer
   Step 5: State Your Answer
   Step 6: Read the Answer Choices

2. A	4. D	6. B	8. E
3. E	5. D	7. A	9. A

CHAPTER 18

Poetry Reading Comprehension Drills
1. Step 1: Read the Purpose Question
    Step 2: Read All of the Multiple-Choice Questions
    Step 3: Read the Poem
    Step 4: Reread the Question You Are Preparing to Answer
    Step 5: State Your Answer
    Step 6: Read the Answer Choices

2. B	5. A	8. C
3. D	6. E	9. D
4. E	7. A	10. D

CHAPTER 19

Drama Reading Comprehension Drills
1. Step 1: Read the Purpose Question
    Step 2: Read All of the Multiple-Choice Questions
    Step 3: Read the Drama
    Step 4: Reread the Question You Are Preparing to Answer
    Step 5: State Your Answer
    Step 6: Read the Answer Choices

2. B	4. E	6. E	8. D
3. A	5. D	7. E	

CHAPTER 20

Nonfiction Reading Comprehension Drills
1. Step 1: Read the Purpose Question
    Step 2: Read All of the Multiple-Choice Questions
    Step 3: Read the Passage
    Step 4: Reread the Question You Are Preparing to Answer
    Step 5: State Your Answer
    Step 6: Read the Answer Choices

2. D	4. D	6. D	8. B
3. A	5. B	7. D	

CHAPTER 21

Whole Number and Operations Drills

1. **Step 1:** Read the Problem
   Step 2: Determine What Is Being Asked
   Step 3: Identify Pertinent Information and Key Words
   Step 4: Choose Which Operation(s) to Use
   Step 5: Solve the Problem
   Step 6: Check Your Work

2. A	5. D	8. C
3. B	6. A	9. B
4. D	7. C	10. A

CHAPTER 22

Number Sense Drills

1. **Step 1:** Read the Problem
   Step 2: Determine What Is Being Asked
   Step 3: Identify Pertinent Information and Key Words
   Step 4: Make a Plan
   Step 5: Solve the Problem
   Step 6: Check Your Work

2. D	5. B	8. C
3. E	6. A	9. B
4. D	7. A	10. D

CHAPTER 23

Decimal Numbers and Operations Drills

1. **Step 1:** Read the Problem
   Step 2: Determine What Is Being Asked
   Step 3: Identify Pertinent Information and Key Words
   Step 4: Choose Which Operation(s) or Steps to Use
   Step 5: Solve the Problem
   Step 6: Check Your Work

2. C	5. B	8. A
3. C	6. C	9. D
4. D	7. B	10. B

CHAPTER 24

Fractions and Operations Drills

1. **Step 1:** Read the Problem
   Step 2: Determine What Is Being Asked
   Step 3: Identify Pertinent Information and Key Words
   Step 4: Choose Which Operation(s) or Steps to Use
   Step 5: Solve the Problem
   Step 6: Check Your Work

2. B	5. D	8. A
3. C	6. B	9. C
4. C	7. D	10. B

CHAPTER 25

Number Relationship Drills

1. **Step 1:** Read the Problem
   Step 2: Determine What Is Being Asked
   Step 3: Identify Pertinent Information and Key Words
   Step 4: Make a Plan
   Step 5: Solve the Problem
   Step 6: Check Your Work

2. D	4. A	6. C	8. C
3. C	5. B	7. B	

CHAPTER 26

Statistics Drills

1. **Step 1:** Read the Problem
   Step 2: Determine What Is Being Asked
   Step 3: Identify Pertinent Information
   Step 4: Choose Which Operation(s) or Steps to Use
   Step 5: Solve the Problem
   Step 6: Check Your Work

2. A	4. B	6. C	8. D
3. D	5. C	7. D	

CHAPTER 27

Percent Drills

1. **Step 1:** Read the Problem
   Step 2: Determine What Is Being Asked
   Step 3: Identify Pertinent Information and Key Words
   Step 4: Make a Plan
   Step 5: Solve the Problem
   Step 6: Check Your Work

2. C	5. B	8. D
3. D	6. C	9. A
4. E	7. C	10. B

CHAPTER 28

Probability Drills

1. **Step 1:** Read the Problem
   Step 2: Determine What Is Being Asked
   Step 3: Identify Pertinent Information and Key Words
   Step 4: Make a Plan
   Step 5: Solve the Problem
   Step 6: Check Your Work

2. E	5. E	8. A
3. C	6. B	9. B
4. A	7. D	10. B

CHAPTER 29

Data Analysis Drills

1. **Step 1:** Read the Problem and All Related Information
   Step 2: Determine What Is Being Asked
   Step 3: Identify Pertinent Information and Key Words
   Step 4: Make a Plan
   Step 5: Solve the Problem
   Step 6: Check Your Work

2. C	5. A	8. B
3. C	6. E	9. C
4. B	7. D	10. A

CHAPTER 30

Algebra Drills

1. **Step 1:** Read the Problem
   Step 2: Determine What Is Being Asked
   Step 3: Identify Pertinent Information and Key Words
   Step 4: Make a Plan
   Step 5: Solve the Problem
   Step 6: Check Your Work

2. A	4. E	6. E	8. B
3. C	5. A	7. C	

CHAPTER 31

Measurement Drills

1. **Step 1:** Read the Problem
   Step 2: Determine What Is Being Asked
   Step 3: Identify Pertinent Information and Key Words
   Step 4: Make a Plan
   Step 5: Solve the Problem
   Step 6: Check Your Work

2. A	4. D	6. D	8. D
3. B	5. E	7. C	

CHAPTER 32

Geometry Drills

1. **Step 1:** Read the Problem
   Step 2: Determine What Is Being Asked
   Step 3: Identify Pertinent Information and Key Words
   Step 4: Make a Plan
   Step 5: Solve the Problem
   Step 6: Check Your Work

2. A	4. C	6. B	8. D
3. B	5. B	7. C	

CHAPTER 33

Formulas Drills

1. **Step 1:** Read the Problem
   Step 2: Determine What Is Being Asked
   Step 3: Identify Pertinent Information and Key Words
   Step 4: Make a Plan
   Step 5: Solve the Problem
   Step 6: Check Your Work
2. **C**   3. **C**   4. **C**   5. **B**   6. **D**   7. **D**   8. **B**